The CASSELL

GUIDE to
COMMON ERRORS IN ENGLISH

The CASSELL

GUIDE to COMMON ERRORS IN ENGLISH

HARRY BLAMIRES

CASSELL

This edition first published in the UK 1997

by Cassell Wellington House 125 Strand London WC2R 0BB

Copyright © Harry Blamires 1997

Reprinted 1998 (twice)

The right of Harry Blamires to be identified as the author of the work has
been aserted by him in accordance with the Copyright, Designs and Patents
Act 1988.

British Library Cataloguing-in-Publication Data
A catalogue record for this book is available from the British Library

ISBN 0–304–34941–0

Designed and typeset by Gwyn Lewis

Printed and bound in Great Britain by
Mackays of Chatham PLC, Chatham, Kent

Preface

'Every other author may aspire to praise,' Dr Johnson lamented; 'the lexicographer can only hope to escape reproach.' What applies to the lexicographer surely applies to the compiler of a guide to faults in English usage. He cannot expect universal acclaim from readers. There will be those who are offended because he has treated too lightly their pet stylistic aversions. There will be those who regard his criticisms of fashionable practices as evidence of insensitive pedantry.

Indeed to try to lay the law down about English usage today is to enter a minefield. There are even voices to be heard implying that the mother tongue is a free-for-all, an area of experience over which no one has the right to impose restrictions in the name of grammar, logic or tradition. But compilation of a guide to error starts from the presupposition that there are standards to be upheld which are not being upheld. By its very nature, this book must be packed full of recommendations and implicit prohibitions. It cannot be expected to delight every reader.

That being said, our language is of course a changing medium. One cannot immerse oneself in the study of error without learning how much change there is in usage from decade to decade. It would be absurd to identify the defence of standards with resistance to all change. Sometimes a general change is made which cannot possibly please lovers of the language but which establishes itself nevertheless, and there is then no point in continuing to resist it. I suppose the current use of 'hopefully' is a case in point. One may regret the development, but it scarcely deserves to be for ever treated as the purist's *bête noire*. As for split infinitives and prepositions at the end of sentences, I have never been able to understand what all the fuss was about, for the condemned usages seem to be natural to the language.

What seem to me to be really damaging are changes which deprive us of a useful word or which blur useful distinctions of meaning. Such, for instance is the current failure now to distinguish the verb 'avoid' from the verbs 'prevent' and 'forestall'.

Since I first began collecting faulty sentences from the press and from the radio, I have accumulated well over 5,000 specimens of error. Roughly 1,250 of them were used in my previous book, *The Queen's English*, which examined the current state of English usage, more especially focusing on prevalent practices in sentence structure that are ungrammatical or illogical. The more I have worked in this field, the more I find myself fascinated by something over and above the issue of bad grammar. There is plenty of that about of course, but there is also plenty of error of a non-grammatical kind. When a journalist writes, of expert marketing, that 'it is about finding the right solutions to a myriad of opportunities' he does not offend grammatically, but the loose use of words deserves criticism none the less. 'Opportunities' do not demand solutions. On the contrary they open up possibilities. Similarly when a spokesman declares of a Criminal Justice Bill, that 'it will fail to tackle the real target of reducing crime', there is again no grammatical error, but, strictly speaking, we do not 'tackle' targets; we aim at them. We may tackle a problem or hit a target, but the verbs are not interchangeable.

Now obviously the writer who talks of tackling targets is not committing a grave offence against literacy. But the compiler of a book on usage must assume that his readers are not just anxious to avoid gross howlers. Presumably they are also anxious to avoid literary practices which mark writing as inexact or unpolished. This anxiety too has to be catered for. Even in correcting students' work in English, the same red ink may be used at one moment to ring a howler, at the next moment to underline an infelicity. So no excuse should be needed for my determination in this book to cast the net widely over contemporary usage and not restrict myself to judgments which every reader will immediately agree with. Moreover, it will be evident at many points throughout this book that a given faulty practice may appear at very different levels of seriousness. Indeed, I sometimes think that the ideal way to present errors would be to tabulate them rather as wine clubs tabulate their various vintages, assessing the errors on a scale of increasing grossness from 1 ('Just acceptable') to 6 ('Totally illiterate').

Even when error can be defined in grammatical terms, the issue is generally as much a matter of common sense offended as of grammatical rules broken. We read, 'A keen fisherman, the peace of the river Test was an antidote to a stormy marriage.' The writer here seems to turn the peace of the river Test into a keen fisherman. Similarly 'A Yorkshireman and a professional, time off from work is not to be wasted' seems to turn time off into a Yorkshireman. We do not really need recourse to grammatical rules governing apposition before recognising that it will not do seemingly to identify the peace of the river as a keen fisherman and time off as a Yorkshireman.

This kind of error is not rare. Let me cite a parallel instance from a *Times* third leader. 'Too lazy to walk or bicycle, the proportion of short journeys taken by car has doubled in the past 20 years.' Again we scarcely need the grammarian's technical know-how about appositional phrases to be unhappy with this. Calling a proportion of short journeys lazy, as the writer does, was not what was really meant. But readers who are uncomfortable with this do not necessarily have grammatical terms like 'apposition' floating around in their minds as they react to it. They sense that something has gone wrong with the logical sequence.

Straight thinking nurtures grammatical accuracy. Indeed the two are inextricably bound together. If what is going on in our heads is indisciplined by the basic logic which we call common sense, then the discipline of grammar will be lost too. Yet we are tempted to comfort ourselves by pretending that ignorance of something technical called 'grammar' is the deficiency most evident in current faulty usage. It is comforting because there are those who tell us that 'grammar' is something that only pedants worry about – the kind of people who would stultify vital change and growth in living language. We don't want to be told that the main deficiency is simply incapacity to think straight. But look at this from the *Guardian*'s 'Comment' column. 'On Sunday the Israeli cabinet decided to import 18,000 foreign workers to fill the most essential gaps.' There is no grammatical error there, and not a single individual word is misunderstood, but the use of words goes badly astray. If the gaps are 'essential', the last thing you must do is to get rid of them by filling them.

My illustrations but touch thoughtlessness where it is easiest to spot. But even when error threads its way through a complex sentence, so that rules for the manipulation of this or that subordinate clause are broken, we shall generally find that there is a core of irrationality which applied common sense can pinpoint without necessarily referring to the rules of grammar. And since grammatical failure, generally speaking, is secondary to failure to think straight, since indeed it is usually a product of failure to think straight, then the prescription for our ills requires us to discipline ourselves in mental precision. We need to make sure, word by word, that we are saying what we want to say.

This book, therefore, is a guide to what goes wrong in our use of English, examined word by word. Making use of some 2,000 specimens of error from the press and the radio, it lists in alphabetical order words which are misused through verbal insensitivity or lack of logicality and words whose use tends to lead writers into error. The largest proportion of entries deals with individual words. Mixed with these entries, however, are more general headings (with headwords in *Italics)* under which slack verbal habits are illustrated. There are also entries (again with headwords in *Italics)* which explain and illustrate the technical terminology of grammar. And lastly, there is a sprinkling of entries which distinguish sometimes confused pairs of words such as 'immanent' and 'imminent'.

The practice I have followed is to correct faulty sentences in such a way as to shed light on the original misuse. This is sometimes a different process from re-writing them in such a way as to produce the most elegant English possible.

Something should be said about the sources of my material. There are over 150 different sources named in the text, but I have not been interested in weighing the literacy of one publication against another's. My selection of journals has been random. The fact that just over 400 sentences, from a total of about 2,000, derive from *The Times* indicates only that *The Times* is the newspaper I happen to read, and the fact that almost as many sentences derive from *Radio 4* indicates my listening habits. Obviously not everything deriving from *Radio 4* is the responsibility of the BBC. However, I have for the most part concentrated on scripted news items and only rarely picked out instances where speakers were forming their sentences as they spoke.

It has to be admitted that some of the sentences under judgment in this book exemplify errors to which frequent usage is now giving a specious authority. Readers will be surprised, as I have been surprised, by the sheer quantity of error under certain heads and by the way certain careless usages seem to have established themselves. What is the point at which those who pass judgment on usage have to say 'This or that practice is now so widespread that it must be accounted correct'? The truth is that a certain usage can become extremely widespread in journalism and the popular media, and yet all but impossible to track down in the work of good writers. Such is the situation, for instance with the abuse of the words 'like' and 'unlike'. I have just heard an instance on the radio. 'Like any other violent crime, a man who beats up his partner should be arrested and charged.' Plainly a man cannot be described as 'like' any other violent crime. What is needed is 'Like any other violent criminal, a man who beats up his partner should be arrested and charged.' Even the person who said it would, I suppose, nod her head in agreement if this were pointed out to her. Such too is the case with the construction which

I have called the 'Gerciple'. I try to judge in these instances by the criterion of common sense. 'He disliked me using make-up' will not do when what is meant is 'He disliked my using make-up'. All instances of the now commonly abused participle and gerund ultimately fail the test of reason.

No reader who takes an interest in the current state of English usage will be surprised at the length of the entry under the heading 'Apostrophe'. But many may be surprised to find that analysing current misuse of the words 'apart from' takes up even more space, and that dealing with the misuse of 'as well as' takes even more space still.

It remains necessary to draw attention to those still frequent confusions between such pairs as 'flaunt' and 'flout', 'militate' and 'mitigate'. This book has its share of such slips. Sometimes they are amusing. We are tickled by the journalist who tells us that a certain lady 'became a prodigy of the Duchess of Devonshire' when plainly he means that she became a 'protégée of the Duchess of Devonshire', but that kind of malapropism does not indicate any oddity in the writer's thought processes. It merely indicates a kind of factual ignorance or forgetfulness. More interesting, and more relevant to the issue of straight thinking is the laxity of the writer who tells us that 'the photograph of the tree in Berkeley Square is not an oak; it is a plane'. Clearly the photograph is neither oak nor plane. If someone is talking about a photograph, he or she is not talking about a tree.

It is a small step from this kind of laxity to the now all too common error which I have exemplified under the heading '*Possessive Trap*'. 'Shy and retiring, modest and hard-working, this man's knowledge and experience is quite immense.' The writer who was talking about a photograph when he thought he was talking about a tree made a very similar mistake to the writer who talks about a man's 'knowledge and experience' when he thinks he is talking about the man himself. Clearly it was not the knowledge and experience that were 'shy and retiring', as the sentence would seemingly convey. Having got as far as 'Shy and retiring, modest and hard-working', the writer ought not to have forgotten that his sentence was about a man and not about his knowledge or experience. The sentence should have read: 'Shy and retiring, modest and hard-working, this man quite clearly has immense knowledge and experience.'

As errors accumulate in my card-index, I am naturally tempted to ask myself such questions as 'Which are the battles already lost?' and 'Which are the battles still undecided?' It would seem that the distinction which preferred 'whether' to 'if' in indirect statement ('We asked them whether it was true') is no longer current. There is an ever more popular assumption that participles such as 'using' and 'looking' can be used independently of proper reference to the one who is using or looking. ('Looking sideways, the hill is just visible', we are told, when in fact the hill is not looking sideways at all.) Perhaps we can still rescue 'avoid' from those who would use it for 'prevent', and 'convince' from those who would use it for 'persuade'. Perhaps we can even restore the meaning of 'substitute' and 'substitution'. But I would confess total defeat in my seemingly single-handed attempt to stop people referring (highly ungrammatically) to 'Basher, as he is known' instead of 'Basher, as he is called'.

When I first began my investigations into current usage, I was anxious to answer the questions: What kind of mistakes are people making? How can the most frequent errors be categorised? What prescriptive grammatical caveats then can be put before writers seeking to avoid them? My first book, therefore, for the most part concentrated on assembling blocks of sentences related together by the character of their erroneousness, and putting them under appropriate headings. My researches soon convinced me that, quite aside from the grammatical ignorance or carelessness underlying faulty sentence structure, a current of mental laxity underlay the choice of words in the press and on the radio. There was a stage, quite early on in my researches, when I invented the category '*Any Word Will Do*' as the repository for certain of my discoveries. The number of sentences under that heading escalated. It was not long before I realised that the collection was becoming a vast reservoir that, if tapped, would quite swamp what I was about in my first book in defining constructional weaknesses in largely grammatical terms. But the 'any-word-will-do' attitude, as exemplified in some of the instances I have quoted above, is one of the demons that this present book sets out to exorcise.

Commentators on the current scene have lamented the growth of 'anything-goes' attitudes in various departments of life. How gravely these attitudes are affecting our culture is not a matter for discussion here, but I have no doubt that they have their verbal equivalent in what I have called the 'any-word-will-do' attitude. In the popular mind a degree of 'authority' attaches itself to the utterances of those who regularly use our language to communicate with the public. To urge them to get the verbal nuts and bolts right in their utterances is not perhaps going to do much immediately for our cultural condition, but the effort to alert them to their larger responsibilities is in the long run surely worth making.

Harry Blamires

A

ability. This word is used of human skill and competence. 'Hopefully increasing awareness of the syndrome and its ability to be treated can lead the sleeping midnight feeders away from the fridge.' (*New Woman*) No syndrome has any 'ability' at all: *Hopefully increasing awareness of the syndrome and its susceptibility to treatment.*

'Small but significant changes would enhance the overall ability of the land to hold game.' (*Shooting Times*) Land does not have ability either. *Small but significant changes would make it possible for the land to hold more game.*

'Animals are sentient beings with the ability to suffer.' (*Radio 4*) It is not possession of any skill or proficiency ('ability') that makes suffering possible for a being. *Animals are sentient beings susceptible to suffering.*

able. This word is best restricted in application to living beings. 'He is able to walk' is an alternative to 'He can walk', but 'The tree is able to be cut down' is a poor evasion of 'can be cut down'.

'He told the Commons his objective was to ensure that the ceasefire was able to be "turned into a permanent peace".' (*The Times*) This should be: *to ensure that the ceasefire could be turned into a permanent peace.*

Similarly 'The fault line in the Tory party doesn't seem able to be bridged' (*Radio 4*) should be: *The fault line in the Tory party can apparently not be bridged.*

The words 'to be able' should be firmly connected to a suitable agent. 'The mains connection lead should have enough slack on it to be able to pull the fridge clear and lay it on the floor.' (*Caravan Magazine*) Someone may have enough leisure to be able to take a holiday, but a mains connection lead cannot have enough slack to be able to pull a fridge about. Some person must do that. *The mains connection lead should have enough slack for one to be able to pull the fridge clear.*

abolish. 'A radical diet based on extremely high-fat meals can abolish seizures in many young children with severe epilepsy.' (*Bella*) To 'abolish' is to do away with something that already exists. It is not possible to 'abolish' something that might happen in the future: *A radical diet based on extremely high-fat meals can prevent seizures.*

about. 'It's the right way to go about the problem.' (*Radio 4*) People do not 'go about' problems. *It's the right way to tackle the problem.*

absurdity. This is one of several nouns that lure the writer to abuse of the gerund. The 'absurdity of believing in astrology' is grammatically correct, but 'the absurdity of me being reclassed as a meticulous and methodical Virgo' (*The Times*) is not. It should be: *the absurdity of my being reclassed*, but better perhaps: *the absurdity of reclassing me. See also* GERCIPLES.

accede/exceed. To 'accede' is an intransitive verb meaning to give agreement or consent: *My father eventually acceded to my request for financial help*, and more technically of entering upon an office: *The heir acceded to the throne.* It must not be confused with the transitive verb to 'exceed', which means to be greater than: *The offer was so generous that it exceeded all our expectations.*

accept/except. The verb to 'accept' is used of receiving something (*He readily accepted my offer of help*) or of responding in agreement (*She accepted my claim to be heard*). It must not be confused with the verb 'to except', which means to exclude or omit: *There will be a charge for use of the hotel bathing pool, resident guests excepted.*

access (noun). 'Access to 80 square miles of moorland in the Peak District has been reopened to walkers.' (*Trail*) 'Access' is the right of entry. It is the paths that have been 'reopened': *access has been restored.*

access (verb). It has become fashionable in the business world to use 'access' as a verb. 'If stone could be accessed and worked readily, it was always the first choice.' (*Cottage & Castle*) In this comment on building cottages the word is out of place: *If stone could be readily obtained.*

accessorise. 'The personal shopping consultant from Harvey Nichols will be on hand to show you some of the newest fashion looks for spring and summer and demonstrate clever ways of accessorising.' (*Woman's Journal*) Innovations ending in '-ise' tend to follow a pattern. The word 'marginalise' means to render something marginal; the word 'prioritise' means to turn something into a priority. On that basis 'accessorise' would mean to turn something into an accessory. What the writer wants, presumably, is a word that means to equip with accessories. The innovation is not a happy one. *See also* COINAGES.

accompany. To accompany someone is to go along with them in the sense of keeping company with them. 'Once this garden would have produced fruit, nuts and vegetables for the large household that accompanied an important country house.' (*In Britain*) The household did not 'accompany' (go along with) the house. Why not *inhabited*?

'A ten-hour flight accompanied by two energetic children isn't the best way to start a holiday.' (*She*) It was not the flight that was accompanied by children, but the parents. *To fly for ten hours in the company of two energetic children isn't the best way to start a holiday.*

account. 'The Security Council is demanding proper accounting of all missing people.' (*Radio 4*) The Security Council surely wants a proper record for identification, which is a matter of *accounting for*, not 'of'.

accurate. 'With the situation as chaotic as it is, it's impossible to be too accurate.' (*Radio 4*) It is always impossible to be 'too' accurate. Accuracy does not admit of increase or reduction by degrees. *The situation being as chaotic as it is, it's impossible to be accurate. See also* WITH.

accusation. 'We hear from witnesses who say MPs are guilty of all these accusations and more.' (*Radio 4*) One may be guilty 'of' a crime, but an accusation is not a crime to be guilty 'of': *MPs are guilty on all these counts*.

accuse. 'It doesn't matter if this . . . is fuzzy-headed or, as he is accused by a group of Jacobin feminists, "self-cancelling".' (*Guardian*) Sometimes turning a construction into the passive causes the mind to jump a step. One may say 'He is accused of murder' because 'murder' is a noun. One may say 'He is accused of being selfish', where 'selfish' is an adjective. But this construction cannot be twisted round into 'That is selfish, as he is accused by his friends'. 'That is selfish, as he is accused of being' would be correct but awkward. The construction needs to be changed. *It doesn't matter if this is fuzzy-headed, or "self-cancelling", to use the label given him by a group of Jacobin feminists.*

achieve. 'Their failure means that one of the last great aeronautical challenges remains unachieved.' (*Radio 4*) A challenge can be taken up, answered, or rejected, but it cannot be 'achieved'. If the notion of non-achievement is to be kept, then the noun 'challenge' must go. *Their failure means that one of the last great aeronautical aims challenging us remains unachieved.*

achievement. 'The achievement of ambition is one of the most satisfying feelings in the world.' (*Nursing Standard*) The achievement is not itself a feeling and it should be distinguished from the 'feeling' it produces. *The achievement of ambition is one of the most satisfying experiences.*

acquiesce. 'She hated the way he dominated the leaders, who idolised him and acquiesced to his abuse of power.' (*Sunday Times*) This use of the preposition 'to' after 'acquiesce' appears to reintroduce an obsolete usage: *who idolised him and acquiesced in his abuse of power.*

acute. 'Those who need acute hospital care should have it.' (*Radio 4*) This is a curious usage. The hospital is not 'acute'; neither is the 'care'. Only the need for treatment may be 'acute'. *Those whose need for hospital care is acute should have it.*

adamant. 'It is typically British not to be adamant about our sporting success.' (*Radio 4*) To be adamant is to be unshakeably determined. It is not what the speaker intended here. *It is typically British not to boast of our sporting success.*

address. This verb is being overworked. 'These articles went some way towards addressing an area that I feel is lacking in British game-fishing, and that is adventure.' (*Trout & Salmon*) The notion of addressing an area is a curious one, unless it is a matter of supplying a post code. *These articles raised a topic that I feel is neglected in British game-fishing.*

adequacy. 'Nurses are concerned about the adequacy of casualty facilities in Edinburgh following the recent closure of the accident and emergency unit at the city's Western General Hospital.' (*Nursing Standard*) There is a tendency to speak of worries about 'adequacy' when what is meant is that there are worries about possible inadequacy. This is a case in point. *Nurses are concerned that casualty facilities in Edinburgh may be inadequate as a result of the recent closure.*

adhere. One of the government's conditions for negotiations, we are told, is 'that Sinn Fein is also prepared to adhere by democratic principles'. (*Radio 4*) Adhesion is a matter of sticking together. The postage stamp does not adhere 'by' the envelope but 'to' it: *prepared to adhere to democratic principles.*

Adjectives. An adjective is a part of speech which qualifies a noun, clarifying its meaning. It may be adjacent to the noun it qualifies (*a pink blouse*) or separated from it by the verb 'to be' or some other verb (*the blouse is pink; the blouse looks pink*). The present and past participles of verbs are used adjectivally. The present participle of the verb 'to sleep' is used in the expression *a sleeping child*, and the past participle of the verb 'to break' is used in the expression *a broken home*. There is a tendency for adjectives and participles to drift from their proper moorings. For instance, *see* CONSCIOUS, DISABLED. On the placing of adjectives, *see* WORD ORDER: SINGLE WORD MISPLACED. *See also* COMPARATIVES AND SUPERLATIVES.

administer. 'We shall draw up rules setting out specific criteria to be administered by the Advisory Committee on Business Appointments.' (*Radio 4*) An estate might be 'administered' (managed), but not criteria: *setting out specific criteria to be applied/observed by the Advisory Committee.*

admission. An admission (e.g. of guilt) is a confession or acknowledgment. 'Worries about factory closures and unemployment, coupled with an admission of different tastes to the West Germans have prompted the new Bundesburger to buy their own products again.' (*Marketing Week*) Here what is admitted is 'that' East German tastes differ from West German tastes. 'Admission' is not the best word. *Worries about factory closures and unemployment, coupled with recognition that they have different tastes from the West Germans have prompted the new Bundesburger. . . . See also* DIFFERENT.

advantage. 'There are, however, advantages to being a redhead.' (*Company*) Accepted usage would eschew 'to': *advantages in being a redhead.*

Adverbs. An adverb is a part of speech which modifies a verb (*He spoke wildly*) or an adjective (*She was wildly incoherent*), affecting its meaning. Some few, but much used, adverbs, such as 'very' and 'extremely', modify other adverbs (*very cheerfully, extremely cautiously*). Most adverbs end with '-ly', added to an adjective (*wild-ly*). Where an adjective happens to end in '-ly' (*It was a lovely day*) no corresponding adverb can be formed from it ('lovelily'). One must say 'beautifully'.

The comparative and superlative forms of the adverb are formed by use of 'more' and 'most' (*more hopefully, most gratefully*). The few irregular monosyllabic adverbs, such as 'fast' and 'soon', form their comparatives and superlatives as adjectives do (*They arrived sooner than expected*).

On the need to place adverbs satisfactorily in relation to the verbs they modify *see* WORD ORDER: SINGLE WORD MISPLACED.

adverse. 'It's even grimmer if you are elderly and want to think medium rather than long term, and if you are adverse to taking any risk.' (*The Times*) This word means unfavourable or hostile and is used of circumstances that are inimical to the efforts one is making. Misuse of it is now not uncommon. The word meaning personally disinclined is 'averse': *and if you are averse to taking any risk*.

advertise. 'This is "550 feet of never-ending free fall!", as the Adventure World of Interlaken proudly advertises.' (*Adventure Travel*) This is a strained use of 'as': *to quote the proud advertisement of the Adventure World*.

advice. 'She finds herself in the middle of another medical story: breast cancer, its conflicting advice and uneven availability of treatments'. (*The Times*) It is correct to speak of the doctor's advice, but not of breast cancer's advice. Breast cancer is incapable of giving advice. The 'its' must go: *conflicting advice given to patients*.

affect. There is a noun 'effect' and a verb 'effect', but there is no noun 'affect', only the verb meaning to influence or to assume a pose.

'Mr McLoughlin attributes the miracle to the beneficial affects of two meals a week of black beans and rice' (*The Times*) should be: *to the beneficial effects of two meals a week*.

'No powders or chemicals. No affect on birds or other pets.' (*The Times*) This advertisement should read: *No effect on birds or other pets*. See also EFFECT.

after. When 'after' is followed by a gerund, there is the danger that grammatical error will ensue. Someone might say 'After reading the book, I went to bed', because 'I' both read the book and went to bed. But it will not do to say 'After reading the book, the fire went out', because the fire did not read the book. Nevertheless sentences on this pattern appear in the press regularly.

'Living in denial? After reading about Jennifer Jason Leigh in the numerous articles . . . this statement takes on a peculiar resonance.' (*Vogue*) The erroneous construction slips through more easily in a longer sentence. 'This statement' is said to have read about Jennifer Jason Leigh. It must be made clear who did. *After I read about Jennifer Jason Leigh . . . this statement took on a peculiar resonance*.

There is a special danger of falling into this error when describing localities and routes. 'After nearly ten minutes of walking the cliff path began to slope gently downhill' (*Novel*) implies by the grammatical construction that the cliff path was walking. *After we had walked for nearly ten minutes, the cliff path began to slope. See also* ROUTES.

aggravate. 'There is no point in this disharmony aggravating into something worse.' (*Radio* 4) To 'aggravate' something is to make it worse. To 'aggravate' someone is to irritate them. There is no intransitive use of the word. It is not an alternative to the word 'deteriorate'. Moreover, the interviewer did not mean what she said in the words 'There is no point', i.e.: 'There is no purpose'. She meant: *This disharmony should not be allowed to turn into something much worse.*

aggressive. This is now a vogue word, loosely exploited. When a spokesman speaks of 'the way charity money is becoming much more aggressive to get hold of' (*Radio* 4) we see its meaning disintegrating. Money cannot be 'aggressive': *the way charities are much more aggressive in their appeals.*

'The chief executive said the restructuring was needed to achieve aggressive performance targets.' (*Radio* 4) This is business-speak at its worst. No target could ever be 'aggressive'. *The chief executive said the dismissals were needed to increase profits.*

aid. 'Noisy revellers and animals did not aid in a good night's sleep.' (*Complete Traveller*) One might aid someone 'in' rescue work, but not 'in' their sleep. This is misplaced evasion of the obvious: *did not help us to get a good night's sleep.*

aim (noun). 'Significant change has taken place at the Legal Aid Board with the aim of improving the quality of service provided.' (*The Times*) Something which just 'takes place' (or 'occurs') cannot do so with any special aim, because 'aim' suggests a human agency and human purpose. *Significant change has been made at the Legal Aid Board with the aim of improving the quality of service provided.*

aim (verb). 'There's a growing trend in skincare for protection products – ones that aim to prevent premature aging rather than just attempt to repair the damage.' (*New Woman*) Products themselves cannot 'aim' or 'attempt': *ones that are designed to prevent premature aging rather than just to repair the damage.*

align. 'Over 80 full-time academic staff are aligned to the faculty.'

(*Guardian*) When things are 'aligned' they are drawn up in a line. The verb is also used of reaching agreement ('They have aligned themselves with our cause'). It is followed by the preposition 'with'. The writer must have meant either: *Over 80 full-time academic staff are associated with the faculty*, or: *have been assigned to the faculty*.

all. One must beware of using 'all' where 'each' is needed.

'All the models on offer cost only £89.95.' (*Woman*) If this were so one could buy the job lot for £89.95. *Each of the models on offer costs only £89.95.* The word is used loosely in conversation in other ways but the same liberty should not be allowed in print.

'Masters from the nine packs who hunt all or partly in the county rallied immediately.' (*Horse & Hound*) There are many idiomatic expressions involving 'all', but none of them allows for this confusion between 'all' and 'wholly' or 'exclusively'. One might say: *who hunt wholly or partly in the county*, but it would be better to say: *who do all or some of their hunting in the county*, and better still to say: *who do some or all of their hunting in the county*.

'The winner will have a standard cabin which all have private bathrooms.' (*The Times*) 'All' cannot refer back to the singular 'cabin'. *The winner will have one of the standard cabins which all have private bathrooms.*

NEGATIVES AFTER 'ALL' One would not say 'All my friends have not turned up', but 'None of my friends has turned up'.

'All the locals, from the trappers to the mayor, could not have been more hospitable.' (*Shooting Times*) A more acceptable usage would be: *None of the locals could have been more hospitable.* If 'all' is kept, the negative could be avoided: *All the locals treated us with the maximum hospitality.*

Similarly 'All of us present at the farewell dinner . . . will never forget the unscheduled 20-minute speech' (*Hunting*) would better be: *None of us present at the farewell dinner will ever forget.*

There is good authority, however, for breaking this rule: 'All they that put their trust in thee shall not be ashamed.' (*Book of Common Prayer*)

all right/alright. 'All right' is the only generally acceptable form.

allowing. In 'The door was open, allowing him to enter' it is clear by what agency the entry is permitted. The door allowed entry. 'In an age of increasing specialisation Hambly remained broadly based, allowing him to tackle an exceptionally wide range of engineering problems.' (*The*

Times) Here there is no real issue of 'allowing'; the participle has no anchorage. *Hambly remained broadly based and was thus able to tackle an exceptionally wide range of engineering problems.*

It is wrong to try thus to turn the participle of the verb 'to allow' into a pseudo-conjunction. 'They were added before the undercoats had totally dried, allowing the different colours to run and mix slightly.' (*Artists & Illustrators Magazine*) This should be: *so that the different colours could run and mix slightly.*

Where the issue is a general one of result or of cause and effect the writer should think twice about using 'allowing'. 'Because of their flexible fine tip, you have more control over the medium than with a conventional palette knife, allowing for finer details to be achieved.' (*Artists & Illustrators Magazine*) This should be: *so that finer details can be achieved.*

along with. This construction is misused in a variety of ways.

FAILURE OF BALANCE This expression functions like a hinge on which two matching items are balanced. 'Along with their 100 per cent cotton classic corduroy and moleskin trousers, a wide selection of shirts, knitwear, ties, shoes, socks, and accessories, Cordings are the complete country outfitters.' (*Shooting Times*) This is tantamount to writing 'Along with his beefsteaks, Smith is a flourishing butcher'. Cordings are not outfitters 'along with' their shirts any more than Smith is a butcher along with his beef. The construction must be changed. *Supplying 100 per cent cotton classic corduroy and moleskin trousers . . . Cordings are the complete country outfitters.*

'ALONG WITH' FOR 'AS WELL AS' 'Scott had previously whipped-in and, along with designing and building cross-country fences, he is in full swing as a youthful, experienced and enthusiastic horseman.' (*Hunting*) Here 'along with' is used where 'as well as' is intended. *Scott had previously whipped in and, as well as designing fences, he is in full swing as a horseman.*

'ALONG WITH' FOR 'AND' Do not substitute 'along with' where 'and' should introduce a new clause. 'American air power in the region [Kuwait] will be beefed up along with more military training exercise.' (*Radio 4*) This does not mean that training exercises will be beefed up along with the air power, which would justify the use of 'along with'. The newswriter presumably means that *American air power in the region will be beefed up and military training exercises will be increased.*

'ALONG WITH' AND SINGULAR VERB Care must be taken with the verb after 'along with'. 'Withdrawn in 1905, the coach, along with a 30ft Third

Class coach (built in 1881), were used side by side as the main part of a bungalow.' (*Old Glory*) 'Along with' does not work like 'and'. We say 'John and his brother James were [plural verb] present', but 'John, along with his brother James, was [singular verb] present'. *Withdrawn in 1905, the coach was used alongside a 30ft Third Class coach as the main part of a bungalow.*

alright. See ALL RIGHT.

alternative. 'Here, cross-country skiing on the frozen lake is a popular alternative to downhill.' (*Country Living*) Skiing may be an alternative to sledging but, wherever it takes place, it cannot be an alternative to 'downhill': *is a popular alternative to skiing downhill.*

although. This word should introduce a genuine contrast. 'Although it was raining heavily, we continued to bat' makes sense, where 'Although it was warm and sunny, we continued to bat' does not, because the antithesis expected after the word 'although' does not follow.

 MISUSED IN ABSENCE OF ANTITHESIS 'It is apparent that the children are very happy here although they still display an enormous amount of respect for their teachers.' (*Country Talk*) The suggested surprise that children should be both respectful and happy is out of place. 'Although' must go: *children are very happy here and display an enormous amount of respect.*

'Although Alastair has taught there periodically over the last three years, he has now taken the place over completely.' (*Vogue*) The same applies here. There is no antithesis between teaching for a time at a cookery school and then beginning to run it. *Alastair has taught there periodically over the last three years and has now taken the place over completely.*

'Although the recession seems to be blamed for absolutely everything, I have to say that it is the most likely cause of the problem.' (*Caravan Magazine*) There is no proper contrast here. It is like saying 'Although it is usually wet here, I have to admit that it is raining'. 'Although' is the wrong word. *The recession seems to be blamed for absolutely everything and I have to say that it is the most likely cause of the problem.*

Sometimes the introduction of 'although' is mystifying. 'One British woman was reported to be in a serious condition although another three, including a six-year-old boy, had to have emergency surgery.' (*Radio 4*) 'Although' must go, and it must not be conveyed that a 'six-year-old boy' is 'another' woman, so the sequence from 'one' to 'another' must be changed. *A British woman was reported to be in a serious condition, and three other people, including a six-year-old boy, had to have emergency surgery.*

'ALTHOUGH' FOLLOWED BY DESCRIPTIVE PHRASE When 'although' introduces a descriptive phrase, care must be taken to preserve accuracy in matching. 'Although a very young man, he had bad health' is correct. 'Although a very young man, his health was bad' is incorrect because his health was not a young man.

'Although a Muslim, his audience was overwhelmingly Christian' (*The Times*) will not do because the Muslim is not identified. *Although he was a Muslim, his audience was overwhelmingly Christian.*

'Although not a very rapid swimmer, capable of reaching speeds of around 6–8km/h, the streamlined shape of the penguin's body means it can twist and turn quickly in pursuit of its prey.' (*Wild Life Fact File*) The shape of the body, instead of the penguin, is said to be a not very rapid swimmer. *Although not a very rapid swimmer, the penguin has a body streamlined so that it can twist and turn quickly.*

Ambiguity. Sometimes a false, even absurd, meaning can be conveyed through carelessness over word order or punctuation.

'Some 200 criminal investigations have been launched against former East German guards suspected of shooting dead people trying to flee to the west.' (*Independent*) Talk of 'shooting dead people' is clearly ambiguous. The words must be re-ordered: *suspected of shooting people dead who were trying to flee to the west.*

'For example, what does it mean if your boss never looks you in the face or peers over her glasses at you?' (*Living*) The punctuation being what it is (there being no comma after 'face'), there would appear to be two problems – that the boss never looks the writer in the face and never peers over her glasses at her. In order to prevent such misunderstanding the word 'if' should be repeated. *What does it matter if your boss never looks you in the face or if she peers over her glasses at you?*

'Sunlite Leisure Caravans is a new dealership opened in the Wirral by the river Mersey.' (*Caravan Magazine*) The word 'by' is often used after 'opened', and its placing here suggests that the river Mersey performed an opening ceremony. It should be changed: *a new dealership opened in the Wirral near the river Mersey* or *on the bank of the river Mersey.*

'Only the high areas [of a non-stick pan] are exposed to wear and tear, which naturally extends the life of the pan.' (*Prima*) Although the singular verb ('extends') should prevent misreading here, 'which' follows directly on 'wear and tear', suggesting the opposite of what is intended. *Only the high areas are exposed to the wear and tear which naturally shorten the life of the pan.*

CAUSAL SEQUENCES In causal sequences after a negative verb ambiguities sometimes arise. 'I am not going because I am ill' might mean that illness is keeping me away or that illness is not the cause of my going. A comma after 'going' would indicate the first interpretation.

In 'Exact details aren't being released for security reasons' (*Radio 4*) the same ambiguity is present. The details are perhaps being released for reasons other than those of security. A comma after 'released' would clarify it, or a change in word order. *For security reasons exact details are not being released.*

'We've been married for 10 years, I'm 35, my husband's 37, and we have no children through our own choice.' (*Woman*) There is ambiguity here. The sentence might apply if the couple had lots of children, but none of them by design. Presumably something other is intended: *and, through our own choice, we have no children.*

In 'No school will start the new term on Monday because of extensive damage to water and heating systems' (*The Times*) the message is not likely to be misinterpreted but the word order produces awkwardness. *Because of extensive damage to water and heating systems no school will start the new term on Monday.*

amenable. 'I was very interested in what John had to say about this possible connection [of the IRA] with East End villains who might be amenable to money.' (*Radio 4*) 'Amenable' means susceptible to being influenced, and therefore villains might be said to be 'amenable' to persuasion by those offering money, but they are not amenable 'to' the money itself. Unless the sentence is to be expanded, the word 'amenable' must be changed: *this possible connection with East End villains who might be tempted by money.*

amend/emend. The verb to 'amend' is in general use, meaning to improve or correct: *The parliamentary bill was amended to meet the objections of back-benchers.* The verb to 'emend' is used restrictively of correcting a literary text: *The new editor emended the faulty first edition.* The corresponding nouns are 'amendment' and 'emendation'.

among. 'These are among the best pictures in the collection' is a perfectly acceptable usage. It is inadvisable to stretch this usage as follows. 'The hotel has undertaken major renovations and can offer among the most comprehensive accommodation and business facilities in the country.' (*Vogue*) It would be difficult to justify the use of 'among' here. To use it is to evade the simplest and most natural wording: *can offer some of the most comprehensive accommodation and business facilities in the country.*

'Among' can also be a risky word to use at the beginning of a sentence. 'Among the older wines, some of which were considered outstanding for their finesse and ageing nutty delicacy, the general consensus was that they are certainly worth tasting.' (*Decanter*) Here the word 'among' seems to be forgotten. We expect something like 'Among the older wines, there was a 1916 Madeira'. Instead the writer seems to cite 'the general consensus' as 'among the older wines'. *As for the older wines, the general consensus was that they are certainly worth tasting.*

amount. 'There was also a large amount of beggars and young children with missing limbs and disabled bodies.' (*Cumbria Life*) Human beings are not quantified in 'amounts'. *There was also a large number of beggars.*

Anacoluthon. When a writer starts a sentence with a construction that is never completed, but succeeded incongruously by words that belong to a totally different construction, the resulting incoherence exemplifies 'anacoluthon'.

'In these [tests], a dog and owner are tested on their ability to heel when on the lead, heel off the lead, calling the dog from a distance, and finally "sit and stay".' (*Wild About Animals*) Plainly the 'owner' cannot be tested on ability to heel either on or off the lead. Nor can the dog be tested on 'calling'. But the sentence attributes all these processes to the 'dog and owner'. *In these tests for dog and owner the dog must come to heel obediently with or without lead, respond to calls from a distance, and obey the order to 'sit and stay'.*

'When you realise that over 350 pack-horses on long haul routes passed through Kendal in one week, and to that a much larger number of local trade horses must be added, the traffic must have been considerable.' (*Cumbria Life*) This will not do. 'When you realise' introduces a sequence that is not completed. The traffic was considerable before you realised anything and would have been so whether you had realised it or not. 'When you realise' must go. *Since over 350 pack-horses passed through Kendal, the traffic must have been considerable.*

A very large proportion of the sentences quoted in this book exemplify anacoluthon in its numerous forms. In particular, *see also* LOSS OF VERBAL CONTROL.

and. The word 'and' is a link word. 'He ate fish and' we read, and prepare for 'chips'. The writer is not likely to go astray over links so simple as that, but in more complex sentences even the word 'and' can send the writer into supposedly related sequences that do not in fact match.

'The Stroke Association has been in existence for over 90 years and now concentrates on caring for people who have had strokes and vital research.' (*The Stroke Association Appeal*) The trouble here is that 'and' establishes the wrong connection between 'strokes' and 'vital research', as though they were two kinds of affliction. Moreover, once the reader has brushed that false connection out of the way, another false connection asserts itself between 'people who have had strokes' and 'vital research', as though they were parallel objects of 'caring'. To avoid confusion, the writer needs to underline the connection between the two things that the association 'concentrates on'. This can be done by repeating the word 'on': *and now concentrates on caring for people who have had strokes and on vital research.*

'We want all our children to be a picture of health and to make sure that we are giving them a nutritious diet.' (*Parents*) Here 'and to make sure' appears to be something the children must do. The verb 'want' must be repeated: *We want all our children to be a picture of health and we want to make sure.*

'Like its competitors it has suffered from weak retail sales and too many shoe shops on the high street.' (*Investors Chronicle*) Once you have written 'it has suffered from (1) weak retail sales and (2)', then what follows (2) must match what follows (1) in construction: *it has suffered from weak retail sales and an excess of shoe shops in the high street.*

'He has commemorated further great royal events and even landmarks in his own family life, celebrating anniversaries and when each of his four children were born.' (*Best of British*) Here the construction again changes after 'and': *celebrating anniversaries and the birthdays of his four children.*

'The lane seemed to wind in a series of unnecessary loops. There were no hills for it to circumvent and the river to flow in the opposite direction.' (*Novel*) Someone might say 'There was no bacon for me to cook and the children to eat', where the two infinitives, 'to cook' and 'to eat', have the same object, 'bacon'. But no one would say 'There was no bacon for me to cook and the children to be late for school'. Similarly 'hills for the lane to circumvent and the river to flow' will not do: *no hills for the lane to circumvent and the river to flow away from in the opposite direction.*

Sometimes 'and' is simply the wrong word to use. 'The things you can still buy and still care about the environment are reducing every day.' (*Annabel*) One might speak of the 'things you can buy and sell', but not of things you can buy and care about the environment. *The things you can still buy while caring about the environment are being reduced every day.*

animal. 'The RSPCA yesterday called for harsher penalties for animal cruelty.' (*Independent*) 'Human cruelty' would be cruelty practised by human beings. 'Animal cruelty' ought therefore to mean cruelty by animals: *called for harsher penalties for cruelty to animals.*

answer (noun). An answer is a response to a question. 'Shared use could be answer to success.' (*Lake District Guardian*) A certain freedom can be allowed to writers of headlines, but a writer ought not to imply that success calls for an answer. *Shared use may bring success.*

'New Covent Garden Soup Company has the perfect answer to a quick and tasty meal at any time of the day.' (*My Weekly*) A quick meal does not call for an answer: *has the perfect recipe for a quick and tasty meal.*

'This is the answer to some of their previously inexplicable behaviour' (*Wild About Animals*) should be: *This is the explanation for their previously inexplicable behaviour.*

answer (verb). 'But now cheese specialist Peter Gott has answered our plight.' (*The Times*) A plight is not a question to be 'answered' but a condition of extreme distress: *Peter Gott has saved us from our plight.*

Antithesis. Effective writing often relies on contrasting one thing with another. 'Deeds matter more than words.' There an effective antithesis is presented. We know exactly what is being contrasted with what. And we recognise that in the context speech is being denigrated while action is praised. Provided that action and speech are genuine alternatives the logic is sound. Unfortunately this device of antithesis can be abused when in verbal form contrast appears to be present but the genuine substance of contrast is absent.

'People matter – not their accents.' (*Daily Express*). Thus the paper headlined a piece in defence of regional accents on radio. There can be no possible contrast between people and their accents, because all people have accents. It is like saying 'Grocers' shops matter, not cheese and bacon'. Without people there would be no accents. But the writer has inserted into the reader's mind the notion that worrying too much about accent involves denigrating something of more vital human worth. The propaganda value of this technique of misrepresentation is considerable.

any. It is not permissible to follow 'any' with a negative verb. 'Flu viruses are unstable, so any immunity people may have acquired to the old strains will not help them when they come across new ones.' (*Living*) In such sentences 'any' should become 'no/none': *so no immunity people may have acquired will help them.*

'During that time any changes in the income don't affect the benefit paid.' (*Radio 4*) Here, where 'any changes' means 'any changes that may be made' the implicit meaning must be clarified. *During that time no changes made in the income would affect the benefit paid.*

'From tomorrow any new employee at Railtrack will no longer be entitled to a full range of travel benefits.' (*Radio 4*) This should be: *From tomorrow no new employee at Railtrack will any longer be entitled to a full range of travel benefits.*

anyone. 'Anyone who hands in a gun will not be prosecuted.' (*Radio 4*) 'Anyone' cannot be followed by a negative verb. *No one who hands in a gun will be prosecuted.*

apart from. In the proper use of these words, 'Apart from a few sweets, I did not buy anything', they isolate an item ('a few sweets') as exceptional in relation to a statement. The expression is misused in a variety of ways.

IMPROPERLY CONNECTED 'Apart from a television broadcast, where he justified a military solution, he has failed either to assume public command of the crisis or to explain adequately how Russia will reimpose its political will.' (*The Times*) This leader does not link the first phrase grammatically with what follows. It is like saying 'Apart from breakfast he failed to look after himself.' *Apart from giving a television broadcast, he has done nothing either to assume public command of the crisis or to explain adequately how Russia will impose its political will.*

'Apart from the water companies, with their special problems of coping with neglect and robbery by previous governments of whichever complexion, prices are much lower than before privatisation.' (*The Times*) If 'apart from' is kept, 'prices' must go. *Apart from the water companies, utilities have much lower prices than before privatisation.*

'Apart from several operations on her teeth, her friends say she is not the exhausted and bitter woman portrayed by her detractors, but is staggeringly fit for a septuagenarian.' (*The Times*) If the sentence had run 'Apart from several operations on her teeth, she has not had any hospital treatment', the use of 'apart from' would have been justified. As it is, the expression does not make sense in relation to what follows, and should go: *Her friends say she is not the exhausted and bitter woman portrayed by her detractors and, though she has had several operations on her teeth, she is staggeringly fit for a septuagenarian.*

Sometimes it seems impossible to account for the writer's use of this expression. 'Apart from lack of evidence, it defies logic to suggest that anyone smuggling drugs is going to land on Gibraltar's heavily controlled coastline.' (*Radio 4*) Here the expression 'apart from' has nothing to link with since it does not isolate an exception in relation to 'it defies logic to suggest'. *Even if we ignore the lack of evidence, it defies logic to suggest that anyone smuggling drugs is going to land on Gibraltar's heavily controlled coastline.*

USED INSTEAD OF 'ALTHOUGH' 'Apart from moving to a new office in lovely Lincolnshire, *Best of British* will remain very much the same excellent magazine.' (*Best of British*) Here the writer tries to make 'apart from' do the work of 'although'. *Although moving to a new office in lovely Lincolnshire, Best of British will remain very much the same.*

USED INSTEAD OF 'AS WELL AS' 'Apart from being far less crowded, Spring in Corfu is very special.' (*Sunmed Holidays*) This quite common usage tries to equate 'apart from' with 'as well as'. *As well as being less crowded, Spring in Corfu is very special.*

'Apart from the more obvious pleasures of holidaying in splendid properties, cottage breaks are a very effective way to test drive an area where you might consider living.' (*Cottage & Castle*) Nothing here links grammatically with 'apart from the pleasures': *As well as giving you the pleasure of holidaying in special properties, cottage breaks are a very effective way.*

'Apart from a strong sense of humour, her submissions displayed a passion for the clinical aspect to her role.' (*Nursing Standard*) The misuse of 'to' should also be noted here. *As well as a strong sense of humour, her submissions displayed a passion for the clinical aspects of her role.*

USED INSTEAD OF 'IN ADDITION TO' 'Solas comes with either fixed or loose covers, but apart from choosing a colour and pattern you like, the fabric must meet flammability regulations.' (*OK! Homes*) Here again it is a matter of citing not an exception but an addition: *in addition to choosing a colour and pattern you like, you must see that the fabric meets flammability regulations.*

'What made the finalists stand out? Apart from expressing themselves clearly, they convinced the judging panel that they had potential to develop further.' (*Nursing Standard*) Clearly this should be: *In addition to expressing themselves clearly, they convinced the judging panel that they had potential.*

USED INSTEAD OF 'NOT ONLY' 'Apart from browsing along river banks and quaysides, any wet surface now became a valid study.' (*Artists & Illustrators Magazine*) This artist appears to mean: *Not only did I browse along river banks and quaysides, I also found that any wet surface became a valid study.*

Apostrophe. SINGULAR NOUNS ENDING IN 'S' Where a singular noun has the letter 's' as its final letter, there is a tendency to omit the apostrophe in the possessive case. This practice is condemned by many grammarians. If their precepts are followed, then 'St Thomas' Tower' (*History Today*) should be *St Thomas's Tower*, 'captured by their hostess' camera' (*Traditional Homes*) should be: *captured by their hostess's camera*, 'Jill Curtis' broad outline' (*New Woman*) should be: *Jill Curtis's broad outline*, 'Charles' rule' (*History Today*) should be: *Charles's rule*, 'Dickens' circumlocution' (*Gentlemen's Quarterly*) should be: *Dickens's circumlocution*. 'Michael Ross' wayward son' (*Woman's Own*) should be: *Michael Ross's wayward son*. However, comprehensive application of this rigid rule is not easy, for there are names such as 'Zeus' which look absurd when the rule is followed ('Zeus's') and indeed the King James Bible does not apostrophise 'Jesus' with an extra 's' ('She had a sister called Mary, which also sat at Jesus' feet').

PLURAL NOUNS ENDING IN 'S' Where a plural noun ends in 's', as most of them do, then it is proper to add the apostrophe without a further 's'. 'The second and final sections consider inheritance from the beneficiaries viewpoint' (*Meridian*) should be: *from the beneficiaries' viewpoint*, 'a new retail outlet specialising in ladies leisure footwear' (*Lancashire Life*) should be: *specialising in ladies' leisure footwear*.

PLURAL NOUNS GENERALLY Where a noun is in the plural and it is not possessive, it is bad to insert an apostrophe before the final 's'. 'The under five's need certain things to help them' (*Good Housekeeping*) should be: *The under fives need certain things*, 'Smart girl's get more!' (*Marketing Week*) should be: *Smart girls get more!*, 'You get personal tips that have taken the pro's years to evolve' (*The Times*) should be: *tips that have taken the pros years to evolve*, 'Levi's encase long, coltish legs' (*Tatler*) should be: *Levis encase long, coltish legs*, 'Detailed transaction recording is available for single or multiple portfolio's' (*Moneywise*) should be: *multiple portfolios*, 'From your favourite photo's' (*Wild About Animals*) should be: *favourite photos*, 'Pharmacist's spend years learning their profession' (*New Woman*) should be: *Pharmacists.*'Monday's to Saturday's: Enjoy a meal in our relaxing lounge' (*Stakis Lodore Hotel*) should be: *Mondays to Saturdays*. These errors would merit poor assessment in the junior school.

AGES AND DECADES ETC IN FIGURES 'The shepherd seemed to be in his 30's' (*Outdoors Illustrated*). Again there should be no apostrophe: *30s*. This applies to calendar years too. Reference to 'a farmhouse dating from the 1960's' (*Allerdale Outlook*) should be: *1960s*. 'Local MPs Michael Jopling and John Hutton donned 1920's helmets' (*Lancashire Life*) should be: *1920's helmets* or possibly: *1920s' helmets* (i.e. helmets *of* the 1920s).

What applies to dates applies to scores in games. 'Another unusual feature of the course is two consecutive par 5's' (*Lancashire Life*) should be: *par 5s*.

BEYOND THE PALE We reach the nadir of illiteracy in reference to 'the Foreign Office list of country's [*countries*] British citizens are recommended to avoid' (*Adventure Travel*) and in reference to 'specialist activity insurance's [*insurances*]'. (*Adventure Travel*)

appearance. 'Women are startled when this sometimes wild appearanced character leaps to his feet.' (*Woman's Journal*) There is no verb 'to appearance' and therefore no participle 'appearanced': *when this sometimes wild-looking character leaps to his feet.*

application. One application of a given principle may be compared to another application, but the word should not be treated as though it were synonymous with 'specimen' or 'example'.

'The NHS is regarded as the most successful application of the citizen's charter initiative' (*The Times*) should be: *The NHS is regarded as most successfully exemplifying the citizen's charter initiative.*

'All the gear we tested on this expedition has many applications.' (*Adventure Travel*) The obvious words here are: *has many different uses.*

'A typical application of a performance fabric in use is a hot air balloon' (*Trail*) should be: *The hot air balloon exemplifies how a performance fabric can be used.*

'The most familiar supersonic craft are military in their application.' (*Focus*) Here the expression 'in their application' adds nothing and should be omitted.

appointee. 'These powers often included also being President of the Civil and Criminal Courts, Coroner, Keeper of the local Jail, sole appointee of offices . . . ' (*Allerdale Outlook*) As an employer is one who employs others and an employee is among those employed, so an 'appointee' is a person appointed: *sole appointer of officers* [sic].

Apposition. In 'Mr Brown, the baker', the words 'the baker' stand in apposition to 'Mr Brown'. Words or phrases which perform this function must match the noun they parallel. As sentences lengthen, the danger of a mismatch increases.

'A compact and well-armed design, mounting a variety of missile, gun and torpedo systems, they are still the frontline ships of the Belgian Navy.' (*The Times*) 'A compact design' cannot stand in apposition to 'they . . . the frontline ships'. The ships are not a design. A simple change would correct this. *Compact and well-armed in design, they are still the frontline ships. See also* PARALLELS THAT FAIL TO MATCH.

appraise/apprise. The word 'appraise' is now commonly misused by confusion with 'apprise'. To 'appraise' something is to estimate its value: *The inspectors came to appraise the school's performance.* To 'apprise' is to inform: *The police were officially apprised of her disappearance.*

apprehend/comprehend. These two verbs both mean to 'understand', to 'grasp' mentally. The difference between them can best be indicated by recalling that to 'apprehend' is also to seize or arrest (*The criminal was apprehended*), and to 'comprehend' is also to comprise or include (*This list comprehends the contents of all previous lists*). The corresponding adjectives have drifted apart in meaning. Where 'comprehensive' means fully inclusive, 'apprehensive' means somewhat fearfully expectant. The two processes of seizing something with the mind ('apprehending' it) and fully embracing something with the mind ('comprehending' it) clearly overlap.

apprise. *See* APPRAISE.

approach. This is one of the most carelessly used words today. 'I would like to add a new approach to the power war where "manufacturers pay and retailers benefit" – cooperation.' (*Marketing Week*) An approach is not something that can be 'added'. *I would like to propose the adoption of a new attitude.*

approaching. The participle 'approaching' is sometimes used as an alternative to 'nearly' (a sum of money 'approaching' £1m). It is better avoided.

'Approaching 200 dogs from all over the country entered this year's pilot event.' (*Dogs Monthly*) Nothing is gained by not saying: *Nearly 200 dogs.*

appropriateness. This is one of those abstract nouns which are often better avoided. 'It also brought him to the fore of a fierce public debate about the appropriateness of prisoners making money from the sale of pictures.' (*The Times*) The gerciple, 'of prisoners making money', is a poor alternative to: *public debate about whether it was appropriate for prisoners to make money.*

arcane. 'But what should have been a straightforward, if not arcane, debate about computer data is overshadowed by a furious row.' (*Radio 4*) This is like saying 'The occasion was a happy, if not sad one'. The words 'straightforward' and 'arcane' point in opposite directions. The word 'arcane' is applied to what is esoteric, what requires secret knowledge if it is to be understood. If something is straightforward it cannot possibly be arcane: *But what should have been a straightforward, far from arcane, debate about computer data.*

area. Fashionable misuse of the word 'area' is destroying its meaning. 'Nappy changing is another area which requires special care.' (*Parents*) Changing nappies is an act, not an area: *Nappy changing is another process which requires special care.*

Changing nappies is not the only process to be dubbed an 'area'. 'Choosing colour schemes is a fun area for Stafford' (*Home Style*) should surely be: *Choosing colour schemes is something Stafford enjoys.*

Solid artefacts also get called 'areas'. 'Boots are an area in which much change has been seen and many people now wear rubber ones.' (*Horse & Hound*) Here the first eleven words can be reduced to six by abandoning use of the word 'area'. *Fashion in boots has changed greatly and many people now wear rubber ones.*

Advice about buying antiques, 'Pick one or two areas that you are particularly drawn to, whether it is plates, toys, or horse brasses,' (*Home Style*) turns various solid articles into 'areas'. *Pick one or two items that you are particularly drawn to.*

Rumours about a cut in maternity pay produced this from a government spokesman, 'There are much more sensible areas where we could cut back.' (*Radio 4*) Again removing 'areas' cuts out waste words: *There are costs we could more sensibly reduce.*

arguable. 'The only arguable problem was the decision of the directors to put the audience on stage and some of the action in the auditorium.' (*The Times*) Since we do not 'argue' problems, they cannot be said to be 'arguable', but a proposed solution to a problem might be 'arguable'. The writer appears to mean: *The only matter which arguably presented a problem was the decision of the directors to put the audience on stage.*

argue. 'And few could argue that the South Africans fully deserved their victory.' (*Radio 4*) Unfortunately (as the context makes clear) this means the opposite of what the cricket commentator wanted to say. To argue that a man is a thief is to maintain that he is a thief. To dispute that a man is a thief is to deny that he is a thief. *And few could dispute that the South Africans fully deserved their victory.*

argument. 'Their old arguments of providing effective and humane vermin control have long since lost all credibility.' (*Green Magazine*) The word 'argument' is not followed by 'of' when the subject of the argument is at issue: *Their old arguments about providing effective and humane vermin control.*

arising out of. The strict use of this expression ('Arising out of the bath, he seized a towel') shows its limitations, and it ought not to be turned into a kind of pseudo-conjunction more or less equivalent to 'as a result of'.

'Arising out of his experiences of warning about potential disasters he persuaded the academy that there was an important need to develop guidelines.' (*The Times*) 'He' was not 'arising', as the grammar implies: *As a result of his experiences of warning about potential disasters.*

around. 'I prefer being around people.' (*She*) This sentence attempts to reverse an idiom that is not reversible. *I prefer having people around me.*

array. 'The traditional array of claxons, hooters and balloons were not in evidence.' (*Radio 4*) 'Array' is a singular noun. *The traditional array of claxons, hooters and balloons was not in evidence.*

articulate. 'We are prepared to stick to this ground and, what's more, articulate it.' (*Radio 4*) 'Ground' (when the word is used metaphorically thus) can be 'covered' or 'explored', but it cannot be 'articulated'. If 'articulated' is to be kept, the word 'ground' must be replaced. *We intend to stick to this belief/principle and articulate it.*

as. Where 'as' is used to introduce appositional phrases the connection between the phrase and the subject it amplifies must be carefully preserved. This applies whether the 'as' phrase succeeds the subject it parallels ('He was a failure as a businessman') or precedes it ('As a businessman he was a failure').

SUBJECT FOLLOWED BY 'AS' PHRASE 'His life-long connections with the Holcombe Hunt began as a small boy.' (*Horse & Hound*) His 'connections' did not begin as a small boy: they were never a small boy. *He began his lifelong connection with the Holcombe Hunt as a small boy.*

'Nerylla Taunton's interest in antiques began with collecting thimbles as a teenager.' (*Country Living*) Her 'interest' did not begin as a teenager. *Nerylla Taunton's interest in antiques began with collecting thimbles when she was a teenager.*

'She caused a laugh by describing Alison's theft, as a toddler, of the family trifle.' (*Guardian*). The theft must not be described as 'a toddler': *by describing how, as a toddler, Alison stole the family trifle. See also* POSSESSIVE TRAP.

SUBJECT PRECEDED BY 'AS' PHRASE Beginning a sentence (or a clause) with 'as' can easily lead to error. 'As a self-employed business woman, Jill Hadfield's car is her second home.' (*Radio 4*) The car must not be said to be a businesswoman. If the sentence begins with 'As a self-employed businesswoman', the following statement must begin with Jill Hadfield, not with her car. *As a self-employed businesswoman, Jill Hadfield finds her car is her second home.*

'As a public speaker he excelled' is correct because 'he' is the public speaker. 'As an outstanding trainer of curates his greatness lay in the capacity to allow junior colleagues to do things their own way' (*The Times*) is incorrect because 'his greatness' did not train curates. *As an outstanding trainer of curates, he excelled because he allowed junior colleagues to do things in* [sic] *their own way.*

'As the organisation which drew up the poster mentioned in the article, the complexities and cost of the new legislation are all too apparent.' (*The Times*) This is like saying 'As a boy of twelve, the countryside was beautiful'. There is no word to balance the phrase 'as the organisation'. *As the organisation which drew up the poster mentioned in the article, the Institute of Actuaries finds the complexities and cost of the new legislation all too apparent.*

'One woman who has made it to the top says that as a woman, corporate finance departments and bond markets "are the nicest areas" in which to work.' (*The Times*) This tells us that corporate finance departments and bond markets are the nicest areas when they are a woman. The word 'as' must be changed: *that, for a woman, corporate finance departments and bond markets "are the nicest areas" in which to work.*

as a result. Something can be said to occur or happen 'as a result of' some event or cause, but the words cannot follow the verb 'to be'.

'Some of the difficulties facing Gibraltar at the moment are as a result of the actions of both Spain and the United Kingdom.' (*Radio 4*) Some other verb than 'are' should be used here: *Some of the difficulties have arisen as a result of the actions*. Alternatively the word 'as' may be taken out: *Some of the difficulties are a result of the actions*. Best of all might be to get rid of 'result': *Some of the difficulties have arisen from the actions*.

as easily as (etc.). In 'The puppy was as easily caught as the kitten' the comparison is straightforward. Puppy and kitten can be easily caught.

'The Dehaene supporters seem to believe that the British veto is as easily overturned as the last time a stand on principle was attempted.' (*The Times*). Now the British veto might be as easily overturned as a milk jug, but not 'as the last time'. The precise comparison must be made clear. *Now the British veto is as easily overturned as it was the last time*.

as far as. We say 'He drove as far as he could' but 'He went so far as to call me a fool'. 'Israel's Prime Minister, Yitzhak Shamir, went as far as comparing his erstwhile enemy, President Assad of Syria to the late Egyptian leader, Anwar Sadat.' (*The Times*) The construction 'so far as' would be better here and 'to compare' would be better than 'comparing': *went so far as to compare his erstwhile enemy*.

as . . . go. 'As religious seekers go, Elgar's *Gerontius* has always pipped *King Olaf* at the post.' (*The Times*) It would be correct to say 'As religious seekers go, Luther was unique' because Luther was a religious seeker. But Elgar's *Gerontius* was not a religious seeker. The idiom is the wrong one. *For religious seekers* Gerontius *has always pipped* King Olaf.

as he was known. 'The butcher of Islington, as he was called' is correct because he was indeed called 'the butcher'. 'The butcher of Islington, as he was known' is incorrect, because he was not known 'the butcher' but 'as the butcher'.

Thus 'The "pilots" as they came to be known, still meet annually for a reunion' (*The Times*) should be: *The 'pilots' as they came to be called*.

'"Hinch" as he was invariably known in the House' (*The Times*) should be: *'Hinch' as he was invariably called in the House*. See also KNOW.

as in. 'As in every other field of human endeavour, livestock husbandry has its fashion trends.' (*Country Talk*) It is ironic that while 'like' is often used where 'as' would be better, the converse often applies too. There is nothing here for 'as in' to latch on to. *Like every other field of human endeavour, livestock husbandry has its fashion trends.*

'Top-level success in British dressage, as in the rest of the world, is now virtually dependent on the fact that one has a trainer.' (*Tatler*) One might say 'in Britain as in the rest of the world' or 'in British, as in French dressage', where in each case what follows 'as' matches what precedes it, but 'in British . . . as in the rest of the world' will not do: *Top level success in dressage in Britain, as in the rest of the world.*

as of. These words are being used together where they do not make sense. 'But the fact remains that as of this minute, if you so choose, you can start the long haul back to dental health.' (*Country Living*) Here 'as of' appears to be used to give a kind of special emphasis to 'this minute'. It is not grammatically fitted to do so. *But the fact remains that from this very minute you can start the long haul.*

as quickly as. 'A divorce can be arranged as quickly as three months.' (*The Times*) A divorce can be arranged as quickly as a wedding, but months cannot be arranged at any speed. *A divorce can be arranged within three months.*

as soon. 'Personally, I'd just as soon watch or listen to what people do than read about them.' (*Me*). In the idiom used here ('I'd just as soon go as stay') 'as soon' must be followed by 'as', not by 'than'. *I'd just as soon watch or listen to what people say as read about them.*

as such. 'All three of these charities are pressure groups which aim to influence public policy. As such, their activities and promotional campaigns verge on the political.' (*The Times*) 'As such' is here made to agree falsely with the activities of the groups instead of with the groups themselves. If 'as such' is kept, the subject of the second sentence must be changed. *As such, they verge on the political in their activities and promotional campaigns.*

as well as. This is an expression variously misused.

GRAMMATICAL MISMATCH The words bind two items closely together. They must be so placed that there can be no doubt about what those two items are. What follows 'as well as' must parallel what precedes it ('I like rice as well as potatoes', 'He used to sing as well as to play the fiddle').

'White or a weak grey helps to give the room a light, spacious feeling as well as providing a neutral background colour against which to view your work.' (*The Artist*) Here 'to give' is improperly matched with 'providing': *helps to give the room a light, spacious feeling as well as to provide a neutral background.* To be more pedantic, the 'feeling' is not really given to the room: *helps to give the room light and spaciousness.*

'Soap flakes can be used to do the washing up, as well as washing clothes' (*Essentials*) should be: *to do the washing up as well as to wash clothes.*

Where the sentence is longer it is easier to slip up. 'The Variety Club wants to raise £3 million to help children's hospitals, special schools and needy children all over the UK, as well as buying more Sunshine coaches to take housebound children on outings.' (*Family Circle*) should be: *to help children's hospitals all over the world as well as to buy more Sunshine coaches.*

'Fruit and vegetables make ideal finger foods and snacks as well as being served with meals.' (*Parents*) Again the construction 'as well as being served' should go, and the sentence should read: *Fruit and vegetables make ideal finger foods and snacks, as well as part of a meal.*

Similarly 'Smallbone designers can talk through different design schemes and price options as well as explaining the complex installation service' (*Country Living*) should be: *can talk through different design schemes and price options and also explain the complex installation service.*

USED INSTEAD OF 'BOTH ... AND' 'Maggie Gee explores Alma's gradual recovery from this nightmare, and in doing so depicts with painful honesty the difficulty of letting go of one's own childhood as well as the true nature of parenthood.' (*Vogue*) Here 'the true nature of parenthood' is seemingly bound to 'one's own childhood', as though one has to let both these things 'go'. The verb 'depicts' is too far off for 'as well as' to do its proper job in relation to it. It would be better to substitute 'both . . . and': *depicts with painful honesty both the difficulty of letting go of one's own childhood and the true nature of parenthood.*

USED INSTEAD OF 'LIKE' 'As well as Londonderry, tomorrow's republican march and rally in Belfast could prove to be a flashpoint.' (*Guardian*) No one would write 'As well as the kitchen, dinner in the bedroom makes a mess'. The constructions should be changed. *Like those in Londonderry, tomorrow's republican march and rally in Belfast could prove to be a flashpoint.*

OVERKILL 'As well as our Carefree Travel Service there are many more excellent Club Services.' (*Camping*) 'As well as' must not be combined with 'more'. *As well as our Carefree Travel Service there are many excellent Club Services.*

WILD MISUSE 'As well as the civilised life of its owners there was in residence the Kurt Jooss ballet company.' (*The Times*) This obituary is listing the advantages for a sculptor of living at Dartington Hall. It tells us that somebody's civilised life was in residence there along with a ballet company. 'As well as' leads the writer to grammatical disaster: it is best to sacrifice the phrase. *The owners led a civilised life, the Kurt Jooss ballet company was in residence.*

'As well as his regular workshops at home in Clanna Gardens he is a prolific author and is now working on his 23rd book.' (*Artists & Illustrators Magazine*) He is not regular workshops 'as well as' a prolific author. *As well as running regular workshops at home in Clanna Gardens, he is a prolific author.*

as with. It is bad to use 'as with' loosely as a substitute for 'like'. 'Bartex is a strong, waterproof, lightweight material. As with most nylon based materials, it is immensely hardwearing.' (*Shooting Times*) As so often, the simplest choice of words is the best. *Like most nylon-based materials, it is immensely hard-wearing.*

This bad usage is on the increase. 'As with fresh milk, Longlife is more thirst quenching when chilled' (*Living*) should be: *Like fresh milk, Longlife is more thirst-quenching.*

'As with most carmakers, Vauxhall produces hundreds of models each year that are never sold' (*The Times*) should be: *Like most carmakers.*

'As with people, rodents are individuals' (*Wild About Animals*) should be: *Like people.*

'As with many recent books it emulates the picture book format of Bob Allan's "High Lakeland Fells"' (*The Great Outdoors*) should be: *Like many recent books.*

ask. We use the verb 'ask' for what are called 'indirect questions', such as 'We asked him how far it was to London'.

'I asked him the extent to which the plague is now spreading from its original source.' (*Radio 4*). Usage allows us to ask a passer-by or to ask a question, but it does not permit us to ask anyone an extent. *I asked him to what extent the plague is now spreading from its original source,* or *I asked him how far the plague is now spreading.*

'Some general questions to ask of your software include the following.' (*Computer Weekly*) Anyone can ask a favour 'of' someone, and might idiomatically 'ask' (i.e. 'expect') certain uses of their software, but questions cannot be put to software: *questions to ask about your software.*

aspect. This word is appropriately used for the appearance of a thing or for a distinct feature. 'This place [the Black Country Museum] seems to improve every time I call. The canal aspect becomes more varied.' (*Waterways World*) This represents a fashionable misuse of the word. *The canal section becomes more varied.*

assumption. The word 'assumption' is used in two different constructions. 'His assumption of superiority was irritating' tells how he adopted a certain pose. 'His assumption about my career was false' tells how he misjudged something.

'This was work which challenged assumptions of the physical – impermanent, "impractical" work which could not be accommodated within the conventional art gallery.' (*Vivid*) It is the latter of the two usages which the writer of the above should have adopted, and 'of' will not do: *This was work which challenged assumptions about the physical.*

at. 'That house was at 25 Cromwell Street.' (*Guardian*) The house was not 'at' 25. *That house was 25 Cromwell Street.*

at least. 'We won't know the result until at least tomorrow' (*Radio 4*), it is announced of the Irish referendum. Neither 'at least' nor 'at most' can be used here. It is not a question of most or least but of time when. *We won't know the result until tomorrow at the earliest.*

at once. In its most common usage, this expression means 'immediately', but it is also used as a condensed version of 'at one and the same time' ('He is at once judge and jury').

'He is at once head of state as well as head of government.' (*Radio 4*) The expression cannot be thus combined with 'as well as', which becomes redundant. *He is at once head of state and head of government.*

at the age of. This is one of those phrases which require anchorage. The text must make plain whose age is at issue. 'At the age of six, Massey's parents divorced.' (*The Times*) Clearly the parents were older than that. *When Massey was six, his parents were divorced.*

attach. The word means to fasten or connect and should not be employed in contexts where notions of connection are absent.

'There are no grand or noble origins attached to Finsbury Park.' (*British Railways Illustrated*) The subject is the railway station. The word 'attached' is out of place. Nothing has an origin 'attached' to it. The writer is following the now unfortunate tendency to equate 'attached to' with 'associated with', but either expression would be pretentiously redundant here. *There was nothing grand or noble about the origin of Finsbury Park.*

attack. 'The shootings are the latest in a series of sectarian attacks between the Shia and Suny communities.' (*Radio 4*) There can be an attack 'on' someone or 'against' someone, but there cannot be attacks 'between' people. The noun must be changed: *a series of sectarian clashes between the Shia and Suny communities.*

attempt. 'The main mortgage rate is up only a quarter per cent in an attempt to limit the pain.' (*Radio 4*) The rate is clearly not 'up' in an attempt to limit pain. There must be an appropriate verb for the words 'in an attempt to' to latch on to. *The rise in the main mortgage rate has been restricted to a quarter per cent in an attempt to limit the pain.*

attention. 'Focus is about bringing attention to the business or businesses that you run.' (*Radio 4*) In received usage we 'bring' things to people's attention and 'draw' their attention to things. *Focus is a matter of concentrating attention on the business you run.*

So too 'Civil servants didn't draw this immediately to Mr Howard's attention' (*Radio 4*) should be: *Civil servants didn't bring this immediately to Mr Howard's attention*, or: *didn't draw Mr Howard's attention to this immediately.*

attribute (noun). 'Investment Trust Warrants allow you to enjoy the market movement attribute to a much larger investment.' *(Moneywise)* This means that advantage will be taken of movements in the market, which represent one among the various causes of profit or loss that have to be balanced against each other. But there is nothing here than can be fitly called an 'attribute'. We must not use the word as though a given process might be a collection of attributes as a machine is a collection of 'components': *enable you to take full advantage of market movement.*

'In fact money-making was not one of his many attributes.' (*Cumbria Life*) An attribute (of a person) is a characteristic or gift, not a function or process: *money-making was not one of his many interests.*

'He is a team player: a rarer attribute at present than it ought to be.' (*The Times*) A team player is a person, and a person cannot be an 'attribute'. Something must be mentioned that can be an 'attribute'. *He has the true team spirit: a rarer attribute at present than it ought to be.*

attribute (verb). 'There have been plenty of bad writers who have been attributed above their station.' (*Radio 4*) People may 'attribute' a piece of music to Chopin, and the piece of music 'is attributed' to Chopin, but Chopin cannot 'be attributed' anything. *There have been plenty of bad writers who have been ranked above their station.*

'Even a very good one [first novel] is rarely attributed with more merit than a clever opening gambit.' (*The Times*) Critics 'attribute' *Hamlet* to Shakespeare, and indeed they 'attribute' genius to Shakespeare, but neither *Hamlet* nor Shakespeare can be 'attributed with' anything: *Even a very good one is rarely credited with more merit.*

aural/oral. Confusion between these two words springs from the fact that they are usually indistinguishable in pronunciation. The one ('aural') derives from the Latin word for 'ear', the other ('oral') from the Latin word for 'mouth'. Thus the adjective 'aural' relates to the sense of hearing and 'oral' is concerned with speech. An *oral* examination tests the candidate in actual utterance. An *aural* examination might test the candidate's ability to take down on paper 'by ear' music played on keyboard of which the candidate has no previous knowledge.

automatic. 'Many middle-class voters will return to the fold on election day. But that is not automatic.' (*The Times*) An automatic action is performed without conscious volition. Careless use of the word weakens it. What is meant is: *But that cannot be taken for granted.* In any case there is a failure of logic. If many middle-class voters may not after all return to the fold, then why say that they will in the first place? *Many middle-class voters may return to the fold.*

availability. This is one of those words (like 'adequacy') which tends to be used where its opposite in intended.

'The prices currently paid by the generators are approaching 50 per cent higher than for imported coal, although the latter has certain disadvantages such as poorer quality, long-term availability and the cost of transport.' (*The Times*) 'Poorer quality' may be a disadvantage, but 'long-term availability' could not possibly be a disadvantage. On the contrary, it is the question mark over availability – and the possibility of unavailability – that is presumably a disadvantage: *certain disadvantages such as poorer quality, uncertainty over long-term availability and the cost of transport.*

available. 'Voyagers are available in both Gents and Ladies backs.' (*Adventure Travel*) 'Available in' is the wrong expression here. The things are not available in people's backs. The preposition 'in' is out of place. *Voyagers are designed for both Gents' and Ladies' backs.*

'Details are available by calling this number' (*Radio 4*) we are told, but they are presumably available whether we call it or not. *Details can be obtained by calling this number.*

avenge. 'Terrorist leaders spoke of avenging blood for blood.' (*Radio 4*) Someone may 'demand' or 'desire' blood 'for' blood, but the preposition 'for' is quite wrong with 'avenge'. *Terrorist leaders spoke of avenging blood with blood.*

averse. *See* ADVERSE.

avoid. This word should not be used where the issue is one of prevention rather than evasion.

'Their objective is to avoid a proposed new shopping centre swamping the canal and drydock in the way that the bus station, which it will re-place, was constructed on the site of Banbury's basins and warehouses.' (*Waterways World*) 'Avoiding' a shopping centre is a very different thing from preventing one from swamping a neighbourhood. And we must not say 'The new building is swamping the area in the way that the previous building was constructed', because swamping and constructing are different processes. It is like saying 'Her new hair-style transforms her appearance in the way previous outfits were bought.' *Their objective is to prevent the proposed new shopping centre from swamping the canal and drydock as the bus station, which it will replace, swamped the site of Banbury's basins and warehouses.*

Similarly 'Basedow picks early to avoid the wine becoming fat and blowsy' (*Oldie*) should be: *picks early to prevent the wine from becoming fat and blowsy.*

'It is expected that behind the scenes agreements will be sought to avoid the bill failing to get royal assent' (*Radio 4*) should be: *to prevent the bill from failing to get royal assent.*

Advice about what should be done 'in the interests of avoiding pollu-tion' (*Meridian*) is misleading since you 'avoid' pollution by by-passing the area of pollution: *in the interests of preventing pollution.*

Similarly in recommending tools which 'avoid the problem of one joint coming undone when you solder the next one' (*Railway Modeller*) the writer needs 'forestall' and an active verb: *which forestall the prob-lem that one joint will come undone.*

'VyrBrit can help avoid embarrassing cold sores' (*New Woman*) should be: *can help to prevent embarrassing cold sores.*

'We needed a path built around the lawn which would avoid us having to walk on the water-logged grass' (*Living*) should be: *which would save us from having to walk*.

'The wearing of shoes or boots with heels, to avoid a foot trapped in the stirrup, will be second nature.' (*The Field*) To avoid a trapped foot would not test the resources of most people; trapped feet do not often appear in one's footpath: *to forestall trapping a foot* or *getting a foot trapped*.

'To avoid personal opinion taking too strong a hand, in most cases I consulted a panel of advisers to arrive at a conclusion.' (*The Author*) This, alas, is the author of a book on usage writing about his work. In the first place, 'avoid' should be 'prevent'. In the second place, 'opinion taking' is inadmissible as the direct object of 'avoid' ('personal opinion's taking too strong a hand' would be correct, though ugly). In the third place, the re-peat of the infinitive construction ('to avoid . . . to arrive') is unfortunate. *To prevent personal opinion from taking too strong a hand, in most cases I consulted a panel of advisers before reaching a conclusion.*

award. 'The Directors were awarding themselves with handsome salary and share option packages.' (*Radio 4*) As we give someone a present, so we award someone a silver cup, not 'with' it: *awarding themselves handsome salary and share option packages.*

B

babysit. This may be accepted as a useful new intransitive verb. ('She is babysitting for her friend.') 'Derrick Morris will spend today with his wife Beryl, babysitting two grandchildren he might never have seen.' (*The Times*) A certain freedom is allowed with the verb 'sit' in that you may sit a baby on a potty, but 'babysit' cannot happily take an object: *looking after two grandchildren he might never have seen*.

badly. 'Lawyers believe that if he'd been able to sue he might have received three times as much compensation, money that Mr Bennett and his wife could badly use.' (*Radio 4*) The newswriter here confuses the expression 'well use' with the expression 'badly need': *money that Mr Bennett and his wife could well use.*

ballot. 'Today, as he cast his ballot, Mr Yeltsin said no circumstances would force him to abandon the course of reform.' (*Radio 4*) The ballot is the organised exercise of voting, the list of candidates, or the total number of votes cast: *Today, as he cast his vote.*

Newswriters continue to get this wrong. 'Up to fifty-five per cent of the voters have already cast their ballot' (*Radio 4*) should be: *have already voted.*

ban. 'A Tory MP who yesterday advocated a ban on pensioners retiring to the West Country to ease the rural housing crisis, was immediately attacked . . .' (*The Times*) There are two errors here. The gerciple 'pensioners retiring' should be 'retirement of pensioners'. The word order suggests that pensioners retire to the west country to ease the housing crisis. It must be changed: *A Tory MP who, to ease the rural housing crisis in the west country, advocated a ban on the retirement of pensioners there.*

barrier. 'Yet uncertainty and loss of confidence are the main barriers to Japan emerging from recession.' (*The Times*) They are not barriers to 'Japan emerging', but barriers preventing Japan from emerging: *the main barriers to Japan's emergence from recession. See also* GERCIPLES.

based on. 'Based on government estimates, 12,000 to 13,000 domestic workers enter the country each year.' (*The Times*) A theory may be 'based on' certain facts or evidence but domestic workers must not be said to be based on government estimates. The construction is the wrong one. *According to government estimates, 12,000 to 13,000 domestic workers enter the country each year.*

battle. 'The crews had to battle a well-developed blaze.' (*Radio 4*) The verb 'to battle' is intransitive. It should be followed by 'with' or 'against': *had to battle against a well-developed blaze.*

be. Misuse of the verb 'to be' occurs often and takes various forms.

OMISSION OF PREPOSITION In this respect what may be acceptable in conversation is not permissible in print. 'A worker for a Christian charity described East Timor as "the most frightening place I have ever been".' (*The Times*) A worker for a charity cannot 'be' a place: *the most frightening place I have ever been to.*

'TO BE' USED FOR OTHER VERBS 'The climax is when "Securiboars" start arresting humans.' (*Green Magazine*) This usage overworks the verb 'to be'. A less vague verb is required. *The climax is reached when "Securiboars" start arresting humans.*

'The advantage of this diversion was following the Lancaster Canal on the other side of the M6.' (*The Great Outdoors*) Here the use of the weak verb 'to be' is even more unfortunate. 'The advantage' must not be said to be following a canal. *The advantage of this diversion lay in following the Lancaster Canal.*

'One oddity though; the very job that calls for two people right around the world – the driver plus fireman – is just one man here!' (*Steam Railway*) It must not be said that the job 'is' one man: *the very job . . . is done by one man alone here.*

'Gavin Ewart's death last October was one of Audrey's last efforts for poetry, as she helped his widow to organise the friends for the funeral.' (*The Times*) To say that the poet's death was one of the good lady's last efforts for poetry suggests an act of murder in the interests of literature. 'Was' is the wrong verb here. *Gavin Ewart's death last October evoked one of Audrey's last efforts for poetry.*

because. This word is often ill-used.

GRAMMATICAL FUNCTION 'Because' is a conjunction. It is correct to say 'He died because he had a weak heart', where 'because' links with the verb 'died'. It is incorrect to say 'His death was because of a weak heart', linking 'because' with the noun 'death'.

'Contrary to Dr Gray, he argues that current problems are not because of free-market ideology run riot, rather the reverse.' (*The Times*) Replace 'because' by 'caused by': *he argues that current problems are not caused by free-market ideology.* (i)

Similarly 'during a shortage of this because of the Korean War' (*The Times*) should be: *during a shortage of this caused by the Korean War.* (ii)

Again 'It offered the soaps giants a new variety of liquid laundry detergent – a technical challenge because of the need to keep the active ingredients suspended evenly throughout each bottle' (*Money Observer*) must become: *a technical challenge caused by the need to keep the active ingredients suspended evenly.* (iii)

In the above three sentences an alternative satisfactory correction would be to replace 'because' by 'due to'. Thus (i) could be: *problems are not due to free-market economy*, (ii) could be: *shortage of this due to the Korean War*, and (iii) could be: *a technical challenge due to the need.* (It is ironic that 'due to' is increasingly used where it is incorrect and increasingly unused where it would be correct.)

'In these children, the attack isn't because they have ingested the toxin, but is a consequence of . . .' (*The Times*) This should be: *In these children the attack is not due to ingesting the toxin, but is a consequence of . . .*

CAUSE AND RESULT 'Because' should not be used where causation is not involved. 'Because of the need to turn the plough and oxen at each end of the strip, the ridge and furrow sometimes acquired a slight "s" shape.' (*Cottage & Castle*) This is not a matter of causation or motivation but of consequence: *As a result of the need to turn the plough and the oxen at each end of the strip.*

CAUSATIONAL OVERKILL 'Mr Ward said a major reason why the right services were not reaching the right people was because of a lack of direction from central government.' (*Nursing Standard*) To say 'The reason he died was because he smoked heavily' is to duplicate causation illogically. The 'reason' is the fact that he smoked heavily. Similarly in the above either 'reason' or 'because' should be removed: *a major reason why the right services were not reaching the right people was the lack of direction from central government*, or: *the right services were not reaching the right people largely because of a lack of direction from central government.*

The same error can occur when a writer starts with 'because'. 'In other words, just because we can think doesn't make us any better than any other creature.' (*The Times*) This should be: *The fact that we can think doesn't make us any better than any other creature.*

'Just because abortion is legal does not mean that it is agreeable' (*The Times*) should be: *That abortion is legal does not mean that it is agreeable.*

'Unfortunately, just because we want something to be, doesn't make it so' (*The Times*) should be: *(The fact) that we want something to be doesn't make it so.*

WILD MISUSE 'Because' must establish a clear causal connection. 'Maqui-Libre is the first ever foundation to liberate the skin, because our silky silicone pearls leave your skin kissed with a fine invisible veil.' (*Company*) Surely the advertisers do not really mean that the effect on your skin is the true cause of the product's primacy. Omit 'because' and insert a semicolon instead.

become. The verb 'become', like the verb 'to be', is followed by a complement, that is to say something that matches the subject. In 'He became king', 'king' matches 'he', complementing it.

'Jonathan Miller became practically everything you can think of from lecturing on medicine to staging operas.' (*The Times*) The writer here states that Miller 'became' lecturing and staging, but that is not what he 'became'. *Jonathan Miller became everything you can think of from lecturer on medicine to producer of opera.*

becoming. 'There is talk about astronauts on board the space shuttle becoming part of the Super Bowl pre-game show.' (*The Times*) 'Talk about people becoming this or that' is slack usage. *There is talk that the astronauts on board the space shuttle may become part of the Super Bowl pre-show game. See also* GERCIPLES.

bedevil. '. . . the need for juggling with an air-lever as engine revolutions rose and fell – a situation which bedevilled so many early carburettors.' (*Automobile*) To 'bedevil' is to harrass or to throw into confusion. It is not something which could be done to a carburettor. Nor is the word 'situation' happily used here. It would be easy to amend this: *a defect from which so many early carburettors suffered.*

befit. 'Maria Perry's latest book, *Knightsbridge Woman*, is published this week and, as befits the title, Ms Perry has been busy signing copies in Harrods.' (*The Times*) It would not befit a title to sign books in Harrods: *and appropriately, in view of the title, Ms Perry has been signing books in Harrods.*

before. In its simplest usage 'before' presents no problems ('You must wash your hands before tea'), but it is important to notice that when 'before' is followed by a verb instead of a noun ('You must wash your hands before eating') the connection between 'you' and 'eating' is crucial. 'Before eating' is the equivalent of 'before you eat'. You are not required to wash your hands before someone else begins to eat. Thus, whereas it is correct to say 'Before eating, you must wash your hands', because the subject 'you' harks back to 'eating', it is poor usage to say 'Before eating, the plates must be clean', because the plates are not going to eat.

'However, before concluding this article there are one or two minor points which are worthy of mention.' (*Steam Classic*) Here is a case in point. The 'other points' are not going to conclude the article. *However, before concluding this article I must mention one or two minor points.*

beg the question. To beg a question is to use an argument which evades the central issue at stake. Thus to defend capital punishment on the grounds that it costs the taxpayer less to kill than to imprison a murderer would be to beg the central moral question at issue. The idiom is now increasingly misused.

'Both have been in trouble with police for stolen vehicles a number of times. It begs the question why were two teenage children with social problems allowed to wander the streets of Plymouth at 4am?' (*The Times*) This police statement appears to misuse the idiom: *It raises the question why two teenage children were allowed to wander the streets of Plymouth.*

BBC newswriters also misunderstand the idiom. 'The coincidence in the timing begs the question whether Saddam Hussein planned all along to leave it to this minute to announce his retreat.' (*Radio 4*) The very opposite is presumably intended: *The coincidence in the timing raises the question.*

Misunderstanding of the expression must now be widespread. Various journals misuse it. 'But her egotistical behaviour begs the question: is she a megalomaniac?' (*OK! Magazine*) should be: *her egotistical behaviour raises the question: is she a megalomaniac?*

'This situation begs the question of whether she has enough work of her own when she has so much time to monitor yours' (*Living*) should be: *raises the question whether she has enough work of her own.*

And the investment advertisement 'All of which begs the question. Wouldn't you be better off with Schroders?' (*The Times*) should also be: *raises the question.*

'We now know the planets circling our Sun are "dirty iceballs" – which begs the question, how have they survived so long?' (*Focus*) should presumably also be: *raises the question.*

begin. 'Pat Keeble began his love for motoring with motorbikes.' (*The Times*) It is poor usage to speak of 'beginning' love. Convention allows either: *Pat Keeble began to love motoring with motorbikes*, or: *Pat Keeble's love for motoring began with motorbikes.*

begin with. This is one of those constructions which lures writers into error. 'Whereas most tapes begin with the narrator taking you into a deep relaxation . . .' (*New Woman*) 'With the writer taking' will not do: *Whereas on most tapes the writer takes you into a deep relaxation straightaway. See also* GERCIPLES, WITH.

behaviour. 'Their ability to perform natural behaviours – nesting and dust-bathing for example – is severely restricted.' (*The Times*) 'Behaviour' is the manner in which beings conduct themselves. The word does not have a plural. *Their ability to perform natural acts is severely limited.*

behavioural. 'During stage two, 36 behavioural eating goals were set in partnership with the patient, for example, to eat two pieces of fruit each day.' (*Nursing Standard*) Does the word 'behavioural' mean anything here? And why not 'agreed' instead of 'set in partnership'? *36 eating goals were agreed with the patient.*

behind. 'George Gardiner and all Conservatives should unite now behind the enemy.' (*Radio 4*) One assumes that this was the newswriter's error in reporting the Chairman of the Conservative Party: *all Conservatives should unite now against the enemy.*

behove. The impersonal verb 'It behoves' means 'It is fitting' or 'It is necessary'. Thus 'It behoves me to be careful about my grammar.'

'If a member of the public, whether royalty or not, is willing to go into a public place in low cleavage, it ill behoves criticism if anyone takes a picture.' (*The Times*) This is a tortuous misuse of the expression: *it ill behoves anyone to criticise if someone takes a picture.*

being. This is a dangerous word to use at the opening of a sentence.

'BEING' MISCONNECTED It is correct to say 'Being an old man, I need plenty of rest', where 'I' am the person 'being' old. It is also correct to say 'Being an old man, the walking-stick is a great help to me', where the walking-stick is not 'being' an old man, but 'me' supplies the word for 'being' to relate to. But it is incorrect to say 'Being an old man, the stairs are a nuisance' where neither 'stairs' nor 'nuisance' can be said to be old.

'Being South Africa, the crash was immediately assumed to be politically motivated.' (*Radio 4*) This news item on the disaster to a commuter train makes the common error. There is nothing here which can 'be' South Africa. The grammar implies that the 'crash' is South Africa. 'Being' must go. *As might be expected in South Africa, the crash was immediately assumed to be politically motivated.*

'Being a front-wheel drive machine, when provoked around corners the driver wheels will eventually start to scrabble for grip.' (*Cumbria Life*) Nothing is mentioned here which can 'be' a front-wheel drive machine. In strict grammatical terms, the driver wheels are cited as 'being' a front-wheel drive machine. As so often it is best to get rid of 'being'. *As it is a front-wheel drive machine, when provoked around corners the driver wheels will eventually start to scrabble for grip.*

'Being the elder son, my future in farming was already set.' (*Home*

Style) This sentence illustrates what we are calling the 'possessive trap'. 'My future' is said to be the elder son. A word must be inserted to which 'being the elder son' truly applies. *Being the elder son, I found my future in farming already set.*

'But, being amateurs, unlike Coward's original 400, Crawford's rehearsal time was limited.' (*The Times*) In this review of a revival of *Cavalcade*, the rehearsal time is said to be 'amateurs'. 'Being' must go: *But, since they are amateurs, unlike Coward's original 400.*

The misconnected 'being' does not always occur right at the beginning of the sentence. 'There's the stunning Cornish countryside to explore – being out of season, it should be blissfully peaceful.' (*Home & Country*) It is best here to eliminate 'being': *out of season it should now be blissfully peaceful.*

Sometimes 'being' is simply the wrong verb. 'Being a total body workout, the NordicTrack Skier burns more calories than other exercise machines.' (*AA Magazine*) The skier must not be said to be itself a workout: *Supplying a total body work-out, the NordicTrack Skier burns more calories.*

'BEING' AFTER PREPOSITION 'The video did not show the full death scenario from the initial grip on the fox to it being torn apart or "broken up" as the hunter describes it.' (*Cumbria Life*) If 'being' is kept here, 'it' must be changed to 'its'. The logic moves from the 'grip' to the 'tearing apart', not from he 'grip' to 'it': *the full death scenario from the initial grip on the fox to its being torn apart.*

'This necessitated straight-line cycling with the route being dictated (on the smallest roads) by a rule being drawn from Paris to Dieppe.' (*Independent*) The first 'with' is redundant, the second 'being' is redundant, and it is not a 'rule' that is drawn. *This necessitated straight-line cycling, the route being dictated (determined) by a line ruled from Paris to Dieppe.*

'He said he was encouraged by gas, electricity, and water supplies being restored to Sarajevo.' (*Radio 4*) He was not encouraged by 'them' being restored, but by 'their' being restored. It is the restoration that gives encouragement. *He said he was encouraged by the restoration of gas, electricity, and water supplies to Sarajevo.*

'There will be valid reasons for these [questions] being asked' (*Options*) should be: *valid reasons for these questions to be asked.*

belong. The word carries overtones of proprietorship and of propriety. It should not be used so as to weaken its significance. 'The NRA is part of the Department of the Environment, belonging to a separate ministry's budget.' (*The Field*) This is a loose use of the verb which ignores its connotation. *The NRA is part of the Department of the Environment, financed by a separate ministry's budget.*

betray. 'He finally married Anne Williams, a solicitor's daughter whose liquid eyes and easy manner betray a robust will.' (*The Times*) In this context to 'betray' is to reveal. Surely the writer does not mean that liquid eyes and easy manner are signs of a robust will. She appears to have used the wrong verb: *whose liquid eyes and easy manner belie her robust will.*

better. 'These [cosmetics] are full sized and couldn't be a better collection to slip into your holiday packing.' (*Prima*) This is like saying 'Our candidate is first-class and couldn't be a better man to elect' instead of 'and there could be no better man to elect'. It should be similarly rephrased: *and there could be no better collection to slip into your holiday packing.*

between. Two main errors recur in the use of this word.

FAILURE IN BALANCE The word 'between' bears upon a relationship involving two points, objects or persons. Where this duality is lacking, 'between' should not be used.

'I merely wanted to do a little light television reporting between looking after our daughter.' (*The Times*) There is no duality here for 'between' to link. It is not possible to do anything 'between' a single process like looking after a daughter. *I merely wanted to combine a little light television reporting with looking after our daughter.* If it cannot be assumed that the reader will know what this means, then it must be spelt out. *I merely wanted occasionally to interrupt looking after my daughter with a little television reporting.*

Care must be taken to preserve strict grammatical balance between the items linked by 'between'. Reference to 'anxiety about striking a balance between that ruthlessness in spending and a caring government' (*Radio 4*) destroys the balance: *between that ruthlessness in spending and the government's concern for welfare.*

'There has been a close link between Liberal Democrat successes in local council elections and where the party has won seats in the Commons such as Bath, North Cornwall and North Devon.' (*The Times*) This awkward intrusion of the word 'where' upsets the balance and could easily be avoided: *close link between Liberal Democrat successes in local council elections and in elections where the party has won seats in the Commons.*

FAILURE IN LINKAGE Distinctions are made 'between' one thing *and* another. 'No longer is there [in modelling] a division between brains versus beauty.' (*The Times*) 'Between' cannot be thus followed by 'versus'. It would be absurd to speak of a fence 'between this house versus next door'. If 'versus' is kept, 'between' must go. *It is no longer a matter of brains versus beauty.* Otherwise it must be: *No longer is there competition between brains and beauty.*

Reference to 'that small bit of carpet between the bar to the strobe arena' (*New Woman*) misuses the word 'to': *small bit of carpet between the bar and the strobe arena.*

The misuse is not rare. Reference to 'the mass of land between the river Duddon in the south to the river Derwent in the north' (*Cumbria Life*) should be: *between the river Duddon in the south and the river Derwent in the north.*

'Typically muggings were committed by gangs of youths aged between 14 to 16' (*Radio 4*) should be either *aged from 14 to 16*, or *aged between 14 and 16.*

bit. 'There is hardly any wind, so it would be wrong to imagine the painter struggling against blizzards and freezing temperatures – the only bit of that which we experienced was two days at the end of our second stay.' (*Artists & Illustrators Magazine*) There are things which can be divided into 'bits' and things which cannot, among them blizzards and freezing temperatures: *the only touch of that which we experienced was on two days at the end of our second stay.*

bite the dust. 'More encouragingly, pairings of older women and younger men are becoming increasingly common, so perhaps this is another myth that will eventually bite the dust.' (*Options*) To 'bite the dust' is to accept a humiliating defeat or recantation. Myths cannot suffer humiliation. In any case what is the 'myth' in question? Presumably the unstated notion that women should not marry men much younger than themselves. This view should be cited: *so perhaps the notion that such pairings are inappropriate has now been exploded.*

blame. 'The man blamed with bringing Barings down, Nick Leeson . . .' (*Radio 4*) A man may be charged 'with' an offence, but he is blamed 'for' it: *The man blamed for bringing Barings down.*

blasphemous. 'Gandhi's descendants want the ashes immersed in sacred water. The bank vault is a blasphemous resting-place.' (*Radio 4*) An act is blasphemous if it is impious or offensive towards what is sacred. It is blasphemous to say a black mass in a cathedral, but that does not make the cathedral itself blasphemous. It is the act that is blasphemous, not the place. *It is blasphemous to leave them in a bank vault.*

blatant/flagrant. These two adjectives both have a condemnatory flavour, the latter especially. A 'blatant' act is conspicuous to an offensive degree: *To turn up for his mother's funeral in a track suit was blatant bad taste.* The word 'flagrant' describes an act which is not only blatant but also somewhat beyond the pale morally or legally: *To fail to report for duty in an emergency showed a flagrant disregard for duty.* See also FLAGRANT.

blow. 'Hard on the heels of the suggestion that children should take their mother's surname rather than their father's comes another blow for women's rights: pensions for housewives.' (*The Times*) This reveals ambiguity in the use of the words 'blow for'. In 'Her husband's death was a great blow for her' we see one usage. In 'Strike a blow for freedom' we see another. The latter is perhaps the rarer usage and for that reason would be better avoided where there might be ambiguity: *another blow on behalf of women's rights.*

boast. The intransitive verb 'to boast' (to make proud claims) is followed by 'of' ('boasted of his skill') or 'about' ('boasted about his wealth'). The transitive verb 'to boast' (proudly to possess something) is not followed by 'of'.

'The building today can boast of a new tiled roof' (*Lancashire Life*) should be: *The building today can boast a new tiled roof.*

bore. 'People were getting bored of realism.' (*The Times*) We say 'tired of' but it is an instance of false transference to apply this construction to 'bored'. *People were getting bored with realism.*

born. When beginning a sentence with 'born', care should be taken to ensure that it is matched in what follows.

'Born in France in 1903, of a Danish Cuban mother and Catalan father, Nin's early years were troubled and insecure.' (*The Times*) This tells us that Nin's early years were born in France. *Born in France ... Nin was troubled and insecure in her early years.*

both. It is correct to say 'I like both my sisters', but it would be incorrect to say 'I should not like to quarrel with both my sisters' if what was really meant was 'I should not like to quarrel with either of my sisters'.

Nevertheless on a news bulletin it was announced, in connection with IRA bomb attacks on Bognor Regis and Brighton, that the police would like to hear from people who might have taken photographs 'of both resorts' (*Radio 4*). Plainly one did not have to have taken photographs of both resorts in order to be of interest to the police: *photographs of either resort*.

The instance is unfortunately not an isolated one. 'The redemption of the Prime Minister's pledge will not be easy both in terms of the money available and where it's spent.' (*Radio 4*) This use of 'both' is bad. And so is the misplacing of 'both' before, instead of after, 'in terms of'. *The redemption of the Prime Minister's pledge will not be easy in terms either of the money available or of where it is spent.*

Similarly 'Didn't he know that the LMS and the LNER both employed more people than today's entire railway industry?' (*Steam World*) appears to mean: *Didn't he know that the LMS and LNER each employed more people than today's entire railway industry.*

'Both sets of brushes are very similar' (*Artists & Illustrators Magazine*) is tautologous. Set 1 cannot be similar to set 2 unless set 2 is similar to set 1, so 'both' is misplaced. *The two sets of brushes are very similar.*

breach. To breach is to break or break through. 'The gulf between relatively sedate county championship cricket and the Test arena has to be breached, and soon.' (*The Times*) One cannot 'breach' a gulf. Presumably what is meant here is: *The gulf between relatively sedate county championship cricket and the Test arena has to be bridged.*

break up. 'After the game police with riot shields and batons had to break up trouble which erupted in the streets near the ground.' (*Radio 4*) 'Trouble' can 'break out' but it is not something that can be either 'broken' or 'broken up'. Nor does trouble 'erupt'. *Police with riot shields and batons had to quell disorder that erupted near the ground.*

breathtaking. There is an adjective 'breathtaking' to describe what takes one's breath away. There is also an adverb 'breathtakingly'.

'Two years later Disraeli was breathtaken.' (*The Times*) There is no verb 'to breathtake'. *Two years later Disraeli was flabbergasted.*

build. 'This morning the meeting was to have concentrated on building closer ties between Britain and Germany.' (*Radio 4*) Ties are not 'built': *the meeting was to have concentrated on strengthening the ties between Britain and Germany.*

burn. 'As business picked up, Andrew decided to burn his bridges and gave up his job.' (*Cumbria Life*) The conventional expression would be: *Andrew decided to burn his boats.* No doubt burning bridges behind one is equally decisive. So is 'crossing the Rubicon'.

by. Care must always be taken to ensure that the word 'by' is correctly attached in its context. There are two constructions which lure to error.

'BY' AND GERUND A commentator says of McDonald's decision to ban beef 'Simply by taking this decision people are going to say "Wow"'. (*Radio 4*) This tells us that the 'people' have taken the decision and by taking it have said 'Wow'. It should become either: *Simply by taking this decision they will astonish people,* or *On hearing this decision people are going to say 'Wow'.*

'He will be suspicious at first, but by spending time by the cage talking to him, reassuring him, and offering little bits of food, he should soon come to trust you.' (*Wild About Animals*) The word order here implies that by doing this and that 'he' will learn to trust you. The words 'by spending time' etc. attach themselves to 'he' instead of to the more distant word 'you'. *He will be suspicious at first, but by spending time by the cage talking to him, reassuring him . . . you should soon gain his trust.*

'My obsession started at the age of ten by watching a children's TV show.' (*Dogs Monthly*) This sounds as though the obsession was ten years old and watched TV shows. 'By watching' must be properly anchored. It would be better here to remove 'by'. *My obsession started when I was ten and watching a children's TV show.*

The longer the sentence the more easily can error of this kind be concealed. 'The Crown Prosecution Service says it hopes that by making its guidelines widely available the public will understand the legal requirements that have to be satisfied in deciding what charges are brought against drivers.' (*Radio 4*) This implies that the public makes the guidelines available. *The Crown Prosecution Service says that by making its guidelines widely available it will enable the public to understand the legal requirements.*

'BY' AND GERCIPLE It is dangerous to use 'by' followed by a noun or pronoun and then a seeming gerund or participle. It is correct to say 'We succeeded by working hard.' It is incorrect to say 'The success was achieved by the management working hard' because the working hard of the management is 'the management's working hard', not 'the management working hard'. The best way to avoid this trap is to use the noun 'work' instead of the verb: *The success was achieved by the hard work of the management.*

'German consumers like their yolks deep crimson-orange, a colour produced by the hen eating grass' (*Country Living*). To avoid the awkwardness of the straightforward correction ('a colour produced by the hen's eating grass') change the construction: *a colour produced by the hen's consumption of grass.*

'London Health Emergency, a health watchdog, said the 6 per cent fall in London's population – widely believed to be distorted by people failing to register for the poll tax – could mean a £97m cut.' (*Nursing Standard*) Here the 'fall' is said to have been distorted 'by people failing' to register, but it is not the fall, it is the figure of 6 per cent that may have been so distorted, and it was not distorted 'by' the people but by their failure to register for the poll tax. *The London Health Emergency said that the reported fall of 6 per cent – a figure widely believed to be distorted by the failure of people to register for the Poll Tax – could cause a £97m cut.*

'BY' OR 'WITH' *See* WITH.

C

campaign. 'Both Windsor Castle and the Tower of London were part of William's campaign to establish himself as the undisputed King of England.' (*Majesty*) The buildings were not 'part' of a campaign. It was the construction of the castles that was part of William's campaign. *Both Windsor Castle and the Tower of London were constructed as part of William's campaign.*

Capital Letters. The modern tendency is to use capital letters sparingly. Proper nouns, that is names of individual persons, places or institutions etc., need initial capital letters (*John Smith, Birmingham, the House of Commons*).

The names of specific historical events, like the French Revolution or the Reformation, require initial capital letters, though of course the ordinary words 'reformation' and 'revolution' generally do not. This illustrates the basic difference between specific titles and general use (*He is a duke*; *he is the Duke of Devonshire*: *He is a bishop*; *he is Bishop of London*).

career. 'His career spanned 24 years at the Conran Design Group, starting as a junior designer to becoming the Creative Director of the company.' (*Home Style*) His 'career' did not start as a junior designer and become the Creative Director. The subject of the sentence must be changed. *In a career of 24 years at the Conran Design Group, he started as a junior designer and eventually became Creative Director.*

carry. We have certain idiomatic uses of this verb, notably in the various meanings of 'carry on'. Idiomatic freedom of this kind ought not to be abused.

'The idea of underwater diving has carried through to the 20th century to its present sophisticated form, via snorkelling.' (*Outdoors Illustrated*) The point is, not that the 'idea' of diving has survived, but the practice. It has not 'carried' anything 'through', it has evolved or developed. *Underwater diving has developed into its present sophisticated form in the 20th century through the use of snorkels.*

carry out. 'Now you can have soft, natural looking breasts, the shape and size you've always dreamed of, carried out by our experienced FRCS surgeons.' (*The Times*) It seems unlikely that many women will want to have their breasts, even new ones, 'carried out' by anyone. Perhaps the advertisers fought shy of the word 'manufactured'. One may venture: *Now you can have soft, natural looking breasts, the shape and size you've always dreamed of, moulded by our experienced surgeons.* But perhaps it would be more delicate to say: *after treatment by our experienced surgeons.*

'The offences carried out by John Allen went on for 12 years.' (*Radio 4*) A commission or an order may be 'carried out', but not an offence: *The offences committed by John Allen.*

'I know how much lobbying has been carried out.' (*Radio 4*) Lobbying is not something that is 'carried out'. *I know how much lobbying there has been.*

case. 'Each case [request for a bank loan] will be viewed on its merits and depend on whether you are a first-time buyer or already own a property.' (*Meridian*) The thing which will be viewed on its merits (the 'case') is not the thing (i.e. the outcome of the case) which will depend on the client's status. So 'case' cannot be the subject of the verb 'depend'. *Each case will be viewed on its merits and the outcome will depend on whether you are a first-time buyer.*

case of. This expression lures writers into error. It is correct to speak of 'a case of disliking meat' but not 'a case of people disliking meat' because strictly it is a matter of 'their' disliking, not 'them' disliking.

'Here was one of the clearer cases of the work itself addressing issues of immediate concern.' (*The Times*) This should be corrected by a change of the construction: *Here was one of the clearer cases in which the work itself addresses issues.*

'He said the case of Susan Edwards, who had a baby while shackled to a guard, should not have happened.' (*Daily Express*) A case does not 'happen'; it may 'arise'. It is the event itself that should not have 'happened'. Until something has actually happened it cannot become a 'case', i.e. a matter of discussion and possible controversy. *He said the incident in which Susan Edwards had a baby while shackled to a guard should never have occurred.*

cast. 'It will, he says, cast doubt about the press system of self-regulation.' (*Radio 4*) There is an idiom, to 'cast about', used generally of seeking rather wildly for something, but here the preposition 'about' is wrong: *It will cast doubt on the press system.*

cater. 'They've been catering to smokers since 1869.' (*Radio 4*) Since to cater is to provide 'for', the modern (American) usage of catering 'to' is not recommendable: *They've been catering for smokers.*

cause (noun). 'The commonest cause of normal hair loss apart from that due to ageing is androgenetic alopecia.' (*Lancashire Life*) There is no need here to introduce the awkward expression 'that due to'. *The commonest cause of normal hair loss, apart from ageing, is androgenetic alopecia.*

cause (verb). 'Scientists think they've found a way to cause little or no scarring after an operation.' (*Bella*) Although we say 'He caused no trouble', negatives after 'cause' are not always felicitous: *found how to operate and leave little or no scarring.*

caused by. When 'caused' is used as a participle, it must hang on a noun, as in 'The flood, caused by the sudden storm, swept through the village'. Here 'caused' qualifies the noun 'flood'.

'The infant mortality rate is still high – caused by a poor diet and the severe climate.' (*Marie Claire*) This is not good because 'caused' appears to be hanging on the adjective 'high'. It should be firmly connected with a noun. *There is still a high infant mortality rate – caused by a poor diet.*

'I preferred a more sedate pace caused partly by a lack of "bottle" and partly by the fact that most of the time I couldn't see further than the glass in my goggles.' (*Complete Traveller*) Here again 'caused' should relate to a noun, not a verb. Either supply the noun: *My preference for a more sedate pace was caused partly by a lack of 'bottle'*, or substitute 'because' for 'caused': *I preferred a more sedate pace partly because of a lack of 'bottle' and partly because most of the time I couldn't see.*

'Many burns are caused by pan handles being left carelessly pointing outwards.' (*Woman's Own*) It is the careless leaving of the pan handles, i.e. 'the pan handles' (with an apostrophe) being left' that causes the trouble: *caused by carelessly leaving pan handles pointing outwards.* But the sentence is susceptible of further improvement: *Burns are often caused when pan handles are carelessly left pointing outwards.*

cavort. 'Nevertheless the King managed to cavort himself as a kind of "male Gloriana" in costume adapted from the Tudor times.' (*The Times*) To 'cavort' is to prance or caper and the verb is intransitive. No one can cavort 'himself': *the King managed to cavort about as a kind of 'male Gloriana'.*

celebrate. 'She [the Queen] celebrated her twenty-first birthday party in Cape Town.' (*Radio 4*) She did not celebrate her 'party'. Either: *She celebrated her twenty-first birthday with a party*, or: *She held her twenty-first birthday party in Cape Town.*

'There is plenty of wizardry to celebrate over.' (*Radio 4*) We do not celebrate 'over' great achievements, we celebrate them. *There is plenty of wizardry to celebrate.*

'Protesters jeered in the plaza in front of Westminster Cathedral as she [the Queen] celebrated Vespers for St Andrew's Day.' (*The Times*) It is the officiating priest or minister who 'celebrates', not the congregation. The Queen did not perform any religious ceremony. She attended one. In any case, Vespers is not 'celebrated': *as she attended Vespers.*

-centred. It has become voguish to use this suffix, as in 'child-centred educational techniques'. However, reference to 'the government initiative aimed at providing woman-centred maternity services' (*Nursing Standard*) is surely stating the obvious. What other maternity services could there be?

challenge. 'Mr Tatchell is endeavouring to challenge this situation.' (*The*

Times) A 'situation' cannot be subject to 'challenge' (both words are overused), though its fitness may be. *Mr Tatchell is endeavouring to query the justice of this situation.*

'As Master of the South and West Wilts Foxhounds, he bred a pack that was to challenge the size, shape and weight of the modern fox-hound.' (*Hunting*) Parallelism breaks down here. Hound must be matched with hound, or size and weight with size and weight: *he bred a pack to challenge the modern foxhound in size, shape and weight.*

challenging. This long overused word now means little. 'The house-holders gathered to see [from photographs] how their houses had changed in the best part of a century interesting and challenging.' (*The People's Friend*) Neither 'interesting' nor 'challenging' carries any weight here. Both should be omitted.

chance. Unless the construction is brief and simple ('There is no chance of victory') it is always safer to follow this word by 'that' than by 'of'.

'Demand is growing by at least 6 per cent a year and there is little chance of any additional airport infrastructure being developed in the foreseeable future.' (*The Times*) The illicit passive gerciple would be awkward if directly corrected ('of any additional airport infrastructure's being developed'): *there is little chance that any additional airport infra-structure will be developed.*

'The chances of them allowing him to take the boy away from you are virtually nil.' (*Woman's Own*) The same applies here. It must be either: *The chances of their allowing him to take the boy away*, or: *The chances that they will allow him to take the boy away from you are virtually nil.*

change. 'In these cases, your doctor will advise on lifestyle changes like a good diet, no smoking, avoiding obesity, regular exercise, and check-ups on blood pressure.' (*My Weekly*) Not all the items listed are 'changes' but the consequences of changes. It would be better to drop the word: *your doctor will advise on healthier habits such as keeping to a good diet, giving up smoking, avoiding obesity, taking regular exercise and having regular check-ups.*

charge. 'A part that costs £40 may be charged at three times that.' (*AA Magazine*) It is the purchaser who is 'charged', not the purchase. *A part that costs £40 may be priced at three times that.*

chasm. This is a word which has not yet been weakened by inappro-priate metaphorical usage, but the danger is there.

'An employment assistant at Richmond College, her cultural chasm became particularly apparent when her mother died four years ago.' (*Cosmopolitan*) The subject is an Indian woman. If there is a 'chasm' of some kind between you and me, then it is certainly not either 'my' chasm or 'your' chasm. Nor is the chasm between the young Indian lady and the (unmentioned) society she is placed in 'her' chasm. In any case her 'cultural chasm' must not be said to have been an employment assistant at Richmond College. *An employment assistant at Richmond College, she became particularly aware of the cultural chasm separating her from the society around her when her mother died four years ago.*

choice. 'Now they find darker colours make a stronger choice of background for old pictures, which are often yellowed or have faded with age.' (*Period Living*) The word 'choice' is totally unnecessary here: *darker colours make a better background for old pictures.*

'Our choice of pitch for the test was unfortunately well populated with the sort of passers-by who have time on their hands.' (*Camping*) It was not the 'choice' that was well populated, but the site. *The site chosen for the test was unfortunately well populated.*

'You can eat at a choice of twelve restaurants.' (*Woman's Own*) You eat at a restaurant, not at a choice. Either the verb 'choose' should be used: *You can choose between twelve restaurants*, or the construction changed: *You can eat at any one of twelve restaurants.*

Where the word 'choice' is followed by 'between' and itemised alternatives, there must be no grammatical mismatch. 'But the choice should be between investments that pay interest gross, or where tax has been deducted that can be reclaimed.' (*Money Observer*) Here it is necessary to replace 'or' by 'and' and to match 'investments' with a grammatical parallel. *But the choice should be between investments that pay interest gross and investments from which tax that has been deducted can be reclaimed.*

choose. 'The theme park you choose will probably depend on where you live.' (*Moneywise*) This is an increasingly common error. It is not the park that depends on where you live, but the choice. *Which theme park you choose will probably depend on where you live.*

chord. 'The Prime Minister's office has said that the personal manifesto written by the widow of the murdered head teacher has touched a chord that government strategy supports.' (*Radio 4*) Chords cannot be 'supported': *touched a chord to which government policy is responsive.*

claim. Distinguish between claims 'of' and claims (made) 'for'.

'The health claims of many products are at the very least imaginative.' (*Marketing Week*) Products do not themselves make claims. This should be: *The health claims made for various products.*

'One milk drink that claimed to help women grow larger breasts enjoyed short-lived popularity.' (*Marketing Week*) No milk drink is capable of making a claim. The claim was made for it by human beings. *One milk drink which purported to help women to grow larger breasts enjoyed short-lived popularity.*

Coinages. To 'coin' a word is to invent a new word or a new usage. Such innovation, when successful, can illuminate and delight. The writer who fashioned the word 'couth' as the converse of 'uncouth', for instance, showed a sense of humour and provided a useful descriptive term. It can still count as an innovation, for it appears not yet to have found its way into the dictionaries. We should notice, however, that it is a logically conceived and designed word. This is what makes it acceptable.

DIARISE. 'But in the meantime diarise Oct 3–8, the dates of this year's show.' (*Artists & Illustrators Magazine*). It would seem logical that, as to 'prioritise' is to turn something into a priority, so to 'diarise' ought to mean to turn something into a diary. That is not the intended meaning here: *Make a note of Oct 3–8.*

IMPULSE-BUY. 'Resist the temptation to impulse-buy a plant that gives glorious but brief colour.' (*Home Style*) This is not a happy invention. To combine the noun 'impulse' with another noun and speak of an 'impulse-purchase' might not offend the insensitive, but to tack it on to a verb is unacceptable. The heady-minded shopper cannot 'impulse-buy' any more than the thoughtful one can 'reflection-buy'. *Resist the temptation to buy on impulse a plant that gives glorious but brief colour.*

OUTSHOP. '25/0 – the initial 28 outshopped from Darlington . . .' (*Railway Modeller*) Compounds such as 'outstrip', 'outvote', 'outshine' surely set the pattern for new experiments with 'out'. To speak of a new railway engine being 'outshopped' (*turned out from the works*) is like describing a school-leaver as 'outschooled'.

STAY-CLEAN. 'All our ovens are stay-clean.' (*OK! Homes*) This is like saying 'All good children should be stay-quiet'. Nothing seems to be gained by not saying: *All our ovens are easy to clean.*

See also ACCESSORISE, NUANCE.

coincide. In the use of this verb there must be a proper grammatical match between two items, as in 'The bazaar (noun) coincides with my birthday (noun)'.

'The sale of the Rising Sun Hotel at Umberleigh, North Devon, and some of the river Taw which went with it, coincides with more fishing coming on to the market at Taw.' (*Trout & Salmon*) There is no satisfactory noun to balance 'sale' here. 'More fishing coming' is a gerciple. A noun must be provided to balance 'sale'. *The sale of the Rising Sun Hotel coincides with an increase in fishing coming on to the market.*

collaboration. '"The Big Cats" is a collaboration with artist Malcolm Watson on a series of four drawings exploring the world of wild cats.' (*Wild About Animals*) The book is not itself a 'collaboration' but the product of collaboration. *In "The Big Cats" there is collaboration with artist Malcolm Watson.*

Collective Nouns. A collective noun should be followed by a singular verb unless it clearly indicates individuals of the collective.'The audience was large', we say but 'The audience were shouting and stamping their feet'.

'Her office staff were pared – and worked, so they said – to the bone.' (*Independent*) That they were worked to the bone is happily put in the plural, but 'they' were not 'pared', which suggests the peeling off of skin. The plural should be singular. *Her office staff was pared – and they were worked, so they said – to the bone.* See also COUNCIL, GOVERNMENT.

collude. 'A lecturer in a Church of England theological college has accused the Church of colluding with violence against gay people.' (*Radio 4*) To collude is to conspire. One may collude with someone but one cannot collude 'with violence': *has accused the Church of furtively encouraging violence against gay people.*

Colon. The colon marks a slightly stronger break than does the semi-colon and a slightly weaker break than does the full stop. Where it is used to separate clauses (*Too many people these days drive like madmen: some of them finish up in hospital as a result*), it could generally be replaced by a full stop, which would be equally acceptable grammatically. The most common use of the colon is for connecting general statements with specific instances (*The council consisted of twelve members: a chairman, a vice-chairman, a secretary and nine other elected delegates*).

combine. 'Combine . . . with' always requires the two balancing elements of the combination to be clearly cited.

'Modern bathrooms can look absolutely stunning when combined with the right accessories.' (*Home Style*) This is like saying 'A handsome man looks stunning when combined with gleaming teeth'. To combine items is to join them together. Accessories are not 'combined with' a bathroom any more than teeth are combined with a man. *Modern bathrooms can look absolutely stunning when equipped with the right accessories.*

'Finding garden furniture that combines aesthetic charm as well as practicality isn't easy.' (*Perfect Home*) Two constructions are confused here. Either 'as well as' must go: *combines aesthetic charm with practicality*, or 'combines' must go: *has aesthetic charm as well as practicality*.

'These [lists] are in process of being combined in to a master register by English Heritage.' (*Old-House Journal*) The word 'to' is clumsy and unnecessary: *are being combined in a master register*.

combust. 'If I get started on that one I shall spontaneously combust.' (*Cumbria Life*) The innovation may be entertaining, but there is no verb 'to combust'. 'Combust' is an adjective meaning 'burnt up': *I shall explode*.

come. It is best not to overuse the commonest verbs in the language. 'The range of the garden comes from an exceptional variety of growing conditions, all in close proximity.' (*In Britain*) 'Comes' would seem to be the wrong word here. *The range of the garden derives from* would be better, and *the range of the garden is due to* better still. But best of all would be to switch the words 'range' and 'variety' around: *The variety (of produce) in the garden is due to an exceptional range of growing conditions all in close proximity.*

'His alarm at inadequate searching came during an inspection of the jail last October.' (*The Times*) Again, to speak of alarm 'coming' is weak: *His alarm at inadequate searching arose during an inspection.*

coming. There is a tendency to begin a sentence with 'coming' and then to fail to provide a fit word to match it in what follows.

'Coming from a comfortable middle-class background, this has come as a shock.' (*New Statesman*) Here the thing which has shocked ('this') is said to have come from a middle-class background. *Coming from a comfortable middle class background, this has come as a shock to me* links 'coming' with 'me'. *Coming from a comfortable middle class background, I have been shocked by this* links 'coming' with 'I'.

Comma. Effective use of the comma is determined as much by commonsense and by good taste as by grammatical regulation.

FALSE LINKAGES These can easily be created by neglect of commas, especially after the word 'and'. 'Try not to scratch and see your doctor if any reactions persist.' (*Prima*) Here 'scratch' and 'see your doctor' need to be separated because 'see your doctor' should be closely related to what follows it, not to what precedes it. *Try not to scratch, and see your doctor if any reactions persist.*

'Then there's Paignton, with the most stunning wide beaches made for buckets and spades and kiosks selling ice-cream and teas and the most charming and popular steam train in the South West.' (*In Britain*) The lack of a comma here leaves the suggestion that the charming and popular steam train is on sale alongside the ice-cream and the teas, and that the beach is made for kiosks as well as for buckets and spades: *with the most stunning wide beaches made for buckets and spades, kiosks selling ice-cream, and the most charming and popular steam train in the South West.*

'On the GWR this meant donning more utilitarian clothes and the distinctive steel-framed sheds became familiar.' (*British Railways Illustrated*) Again the reader must be protected from even temporarily gathering that utilitarian clothes and steel-framed sheds were donned. *On the GWR this meant donning more utilitarian clothes, and the distinctive steel-framed sheds became familiar.*

'They're marked, as every schoolboy knows, with a blue plaque and tracking them down is quite a voyage of discovery.' (*In Britain*). It would be correct to write 'They are marked with an asterisk and a footnote', but incorrect to write 'They are marked with an asterisk and locating the footnote is easy'. In the first sentence 'and' closely links what follows it to what precedes it, as does the 'and' in 'fish and chips' or 'bacon and eggs'. In the second sentence 'locating the footnote' is not so linked to what precedes it, nor is 'tracking them down' in the sentence above. *They are marked with a blue plaque, and tracking them down . . . is quite a voyage of discovery.* The reader will notice that, had the conjunction 'and' been omitted from the sentence ('They're marked with a blue plaque; tracking them down is quite a voyage of discovery'), then the comma would no longer suffice after 'plaque'. Indeed 'and' or 'but' (preceded by a comma) might often be omitted and a semicolon substituted.

SEPARATING PHRASES Commas are needed to separate phrases from their context. 'We stood by a lone stone wall sipping tea provided by our enthusiastic and helpful host.' (*Outdoors Illustrated*) The participle construction beginning with 'sipping' requires to be separated from what precedes it. *We stood by an old stone wall, sipping tea.*

'Beautiful colour illustrations support a plethora of useful information on every breed recounting the history, appearance and characteristics of each one.' (*Artists & Illustrators Magazine*) What applied to the participle phrase beginning with 'sipping' above applies likewise to the participle phrase beginning with 'recounting' here: *a plethora of useful information on every breed, recounting the history.*

'The old thatch had degenerated into a black rotting mass and for the thatchers removing the wet straw after several days of rain proved to be a filthy job.' (*Old-House Journal*) Here the words 'for the thatchers' need to be separated from what surrounds them: *and, for the thatchers, removing the wet straw proved to be a filthy job.*

When a phrase calls for this treatment, it is important to make sure that the comma preceding the phrase is matched by one at the end. 'Since arriving at Sheffield Park, the engine, preserved in Southern Railway olive green livery has been a stalwart on the line giving many miles' service.' (*Steam Classic*) Here is a case in point. The comma correctly preceding 'preserved in . . . green livery' must be matched by a comma at the end of the phrase: *the engine, preserved in Southern Railway olive green livery, has been a stalwart.* There should also be a comma after 'line': *stalwart on the line, giving many miles' service.*

OVERUSE OF COMMAS The use of commas to separate a phrase clearly from its surroundings must be adopted with restraint. 'An exhibition . . . starts at the Natural History Museum after November's announcement and before it, too, tours.' (*Viva*) There is no need to write 'This, too, offends me' for 'too' can do its work without the protection of surrounding commas. In any case the wording is unsatisfactory. *An exhibition . . . will open at the Natural History Museum after November's announcement, and before that will be on tour.*

WHERE COMMAS ARE INADEQUATE Just as commas are often omitted where they are needed to mark a break in the flow of what is conveyed, so we sometimes find a comma used where the break in question demands a more forceful mark. 'Bouncing back doesn't happen with a bang, it's a gradual process.' (*Company*) Here there is a strong case for a semicolon. *Bouncing back doesn't happen with a bang; it's a gradual process.* Something like a fresh start is made by the word 'it's'.

It should go without saying that the greater the break in the flow, the more forceful must be the punctuation mark. Thus 'I had my first glimpse of the wine list, what a wine list!' (*Lancashire Life*) must be re-written with either a colon or a fullstop after the first 'list'. *I had my first glimpse of the wine list. What a wine list! See also* COLON, SEMICOLON.

comment. 'His sense of humour shone through an opening remark which commented that it was a remote and sparsely populated area about which he was to tell us.' (*Steam World*) A remark cannot 'comment': *an opening remark in which he observed that it was a remote area.*

commentary. 'On the Saturday and Sunday a coach, usually with a commentary, takes the party to see the waterways.' (*Waterways World*) This makes a commentary sound like a piece of equipment sometimes fitted to coaches. *On the Saturday and Sunday a coach, usually supplying a commentary, takes the party to see the waterways.*

commit. 'The Americans say that mass executions were committed by Bosnian Serb forces.' (*Radio 4*) 'Commit', meaning to perform, is used of crimes and errors, not of punishments: *mass executions were carried out by Bosnian Serb forces.*

common. Adjectives which may have a double reference ('The garden is common to our house and theirs') have to be used with great care.

'The introduction of corn-coloured paintwork brings this room to life. Common to all three fabrics, though in small quantities, the corn walls succeed in pulling the whole scheme together.' (*House Beautiful*) The writer here tells us that the corn walls are 'common' to all three fabrics and thus bring the whole room together, when she means that the corn colour is common to them and performs that function. The subject of the second sentence must be changed if the construction is to be kept. *Common to all three fabrics, the corn colour of the walls succeeds in pulling the whole scheme together.*

companion. 'They include ensuring "regulated companion animal access into hospitals, retirement and nursing homes and other centres for the care of people of all ages who are in need of such contact".' (*Nursing Standard*) If the aim is to *let people take their pets with them into hospital*, why not say so? To pretend that the words 'regulated companion animal access' represent a satisfactory alternative way of using the English language is regrettable.

comparable to. 'Tea is comparable to coffee as a cheering drink.' In that sentence the parallelism between the two items, tea and coffee, is firm. Comparisons require that kind of parallelism.

'Modern regional aircraft are . . . highly manoeuvrable. The comfort they offer is comparable to large aircraft.' (*Marketing Week*) The aircraft may be compared or the comfort they offer may be compared, but comparison cannot cross from the one to the other. *They are comparable to large aircraft in the comfort they offer*,

comparatively. When comparisons are made it should not be necessary to underline the fact by use of this word.

'The present hostile economic environment is exposing the weaknesses of comparatively more boards of directors.' (*Independent*) 'More' is a comparative adjective. If there is 'more' of anything, there is 'comparatively' more, because that is what the word 'more' means. Thus the word 'comparatively' is redundant. If reinforcement of 'more' is needed, it can be repeated: *exposing the weaknesses of more and more boards of directors.*

Comparatives and Superlatives. The comparative and superlative forms of regular monosyllabic adjectives are formed by addition of the suffixes '-er' and '-est'. Thus 'long' has the comparative 'longer' and the superlative 'longest'. Where the adjective ends in '-e', the letter is not repeated: 'nice' becomes 'nicer' and 'nicest'. Some very common adjectives are irregular: 'good', 'better', 'best' and 'many', 'more', 'most'.

Many adjectives of two syllables also have comparatives and superlatives formed by adding '-er' and '-est'. There is a slight irregularity with adjectives ending in '-y': 'lively' becomes 'livelier' and 'liveliest'. Adjectives ending in '-le', such as 'gentle' and 'feeble', and adjectives ending in '-er', such as 'slender' and 'clever', follow the general rule. So do most two-syllable adjectives with the accent on the second syllable, such as 'remote', 'acute' and 'intense'.

It is in the case of many two-syllable adjectives that the formulation of exact rules is most difficult. For instance, while 'demure' can become 'demurer' and 'demurest', and 'handsome' can become 'handsomer' and 'handsomest', the adjectives 'active', 'austere' and 'famous' (along with others ending in '-ous') require the use of 'more' and 'most'.

Adjectives of three syllables or more form their comparatives with 'more' and their superlatives with 'most'. Thus 'beautiful' becomes 'more beautiful' and 'most beautiful'. The chief exceptions to this rule are some few of those three-syllable adjectives which are really two-syllable words with a negative prefix added, such as 'insecure', 'unfriendly', and 'ungainly', which can acquire '-er' and '-est' endings.

It should be said, however, that established writers have sometimes used normally unacceptable forms (such as 'beautifullest' or 'cunningest') for stylistic effect.

USE OF THE SUPERLATIVE A writer can sometimes slip up in describing objects or people as being the best of their kind. It is correct to say 'He was the cleverest of his class' but incorrect to say 'He was the cleverest of his classmates' because he was not one of his classmates.

'Of her sisters she was the most able to stand up to him.' (*The Times*) No woman can be classed as one of her own sisters. *Of his sisters she was the most able to stand up to him. See also* MOST.

compare. 'There is no writer alive today who can compare to Shakespeare.' (*Focus*) This usage should surely be discouraged. It is not the writers who 'compare' but those who judge them. *There is no writer alive today who can be compared with Shakespeare.*

Similarly 'The light one spread well, but its taste just couldn't compare' (*Woman*) should be: *The light one spread well but couldn't be compared in taste.*

compared to/with. When the expression 'compared to/with' is used, care must be taken to preserve exact parallelism between the items compared.

'Compared with old technology, the great advantage of a Musto is the way it copes with changing conditions.' (*Shooting Times*) This sentence compares the 'advantage of a Musto' with old technology, instead of with the jacket produced by that technology. *Compared with the jackets made by the old technology, a Musto has the great advantage that it can cope with changing conditions.*

'Compared to the Eighties, more of us visit the dentist at least once a year.' (*Woman's Journal*) It is correct to say 'Compared to the Eighties, the Nineties are . . .' but incorrect to compare the Eighties with 'more of us'. It is advisable in this case to sacrifice the expression 'compared to'. *By comparison with the Eighties, more of us now visit the dentist at least once a year.*

'By the 18th century the town became a fashionable centre with a social season which was even compared with Harrogate and Cheltenham.' (*Lancashire Life*) The social season (at Preston) was not 'compared with' Harrogate, but with Harrogate's social season. Either social seasons must be compared, or towns must be compared: *with a social season which was even compared with Harrogate's and Cheltenham's.*

Even skilled writers can slip up with this usage. 'Compared with the fate of most conservation bodies elsewhere in Europe, the [National] Trust has contrived to stay solvent, avoid scandal, keep its properties occupied and in good repair, and be phenomenally popular.' (*The Times*) Here the writer compares one conservation body with the fate of another;

but fate must be compared with fate or body with body. In fact 'the fate of' is redundant. *Compared with most conservation bodies elsewhere in Europe, the Trust has contrived to stay solvent.*

'820 men complained of sex discrimination while applying for jobs compared to 803 women.' (*Radio 4*) Whether with 'comparing', 'connecting', or 'linking' newswriters display a curious preference for 'to' where 'with' would be more conventionally acceptable: *compared with 803 women.*

Comparisons. In making comparisons it is always necessary to guard against failing to match like with like. 'Mr Clarke emerges as more anxious to cut interest rates than a more cautious Mr George – with Mr Clarke's reading of the economy more downbeat than the Bank of England.' (*Guardian*) Mr Clarke's reading of the economy must be compared with the Bank of England's reading, not with the Bank of England. The word 'with' is ill-used: *Mr Clarke's reading of the economy being more downbeat than the Bank of England's. See also* WITH.

Similarly 'The anger of the architects is matched by the people' (*Green Magazine*) should be: *is matched by the people's.*

'Its doors, 3/4in longer than the three-door Fiesta, are strengthened to help resist side impact.' (*The Times*) If the doors were longer than the Fiesta, the car would be immense: *Its doors, 3/4in longer than the three-door Fiesta's.*

The three sentences above show how many a false comparison can be thus easily corrected by insertion of an apostrophe ('Bank of England's', 'people's', and 'Fiesta's'), but sometimes the shape of the sentence does not allow it. 'The rear of the car has been designed shorter than the 600 series.' (*Tatler*) An apostrophe after 'series' would be clumsy. In cases like this, use 'that of'. *The rear of the car is shorter than that of the cars in the 600 series.*

'Durand's style was unique and the antithesis of the great advocates of the past.' (*The Times*) This again is the same mistake as is made if one says 'Our piano is big and very different from your mother' instead of 'very different from your mother's'. The lawyer's style was not the antithesis of other great advocates, but of their style. *Durand's style was unique and the antithesis of the style of the great advocates of the past.*

'His reading of the crisis has been shrewder than many of his more excitable colleagues.' (*The Times*) The reading is not shrewder than the colleagues, but shrewder than their own readings. *He has read the crisis more shrewdly than many of his more excitable colleagues.*

'It is perhaps too little known that the social benefits of the waterway network are many times greater than the annual government grant.' (*Waterways World*) Benefits must not be described as 'greater' than a certain amount of money, but only as greater than anything the money could buy: *the social benefits of the waterway network greatly exceed in value what the annual government grant amounts to.*

Comparisons often stray more widely into error. 'British Coal's last months seem destined to prove as bizarre as the industry's treatment by the Government has been over the last three years.' (*The Times*) This sentence compares a period of time ('last months') with the Government's treatment of an industry. The subject of the sentence must be changed. *British Coal's experience in its last three months seems likely to be as bizarre as has been its treatment at the Government's hands over the last three years.*

compensate. 'She has been robbed of a mother. Nothing can compensate that.' (*Radio 4*) If a woman has been robbed of something, it is she who can be 'compensated', not her loss. *Nothing can compensate her for that.*

complacent / complaisant. To be 'complacent' is to be self-satisfied or too readily content with situations that are unsatisfactory. *It shows a complacent attitude to be unresponsive to the needs of fellow beings in a famine-stricken country.* To be 'complaisant' is to be agreeably compliant and obliging: *She was complaisant enough to sit down and play the piano as soon as she was asked.*

complain about. 'But most was the usual complaining about successive governments censoring information about nuclear policy, Ulster security, and so on.' (*Daily Telegraph*) It is correct to complain 'about the weather' but not 'about the weather turning bad' (a gerciple). If the object of the complaint is a process, it is safer to follow 'complain' by 'that', not by 'about': *But most was the usual complaining that successive governments censored information.*

complaisant. *See* COMPLACENT.

complement. *See* COMPLIMENT.

complementary. *See* COMPLIMENTARY.

complete. 'Mr Perez will say nothing about the immediate future until Mr Rabin's funeral is completed tomorrow.' (*Radio 4*) To speak of 'completing' a funeral makes it sound as though funerals are a product of manufacturing. *Mr Perez will say nothing about the immediate future until after Mr Rabin's funeral tomorrow.*

compliment/complement. A compliment is an appreciative tribute to someone; a complement is something which satisfyingly balances something else. As verbs, the two words are similarly differentiated.

'Marks and Spencer's white embossed range is the perfect compliment to patterned tableware' (*OK! Homes*) should be: *the perfect complement*.

Similarly 'Brookmans offer a unique service to clients looking for an original approach to compliment property and lifestyle' (*Country Living*) should be: *to complement property and lifestyle*.

'Ones own emotions have not been substituted by professional physiotherapeutic interventions and actions but simply complimented by them.' (*Good News Magazine*) There are three errors here, involving 'ones', 'substituted' and 'complimented'. *One's own emotions have not been replaced by professional therapeutic interventions and actions but simply complemented by them.*

complimentary/complementary. The same confusion occurs here as occurs with 'compliment' and 'complement'. A remark or an act which is 'complimentary' gives praise or congratulation. An item which is 'complementary' to another one balances it as 'a postman' grammatically balances 'my father' in the sentence 'My father is a postman'.

'This unusual hardwood conservatory is a really complimentary addition to a Victorian townhouse' (*Prima*) should be: *a really complementary addition*.

comply. 'According to British Chambers of Commerce the heads of small firms are spending on average 10% of their time complying with regulations.' (*Radio 4*) This seems to suggest that the firms spend 90% of their time failing to comply with regulations. Presumably it should be: *spend 10% of their time on paperwork required by regulations*.

component. 'Undoubtedly the "young persons' shoot" is a vital component of the shooting calendar.' (*The Field*) The word 'component' has associations with machinery which make it inappropriate in many nonmechanical contexts. A word less technical in its associations is required here, and a word consonant with the word 'calendar': *a crucial date on the shooting calendar*. Alternatively the construction may be changed. *The shooting calendar is undoubtedly incomplete without the "young persons' shoot"*.

comprehend. *See* APPREHEND.

Compression overdone. The attempt to condense utterance can lead to lax English. 'We thought we would look at some of the non Gore-Tex jackets, which do a good job and cost half as much.' (*Outdoors Illustrated*) Half as much as what? Non-Gore-Tex jackets have been mentioned, but not Gore-Tex jackets. *We thought we would look at some jackets other than those of Gore-Tex and costing half as much.*

'People don't speed because they don't know what a 30-mile limit sign means.' (*AA Magazine*) This appears to explain why drivers do not speed. Something very different was meant. *It is not because they don't know what a 30-mile limit sign means that people speed.*

'A spy with no name was yesterday sued by the woman he tricked into believing was his long-lost mother' (*Sun*) should be: *the woman whom he tricked into believing that she was his long-lost mother.*

'I've been given a second chance. Others might not.' (*The Great Outdoors*) 'I have recovered from the accident: others might not' is correct because 'might not' implies 'recover'. The passive verb 'have been given' requires a passive parallel, and 'might not' is active. The wording needs to be filled out: *Others might not be so lucky.*

'Medical cover is essential travelling abroad.' (*Adventure Travel*) It is not the medical cover that travels. *Medical cover is essential when you are travelling abroad.*

comprise. No 'of' is required after the verb 'comprise'. In this respect it differs from the verb 'consist'.

'The company retained a board of management trustees, comprised of well-known names.' (*The Times*) We need either: *a board of management trustees consisting of well-known names,* or *comprising well-known names.*

The advertisement for a cutlery set 'comprising of 6 table knives' etc. (*House of Fraser*) should be: *comprising 6 table knives.*

'The sack has an Ergoform back system which comprises of a padded back overlaying two internal malleable bars' (*Trail*) should be: *which consists of a padded back.*

compromise. 'When you demand style, quality, and an innovative design to create an ambiance [sic] that says so much about you, then a compromise to perfection is beyond consideration.' (*Lancashire Life*) We compromise 'with' someone, not 'to'. It is not absolutely clear what the writer of this advertisement means, but surely it should end: *then a compromise with perfection is out of the question.*

concede. 'They are demanding a full Commons debate on the subject, something the government is still not conceding on.' (*Radio 4*) To 'concede', in this context, is to grant and takes a direct object: *something the government is not conceding.*

conceive. To conceive is to become pregnant with a child and hence to give birth to an idea. 'This proved he had a very low sperm count and would be virtually unable to conceive.' (*Marie Claire*) Even some women writers seemingly need to be told that no man can conceive: *and would be virtually unable to father/beget a child.*

concept. There is a tendency to use this word, which is strictly concerned with what the mind can grasp, as though it were an alternative to words such as 'thing' or 'item'.

Thus, describing how strawberries have been added to the recipe for a new beer, a spokesman says 'While adding a new concept we have kept to traditional brewing methods'. (*Best of British*). This is abuse of a useful word. *While adding a new ingredient we have kept to traditional brewing methods.*

conclusion. 'However, the Board of Banking Supervision will not complete even the first stage of its enquiries before the end of this month and its full conclusions will take even longer.' (*Radio 4*) It is not the 'conclusions' that will take longer, but the process of arriving at them: *and reaching full conclusions will take even longer.*

condemn. 'The opposition parties have condemned the news that Lord Wakeham is to become director of a merchant bank closely involved with the privatisation of the electricity industry.' (*Radio 4*) They did not condemn the 'news' (the factual information), but what that news conveyed. Either the verb must be changed: *The opposition parties have reacted critically to the news*, or the noun must be changed: *have condemned the appointment of Lord Wakeham.*

'Labour has condemned figures showing nurses' pay rising at half the rate of hospital chiefs.' (*Radio 4*) Again it was not the figures that Labour condemned but the facts that the figures revealed. Since the facts are facts which only calculation could establish, why mention the calculation (the 'figures')? *Labour has been shocked that nurses' pay has risen at half the rate of hospital chiefs'.*

Conditions. English usage allows us to say either 'If it rains, I shall stay at home', or 'Should it rain, I shall stay at home'. It is important not to abuse this freedom.

'Many local authorities and the emergency services remain on standby, should the weather worsen further.' (*Radio 4*) But the local authorities will remain on standby even if the weather does not worsen, so the simple conditional 'should' is misplaced: *emergency services remain on standby for fear the weather should worsen.*

'Already there was a local bus on board and even when we joined it, there was room for several more, had they suddenly materialised out of the desert.' (*Outdoors Illustrated*) The conditional tense 'had they materialised' requires to be matched in the main verb: *there would have been room for several more, had they suddenly materialised.*

confirm. 'The officials have asked me to say that this was a tragic accident confirmed by the evidence and the jury's decision.' (*Radio 4*) It was not the accident itself that was 'confirmed', but the assumption that the tragic event was an accident. *The officials have asked me to say that this was a tragic accident, a view confirmed by the evidence and the jury's decision.*

conjure. To 'conjure' is either to practise the art of conjuring or solemnly to implore. 'The accent conjures a more mellifluous Henry Kissinger.' (*Independent*) To bring someone or something before people's eyes by magic or trickery is to 'conjure up'. *The accent conjures up a more mellifluous Henry Kissinger.*

connect. 'Other allegations against the Attorney General connect him to repeated attempts to interfere with investigations into drug traffickers.' (*Radio 4*) A radio set may be connected 'to' the mains supply, but suspicious people connect an individual 'with' a crime: *Other allegations against the Attorney General connect him with repeated attempts to interfere.*

connive. 'If Maggie had been killed, then somehow she had been persuaded unwittingly to connive in her own death.' (*Novel*) To connive at something is to shut one's eyes to it, as though it were not happening. It is an essentially conscious process. It is impossible for anyone not to know that they are conniving, so 'persuaded unwittingly to connive' is a contradiction in terms. Moreover, usage requires 'connive at' not 'in'. The verb should be changed: *then somehow she had been induced unwittingly to acquiesce in her own death.*

connote/denote. What a word 'connotes' is what it signifies in the fullest sense. *The word 'gentleman' connotes not just a male human being, but one with some social graces and perhaps some standing in the world.* What a word 'denotes' is what it signifies literally. Hence it is used of what something designates or indicates: *An over-ruddy complexion may denote a fondness for the bottle.*

conscious. A letter to the press quotes the guarantee on a Christmas card that it is 'printed on environmentally conscious paper'. (*The Times*) Only living beings have consciousness. It is not within the power of a sheet of paper to be 'environmentally conscious': *printed on paper manufactured without damage to the environment.*

'It is vital to remember that everything we do in the health service has to be gender conscious.' (*Nursing Standard*) Again jargon departs from commonsense. People can be 'gender conscious' but things 'we do' cannot.

If the jargon is worth preserving, this must be: *It is vital to remember that in everything we do in the health service we must be gender conscious.*

conservative. 'A leading loss adjuster estimated that the bill was a "conservative £500 million".' (*The Times*) There is no such thing as a conservative sum of money. It is the estimate that is conservative: *estimated that the bill would be at least £500 million.*

consist of. *See* COMPRISE.

consistent. 'The official said the disturbed earth was consistent with mass graves.' (*Radio 4*) The compression here is tortuous. It is poor use of words to say 'The empty shelf is consistent with the theft of goods'. It is the fact that the earth is disturbed that is consistent with the theory that there are mass graves. *The official said that the disturbed earth might mark mass graves.*

'The find [of arms] appears to be consistent with some kind of training camp.' (*Radio 4*) Here again the verbal short-cut abuses the word 'consistent'. The presence of the arms may be consistent with the theory that there is a camp near by, but the introduction of the notion of consistency is quite unnecessary. *The find appears to indicate the site of some kind of training camp.*

construct. 'I'm trying to construct the circumstances where we have a normal relationship with Argentina.' (*Radio 4*) Talk of 'constructing circumstances' is typical of clumsy political discourse. *I'm preparing the ground for a normal relationship with Argentina.*

construction. 'The construction, whilst not being the simplest, is still very easy to assemble.' (*Adventure Travel*) Construction is not something that can be assembled; it is the process of assembling. *Construction is not child's play, but the tent is easy to assemble.*

construe. 'Take clothes; the tartier the wardrobe, the more the wearer insists that the intention is not to give sexual messages and the more offended she is that such a thing could be construed.' (*The Times*) To construe is to interpret. It is wrongly used here, for what is the 'thing' that is being 'construed', i.e. interpreted? Either the verb must be changed: *the more offended she is that such a construction should be put on it,* or the subject of the verb 'construe': *the more offended she is that her behaviour should be so construed.*

contact. 'The Welsh Rugby Union said that no formal contact about the breakaway had been received.' (*Radio 4*) A 'contact' is what brings one body into relationship with another. It is not something that can be 'received'. Either 'contact' should be changed: *The WRU said that no formal approach about the breakaway had been received,* or 'received' must be changed: *The WRU said that no formal contact about the breakaway had been made.*

contemptible /contemptuous. Something which is 'contemptible' merits contempt. *He knocked the child down on a pedestrian crossing and drove away: it was contemptible behaviour.* Adjectives ending in '-able' or '-ible' tend to have this passive sense ('despicable', fit *to be despised*; 'credible', fit *to be believed*), though there are exceptions. Someone who is 'contemptuous' of an act is scornful of it. *He dismissed the applicant with a contemptuous sneer. See also* DERISORY.

contemptuous. *See* CONTEMPTIBLE.

contend. 'To contend' is to struggle or compete and the verb is intransitive.
'Periodic outbursts of Francophilia such as our ambassador's "Towards a New Entente" are not usually worth contending.' (*The Times*) It is incorrect to speak of contending someone or something: it is a matter of contending 'against' them: *are not usually worth contending against.* Alternatively the verb could be changed: *are not usually worth contesting.*
'On the day the natural amphitheatre shape will mean that players will

have to contend with the large numbers of spectators around the field.'
(*Lancashire Life*) A word may be used, not in its primary sense, but with
an imaginative freedom which stretches connotation away from its true
base. Thus we may say that a climber has to 'contend' with bad weather.
Here the image of sportsmen 'contending' with spectators jars by being
conjoined with the literal account of their contention with each other.
*Because of the natural amphitheatre shape players will have to cope with
large numbers of spectators.*

continue. 'This continued her role as college historian.' (*Independent*)
'This' is a book written by the deceased, whose obituary we quote. But
the book could not possibly 'continue' her role. Either the verb must be
changed: *This showed her still in her role as college historian*, or the construction must be changed: *Thus she sustained her role as college histo-
rian/Thus she continued in her role.*

'He plans to continue his love of music by playing the trumpet.' (*The
Times*) This usage is at best infelicitous. 'Continue to love' and 'continue
loving' are both more natural expressions. *He plans to sustain his love
of music/to satisfy his love of music.*

continuing. A bad habit is now widespread of beginning a sentence with
'continuing' and then failing to supply a subject to match it. 'Continuing
along the lane, there are fine views of the whole of Blagdon Lake' (*Down
Your Way*) should be: *Continuing along the lane, we/you have fine views
of Blagdon Lake. See also* ROUTES.

continuously. 'The railways have suffered for 20 or 30 years from governments continuously cutting back on investment.' (*Radio 4*) 'Continuously' is the wrong word here, for it means unceasingly; 'continually'
means repeatedly. *The railways have suffered from governments who
have continually cut back on investment.*

'Late afternoon saw a peak of activity through the station with
passenger and freight trains passing continuously.' (*Steam World*) Again
the trains did not pass through unceasingly but repeatedly: *passenger
and freight trains passing continually.*

contract. 'Walter only wishes his contract had paid him 10 per cent of
the takings.' (*Daily Star*) But a 'contract' can never pay one anything. It
may signalise a promise to pay. *Walter only wishes the contract had
assigned him 10 per cent of the takings.*

Contradiction. Contradiction can occur even though there is no misunderstanding of a particular word. Very often it arises through sheer lack of logic.

'He said that most of the tariffs to be abolished would help British exports.' (*Radio 4*) The writer says that the tariffs 'would help' British exports when he means that their abolition would thus help. 'Tariffs' must not remain as the subject of 'would help'. *He said that in most cases abolition of the tariffs would help British exports.*

'Savage replies that La Rue is a classic old dinosaur and "a good example of taking early retirement before you get addled and bitter."' (*The Times*) It is clear from the context that this piece of vituperation fails because, by omitting the crucial word 'not', it contradicts what it intends to say. *La Rue is a classic old dinosaur and exemplifies the consequences of not taking early retirement before you get addled and bitter.*

Sometimes neglect of punctuation can cause a contradiction. 'Let's hope the British team selectors don't get cold feet and reward the shooters' achievements with team places at the forthcoming Olympic Games.' (*Shooting Times*) A comma is necessary after 'feet': otherwise 'don't' applies to 'reward the shooters'. 'And' should be changed to 'but': *Let's hope the British team selectors don't get cold feet but reward the shooters' achievements.*

'It's just as well that we stay a little modest in our presentations [on the subject of Nigeria], much less our demands.' (*Radio 4*) What the American spokesman meant was: *much more (so) in our demands.*

There are certain words which, if carelessly, used, may lead the writer into saying the very opposite of what was intended. *See also* ADEQUACY, AVAILABILITY, DEROGATORY, ESSENTIAL, OBJECTIVITY, SPEED.

contrary. 'Contrary' is an adjective ('I take the contrary viewpoint'). 'Contrary to the stereotypes currently in circulation, the nature of Essex is neither bland nor boorish.' (*BBC Wildlife*) It is a pity that people have begun to misuse the word thus. 'Contrary' will not do here: *In spite of the currently fashionable stereotypes.*

'Our experience on the Cotswolds may have been contrary to other areas, but foxes seemed to be more adventurous early this season.' (*Hunting*) The experience is not contrary to other areas but to the experience in other areas: *may have been contrary to that in other areas.*

contrast. 'He [President Clinton] contrasted his own forward-looking approach to the conservative stance of his republican challenger.' (*Radio 4*) Although it is correct to say 'in contrast to', the word 'to' is not used after the verb 'contrast'. *He contrasted his own forward-looking* *approach with the conservative stance of his republican challenger.*

contribute to. Very often the use of 'contribute to' leads to grammatical error. 'Among the string was Silver Buck, who contributed to Tony winning the trainers' championship.' (*Independent*) What Silver Buck 'contributed to' was not 'Tony' but the 'winning'. It would be awkward to write (correctly) 'contributed to Tony's winning', though satisfactory to write 'contributed to Tony's victory', but in fact it is a good idea to avoid the construction 'contribute to': *Among the string was Silver Buck, who helped Tony to win the trainers' championship.*

Similarly 'the success of Big Break which has contributed to an extra 130,000 readers taking the *Daily Mirror* on a Saturday' (*Marketing Week*) should be either: *which has helped to gain an extra 130,000 sales of the* Daily Mirror *on a Saturday*, or *which has contributed to an increase of 130,000 in sales of the* Daily Mirror. *See also* GERCIPLES.

contribution. This has become a loosely-used and overused noun. 'Whiskas, Britain's favourite catfood, is the perfect example of Waltham's continuing contribution.' (*Living*) Hearing that something is a 'contribution' without learning to what it contributes adds nothing to our knowledge. Perhaps the advertisers meant: *Whiskas is the perfect example of Waltham's continuing contribution to animal health*. On the other hand, perhaps they just meant: *Buy Whiskas for your cat.*

convenient. 'As with all these ways of buying or borrowing a car, it is more about saving effort than making the best use of your money. The future looks convenient but it won't be cheap.' (*Moneywise*) Even chatty journalism ought not to describe the 'future' as convenient when it really means that some process is going to be more convenient in future. *In future it is going to be easier, if not cheaper.*

conversion. 'There are also two cottages named naturally Heron and Curlew, as well as Kingfisher House, the conversion of traditional farm buildings to form a three bedroom family house.' (*Lancashire Life*) To be strict, a building cannot be a conversion. 'Conversion' is the act or process of converting. The pedant would tell us that the building is the product of conversion: *Kingfisher House, a three bedroom family home converted from traditional farm buildings.*

convince. To convince a person is to bring them to full acceptance of what is said. A bad habit has developed of using 'convince' as a straight alternative to 'persuade'.

'Supporters of Private Clegg say they have new evidence that should convince the Northern Ireland Secretary to release the private immediately.' (*Radio 4*) This is not a matter of straight conviction but of persuasion: *they have new evidence that should induce/persuade the Northern Ireland Secretary to release the private.*

'Although Alex was married at the time to his first and only monogamous wife, Shirley, he convinced her to accept two polygamous wives, Diane and Margaret.' (*Woman's Journal*). 'Convinced' is again out of place. We 'convince' people of facts; we 'persuade' them to act. *Although Alex was married at the time to Shirley, he persuaded her to accept two other wives polygamously.*

'The black democratic incumbent will have to convince enough white voters to cross the racial lines' (*Radio 4*) should be: *will have to persuade enough white voters to cross the racial lines.*

cooperation. 'The police in Northern Ireland say they are giving every cooperation to the government.' (*Radio 4*) It sounds somewhat inelegant to speak of 'every' cooperation, likewise to speak of 'giving' it 'to' someone. *The police in Northern Ireland say they are cooperating fully with the government.*

co-ordinate. 'One of the main changes over the past couple of seasons is that people don't want to be dressed head to toe in one co-ordinated label.' (*The Times*) It is hard to picture a person dressed in a label. It is hard too to picture a co-ordinated label. Co-ordination is like partnership: it involves a minimum of two in relationship. Compression here gets out of hand: *people don't want to be dressed head to toe in the style of one fashion house.*

cope. 'Some people are able to cope well against these forces, others are driven to desperation.' (*Lancashire Life*) 'Cope' means to deal successfully and cannot be appropriately followed by 'against': *Some people are able to cope well with these forces.*

corollary. A 'corollary' is a proposition that follows directly on another proposition, and the word is thus used of an obvious deduction or a natural consequence.

'That was the corollary of the executive agencies proposed for Whitehall under the Next Step initiative.' (*The Times*) But 'executive agencies' cannot themselves have any natural consequence. It is their establishment or the proposal to set them up that might have such a consequence, and that proposal to set them up is not the same as the 'proposed' agencies: *That was the corollary of the proposal to set up executive agencies.*

cost. 'Moreover the price of a doorstep pint now costs up to 40p compared with 28p in the superstores and even less in the discount supermarkets.' (*The Times*) Illogicalities abound here. The 'price' cannot be said to 'cost' 40p. It is the milk that costs 40p. Moreover, one cannot say (as here) that the doorstep pint costs 28p in the superstores, because the doorstep pint is sold only on the doorstep. *A pint of milk now costs up to 40p on the doorstep compared with 28p in the superstores.*

couch (verb). 'Mr Coulson presented a rescue package to Bank of Scotland last week, but it was couched with a great deal of uncertainty about the UK shoe business, which has been hit by the collapse of the Facia group.' (*The Times*) To 'couch' is generally used of expressing something unpalatable in words which slightly veil the situation. It requires the preposition 'in' ('He delivered a rebuke but it was couched in superficially friendly terms'). The writer here appears to be thinking of cohabitation rather than of simulation. One cannot speak of a report 'couched with' uncertainty. The verb is the wrong one: *but it expressed a good deal of uncertainty about the UK shoe business.*

council. When this word is used of a public body, it may be followed by a singular verb or a plural verb according to the context, but consistency must be maintained.

'Kingswood Borough Council have won the good dog award for its outstanding progress in the promotion of responsible dog ownership.' (*Dogs Monthly*) Here the plural 'have' gives place to the singular 'its'. Use one or the other consistently: *have won the award for their outstanding progress*, or: *has won the award for its outstanding progress.* See also GOVERNMENT.

count on. This verb attracts misuse of the gerund. 'He hadn't counted on Hyacinth volunteering.' (*Woman's Own*) Strictly this should be: *He hadn't counted on Hyancinth's volunteering.* But it would be just as satisfactory to say: *He hadn't calculated that Hyacinth would volunteer.*

coupled with. The expression 'coupled with' must link two compatible items.

'Coupled with the appreciable increase of individuals wishing to establish their own businesses, the industry is growing fast and enjoys an appreciative general public.' (*Money-Maker*) (The industry in question is that of mobile wayside catering.) Here the industry is incorrectly 'coupled with' the increase of individuals. In fact, the issue is not so much one of coupling as of coincidence. *At the very time when more and more individuals are wishing to establish their own businesses, the mobile catering industry happens to be growing rapidly.*

'Carling Black Label reaped rewards in 1994, coupled with sponsorship of Premier League Football.' (*Marketing Week*) The rewards and the sponsorship were linked but not 'coupled': *reaped rewards in 1994, attributed to sponsorship*, or: *associated with sponsorship.*

'Light and airy, the walls have been adventurously painted using yellow cadmium on fresh plaster. Coupled with deep green paintwork, the effect is striking.' (*Perfect Home*) Here 'the effect' is said to be coupled with deep green paintwork. 'Coupled with' is out of place. *Light and airy, the walls have been adventurously painted with* [sic] *yellow cadmium on fresh plaster. Alongside the deep green paintwork they produce a striking effect.*

cover. '"A Concise History of Greece" . . . which covers the later eighteenth century (the first stirring of the national movement) to the present day.' (*History Today*) One can 'cover' last year or this year, but not last year 'to' this year: *which covers the period from the later eighteenth century. . . to the present day.*

'The cash could be useful to cover for any further eventualities.' (*Moneywise*) Perhaps there is here confusion between the verb 'cover' and the verb 'cater (for)'. There are two alternative corrections: *to cover any further eventualities*, or: *to cater for any further eventualities.*

create. Like 'creative' this has become a vogue word and suffered loss of meaning. 'To create Melanie's eyes, Bobbi used a neutral shade of brown.' (*Company*) No act of creation is involved here: *To beautify Melanie's eyes.*

credible. 'There's nothing more cool, comfortable, and hill credible than a new waterproof jacket.' (*Trail*) The overuse of this word produces absurdities such as this: *nothing more reliable on the hills.*

crescendo. 'With clever writing you can build up the point to a crescendo.' (*Successful Creativity & Direct Marketing*) A crescendo is a gradual increase in loudness. It is not something you can 'build up to' because it is the process of building up. The main error could be corrected by: *With clever writing you can build up the point to a climax*, or: *you can build up the point to a fortissimo*, but the word 'point' would still jar.

criterion. 'God forbid that there should be only one criteria.' (*Radio 4*) The rules of language forbid that there should ever be 'one criteria', for 'criteria' is the plural form of the noun 'criterion'. *God forbid that there should be only one criterion.*

critical. 'The following wiring diagram shows how I wired up the circuit. However, it isn't critical to follow this format as long as siren polarity is respected.' (*Caravan Magazine*) When a person in hospital is in a critical condition, it becomes a matter of life and death, but to deny that kind of urgency to a matter of this kind smacks of gross exaggera-. tion. *However, it isn't essential to follow this format.*

crucial. Care must be taken to follow 'crucial to' with a noun or noun-equivalent. The Foreign Secretary spoke of 'the economic reconstruction in Bosnia which is crucial to peace actually succeeding'. (*Radio 4*) 'Peace succeeding' is a gerciple: *crucial to the success of the peace.*

culture. 'People began to have pets, and no culture doted on their pets more than the English.' (*Academic Book Collection*) 'Their' cannot refer back to the singular noun 'culture'. The word should be removed. It is now overused. *No people doted more on their pets than did the English.*

current. 'This is vital research, part of a very current debate going on.' (*Radio 4*) Something which is 'current' is of the immediate present and the qualification 'very' is logically redundant: *part of a very topical debate.*

curtail. 'Nick Leeson's desire to leave Frankfurt was curtailed.' (*Radio 4*) To curtail is to cut short. It was clear from the context that the desire was not mutilated but disappointed. *Nick Leeson's desire to leave Frankfurt was thwarted.*

customer. This noun, along with many others, is increasingly used as an adjective in the business world. When I read my 'customer number' on my electricity bill, I understand the appropriateness of the usage. But on the same bill is a section headed 'Customer Information', and instead of specifying my age, height, colour of hair, etc., it quotes a telephone number at headquarters that I may call for information. In fact, everything on the bill is directed at the customer, but it doesn't say 'Customer Address', 'Customer Consumption', 'Customer Account', or 'Customer Total'.

Yet there are worse usages than those of Norweb. 'The new-style Al-Ko side-mounted caravan jack was also on display . . . Unfortunately it is not available as a customer retro-fit.' (*Caravan Magazine*) A 'customer retro-fit' sounds to the uninitiated like something to be worn like a rucksack. *Unfortunately it cannot be fitted to your present caravan after purchase.*

'As a customer convenience the page at the back of the book is printed for your personal notes.' (*Halifax Building Society*) Surely a 'customer convenience' would be the toilets provided by large stores.

'We're enhancing our training programme in customer care.' (*AA Magazine*) This, from the AA, suggests that the motoring organisation is diversifying into social service work. Why not: *our training programme in courtesy*, if that is what is meant?

What is the advantage of speaking of 'a jump in the number of customer complaints' (*Radio 4*) against British Gas instead of: *a jump in the number of customers' complaints*?

cut. 'Cutting the tax that we want to cut can't be cut all in one go.' (*Radio 4*) The minister's repetition of the word 'cut' is unfortunate. It's the tax that has to be cut, not the cutting. *Cutting the tax that we want to cut can't be done all in one go.*

D

damaging. 'Whatever the government says, the outlook for tradesmen is damaging.' (*Radio 4*) An outlook, as the word is used here, is like a statement, in that it must be distinguished from the message it conveys. If a tornado is forecast, the tornado may well prove to be 'damaging', but the forecast itself is not 'damaging'. Indeed, in so far as it helps people to prepare for the worst, it is helpful. Even so the actual 'outlook' here is not damaging anyone: *the outlook is discouraging*.

danger. This is one of a group of nouns (including 'risk' and 'possibility') that encourage recourse to the gerciple.

'The danger of a dyke bursting will remain high.' (*Radio 4*) 'The danger of a dyke's bursting' would be grammatically correct but, except where what follows 'danger' is very simple ('the danger of fire'), the best way to avoid trouble is to use 'that' after 'danger' instead of 'of'. *The danger that a dyke will burst remains high.*

'Paul, says Carla, is an extreme example of the potential dangers awaiting all long-term users of prostitutes.' (*Company*) Paul is not an example of the dangers but he exemplifies the damage that can be done by not heeding them. *Paul shows what can happen to a long-term user of prostitutes.*

date. 'The bridge dates in its present form to 1884.' (*Radio Carlisle*) Commonsense rules out 'to': *dates from 1884.*

dated. 'I found this shopping list dated from 1941.' (*Best of British*) This should be: *dating from 1941.*

deal. 'Some are exported, others sold by retailers and in supermarkets, but a great deal goes by mail and are bought by vineyard visitors.' (*Best of British*) It is incorrect to write 'a great deal goes . . . and are', shifting from singular to plural. 'A great deal' is useful in such expressions as 'a great deal of trouble' or 'of expense', but 'trouble' and 'expense' are both singular nouns and applied as here to a plural collection (bottles of wine), 'deal' does not work: *but a great many go by mail order and are bought by vineyard visitors.*

debate (noun). 'The debate about men costing society more has been ongoing here.' (*New Woman*) Thus the expression 'debate about' tends to lead to ungrammatical use of the gerciple ('men costing society more'). It would help to make 'debate' the verb. *The question whether men cost society more has been continually debated here.*

debate (verb). 'Women, whose presence in some areas of the US military has recently been hotly debated, said that they were reluctant to come forward.' (*The Times*) Topics and questions can be 'debated', but not someone's presence or absence. *Whether they should be present in certain areas of the US military has recently been hotly debated, but women were reluctant to come forward.*

decide. 'The other troops in the British-led sector are still being decided.' (*Radio 4*) It is incorrect to speak of 'deciding' troops. What the newswriter meant was: *Which other troops will be in the British-led sector is still to be decided.*

decimate. The verb 'to decimate' was used of the Roman military practice of killing every tenth man, and has thus come to be used of destroying a substantial proportion of any body. A judge, addressing a murderer, said, 'You have also decimated the lives of your victims' families.' (*The Times*) This illustrates the worst form of misuse of 'decimate'. *You have also severely damaged the lives of your victim's families.*

decision. 'When Mrs Graham took over the paper in 1963, her first important decision was hiring Ben Bradlee.' (*Vanity Fair*) 'Hiring' is not a 'decision'. One might say (though it would not be felicitous) 'her first act was hiring', because 'hiring' is an act, but the decision is 'to hire': *her first important decision was to hire Ben Bradlee.*

declare. 'Earlier this year, 12,000 acres of Lancashire's coastal salt marshes were declared as the Ribble Estuary National Nature Reserve.' (*Country Lovers Magazine*) It is correct to define an area 'as' a reserve, but not to 'declare' it 'as' a reserve: *were declared to be the Ribble Estuary National Nature Reserve.*

dedication. 'I have been reading some of the interviews you have been giving to newspapers and what comes over is the extraordinary dedication you have for this job.' (*The Times*) People dedicate themselves 'to' jobs, not 'for' them: *what comes over is the extraordinary dedication you have to this job.*

defective /deficient. Anything which has a defect or an imperfection is 'defective': *An electric bulb that fails to give light must be defective.* A 'deficient' thing lacks something that would make it adequate and complete: *A thief who robs a poor pensioner must be deficient in moral rectitude.*

deficient. *See* DEFECTIVE.

definite /definitive. Something which is clearly defined is 'definite', and so is an intention which is not going to change: *He will certainly never give way; that is definite.* Where the word 'definite' is used for what is exact and firm, 'definitive' is used for what is not only decisive but also final and conclusive: *This book gives us the definitive judgment on Stalin.*

definitive. *See* DEFINITE.

defraud. To defraud a person is to cheat or deprive them of something. 'Money is being defrauded.' (*Radio 4*) One cannot cheat money. Either the verb must be changed: *Money is being embezzled*, or the subject: *People are being defrauded.*

degree. 'He took a degree from Oxford' (*The Times*) makes it sound as though some act of deprivation is involved in examination success. One would expect: *at Oxford*.

deliver.'When people transgress they learn by their mistakes and seek better in the future to deliver the obligation that is imposed upon them by the legislation.' (*Radio 4*) A letter or a baby may be 'delivered', but not an obligation: *seek better in the future to fulfil the obligation imposed on them*.

'Expectant mothers due to deliver' (*Private Eye*) will not do. The midwife delivers the baby; the mother 'is delivered of it': *Expectant mothers due to give birth*.

demand (noun). 'Newbury is a town that has been much neglected in terms of demand management strategy.' (*Radio 4*) The piling up of nouns ('Demand management strategy') is a feature of today's business jargon. The vastly overused and ill-used expression 'in terms of' (where 'terms' anyway are not in question) lures to the use of jargon. *How to give Newbury people what they need has not been properly considered*.

demand (verb). Like all verbs of speaking and requesting 'demand' often needs to be followed by 'that'. 'She demanded I stop seeing them and in the end I compromised.' (*New Woman*) This is a curious construction. The natural thing to say would be 'She demanded that I should stop seeing them'. The verb 'demanded' requires a direct object. 'I stop seeing them' cannot function as such: *She demanded that I should cease to see them*. See also THAT.

demise. 'Over the years Silloth's role as a seaside resort has demised.' (*Allerdale Outlook*) The noun 'demise' means failure or termination. The verb 'demise' is used of transferring titles or leasing property. It is the wrong word here: *Silloth's role as a seaside resort has diminished*.

demolished. 'One of our Rhu residents spotted [in a photograph] Rosneath Castle, a beautiful building visible just over Gareloch. Demolished in the 1960s this is now a caravan park.' (*People's Friend*) But the demolished castle is not the caravan park: *It was demolished in the 1960s and the site is now a caravan park*.

denote. *See* CONNOTE.

deny. Michael Heseltine assaulted Tony Blair's 'hypocrisy' in being prepared 'to deny to 70,000 children, talented like him, to escape as he escaped' from the State school system. (*The Times*) The verb 'to deny' cannot be followed by the infinitive 'to escape': *hypocrisy in being prepared to deny to 70,000 children an escape like his own child's.*

'Although strenuously denied by the local council, a walk along the towpath does confirm the rather uncomplimentary comments in the *WW Guide to the Oxford Canal.*' (*Waterways World*) What is conveyed here is that a walk along the towpath has been strenuously denied. The word order must be changed to make clear what has been 'denied'. *Although strenuously disputed by the local council, the rather uncomplimentary comments in the* WW Guide to the Oxford Canal *are confirmed by a walk along the towpath.*

depend on. A habit has developed of using 'depend on' where 'determined by' would be better. For something to be 'dependent on' something else is not the same as for it to be 'determined by' something else.

'The type of treatment required will depend on mental and emotional needs, the severity of the problem and the amount of time and money available.' (*Family Circle*) The sentence should run either: *The type of treatment required will be determined by mental and emotional needs,* or: *Which kind of treatment is required will depend on mental and emotional needs.*

dependant. This is the noun form ('Children and other dependants'). The adjective is spelled with an 'e' ('I am dependent on my father').

'The same area can produce an entirely different answer dependant on the previous night's weather'. (*Hunting*) Here the spelling should be 'dependent' but the construction could be improved, and since the issue is the supply of huntable foxes, 'answer' is an inappropriate word: *an entirely different result according to the previous night's weather.*

'Dependant on location, this would allow for 20–30 extra lights.' (*Allerdale Outlook*). Again the correct spelling would be 'dependent', and a better construction would be: *According to location.* See also DEPENDING ON.

depending on. Very often this construction is used where 'according to' would be better.

'Investment trust spreads will vary depending on the trust and with the amount you are investing.' (*Moneywise*) It is bad to say 'depending on this and with that' instead of 'depending on this and on that', so 'with' must go. But 'depending on' is misused too, for there is no word for 'depending' to depend on. When tempted to write 'depending on', one should always ask whether 'according to' would not be better. *Investment trust spreads vary according to the trust and to the amount you are investing.*

'Space plants 10–15" apart, depending on the variety.' (*Practical Gardening*) The case here is exactly the same. *Space plants 10–15" apart, according to the variety.*

'There are four categories of hair colorant depending on how long you want your new colour to last.' (*Living*) Clearly there is no issue of dependence here. 'Depending' should go. *There are four categories of hair colorant to choose from, according to how long you want your new colour to last.*

'Depending on the exchange which serves your area, they may be able to trace the calls.' (*Catch*) Here 'they' ought not to be said to depend on anything. A conditional clause is called for. *If your local exchange is so equipped, they (it?) may be able to trace the calls.*

In 'many single women still operate on the basis that their whole lives may change depending on who they marry' (*Vogue*) 'who' should be *whom*, and the ungrammatical 'depending on whom they marry' says no more than *when they marry.*

derisory. This word means 'contemptuous', not 'contemptible'. 'Childcare facilities are so derisory in this country.' (*Vogue*) This should be: *Childcare facilities are so derisible (contemptible) in this country.* See *also* CONTEMPTIBLE.

derogatory. 'I make no apologies for not immediately replying to the front page article which highlighted in derogatory terms totally untrue remarks made in a report on my school by government inspectors.' (*Times Educational Supplement*) If a man writes about something in derogatory terms, he disparages or ridicules what is said. And if the article thus disparaged the untrue remarks of the inspectors, the writer ought to be highly gratified at this defence of his position. He has used the wrong word: *the front page article which blatantly highlighted totally untrue remarks.*

descending. Like other participles this word must be accurately connected in descriptions of routes.

'Descending to the town once more, the falling waters of the Carrowbeg, by the weir, appeared yellow.' (*Country Lovers Magazine*) The falling waters must not be said to be 'descending to the town': *As we descended to the town, the falling waters appeared yellow.* See also ROUTES.

description. 'Her description had been circulated'. (*Radio 4*) It is correct to speak of Dickens's description of London, but not of London's description by Dickens, so better here would be: *A description of the woman had been circulated.* See also PSEUDO-POSSESSIVES.

deserve. The verb 'deserve' should be followed by the infinitive ('They deserve to die').

'We deserve being packaged with a name that denies our artificial nationalisms.' (*Complete Traveller*) The verb 'deserve' cannot be followed by 'being packaged'. And anyway things are not packaged 'with' wrappings but 'in' them. *We deserve to be labelled with a name that denies our artificial nationalisms.*

deservedly. 'Everton's goal was deservedly scored by Ferguson.' (*Radio 4*) A child may deserve punishment and therefore be 'deservedly punished', but a goal cannot possibly deserve anything. *Ferguson deserved the goal he scored for Everton.*

design. 'My grandson Christopher, five, was thrilled to wear his grandad's design of sun hat.' (*Woman*) It was the hat he wore not its design: *thrilled to wear the sun hat designed by his grandad.*

This error of confusing an item with its design is not rare. 'The Trail shirt is a conventional design.' (*The Great Outdoors*) The shirt is not a design. *The trail shirt is conventionally designed.*

'At that stage 604 was flying the Blenheim 1F, a bomber design already obsolete even for that function.' (*The Times*) What they were flying was a bomber, not a design. Either this should be corrected directly: *604 was flying the Blenheim 1F, whose design was already obsolete*, or the word 'design' removed: *the Blenheim 1F, a bomber already obsolete.*

despite. 'Despite' is a preposition. ('Despite the rain, I went out.')

'Auberon Waugh failed to mention *The Oldie* . . . despite Littlejohn feeding him a gift question.' (*Oldie*) It would be correct, but ugly, to say 'despite Littlejohn's feeding him a gift question', for it is that 'feeding' of a question which has to be discounted, not Littlejohn himself. The gerciple can be removed by use of 'although': *although Littlejohn fed him a gift question.*

'Despite committed landowners, tenant farmers and gamekeepers making their contribution, each season's sport is still a bit of a lottery.'

(*Shooting Times*) Again 'despite' leads to use of the gerciple ('farmers and gamekeepers making') which could easily be avoided: *Despite the contribution of committed landowners, tenant farmers and gamekeepers.*

'Despite the cats spending lengthy sessions on washing themselves, human help is still essential' (*Wild About Animals*) should be: *Although the cats spend much time in washing themselves.*

'The Cancer Research Council has said it will continue its work with Cambridge University, despite the institution having received funds from the tobacco industry.' (*Radio 4*) This sentence illustrates the problems raised by use of 'despite'. In strict grammatical terms 'despite the institution having received' is an unacceptable gerciple. To correct it directly ('despite the institution's having received') would probably seem to most people to be overpedantic. As so often, the neatest way out is to use 'even though' or 'although' instead of 'despite': *it will continue its work with Cambridge University even though the institution has received funds from the tobacco industry.*

detect. 'This was an awful crime in which an innocent man was clubbed to death. We must detect this crime.' (*Radio 4*) To 'detect a crime' is to discover that a crime has been committed. It is the wrong verb here. *We must get to the bottom of this crime.* Alternatively the word 'crime' could be changed too. *We must identify the criminal.*

determine. 'They now have the evidence that will determine the cause of the worst mid-air collision in aviation history.' (*Radio 4*) Evidence may indicate the cause, but only human interpretation of that evidence can fully establish ('determine') the cause: *They now have the evidence that will reveal the cause.*

devastated. 'Devastated by fire in 1989, its restoration has represented the National Trust's largest ever building conservation project.' (*Country Talk*) This sentence avers that a restoration was devastated by fire. Either the word 'devastated' must be sacrificed: *After destruction by fire in 1989, the restoration has represented,* or a word must be supplied to agree with it: *Devastated by fire in 1989, the restored building has represented the National Trust's largest ever building conservation project.*

devastating. 'The Princess's description of royal life was devastating of the Royal Family idea that has sustained the monarchy for 50 years.' (*The Times*) There is no such construction in English as 'devastating of'. An adjective must be substituted for 'devastating'. *The Princess's de-*

scription of royal life was destructive of the idea of the royal family [sic]
that has sustained the monarchy.

deviate. 'The principle is that a magnetic field deviates the path of an
electric current.' (*Focus*) The verb 'deviate' is generally used intransitively, and (though it cannot be said to be incorrect) there seems to be
little reason to use it transitively when there is a perfectly good transitive
verb. *The principle is that a magnetic field diverts the path of an electric
current.*

devolve. When something is devolved it is passed down to a successor
or subordinate. 'The availability of firearms is increasingly being devolved to a lower level.' (*Radio 4*) This comment on drug gangs in
Toxteth represents a tortuous police idiom. To speak of 'devolving availability' is both pretentious and inexact. *Firearms are becoming more
widely available.*

diagnose. 'This was the case for Corrine, 29, who was 15 when her
mother was diagnosed with cancer.' (*She*) To diagnose a disease is to
identify it by examination. It was the cancer that was diagnosed not
Corinne's mother. *This was the case for Corrine who was 15 when her
mother's cancer was diagnosed.*

'They are designed to temporarily replace your income when you are
diagnosed with a serious illness.' (*Moneywise*) This should be: *when a
serious illness is diagnosed* or *when you learn that you have a serious
illness.*

'She was later diagnosed with ME' (*Daily Telegraph*) should be: *She
was later found to have ME.*

After these examples of the usage 'to diagnose with' we cite an example of 'to diagnose as'. 'More people than ever are being diagnosed as
insulin-dependent' (*Sunday Times*) should be: *More people than ever are
being classified as insulin-dependent.*

The mistake takes various forms. 'At 25, she was correctly diagnosed'
(*Sunday Times*) should be: *At 25 her complaint was correctly diagnosed.*

diarise. *See* COINAGES.

die. This is what is thrown in a game of chance. The plural form is 'dice'.

'The dye is cast already.' (*Hunting*) 'Dye' is the substance that colours
material. *The die is cast.*

diet. 'The staple diet of every magazine at this time of year are the
Christmas-present pages.' (*The Times*) Although 'pages' attracts a plural

verb ('are'), 'diet' requires a single one. In any case the use of the image makes it sound as though magazines eat their own pages. It is surely the reader's 'diet' that is at issue. *The staple menu of every magazine at this time of year includes Christmas-present pages.*

differ. 'The Director of the Inquiry described how the Assured Pension would differ to the existing system.' (*Radio 4*) It is considered pedantic to insist on 'different from' as opposed to 'different to', but the verb 'differ' should be followed by 'from'. It would be bad to say 'I differ to you in that respect'. *The Director described how the Assured Pension would differ from the existing system.*

difference. 'In an increasingly competitive world, finding a genuine point of difference is becoming more difficult.' (*Marketing Week*) As the opening sentence of an advertisement, this is scarcely self-explanatory. What is a 'point of difference'? In another context it might mean a matter of dispute. Judging from the context here, I take it that what is meant is: *In an increasingly competitive world, distinguishing oneself from rivals is becoming more difficult.*

'Working with children is no different from working with the elderly. Neither should it be of any difference to working with the disabled or able-bodied.' (*Good News Magazine*) The expression 'of any difference' is unEnglish, and the word 'or' seems to be out of place. One suspects that something straightforward is intended: *Nor should working with the disabled be different from working with the able-bodied.*

In sentences with the pattern 'There is no difference between A and B', care must be taken to ensure that A and B are exactly matched. 'There is no real difference between the type of shoe bought by the trendy advertising executive and the staid stockbroker.' (*The Times*) Here the type of shoe is compared with the stockbroker instead of with his shoes. *There is no difference between the trendy advertising executive and the staid stockbroker in the type of shoes they buy.*

different. This word is often ill-used.

FAILURE OF PARALLELISM When one thing is being declared to be 'different' from another, the two items must be comparable. 'Its style, though clearly magnetic to current Renault 5 users, is not dramatically different to, say, a Fiesta or a Peugeot 205.' (*Esquire*) The style of the Renault must not be compared with the Fiesta or the Peugeot, but with their respective styles. There are three ways of getting rid of this all too common error: *Its style is not dramatically different from, say, a Fiesta's or a*

Peugeot 205's or: *Its style is not dramatically different from that of, say, a Fiesta or a Peugeot 205*, or: *In style it is not dramatically different from, say, a Fiesta or a Peugeot 205.*

'I was only 15, and I'd known her for less than a fortnight, but I knew that what I was feeling was completely different from previous times.' (*More!*) What he was feeling was not different from previous times but from the feelings then experienced: *what I was feeling was completely different from anything I had felt before.*

In common with other words of comparison or contrast which express relationships between periods (such as 'like' and 'unlike') 'different' often leads to this error. 'Living in the countryside in the 1990s is very different from previous decades.' (*Home & Country*) The 'living' is not different from previous decades, but from living in previous decades. Compare living with living or period with period: *Living in the countryside in the 1990s is very different from what it was in previous decades*, or: *The 1990s are very different from previous decades for those who live in the country.*

MISUSED AS PSEUDO-ADVERB 'More and more people are getting into bad habits because no one has shown them any different.' (*Shooting Times*) 'Different' is an adjective and must qualify a noun: *because no one has taught them otherwise.*

'Soon her partner has to get used to a woman who not only looks different, but acts different.' (*Options*) A person can 'look' wise or old or different but the verb 'act' again demands an adverb: *not only looks different but acts differently.*

FOLLOWED BY 'FROM' OR 'TO' 'Entirely different than a brush or any other tool, Colour Shapers' rubber composite tips allow the users to carve and shape colour on the painting surface.' (*Artists & Illustrators Magazine*) 'Different' should be followed by 'from' or 'to', not by 'than': *Entirely different from a brush or any other tool.*

difficulty. 'There are great difficulties for many people to get out [from a besieged city].' (*Radio 4*) It is correct to use the infinitive after the adjective 'difficult' ('It is difficult to succeed'), but incorrect to use it after the noun 'difficulty'. *There are great difficulties for many people in getting out.*

There is a tendency to use this word without any clarity of reference. 'The difficulty of the Sistine Chapel is not simply tourist crowds or matters of restoration.' (*The Times*) Is it (whatever 'it' is) really the Sistine Chapel's difficulty? Even if we fill out the meaning ('The difficulty presented by the Sistine Chapel'), 'difficulty' still seems to be the wrong word. *The Sistine Chapel presents us with a problem, and it is not just matters of tourism and restoration.*

dig. A piece in the press speaks of courses for labourers on how to 'avoid buried cables and pipes and even how to dig a hole correctly, leaving the site as if it had never been touched'. (*The Times*) It is not the correct way of digging a hole that will ensure that the site is left thus, but the correct way of filling it in. A very slight change is needed: *and how to dig a hole correctly and leave the site as if it had never been touched.*

dimension. This word is being vastly overused and ill-used. 'We invite you to enter the new and fascinating dimension of ceramic articles by Paolo Marioni.' (*World of Interiors*) The 'dimensions' (measurements) of the ceramic articles are simply not at issue. As for 'dimension' in its wider sense, the pottery does certainly not exist outside the space-time continuum which we all inhabit. *We invite you to look at new ceramic articles by Paolo Marioni.*

diminish. 'I don't wish to diminish the difficulties the service faces.' (*Radio 4*) Since to 'diminish' is to decrease, the Acting Director General of the Prison Service is denying that he wants to decrease the difficulties facing the service. Plainly he means something else. *I don't wish to underestimate the difficulties the service faces.*

The misunderstanding is not an isolated case. 'And while not wishing to diminish the irritation factor of Mrs Branagh on her home turf, Lettice does strongly suspect that, when she hits American ground, she becomes even more irritating still.' (*OK! Magazine*) The sarcastic tone adopted makes it clear again that 'diminish' (to decrease) was not the word intended: *And while not wishing to underestimate the irritation factor of Mrs Branagh on her home turf.*

disabled. This is a word which increasingly tends to drift from its proper mooring. 'John and Jill Cornish had been invited to the show by United British Caravans, who were displaying two caravans that they had converted for disabled use.' (*Caravan Magazine*) The use is certainly not 'disabled'; the users may be: *converted for use by the disabled.*

discourage. 'Even a small charge would discourage people applying for the voluntary card.' (*Radio 4*) It might be said, of a retiming announcement at an airport, 'The announcement is discouraging people queueing at the gate'. Similarly it might be said, of an announcement about a bomb scare, 'The announcement is discouraging people from queueing at the gate'. It would be helpful to preserve this subtle distinction in what may follow the verb 'discourage'. *Even a small charge would discourage people from applying for the voluntary card.*

discreet. *See* DISCRETE.

discrete. This word means 'distinct' or 'separate'. It should not be confused with 'discreet' which means 'tactful' and hence 'not very noticeable'. 'The discrete alternative to unsightly indoor TV aerials' (*Home Free*) should be: *The discreet alternative to unsightly indoor TV aerials.* *See also* DISCRETELY.

discretely. 'Politicians are discretely wined and dined by lobby journalists every day.' (*Daily Telegraph*) It appears that what is meant here is that the politicians are entertained out of the public eye: *Politicians are discreetly wined and dined.*

disinterest. This word means lack of all bias or partiality. It is not the state of being uninterested.

'Asher, perhaps as a consequence, has a total disinterest in vehicles.' (*The Times*) There is no single word appropriate to replace 'disinterest' here: *has a total lack of interest in vehicles*, but the misused noun can be dropped in favour of an adjective. *Asher, perhaps as a consequence, is totally uninterested in vehicles.*

disinterested. This word does not mean 'uninterested'. It is used of acts that are impartial and wholly devoid of selfish motive.

'After a season or two with one pride, the male [lion] may beome disinterested and fail to resist a challenge from a rival male.' (*Wild Life Fact File*) Since 'become uninterested' is inelegant, it is better to say: *the male lion may lose interest.*

dismantle. 'It finds the claim that the Metropolitan Police had never dismantled its ability to handle this type of incident less than convincing.' (*Radio 4*) We can 'dismantle' (take apart) an organisation, but not an ability. Either the word 'ability' must go: *had never dismantled its organisation for handling this type of incident*, or 'dismantled' must go: *had not impaired its ability.*

dismay. 'But he said nursing staff should not dismay.' (*Radio 4*) The verb 'dismay' is transitive, used of causing apprehension to another.

Intransitive usage is officially obsolete: *But he said that* [sic] *nursing staff should not despair.*

dismiss. 'I have two children who are without defect and do not have the worries at present of the physical or/and mental development deficiencies although it is an area that cannot be dismissed and there are factors that happen without warning.' (*Good News Magazine*) There is a tangle of error here. 'Worries of' should be 'worries about'. It is not clear, because of the absence of a second 'I' before 'do not', whether it is the children or the writer who do not have worries. Moreover, to speak of dismissing an 'area' is poor usage, and 'factors' do not 'happen'. *I have two children who are without defect and I do not at present have worries about their physical or mental development, though one cannot totally forget such concerns when changes are unpredictable.*

disposal. 'Over 50s have such much spending power, or disposal income, as it is known in financial jargon, that they are being wooed by all and sundry.' (*Lancashire Life*) This short sentence contains three errors, involving the words 'such much', 'disposal' and 'as it is known'. It should be: *Over 50s have so much spending power, or disposable income, as it is called.*

dispute. 'The biographies of Sylvia Plath are hotly disputed.' (*New Woman*) A biography is not something that can be 'disputed' any more than a novel can. It is the notions expressed therein that may be disputed. *Claims made in the biographies of Sylvia Plath are hotly disputed.*

dissociate. 'The Tottenham Conservative Association not only completely dissociates itself with the remarks made by Justin Hinchcliffe . . .' (*Radio 4*) It is possible for a body to 'associate' itself with something said, but not to 'dissociate' itself 'with' something or someone: *completely dissociates itself from the remarks.*

distaste. 'Most businesses share the public's distaste with what are apparently excessive pay rises.' (*Radio 4*) There can be dissatisfaction 'with' something, but not distaste 'with' something: *the public's distaste for what are apparently excessive pay rises.*

distinction. When the expressions 'difference between' or 'distinction between' are used, parallelism must be sustained between the items contrasted. We speak of the difference between 'talking and singing' where 'talking' and 'singing' are grammatically parallel.

'What do these words mean? First of all they imply a distinction

between the Union as presently envisaged and it becoming a federation.'
(*Independent*) It is correct to speak of the distinction (difference) between the Union as presently envisaged and what the Union may
become, but certainly not between the Union as presently envisaged and
'it becoming': *they imply a distinction between the Union as presently
envisaged and its future development into a federation.*

distinguish. 'Distinguished from other buildings in the village by hanging green leaves or branches over the door, they were normally located
around the village green along with other valid services.' (*Heritage*) This
is a piece on historical inns. 'He distinguished his house by putting up a
sign' makes sense because he did indeed put up a sign, but 'His house
was distinguished by putting up a sign' does not make sense because the
house did not put up the sign. Nor did the inns hang things over their
own doors: *Distinguished from other buildings in the village by green
leaves or branches hung over the door.*

do. This verb is wrongly used both in connection with nouns and in connection with other verbs.

IN CONNECTION WITH NOUNS There are things which common usage
accepts that people 'do' (like the washing-up or the crossword puzzle)
and there are processes for which the verb is not used. 'House transactions in Scotland are usually done quickly.' (*Cottage & Castle*) Here is a
case in point. Transactions are not 'done'. *House transactions in Scotland are usually effected/completed quickly.*

'As a result, we still think of competition as unfair: to do it against a
man is mean.' (*Company*) Again it is not good usage to speak of 'doing'
competition: *to compete against a man is mean.*

'Go for a walk, clear a cupboard, tidy your flat or do an exercise class.'
(*New Woman*) Likewise an exercise class is not something to be 'done':
attend an exercise class.

'DO' FOR 'TAKE PART IN' 'More children will do at least two hours of
sport within school hours.' (*Radio 4*) This is one of the cases where the
verb 'to do' should be replaced by 'to take part in': *More children will
take part in sport for at least two hours.*

'People are spending their time off doing ever more obscure sports'
(*The Times*) should be: *taking part in ever more obscure sports.*

IN BACK-REFERENCE In using the verb 'do' to refer back to some act
already mentioned, the writer must ensure that there actually is a verb to
which it can properly refer.

'PC Patrick Dunne was killed in a relatively "safe" area of south

London and in a street not known for drug dealing or violent crime. That he did so shows that the distinctions between so-called quiet areas and those regarded as lawless are becoming increasingly irrelevant.' (*The Times*) The words 'That he did so' raise the question 'Did what?' He was killed: that was not something he 'did' but something that was done to him. The active verb 'did' is totally out of place: *That this happened to him shows that the distinctions are becoming increasingly irrelevant.*

'It also makes a pleasant talking point if you can show off flowers from your own garden – or at least choose blooms that look as though they may have done.' (*Perfect Home*) Again the question is raised 'Done what?' There must be a verb for 'may have done' to refer back to: *show off flowers that come from your own garden – or at least look as though they have done.*

'Your own life should take second place to your children and I've never felt able to do that.' (*OK! Magazine*) Here there is once more no verb for 'do that' to refer back to. A verb other than the verb 'to do' is called for. *Your own life should take second place to your children's and I've never been equal to that demand.*

'"A tiny shift by one partner will inevitably bring about a response in the other," explains Denise Knowles. There are many ways you can do this.' (*New Woman*) Do what? Only certain kinds of employees 'do a shift', and that is not the process at issue here: *There are many ways to make such a shift.*

'It is difficult to imagine what further initiatives they can devise, but if they don't then the future of Bosnia looks grim.' (*Radio 4*) Once more 'if they don't' raises the question 'If they don't what?' The meaning needs to be clarified and the verb 'to do' sacrificed: *but if they can't think of one.*

PASSIVE VOICE Comparable errors are made with the verb 'do' in the passive voice. 'They need fresh water every day which can be done last thing at night.' (*Cumbria Life*) Fresh water cannot be 'done'. If the construction is to be kept, something that can 'be done' must be mentioned. *You must give them fresh water every day, which can be done last thing at night.*

'Although events such as the State Opening of Parliament rarely differ from year to year, each one is planned afresh as if it were being done for the first time.' (*Majesty*) 'Each one' refers back to 'events' and an event is not something that people 'do': *each one is planned afresh as if it were happening for the first time.*

do so. 'I would not do so' is an appropriate usage when 'do' refers back clearly to a matching verb. Failure to make such a match occurs all too often.

ACTIVE/PASSIVE CONFUSION 'He beats his children: I would not do so' is correct, but it would be incorrect to write 'His children get beaten: I would not do so' because there is no active verb 'to beat' for 'do so' to refer back to.

'But aesthetics should not be separated from morality; to do so is to pretend that there is no connection between architecture and the society it serves.' (*The Times*) Here, as in the sentence above, there is no active verb 'to separate' for 'do so' to refer back to: *We must not separate aesthetics from morality; to do so is to pretend.*

'The shipping minister said ferries would be made safer as soon as it was practicable to do so.' (*Radio 4*) Either the first verb must be in the active voice: *The shipping minister said that we must make ferries safer as soon as it was practicable to do so*, or 'do so' must go: *as soon as it was practicable (to make them so).*

FAULTY BACK-REFERENCE It is not only in confusing the active and passive voices that the expression 'to do so' fails to connect properly to what has been written.

'All we can do is ensure that anyone who wants good accommodation at the best possible price can do so easily through our new booking system.' (*The Times*) Here 'do so' has no verb to reflect back to. If the sentence had been 'anyone who wants to obtain good accommodation . . . can do so', then 'do' would properly refer back to 'obtain'. As it is, the sentence strictly conveys that anyone who wants good accommodation can go on wanting it ('do so'). The words 'do so' must go: *anyone who wants good accommodation . . . can easily obtain it.*

'It was a rotten corrupt set-up, in need of drastic reform. But what happens when anyone starts to do so?' (*The Times*) Again the question arises, do what? There must be an active verb for 'do so' to refer back to. The noun 'reform' cannot double as a verb. Once more the words 'do so' must go. *But what happens when anyone starts to reform it?*

'Since then I have met many sheep-keepers, whose reasons for doing so vary.' (*Country Living*) 'Sheep-keepers' is not something that people 'do'. A verb must be supplied for 'doing so' to relate back to. *Since then I have met many people who kept sheep and whose reasons for doing so varied.*

dog (verb). 'Ever since the Home Secretary launched his Green Paper two years ago, the whole thing has been dogged with problems of one sort or another.' (*Radio 4*) To 'dog' is to pursue like a dog, hence to harrass. One would not speak of being pursued 'with' a dog and the preposition 'with' is better avoided here: *the whole thing has been dogged by problems.*

donate. A person may 'donate' a sum to a good cause. The verb does not take an indirect object. No one could be said to 'donate a cause a sum' as one might 'give a dog a bone'.

Thus 'Sometimes we are donated a puppy from a litter' (*Dogs Monthly*), is wrong because we are not donated: the puppy is. *Sometimes a puppy from a litter is donated to us.*

douse. 'If you do make a fire . . . when you've finished with it douse it out with water.' (*Trail*) To 'douse' (or 'dowse') is to put out, so 'out' is wrong here: *douse it with water.*

draw (noun). 'For most it's a goalless draw which need never have been played.' (*Radio 4*) The subject is a matter of political diplomacy. To describe a match as 'a goalless draw' is settled usage, but even in metaphorical usage a 'draw' cannot be 'played': *it's a goalless draw in a match which need never have been played.*

draw (verb). 'People are bound to draw similarities between this case and the case of James Bulger.' (*Radio 4*) Established usage allows us to 'draw' a parallel but not a similarity: *People are bound to detect similarities.*

drop. 'Even when heavy items like litre bottles of drink were carried, the comfort factor did not drop.' (*Country Walking*) The word 'factor' is out of place as a measurement of 'comfort'. There is a simple way of putting this: *Even when heavy items like litre bottles of milk were carried, I was no less comfortable.*

due. 'Fokker came close to bankruptcy last month when its majority shareholder Daimler Benz was due funding.' (*Radio 4*) Creditors are never 'due' anything. If money is due to me, that does not make me 'due money': *when funding was due to Daimler Benz.*

'Find out if you're due a rebate from the tax office.' (*Moneywise*) It is the rebate that may be 'due', not you. *Find out if a rebate is due to you from the tax office.*

due to. This expression which should qualify a noun ('The accident was due to negligence') must not be used where there is no noun like 'accident' for 'due' to agree with.

'The Poles who settled here were unable to develop much agriculture due to the uneconomic character of the region.' (*Green Magazine*) Here there is no noun for 'due' to agree with: *were unable to develop much agriculture because of the uneconomic character of the region.*

'A meeting of the British Union for the Abolition of Vivisection has been closed by the police due to unruly scenes' (*Shooting Times*) should be: *because of unruly scenes.*

'Then came a series in February and March, which was extended due to its popularity' (*Wild About Animals*) should be: *extended because of its popularity.*

The BR announcement at Woking, 'Customers should use the front three carriages only due to an outbreak of fleas' (*The Times*) should be: *because of an outbreak of fleas.*

Reference to 'employees who claimed their work had suffered due to work related stress' (*She*) should be: *had suffered through work-related stress.*

'All toilets are closed due to no water supply' (*Public Notice*) should be: *closed through lack of water.*

'Pre-eclampsia occurs because the placenta doesn't develop properly, possibly due to the overactivity of the mother's immune system.' (*Living*) Here we need to avoid repetition of the word 'because': *possibly owing to the overactivity of the mother's immune system.* The use of the neglected words 'owing to' can often save a writer from erroneous use of 'due to'.

The words 'due to' are especially dangerous when used at the beginning of a sentence. 'Due to the devotion of the staff in recovering ledgers and records from smouldering and unsafe buildings, only 15 branches had to have their accounts reconstructed from duplicate records throughout the entire war period.' (*Meridian*) 'Due to' has no noun to attach itself to. *Thanks to the devotion of the staff in recovering ledgers and records, only 15 branches had to have their accounts reconstructed.*

'Due to a previous collision this loco has lost its split head-codes at one end' (*Railway Modeller*) should be: *As a result of a previous collision.*

'Due to the wonderful artists quality of the semi moist pans, its time to switch to St Petersburg Artists' Water Colours.' (*Artists & Illustrators Magazine*) This should be: *If we take into account the wonderful quality of the semi moist pans, it's* [sic] *time to switch.*

'At least partly due to the celibacy rule, would-be priests in America enter Catholic seminaries later in life.' (*The Times*) This should be: *In part because of the celibacy rule.*

Duplication. There is an ugly kind of repetition which sometimes occurs after a writer has begun a sentence with a preposition.

'In this second instalment from well-known watercolourist Alwyn Crawshaw, he introduces the pen and wash technique.' (*Artists & Illustrators Magazine*) Surely no one would write 'In the book from John Bunyan he tells the story of Christian', instead of 'In his book John Bunyan tells the story of Christian'. Yet that is what happens here. *In this second instalment the well-known water-colourist Alwyn Crawshaw introduces the pen and wash technique.*

'I know America where they have always been interested in crafts, but what we do here, it's much better than France.' (*Country Living*) The word 'it' is redundant: *what we do here is much better than what is done in France.*

dwarf. 'Both these names are dwarfed by the Eccles brand when it comes to history.' (*Caravan Magazine*) This advertiser appears to mean that the 'Eccles' commodity has a history longer than that of its rivals. The image of 'dwarfing' is surely overdone. *Neither of these brands can compare with Eccles in their record to date.*

dye. *See* DIE.

E

each. 'Each' is a singular pronoun and must be followed by a singular verb.

'Although each scene is relatively short, they move smoothly from one to the next in connecting interludes.' (*Opera Now*) 'They' cannot refer back to 'each scene'. The plural word 'scenes' should be introduced. *Although each of the scenes is relatively short, they move smoothly from one to the next.*

'Two agents each were standing on running boards on both sides of "Halfback".' (*The Times*) (The occasion is the assassination of President Kennedy.) 'Each' appears to be misplaced. *Two agents were standing on each of the running boards. See also* ALL.

early. 'Despite the Prime Minister's words, an early end to the rebels' isolation still looks a long way off.' (*Radio 4*) If something is or looks 'a long way off' it cannot possibly be also 'early'. Omit the contradictory word: *an end to the rebels' isolation still looks a long way off.*

earn. 'His pragmatism earnt him respect in Ulster.' (*Independent*) The verb to 'learn' has the past tense 'learned' and the alternative form 'learnt'. There is no such alternative form to the past tense of 'earn': *His pragmatism earned him respect.*

eclipse. 'But there was an energy so bright that it eclipsed all of his contemporaries.' (*The Times*) This should be either: *that he eclipsed all his contemporaries*, or: *that it eclipsed that of all his contemporaries.*

effect. 'Too much salt effects the lungs.' (*Health Guardian*) To 'effect' is to bring about ('We effected a change in the organisation'). To have an effect upon someone or something is to 'affect' them. *Too much salt affects the lungs. See also* AFFECT.

effective. 'Nick Shelton has been banned for one month, effective from January 31.' (*Horse & Hound*) Here there is no word for the adjective 'effective' to agree with. No person can be 'banned effective from today' though someone might impose 'a ban effective from today', where it is clearly the 'ban' that is 'effective'. *Nick Shelton has been given a one month's ban, effective from today.*

effort. 'Zaire insists that any aid effort for the refugees must be carried out through the existing Zaire authorities.' (*Radio 4*) An 'effort' is not something that can be 'carried out': *any aid operation for the refugees must be carried out through the existing Zaire authorities.*

effortlessly. 'There's something for everyone at Britain's number one theme park where heritage and fun blend effortlessly.' (*AA Magazine*) Neither heritage nor fun is capable of effort and it is a pity to cheapen the concept of effortlessness: *where heritage and fun blend pleasantly.*

either. Strict grammar allows us to use 'either' only before the first of two alternatives. 'Nearly one in four women are on their own by the time they are 64, either because they have been divorced, separated or widowed.' (*Money Observer*) Here there are three options after 'either', and anyway the word is wrongly placed before, instead of after, 'they have been'. It should be taken out: *because they have been divorced, separated or widowed.*

'Under the Prevention of Corruption Act 1906 any person either remunerating a company employee in return for benefit, or who, as an employee accepts remuneration . . . is guilty of a corrupt practice.' (*Marketing Week*) It is always better to keep grammatical parallels, broken here by the change from 'either remunerating' to 'or who . . . accepts'. In any case the 'person' who remunerates an employee cannot be the same as the one who offends 'as an employee'. Therefore 'either . . . or' is misplaced. *Under the Prevention of Corruption Act 1906 anyone who remunerates a company employee . . . or any employee who accepts remuneration is guilty of a corrupt practice.*

'Because it is always there, and in receipt of its members' money, it is assumed either to be capable of effective action or, if not, it should be.' (*Hunting*) One cannot say 'He is assumed either to be tall or he should be'. The 'to be' introduced by 'either' must be balanced after 'or'. It would be best to substitute 'they assume' for 'it is assumed' and 'that' for 'to be'. *Because it is always there, and in receipt of its members' money, they assume that it is capable of effective action, or, if not, that it should be.*

eke. On its own this is an archaic word meaning 'moreover'. The verb to 'eke out' means with effort to make meagre resources go as far as possible. 'I spent several weeks worrying over character and plot, and practical tips eked from the pages of my two Writer's Workshop books were invaluable.' (*Private Eye*) This does not make sense: *practical tips extracted from the pages of my two Writer's Workshop books.*

elaborate. 'As the party conference proceeds, we asked the three main players to elaborate on their plans for our spending power.' (*The Times*) To 'elaborate' an idea or a plan is to work it out or develop it in detail. Thus it is unnecessary to turn the verb into an intransitive one to be followed by 'on', and it seems a pity that a recent dictionary encourages this use of the verb: *we asked the three main parties to elaborate their plans for our spending power.*

'God created choice, but the Conservative party elaborated on the idea.' (Radio 4). Again 'on' is unnecessary, but 'elaborated the idea' would not be very elegant either: *but the Conservative party extended its application.*

element. 'The rich decorative effect achieved by the wall hangings was an important element within the dwellings of the 16th century.' (*Old-House Journal*) There are various words used for part of something which contributes to its total effect – 'element', 'factor', 'feature', 'component', 'aspect', and the like – but they are not all interchangeable. Each has its appropriate contexts, and 'element' is out of place here for something so concrete and visual: *The rich decorative effect achieved by the wall hangings was an important feature.*

'The fact is that the human element in whose interest we act have not been by nature alert or active in their own defence.' (*Hunting*) Pretentious use of the expression 'human element' leads to error when it is followed by the plural verb 'have': *The fact is that the people in whose interest we act have not been alert.*

eligible. This word means fit or officially qualified for a certain role. 'The £2000 award is eligible to any British artist.' (*Radio 4*) British artists are eligible but the award is not. *The £2000 award is open to all British artists.*

elsewhere. 'For example, some of the spiders found here have never been found elsewhere.' (*In Britain*) This is unintentionally funny. The same spiders could scarcely be found elsewhere. *Certain kinds of spiders found here have not been seen elsewhere.*

embed. 'The concrete had been embedded with glass.' (*Radio 4*) To 'embed' something is to fix it deeply in some surrounding mass. The concrete was certainly not 'embedded' in anything. It was the glass that was 'embedded'. *Glass had been deeply embedded in the concrete.*

emend. *See* AMEND.

emerge. 'Fresh international efforts to find a diplomatic solution to the crisis in former Yugoslavia have emerged during the day.' (*Radio 4*) It is a pity to weaken the verb 'emerge' by overuse thus: *have come to light.*

emphasis. 'But the emphasis has been turned around.' (*The Times*) The mind boggles at the thought of turning round an emphasis. It would be better to say: *The emphasis has now been laid elsewhere.*

'I have no doubt that more emphasis needs in future to be given to teacher training.' (*Radio 4*) Emphasis cannot be distributed here and there. *I have no doubt that greater emphasis needs to be laid on teacher training.*

employ. 'Children are prepared to find solutions to bullying and already employ many ways coping.' (*Children in Focus*) There are 'ways of coping' but not 'ways coping'. To speak of 'employing' ways is turgid. *Children are ready to cope with bullying and find many ways of doing so.*

enact. 'Bo-Bos were early candidates for withdrawal which was duly enacted between 1978 and 1987.' (*Railway Modeller*) The verb to 'enact' is formally used of dramatic presentation or legislative procedure, and it is pretentiously out of place here. *Bo-Bos were early candidates for withdrawal, which occurred between 1978 and 1987.*

enamoured. 'Future generations aren't yet enamoured to the charms of the super information highway.' (*Radio 4*) To enamour is to inspire with love. 'Enamoured' is followed by 'of', not 'to'. *Future generations aren't yet enamoured of the super information highway.*

'Mr Helfrich's book provides the answer to the many questions asked by patients who are enamoured by alternative procedures.' (*The Times*) Enamoured 'by' is only slightly less inappropriate than enamoured 'to': *patients who are enamoured of alternative procedures*. Alternatively the verb may be changed: *patients who are attracted by alternative procedures*.

'Penrose became enamoured with flight at the age of five.' (*Independent*) 'Enamoured with' is a further vagary. Journalists seem determined to avoid the correct construction: *Penrose became enamoured of flight at the age of five.*

encompass. 'Under new rules a "forest" can be as small as half an acre, or 15 metres wide. This encompasses many rural homes, where unused land can be planted with trees.' (*Period Living*) It is not clear what 'this' is, which is said to enclose rural homes within its circle ('encompass' them). *Under new rules a 'forest' can be as small as half an acre in area or 15 metres in width. These dimensions are those of many a rural home.*

encourage. 'The "common declaration" issued by Archbishop Carey and the Pope encouraged their followers that "whenever they are able to give united witness to the Gospel they must do so."' (*The Times*) To encourage is to hearten, embolden, or inspire. It is followed by the infinitive ('My teacher encouraged me to take the examination'). It cannot be followed by 'that' and is the wrong verb here: *told their followers that whenever they are able to give united witness to the Gospel they must do so.*

encroach. 'It is believed that around 1350 BC the people who lived at Flag Fen found their land was being encroached by people from the main fenland region.' (*In Britain*) In modern usage 'encroach' is an intransitive verb like 'intrude'. One may intrude 'on' someone's privacy or encroach 'on' it: *the people found their land was being encroached on by people from the main fenland region.*

end with. 'A high profile rape case has ended with the defendant demanding that he too should be granted the anonymity granted to the alleged victim.' (*Radio 4*) 'To end with a song' is grammatically healthy, while 'to end with the audience departing' is grammatically faulty. Accuracy demands 'with the audiences's departure'. So too the above should be: *A rape case has ended with the defendant's demand that he too should be granted the anonymity.*

enough. 'There was some criticism that the area covered [in a police search] was not sufficiently wide enough.' (*Radio 4*) 'Enough' is redundant. It means what 'sufficiently' means. The two alternative corrections are: *was not sufficiently wide*, or *was not wide enough*.

entitled. 'On February 22, Jonathan Stephenson will be talking about the use of colour and pigments, at the Ruskin Library in Sheffield entitled "Painters and Decorators".' (*The Artist*) But the Ruskin Library is not entitled 'Painters and Decorators'. There must be a noun for 'entitled' to apply to. *Jonathan Stephenson will be giving a talk entitled 'Painters and Decorators' at the Ruskin Library in Sheffield.*

entry. 'Entry to this year's Fair, which will be at Harewood, will be payable by pedestrians on entry.' (*The Field*) 'Entry' is not a sum of money that can be paid and the repetition of the word is unfortunate. *The admission fee to this year's fair will be payable by pedestrians on entry.*

equate. 'The role of a mother is often undervalued in a world that equates earning power as the measure of worth.' (*Prima*) We do not equate something 'as' something else, but 'with' it: *in a world that equates earning power with worth.*

equip. 'Their 200ft trawlers are equipped with the most sophisticated equipment.' (*The Times*) This kind of repetition of verb with parallel noun ('equipped with equipment') is easily avoided: *are fitted with the most sophisticated equipment.*

Errors of Omission. As the mind races forward on its course, it should take care to ensure that the words keep abreast of it. Skipping over a word or words necessary to the strict meaning of a sentence or to its grammatical accuracy may sometimes be acceptable in conversation but not on the printed page. 'Her first visit to the theatre was, predictably, *Peter Pan.*' (*The Times*) The visit is one thing, the play another. *Her first visit to the theatre was to see* Peter Pan. 'One of the most memorable and moving evenings in her six years was the revival of *Guys and Dolls.*' (*The Times*) The evening is one thing, the play another: *One of the most memorable and moving experiences in her six years*. 'One obvious choice would be Wilfried Martens, a former Belgian prime minister, who would be an even worse outcome for Mr Major . . .' (*The Times*) A prime minister must not be defined as 'an outcome': *a former Belgian prime minister, whose appointment would be an even worse outcome*. 'My first winner was just an unbelievable feeling.' (*Majesty*) The jockey has jumped over-hurriedly here. The winner cannot be a feeling. *My first win gave me an unbelievable feeling*.

'Indeed, at one point in the story, physical violence was employed and ended in the dock with a fine.' (*The Times*) Compression leads here to error. The violence must have ended well before the prisoner found himself in the dock. It was not the violence that 'ended' there 'with a fine'. *At one point in the story the use of physical violence led to a criminal charge and a fine*.

'There's an air of prosperity here – and throughout Uzbekistan – that contrasts with the austerity of Moscow, their former masters.' (*Outdoors Illustrated*) Some word is needed to which the words 'their former masters' can properly refer back. *People have an air of prosperity here – and throughout Uzbekistan – that contrasts with the austerity suffered by the Muscovites, their former masters*. 'Dr Robertson also suggested that a large number of birds in each drive affected their willingness to fly.' (*Shooting Times*) What the writer means is that: *the presence of a large number of birds in each drive affected their willingness to fly*.

'Was this not a repeat of the first such licence, awarded last year to a company which had bid nearly three times that of its nearest rivals, only to find that it couldn't raise its start-up capital?' (*Marketing Week*) This piece on radio franchises speaks of a 'repeat' of a licence, when it means the repeat of a process involving the award of the licence. The licence is not repeated. And the words 'that of its nearest rival' will not do, because there is no word for 'that' to relate back to. The verb 'bid' cannot function as the noun 'bid'. *Was this not a repetition of what happened last year, when the first licence was awarded to a company whose bid was nearly three times that of its nearest rival.*

'The company is now living off Ultramar's assets, and any future lies with its smelly gas field in Liverpool Bay, whose developers swear will not pollute the air over the Wirral.' (*Daily Telegraph*) It is impossible to abbreviate 'John is a boy whose mother hopes that he will become a pianist' into 'John is a boy whose mother hopes will become a pianist'. In fact that has happened above: *smelly gas field in Liverpool Bay, whose developers swear that it will not pollute the air.*

'The English critic Arthur Symons referred to Redon as a French Blake, but Redon allied himself more with Turner. Either is appropriate.' (*The Artist*) 'Either' what? *Either identification would be appropriate.*

ABBREVIATING VERB FORMS Failing to complete a verb form can sometimes offend. 'I have not been to Spain, but my brother has' is satisfactory because 'has' recalls 'been'. 'All Labour leaders . . . have pretended that the existing clause is a familiar ritual which no one takes seriously. But plenty of people have, both inside and outside the party.' (*The Times*) There is no word here for 'have' to recall. *All Labour leaders have pretended that the existing clause is a familiar ritual which no one has taken seriously. But plenty of people have.*

erupt/irrupt. To 'erupt' is to break or burst out: *The volcano erupts every few years.* To 'irrupt' is to burst in, to make a violent entry or an inroad. *The city fathers were in conclave when the invading hordes irrupted among them.* The corresponding nouns 'eruption' (bursting out) and 'irruption' (bursting in) are sometimes confused.

especially. 'At first glance it appears too good to be true, especially when you look into it all more closely.' (*Caravan Magazine*) One may say 'The meal was fine, especially the dessert' where 'especially' singles out for emphasis one course of the meal. There is no such logical sequence in the above sentence. Looking at a thing more closely is not an instance of taking a first glance, but a different matter. 'Especially' is the wrong word. *At first glance it appears too good to be true, and even more so when you look into it all more closely.*

essential. People have grown very careless in use of this word and the word 'necessary'.

'On Sunday the Israeli cabinet decided to import 18,000 foreign workers to fill the most essential gaps.' (*Guardian*) The gaps must not be described as 'essential' when what is meant is that it is important that they should be filled: *the Israeli cabinet decided to import 18,000 foreign workers to fill the most glaring gaps.*

essential that. There is a new tendency to put verbs in the wrong tense after 'essential that'.

'The view was that it was essential that momentum is maintained.' (*Radio 4*) The obligatory force of the statement is weakened by use of the wrong tense ('is maintained'): *it was essential that the momentum should be maintained. See also* IMPORTANT.

essentially. 'One reason is that the Eridge had essentially woodland country.' (*Hunting*) Where a noun such as 'woodland' is used as an adjective it is unwise to qualify it adverbially. It is satisfactory to speak of a 'bridge loan' but not so to speak of a 'decidedly bridge loan'. The offending adverb should go.

Similarly in 'the Middle East harbours several essentially "no-go" states such as Libya' (*Adventure Travel*) 'no-go' cannot be happily qualified and 'essentially' should be omitted. *See also* KEY.

eternally. 'The castle is reached by travelling up a dramatic avenue of tall beeches which seem to stretch eternally.' (*Country Lovers Magazine*) What is eternal continues endlessly through time, not through space: *which seem to stretch interminably.*

ethics. 'We've got conditions of grant-giving which cover things like animal ethics committees.' (*Radio 4*) Ethics is the study of the morality of human conduct. 'Medical ethics' is concerned with the moral principles involved in the work of doctors. 'Animal ethics' ought logically to refer to the behaviour of animals. A better expression would be: *animal welfare committees.*

even then. 'Very little is heard about Yemen, and even then it is concerning civil unrest.' (*Trail*) Even when? The word 'then' lacks anchorage. *Only rarely is there news about Yemen, and when there is it concerns civil unrest.*

evolve. 'Dickinson's meticulous eye for a horse evolved through the life of his father George, a Lancashire farmer and noted horsedealer.' (*Independent*) One may doubt whether a person's eye, however 'meticulous', can be said to 'evolve' at all, let alone through the life of his father. *Dickinson's expertise in judging horses developed during the lifetime of his father George.*

Exaggeration. The temptation to say 'enormous' when we mean 'big' is to be resisted chiefly because overuse weakens the force of such terms as 'enormous'. Whenever a highly exaggerated expression is used in serious utterance, that expression is devalued. *See also* FABULOUS, FINITE, IMPOSSIBLE, INCREDIBLE.

examination. A broadcaster speaks of 'the Nolan committee's examination into the outside earnings of MPs'. (*Radio 4*) There may be an investigation 'into' something but not an examination 'into' it: *the Nolan committee's examination of the outside earnings of MPs.*

example. 'Many pet foods contain much more than the animal requires – salt is just one example.' (*Good Housekeeping*) When something is cited as an 'example' the thing it exemplifies must be clearly specified. Here it would appear, grammatically, that 'salt' is a specimen pet food. 'Example' is the wrong word. *Many pet foods contain much more than the animal requires – salt, for instance.*

'One of the difficulties in interpreting the Bible lies in the fact that different bits of it say different things. Hell is a good example.' (*Independent*) The word 'example' is again used carelessly. One asks, Example of what? Of a 'bit' of the Bible? Of one of the 'difficulties'? Hell is neither a bit of the Bible nor a specimen difficulty: *different bits of it say different things on certain matters. Hell is a case in point.*

'Latin American gold and silver in the 16th century and the riches of oil-producing states today are examples of prosperity produced from natural resources.' (*The Times*) The gold and silver and the oil produce prosperity but are not thereby 'examples' of it. *Latin American gold and silver in the 16th century and the riches of oil-producing states today exemplify how prosperity can be produced from natural resources.*

exceed. *See* ACCEDE.

except. *See* ACCEPT.

exception. 'Slowly but surely, with the exception of Discoverys and Jeeps, prices as a whole are dropping.' (*AA Magazine*) Since Discoverys and Jeeps are not prices it would be better to say: *with the exception of Discoverys and Jeeps, models are costing less.*

'But the British are a breed apart from their demonstrative American cousins and rarely exude passion or enthusiasm – football being one of the few exceptions.' (*Nursing Standard*) The question arises: What exactly is football an exception to? Using the word 'exception' correctly, one might say 'I stay in most days, Sunday being an exception' where it is clear what Sunday is an exception to, but it would not be correct to say 'I rarely go out, Sunday being an exception'. The noun 'exception' should be dropped. *The British rarely exude passion or enthusiasm – except for football.*

excise. *See* EXORCISE.

exclude / preclude. To 'exclude' is to debar or leave out items or people where others are being 'included': *Some guest houses now exclude smokers*. Although the verb 'preclude' is sometimes used similarly, its more particular use is for exclusions which are made inevitable by virtue of other inclusions: *Having Smith on the guest list precludes inviting his ex-wife.*

execution. 'An unusual fitting is an open shelf which can be pulled down from beneath the roof locker when required. The idea is good but we judged the execution somewhat flimsy and in need of a bit more thought.' (*Caravan Magazine*) It was presumably the finished shelf that was judged 'flimsy'. The execution calls for a different adjective, perhaps 'inadequate'. And it was rather the original plan than the 'execution' that was in need of more thought. *The idea is good but the shelf was somewhat flimsily constructed without sufficient care to its design.*

exhausting / exhaustive. The word 'exhausting' is the present participle of the verb to 'exhaust', meaning to weary, to draw off resources, to empty completely. Thus in the word 'exhausting' the aspect of wearying is predominant: *The long-distance race proved too exhausting for him.* But in 'exhaustive' the aspect of thoroughly finishing off something is predominant: *The police made an exhaustive check on every young man in the street.*

exhaustive. *See* EXHAUSTING.

existing. 'But ministers are only seeking to renew the [anti-terrorist] legislation for two years, not for the existing five.' (*Radio 4*) The 'years' must not be said to be 'existing'. If the word is kept, it must be properly applied: *not for the existing term of five years*. But that invites simplification: *seeking to renew the legislation for two years, not again for five.*

exorcise. A political spokesman, commenting on a statement, averred that 'a passage was exorcised' (*Radio 4*). To exorcise is to expel evil spirits from a person or a place. It is the wrong word here: *a passage was excised*.

expand. 'The ITA has written to the council to express its concern at the loss of public courts at a time when it is endeavouring to expand the game at all levels.' (*The Times*) To expand is to increase in size. The game of tennis is not something that can be 'expanded', though a single set might be 'prolonged'. A better verb is needed: *at a time when it is endeavouring to advance the game at all levels*.

'Mr Malone also heard that while nurses wanted to expand professionally, they expected to be paid adequately in return.' (*Nursing Standard*) What does it mean to expand professionally, unless one is pursuing a career as a Sumo wrestler? *Mr Malone also heard that while nurses wanted to widen their professional duties they expected to be paid adequately*.

CURRENT USE OF 'EXPAND ON' It seems a pity that, with the backing of a recent dictionary, intransitive use of the verb 'expand' followed by 'on' is taking the place of verbs such as 'enlarge' and 'expatiate'.

'He was expanding on the details of the Government Citizen's Charter.' (*Times Educational Supplement*) He was not 'expanding' (swelling in size). *He was enlarging on the details of the Government Citizen's Charter*.

Regrettably, this is now a common usage. 'The Chancellor, instead, expanded on the provisions of the Maastricht Treaty' (*Radio 4*) should be: *expatiated on the provisions of the Maastricht Treaty*.

'During his statement afterwards, the Chancellor, Kenneth Clarke, expanded on those assurances' (*Radio 4*) should be: *enlarged on those assurances*.

'In a speech today he will expand on the charge that the [Labour] party is the friend of the villain' (*The Times*) should be: *he will enlarge on the charge*.

Even a highbrow reviewer can write 'I'd like to hear him expand on why George Canning "represented the rotten core of conservatism"' (*The Times*) instead of: *enlarge upon*.

The usage is at its most foolish when the 'on' is simply redundant. 'The police have so far refused to expand on their statement that the men have been released on bail.' (*Radio 4*) The word 'on' must be omitted: *refused to expand their statement*.

Similarly 'He expanded on Labour thinking on a variety of issues' (*The Times*) should be: *He expanded Labour thinking*.

expatriate. This word is used of someone who is resident in some other country than that of his birth.

'This man is Jan Stevenson, an expatriot American.' (*Shooting Times*) A man does not cease to be a 'patriot' (a lover of his own country) by going to live abroad: *an expatriate American.*

expectation. 'When I came to Birkenhead in 1969 my expectation was one of hoping to expand the number of jobs.' (*Radio 4*) Is there not a waste of words here? *I hoped to expand the number of jobs.*

expedient / expeditious. An 'expedient' act would be one that is highly appropriate in the given circumstances: *He felt it expedient to close the meeting before further objections were raised.* There is a tendency to use the word somewhat pejoratively of decisions or actions that are based on convenience rather that principle: *The party leader found it expedient to change his view in the weeks before the general election.* An 'expeditious' act is one that is done promptly and effectively: *As the intruder came in by the front door, she made an expeditious exit by the back door.* 'Expediency' has to do with convenience; 'expedition', in this connection, with speed (*cf* the verb to 'expedite').

expeditious. *See* EXPEDIENT.

explain. 'There is definitely a link there [between poverty and ill-health] but explaining it could be due to a number of causes.' (*Radio 4*) It is not the explanation of the link but the link itself that may be 'due' to a number of causes. The word 'explaining' can be removed. *There is definitely a link, but it could be due to a number of causes.*

explicit / implicit. What is 'explicit' is clearly spelt out: *The statement was explicit: No Smoking.* What is 'implicit', by contrast, is conveyed indirectly: *The way she paused before replying carried an implicit dislike of my suggestion.*

exposure. 'The book also examines other factors such as nutrition and pollution . . . and poverty, with its greater exposure to infection.' (*Parents*) Poverty is not exposed to infection. The possessive 'its' is out of place: *poverty, which increases exposure to infection.*

expound. This has until recently been an exclusively transitive verb. One may 'expound a theory'. The new tendency to use the verb intransitively is to be regretted.

'Libby Purves expounded on the consequences of the Trade Marks Act

1994.' (*The Times*) *Libby Purves enlarged on the consequences of the Trade Marks Act.*

Similarly 'He [Clarke] is due to expound to the Conservative Political Centre on the future of Conservatism' (*The Times*) would better be: *due to address the Conservative Political Centre on the future of Conservatism. See also* EXPAND: CURRENT USE OF 'EXPAND ON'.

extend. 'The controls extend to growing only a few well proven grape varieties and to the period and method of maturation for wines to achieve a given status.' (*Meridian*) The controls do not 'extend' to growing grapes. What the writer means is: *The controls limit growers to only a few proven grape varieties and define the period and method of maturation.*

extirpate. 'The long shadow of Thatcherism may be being extirpated slowly.' (*Radio 4*) To extirpate is to pull up by the roots, to root out. Shadows are not susceptible to that kind of treatment. *The long shadow of Thatcherism may be slowly lifting.*

F

fabulous. 'The miniature sofa in green velvet makes a fabulous window seat.' (*Perfect Home*) There is nothing incorrect here, but it is a pity thus to weaken the powerful word 'fabulous', used properly of what relates to fable and is truly extraordinary: *makes an attractive window seat.*

face. 'If children get love, security and support when they are young, they are less likely to face problems in later life.' (*Children in Focus*) The trouble here is one of ambiguity inherent in the word 'face'. 'Less likely to face problems' might mean more likely to run away from them: *they are less likely to encounter problems in later life.*

faced. It is easy to forget that 'faced' is a participle and must be properly anchored.

'Faced with such overwhelming odds, the likely outcome is a military occupation.' (*Guardian*) Here the outcome is said to be faced with overwhelming odds. 'Faced' can be replaced by 'in the face of'. *In the face of such overwhelming odds, the likely outcome is a military occupation.*

facilities. 'You should use the criminal law if you feel strongly that the company made statements or promised facilities that turned out to be false.' (*Good Housekeeping*) Facilities cannot be either true or false. It is the promise of the facilities that may be true or false: *made statements or gave promises about facilities that turned out to be false.*

fact. There is increasing vagueness in the popular use of this word.

'Craig Gibsone stresses the importance of the use of renewable resources. A fact that he believes we will all eventually have to follow.' (*Green Magazine*) 'Facts' are not things that people 'follow': *Craig Gibsone stresses how important it is to use renewable resources; a policy that he believes we shall all eventually have to adopt.*

'I certainly do not accept the fact that Sir Patrick was remotely influenced by the timing of the leadership election.' (*Radio 4*) If someone does not accept a fact, then in their eyes it is not a fact. *I certainly do not accept the suggestion that Sir Patrick was remotely influenced by the timing of the leadership election.*

'The fact that Paul Bailey's new novel, *Sugar Cane*, improves on second reading is not quite the compliment to him that I, an admirer of his writing, should like to have been able to make.' (*The Times*) No 'fact' can ever constitute a 'compliment'. The writer is not talking about a fact, but about an opinion or statement. *My claim that Paul Bailey's novel, Sugar Cane, improves on second reading is not quite the compliment to him that I should like to have been able to make.*

'Fact lies in rather different directions.' (*The Field*) This is a pretentiously absurd way of avoiding the obvious. *That is not the case.*

fair. 'The other novice trekker, Rob, was fairing worse.' (*Trail*) There is no verb 'to fair'. To 'get on' is to fare: *faring worse.*

falter. 'In this long period of time the waterway's annual feast of flounder in the 3–4lb class has never faltered.' (*Sea Angler*) 'Falter' means to move hesitantly, unsteadily, or stumblingly. It is the wrong word to use to characterise fluctuations in fish stocks: *the waterway's annual harvest of flounder in the 3–4lb class has never fallen short.*

fame. 'The wild boar, too, has found fame in recent years and has been appearing on the menus of high class restaurants.' (*The People's Friend*) This is a curious notion of fame. *The wild boar too has become an acceptable dish in recent years.*

Familiar Expressions. There is a temptation to let familiar sayings trip off the tongue without checking their grammatical or logical appropriateness.

For instance, *see* BEG THE QUESTION, FAR CRY FROM, LONG MAY IT REMAIN SO, MAKE A STATEMENT, NO STRANGER TO, NOTHING CAN BEAT, OUT OF ALL RECOGNITION, OUT OF SORTS, WORD OF MOUTH.

far cry from. 'Around the harbour are a number of tavernas and cafes, and the food and cocktails on offer are a far cry from the average Greek island.' (*Sunmed Holidays*) The provisions are not a far cry from any other island, but from the provisions offered on other islands. And an 'average' island is not a tenable concept: *the food and cocktails on offer are a far cry from anything provided on other Greek islands.*

far from. It is correct to say 'Far from needing rest, I need exercise' where the subject 'I' relates back to 'far from needing'. It is incorrect to say 'Far from needing rest, exercise is needed', because the subject 'exercise' cannot so relate back.

'And some experts believe that, far from needing more beds, what is needed are better community support services.' (*Radio 4*) Here again there is neither a noun nor a pronoun to relate back to 'far from needing', and one must be provided. *Far from needing more beds, we need better community support services.*

fare. *See* FAIR.

fascination. To fascinate someone was originally to cast a spell over them. Fascination is the arousal of awesome delight.

'As a young man my fascination was to work as a designer on an island with palm trees swaying in the wind.' (*Green Magazine*) This misuses the word 'fascination'. To work thus was not the writer's fascination: rather it exercised a fascination on him. *As a young man I was fascinated by the idea of working on an island.*

Similarly 'Stafford has a fascination with broken pottery' (*Home Style*) should be either: *Broken pottery has a fascination for Stafford,* or: *Stafford is fascinated by broken pottery.*

'Her war experience had clearly given her a fascination for the sea' (*The Times*) should be either: *As a result of her war experience the sea had a fascination for her*, or: *she was fascinated by the sea.*

A headline describes the biographer of the Duchess of Windsor as having 'a fascination for a dying duchess locked away in a Paris mansion' (*The Times*). This rather implies that the duchess was fascinated by her biographer: *being fascinated by.*

Similarly 'I have a fascination for poultry' (*The People's Friend*) strictly conveys that the hens are spellbound by the speaker, and it should be: *Poultry fascinate me.*

'Mr Corbyn is a man motivated not by money but by a fascination for the science involved' (*The Times*) should be: *motivated not by money but by the fascination of the science involved.*

The word seems to suffer overmuch from experimentation with prepositions. 'She's gone [to France] to talk about employment policy and has discovered a keen fascination in the British experience.' (*Radio 4*) 'In' will not do: *has found the French deeply fascinated by the British experience.*

fatal / fateful. Something (such as an accident or a disease) which is 'fatal' leads to death. An occurrence which is 'fateful' leads to remarkable developments. Thus both words are used of events that turn out to have momentous consequences, but 'fatal' is applied only to those which have tragic consequences, while a man's first meeting with his future wife may be described as 'fateful'.

fateful. *See* FATAL.

feel. 'Flowforms are a relative newcomer to the water garden scene. They have a very contemporary feel.' (*Perfect Home*) This abuses the word 'feel' which properly is a matter of human response. To say something 'produces' a certain 'feel' is more acceptable. Whether a 'feel' anyway can be 'contemporary' is another matter. One word or the other should go. *They have a very contemporary look.*

feeling. 'This technique allows you to build up a painting in blocks of colour to create a broken-textured feeling.' (*Artists & Illustrators Magazine*) It is the painting which is 'broken-textured', not the observer, and the painting does not have feelings: *a broken-textured effect.*

Feminine Titles. In the past English has distinguished between men and women in the names of certain roles and professions. The most obvious case is the distinction between an 'actor' and an 'actress'. This distinction survives, as does the distinction between 'host' and 'hostess', 'waiter' and 'waitress', 'proprietor' and 'proprietress'. Some feminists have objected to such differentiations with the result that certain formerly established terms are now little used. Many of the feminine titles were formed from the masculine terms by the addition of '-ess': 'authoress', 'sculptress', 'instructress', 'editress', 'priestess', but there were variants from this practice. 'Creator', for instance, became 'creatrix' in the feminine. Current practice is generally to prefix the masculine term by the word 'woman' ('woman doctor'). Foreign nouns taken into the language do not always lose their twin terms. 'Masseur' and 'masseuse' are still distinguished. Where a role name has the suffix '-man' as in 'milkman' and 'postman', the feminine versions, 'milkwoman' and 'postwoman' were once in general use. The attempt to change the suffix to '-person' (except perhaps 'spokesperson' instead of 'spokesman' or 'spokeswoman') has never gained universal acceptance.

ferment/foment. To 'ferment' is to stir up, often used of stirring up trouble, and the state produced is a state of 'ferment'. The verb to 'foment' overlaps with 'ferment' in meaning to encourage or instigate. One can 'foment' trouble as well as 'ferment' it, but 'foment' is also used medically of applying heat or moisture to the body to relieve pain.

few. 'Few catalogues are not prefaced by conditions of sale.' (*Homes & Gardens*) In English 'few' is rarely followed by 'not'. It would be unnecessary to say 'Few members will not attend', when it is perfectly natural to say 'Few members will fail to attend' or 'Most people will attend'. *Most catalogues are prefaced by conditions of sale.*

fewer. *See* LESS.

fictional/fictitious. A 'fictional' character or event is an imaginary one such as is found in fiction: *Mr Micawber is a fictional character.* The word 'fictitious' usually carries the pejorative connotation of what is not genuine or authentic: *He invented a fictitious wealthy aunt living in the country.*

fictitious. *See* FICTIONAL.

field. 'Not all physiotherapists work with or in a children's field. Likewise not all physiotherapists work in a field involving gross physical and/or mental impairment.' (*Good News Magazine*) The image of the field should not be stretched too far. To work 'in' a field is understandable, but to work 'with' a field scarcely makes sense. When we get to the field which 'involves physical and/or mental impairment', we fully realise that 'field' is the wrong word. Moreover, it is a superfluous word. *Not all physiotherapists work with children. Likewise not all physiotherapists deal with cases of gross physical and/or mental impairment.*

fight. '. . . Two very different republicans within a few miles of each other fighting very different races.' (*Radio 4*) It is incorrect to speak of 'fighting' a race: *competing in very different races.* Alternatively the context would allow: *fighting very different battles.*

finalise. 'The third objective, to be financially successful, has yet to be finalised.' (*Waterways World*) An objective is a goal or aim. It can be successfully achieved but it cannot be 'finalised'. *The third objective has yet to be achieved.*

find. 'Their main worry is that similar finds may be waiting to be discovered.' (*Radio 4*) A find is something that is discovered. To speak of discovering a find is like speaking of discovering a discovery. The usage is illogical. The discovery makes what is found 'a find'. Until it is discovered it is not a 'find'; therefore there cannot be a find waiting to be discovered. *Their main worry is lest other similar discoveries may be made.*

find favour with. 'Do you find favour with that approach?' (*Radio 4*) The questioner on a phone-in programme repeatedly misused this idiom. To find favour with your boss is to be approved by him, not to approve of him. *Does that approach find favour with you?*

finite. 'My decisions have always been finite.' (*Hello*) The word 'finite' means 'bounded by time and space'. It is a potent word by contrast with the word 'infinite'. It should not be used as synonym for 'limited' or 'moderate'. *My decisions have always been judicious.*

fitout. 'Choice of layout options from our extensive fitout experience.' (*Waterways World*) This advertises equipment for canal boats. The innovation is not felicitous. To 'fit out' is a verb meaning to equip. One would not speak of 'our extensive equip experience'.

fix. 'The mental health unit group decided that the group membership should be fixed to whoever had attended the last of the pre-group meetings.' (*Nursing Standard*) The basic usage of the verb to 'fix' ('He fixed a curtain rail to the wall') makes it unsatisfactory to speak of fixing membership to someone. And 'to whoever had attended' is awkward:

decided that the group membership should be restricted to those who had attended the last of the pre-group meetings.

flagrant. 'There's been a pretty flagrant regard to the safety regulations.' (*Radio 4*) 'Flagrant' means outrageous. What the speaker meant was: *There's been a pretty flagrant disregard of the regulations. See also* BLATANT.

flatter. 'Dr Barnett's sense of history is flattered by the fact that there has been one previous Whitgift headmaster from Oriel.' (*The Times*) It is difficult to be sure what this means. How can one flatter a 'sense'? If it could be done, in what way would the given fact 'flatter' it? Any suggested correction must be hazardous: *Dr Barnett's historical interests would be stirred by the fact.*

'Overall industrial production fell 1.3 per cent, reflecting a big drop in energy output, which tended to flatter the output picture last year.' (*The Times*) If the 'picture' of the output gave a rosier account of things than was justified, then it was the 'picture' that did the flattering. The 'drop' in output did not 'flatter' the 'picture'. It is best to get rid of flattery: *a big drop in energy output, which tended to make the general output figures look healthier than they were last year.*

flattering. 'His command of the 1st Guards Brigade in BAOR from 1958 to 1960 was flattering but almost irrelevant to the subsequent apogee of his career.' (*The Times*) Surely no one's 'command' can be flattering. What is meant, presumably, is that: *His appointment to command of the 1st Guards Brigade was flattering.*

flaunt/flout. These two verbs are often confused. To 'flaunt' a possession or an attitude is to show it off ostentatiously: *He flaunted his aristocratic upbringing in every word and gesture.* To 'flout' is to show contempt, usually for some code or authority: *He flouted every canon of good taste in his dress and his bearing.*

flaw. 'In my view the proposals contain serious flaws which I do not believe can be resolved.' (*Radio 4*) Flaws are blemishes or imperfections. They are not susceptible to being 'resolved': *serious flaws which I do not believe can be corrected/removed.*

flexible. 'The qualifications required are very flexible.' (*Cottage & Castle*) This refers to making a new appointment. It is not the qualifications of candidates that are going to be flexible, but the manner in which the qualifications will be judged. Either: *The qualifications required are* *not rigidly specified*, or *The requirement for qualifications is flexible.*

flicker. 'His [attitude] would not not cause the flicker of an eye.' (*Radio 4*) An unsteady light is said to flicker, but the accepted idiom about expressing astonishment or embarrassment refers to the rapid movement of the eyelid: *would not cause the flicker of an eyelid.*

flout. *See* FLAUNT.

focus (noun). The word is losing all connotative substance through soft-centred overuse in contemporary jargon.

'The challenges of the next century bring the need for success into sharp focus.' (*The Times*) This noisily empty proclamation is part of an advertisement for courses boasting 'Educational Excellence'. *We must do better next century.*

focus (verb). 'After three years in a patient-focused pilot site, I have seen the benefits of generic working.' (*Nursing Standard*) We focus 'on' things. If, in a hospital, nurses focus on the patients, the hospital does not therefore become 'patient-focused'. The jargon is grammatically indefensible. If the sentence is corrected so that it speaks of a hospital in which staff 'concentrate' on patients, it remains unsatisfactory. What else could hospital staff do?

followed by. In using these words it is crucial to define exactly what is followed by what.

'Educated at a public school followed by a period at college, he was employed in a very satisfactory job.' (*Church Army*) A public school cannot be 'followed by' a period at college. The construction must be changed: *Educated first at a public school and then at college, he was employed.*

'Subsequently, he went to Vienna University where he studied mathematics followed by a doctorate.' (*The Times*) The mathematics was not pursued by a doctorate, nor did he 'study' the doctorate: *where he studied mathematics and (then) took a doctorate.*

In more complex sentences use of 'followed by' is even more dangerous. 'Michael Barnes, the ombudsman, said yesterday that the type of legal transaction in which most complainants were involved was buying or selling a house, followed by divorce, property or boundary disputes and probate.' (*The Times*) If someone were recording the relative popularity of various dishes, it would be misleading to write 'Most diners had steak and kidney pie, followed by roast beef, hot or cold turkey and lasagne'. Clearly most diners did not have steak pie 'followed' by the other dishes. Nor were complainants in the sentence from *The Times* involved in buying or selling a house 'followed' by divorce and the rest. The word 'most' must be applied to one of the various transactions, not to the complainants, for it is the transactions that are being placed in order of relative frequency. 'Followed by' must go. *Michael Barnes said yesterday that of the legal transactions in which complainants were involved most concerned house sale or purchase, then divorce, property or boundary disputes and probate in that order.*

'When Italy's greatest Mafia hunter, Giuliano Falcone, and his entourage were blown up on this stretch of motorway outside Palermo three years ago followed closely by the murders of Falcone's colleague, a turning point was reached in Italy's age-old battle with Cosa Nostra.' (*Radio 4*) The man who was blown up was not 'followed'. All writers ought to pause before using the word for this kind of link: *When Italy's greatest Mafia hunter and his entourage were blown up three years ago and Falcone's colleague was murdered shortly afterwards, a turning point was reached.*

following. This word should be used to mean what it says and not as an all-purpose equivalent of 'after'.

'Sir Alastair, 62, who has taken early retirement following a number of shake-ups in the ITN organisation . . .' (*Hello*) Sir Alastair is not 'following' anything or anyone in retiring: *who has taken early retirement after a number of shake-ups.*

foment. *See* FERMENT.

for. 'For' should not be used as an alternative to 'of'.

'The cost for electricity installation was prohibitively high.' (*Country Talk*) should be: *The cost of electricity installation was prohibitively high.*

There is a tendency to overstrain the word 'for'. 'A heavy wire fence, presumably for defensive reasons, made many stretches inaccessible.' (*Complete Traveller*) It is correct to say 'He resigned for personal reasons', where 'for personal reasons' explains 'resigned'. Similarly, one might speak of a 'wire fence erected for defensive reasons', where 'for defensive reasons' explains 'erected', but 'A heavy wire fence, presumably for defensive reasons' puts a burden on 'for' which it cannot bear; and incidentally 'reasons' is the wrong word: *A heavy wire fence, presumably erected for defensive purposes.*

There is also a curious tendency to begin a sentence with the word 'for' and land oneself in pointless repetition. 'For Morrison and Bradford, and so many other compulsive travellers, their wanderings satisfy a powerful need.' (*Complete Traveller*) Whereas the sentence 'For Smith travel satisfies an inner need' is satisfactory, the sentence 'For Smith his travel satisfies an inner need' is not, for the word 'his' is redundant. The same applies above. *For Morrison and Bradford, and so many other compulsive travellers, wandering satisfies a powerful need.*

Similarly 'For some obsessive collectors, they are interested in getting the most endangered species of all' (*Radio 4*) should be: *Some obsessive collectors are interested in getting the most endangered species of all.*

forbid. 'His wife has been forced to leave home and he has been forbidden from seeing their children.' (*Radio 4*) We prohibit, prevent, ban, or bar people 'from' doing something, but the verb 'forbid' is followed by 'to': *and he has been forbidden to see their children.*

force. 'A fierce rivalry between the big supermarket chains has forced a drop in Sainsbury's profits.' (*Radio 4*) It is difficult to picture how a drop can be forced. Either the verb or the noun should be changed: *has caused a drop in Sainsbury's profits*, or: *has forced Sainsbury to reduce its profits.*

forcing. There is a tendency to use this word (like 'prompting') for a function which the adjectival character of the participle does not allow for.

'But the opera house management has been told that the new 2,300-seat theatre will not be ready in time, forcing them to search for alternative sites.' (*The Times*) Who or what is thus 'forcing' them? If 'forcing' is kept, it needs to be anchored. As it is, it hangs on some unspoken words such as 'the delay'. The word is not worth saving: *the management has been told that the theatre will not be ready in time, so they will have to search for alternative sites.* See also MAKING, PROMPTING.

forecast. 'Now here's tomorrow's weather forecast for the United Kingdom.' (*Radio 4*) Strictly speaking it is not 'tomorrow's' forecast (which will deal with the weather on the day after) but today's forecast for tomorrow. *Now here is the weather forecast for tomorrow in the United Kingdom.*

foreshadow. 'As I foreshadowed in this column four weeks ago, the

Government will propose limited changes to the European Court of Justice.' (*The Times*) This is a poor use of the verb 'foreshadow' which means to presage and carries overtones of momentousness. It should not be used as a synonym for 'prophesy' or 'foretell': *As I anticipated in this column four weeks ago.*

form. *See* FORMULATE.

formula. 'The pink, pearlised formula contains light-reflecting particles which give the illusion of a smoother, tauter surface.' (*Bella*) It is not the formula that is pink, and it is not the formula that contains the particles. The substance, the beauty lotion, must be distinguished from the formula, which is not spread on the face but written in a book: *The pink, pearlised lotion contains light-reflecting particles.*

'The gentle non-drip formula smooths through hair, with no mess, leaving a completely natural result.' (*Essentials*) Again it is not the formula but the cream that smooths through hair: *The gentle non-drip creme smooths through hair.*

'As thick and ultra-rich as a moisturiser, the gentle formula contains a unique polymer to protect your hair.' (*Essentials*) The 'formula' is not at all like a moisturiser, nor is it 'gentle': *As thick and ultra-rich as a moisturiser, the gentle lotion contains a unique polymer.*

formulate. 'Cosy indoor shots began to formulate in my mind.' (*Cumbria Life*) To 'formulate' something is to give it systematic expression. The word is not an alternative to 'form': *began to take shape in my mind.*

formulation. 'Its new, tougher, more washable fomulation will keep your room looking like new for longer.' (*Dulux Paint*) The 'formulation' of something is the act of setting it out in systematic terms. Such a process is never 'washable'. The word is unnecessary as well as misleading. *Now tougher and more washable, it will keep your room looking like new for longer.*

frame. 'If we don't see that [improvement] in a very short time-frame, then one has to question the basis of assistance programmes such as this.' (*Radio 4*) The trendy additive 'frame' adds nothing here: *If we don't see that in a very short time.*

fraught. 'Unlike gas, where competition is well on the way, water, with its health implications and absence of a national grid of pipes, is more fraught.' (*Radio 4*) 'Fraught' means either 'full' (a plan 'fraught' with difficulties) or 'tense'. Water cannot be either: *the privatisation of water presents graver difficulties.*

free. Used as the second element in a compound '-free' can be highly ungrammatical. Expressions such as 'fancy-free', 'trouble-free', and 'duty-free' have long been common. But lately a rash of new usages has been evident. 'Nuclear-free' strains our grammar because 'nuclear' is not a noun like 'fancy' and 'duty', but itself an adjective. A worse strain emerges when we read that a given cosmetic is 'cruelty-free'. The strain is too much. A process may be described as free of cruelty, but not a lotion that beautifies the skin. We may suspect that there is cruelty in the manufacture of the lotion, but not in the lotion itself.

from. 'In America a common cause of infant botulism is from spores that have been ingested with honey.' (*The Times*) If someone set fire to a house, the cause of the fire is arson. The 'cause' does not derive 'from' arson. *In America infant botulism is often caused by spores ingested with honey.*

from . . . to. Use of this construction goes astray in more than one way.

FAILURE IN PARALLELISM 'Between them these groups will be visiting 45 countries and investigating a range of environmental topics from the underwater world of the Galapagos, to a study of acute Mountain sickness in tourists on the main trekking routes in the Mount Everest region.' (*Outdoors Illustrated*) The expression 'from . . . to' must introduce parallel terms ('They discussed a range of topics from capital punishment to euthenasia'). It would be incorrect to write 'a range of topics from capital punishment to a study of euthenasia' because a 'study' is not a 'topic' parallel to 'capital punishment'. This is the error committed above: *a range of topics from the underwater world of the Galapagos to acute mountain sickness in tourists.*

'In five years Miss Mulligan rose from working as a nurse in Harley Street to build an international cosmetics company.' (*The Times*) One may rise 'from doing this to doing that', but not 'from doing this to do that'. The items must be made parallel: *rose from working as a nurse in Harley Street to running her own international cosmetics company.*

'What happens rather when a garden moves from serving the delights of family and friends to public pleasure grounds is that it undergoes a shift of focus.' (*The Field*) The initial construction ('moves from serving') must be completed: *moves from serving the delights of family and friends to serving as public pleasure ground.*

FAILURE TO COMPLETE THE CONSTRUCTION 'What a treat that day was – from the ride to Beckwithshaw by charabanc, followed by looking round the farm and playing on a haystack.' (*Dalesman*) Here the junction is signposted, 'from', and then forgotten. The writer never reaches 'to': *from the ride to Beckwithshaw by charabanc to looking round the farm and playing on a haystack.*

CONFUSION OF CONSTRUCTION 'It is a book I was loath to put down, it has selections from such contemporary writers as John Hillaby to Charles Dickens and Sir Walter Scott, and even earlier to the 1698 journal of Celia Fiennes.' (*Country-Side*) Here the word 'from' seems to perform a double function. The words 'selections from' promise a list of contributors ('selections from X, Y, and Z'). But before the ink has dried on the word 'from', it has become the first term in the 'from-to' sequence ('writers from Hillaby to Dickens'). Moreover, the succeeding word 'and' forks into a totally different construction ('writers from X to Y and even to the journal'). It is necessary to rewrite: *selections from writers ranging from such contemporaries as John Hillaby to Charles Dickens and Sir Walter Scott, and even Celia Fiennes, whose journal dates from 1698.*

fuel. The verb 'to fuel' is increasingly used metaphorically.

'The Mirror dismisses the affair [criticism of the Labour party leadership] as gnat-bites for Mr Blair fuelled by sour grapes or thwarted ambitions.' (*Radio 4*) Imagery gets out of hand here in the notion of fuelling gnat-bites with sour grapes. Why not *motivated*?

fulfil. 'There's no point in taking on work that I can't fulfil.' (*Artists & Illustrators Magazine*) One may 'fulfil' an obligation by 'completing' a promised work, but it is not a matter of 'fulfilling' the work: *taking on work that I can't complete*, or: *accepting commissions that I can't fulfil.*

function. 'Increasing levels of car usage are not just a function of higher living standards.' (*Meridian*) They are certainly not. The word 'function' is totally out of place. And 'levels of' is redundant. *Increasing car usage cannot be attributed solely to higher living standards.*

fungus. 'The fungi, once regarded as simple plants, is broken down into poisonous and non-poisonous categories.' (*Wild About Animals*) 'Fungi', as the plural of 'fungus', must have a plural verb: *The fungi, once regarded as simple plants, are broken down.*

further. The phrase 'to go further' is now used with unacceptable looseness.

'Where the lack of expertise has its most fundamental effect is upon the lives of those who must carry the burden of care. For people with learning disabilities, this goes much further than those who are unfortunate enough to find themselves in institutional care.' (*Nursing Standard*) What is it that 'goes further'? And 'further' than what? *In the case of people with learning disabilities it is not just a question of caring for those who live in institutions.*

G

gain. 'What interpretation you, the reader, will put on this view is up to you, but I gained from Guard Sylvester that many railway men of the times thought this [report on an accident] to be a whitewash.' (*Steam World*) To 'gain' does not mean to learn. Either the verb should be changed: *I learned from Guard Sylvester that*, or what follows the verb: *I gained from Guard Sylvester the impression that.*

generate. Used metaphorically, this verb can easily produce absurdity. 'Let's see how much common ground we can generate.' (*Radio 4*) The minister's attempt to be colourful misfires. Human beings cannot 'generate' ground: *how much common ground we can find.*

The word is now being treated as a catch-all alternative to 'make' or 'cause'. Thus we read that 'the genocide' in Rwanda 'has also generated an estimated two million refugees spilling over the borders' (*Adventure Travel*) where notions of generating are totally out of place: *has also caused the exodus of an estimated two million refugees.*

Gerciples. I have coined this word to describe a grammatically illegitimate form which results from trying to combine in one term the function of the gerund, which is a noun, and the function of a participle, which works adjectivally. The practice is now widespread and is offensive to common-sense. In 'I saw my uncle begging for money in the street' the word 'begging' is a participle. In 'Begging for money in the street is forbidden' it is a gerund. In 'We disliked my uncle begging for money in the street', it is neither. Where 'I saw him' is accurate, 'We disliked him' is inaccurate. It was his begging for money that we disliked. So the correct form would be 'We disliked my uncle's begging for money in the street'.

AFTER A VERB As the verb 'dislike' led to the use of the gerciple above, so do many other comparable verbs. 'If we do not want to accept Corsica becoming a mafia society, it is time for the state to stop hiding its face.' (*The Times*) This can be corrected by the means used above: *If we do not want to accept Corsica's becoming a mafia society*, but, as is often the case, it would be better to change the construction: *If we do not want Corsica to become a mafia society*.

Similarly in 'they would not suggest Norma living with them' (*Novel*) the direct correction would be: *they would not suggest Norma's living with them*, but it would be preferable to write: *they would not suggest that Norma should live with them*.

AFTER PRONOUNS Gerciples are often attached to pronouns. 'We will not stage protests when there is a risk of them being high-jacked by the renta-mob.' (*The Times*) To correct this, the pronoun must be put into the possessive case: *when there is a risk of their being high-jacked*.

'Mr Lilley wants to help those at the bottom end of the income scale via in-work benefits in preference to them remaining unemployed.' (*The Times*) Unless the construction is changed this must be: *in preference to their remaining unemployed*.

The same corrective method can often be used when the gerciple follows the pronoun 'it'. 'But they said that no serious discussions had taken place . . . in spite of it now being two years and one month since the couple announced formally that they were to live apart.' (*The Times*) This could be: *in spite of its now being two years and one month*, but it would be better to change the construction: *in spite of the lapse of two years and one month*. Very often the use of a noun (here 'lapse') can help.

'The staff felt their devotion betrayed by Naomi jumping ship' (*OK! Magazine*) should be either: *betrayed by Naomi's jumping ship*, or *betrayed when Naomi jumped ship*. The correct gerund after a noun ('Naomi's jumping') can often thus sound awkward, but the construction is easily avoided.

VERB 'TO BE' The gerciple of the verb 'to be' is best dealt with by changing the construction. Thus 'their talk of the rouble's fall being due to sabotage' (*The Times*) would become very awkward if the gerciple were directly turned into a correct gerund ('their talk of the rouble's fall's being due'), so it is better to change the construction: *their talk that the* *rouble's fall is due to sabotage.* 'It was only the lower stitching points failing which led to water seepage' (*Trail*) should be: *It was only the failure of the lower stitching points.*

Certain words and constructions seem to attract gerciples. *See also* INSTANCE, POSSIBILITY, RECORD, RISK.

germ. 'It was clear that the germs of a compromise policy would have to be sown.' (*Radio 4*) Strictly a germ is a microorganism, generally productive of a disease. It is true that we may speak metaphorically of the origins of some movement as the 'germs of mutiny', but germs cannot be 'sown'. Either 'germs' or 'sown' must go. *It was clear that the seeds of a compromise policy would have to be sown.*

Gerunds. The gerund is a verbal noun. From the verb 'to look', for instance, we form a gerund by adding the suffix '-ing'. In this sentence 'adding' is a gerund and it works properly because of its obvious connection with the subject 'we'. It is 'we' who do the 'adding'.

Mistakes occur when this connection is lost. 'The garden can still look good by filling the gaps with annuals and quick growers.' (*Home Style*) This is incorrect because the garden does not fill the gaps. Something must be provided for 'by filling' to latch on to. *We can still make the garden look good by filling the gaps with annuals.*

'They [exfoliants] all work in two basic ways: physically by rubbing creams and bars containing abrasive particles over your skin.' (*Living*) 'They' do not work 'by rubbing', because they are incapable of rubbing. A human being does the rubbing. As so often 'by'+gerund is an unnecessary construction. *They all work in two basic ways: you rub creams and bars over your skin.*

PASSIVE GERUND Passive gerund constructions must likewise be firmly and appropriately attached. 'Furthermore the MOD was bound by Treasury rules to sell properties within three years of being declared redundant.' (*The Times*) If I am bound to sell my house within three years of being declared bankrupt, it is clearly I and not the house that is likely to become insolvent. The MOD, alas, is not about to be declared redundant: *The MOD was bound to sell properties within three years of their being declared redundant.*

The gerund, which works as a noun, must be distinguished from the participle, which works as an adjective. 'A new house has been built, filling the gap between the two properties.' There 'filling' qualifies 'house' adjectivally. Confusion between the two forms is now a major problem in English journalism. *See also* GERCIPLES.

gibe. 'It was a cabinet that still seemed heavily weighted with Old Etonians (rather than the "Old Estonians" as Macmillan was later to gibe about Margaret Thatcher's).' (*The Times*) One might say '"snake in the grass" as Smith called me' but not '"snake in the grass" as Smith gibed about me', because you cannot 'gibe' anything about anyone: *(rather than the 'Old Estonians', to use Macmillan's mocking description of Margaret Thatcher's).*

give. There is a tendency nowadays to overuse certain common verbs such as 'give', when precision demands something more exact.

'The NGA said investors were reluctant to continue the centre when the employees, the main beneficiaries, were not willing to come forward. It did not give confidence in their future involvement in training.' (*Independent*) People may 'give' confidence 'to' a man when they boost his morale. But the writer here is not speaking of that process. Confidence 'in' a person or a project is something that people 'inspire' or 'stimulate'. And surely 'confidence in their future involvement' really means 'confidence that they will involve themselves'. *It did not inspire confidence that they would respond well to training.*

'A board gives brief historical details and the fact that the construction workers coined the term "Neptune's Staircase".' (*Waterways World*) A board can 'give' details, but not a fact. The word 'fact' is out of place. *A board gives brief historical details and reveals that construction workers coined the term.*

go under. Failure may be described as 'going under' only provided that the context does not make the metaphor ambiguous. 'Investors were shocked by Sir Alistair's blunt warning that Eurotunnel was at risk and could go under.' (*Radio 4*) Clearly a tunnel is designed to 'go under': *Eurotunnel was at risk and could fail.*

goal. A 'goal' is something to be aimed at. 'The traveller understands that progress is relative and by no means a necessary goal.' (*Complete Traveller*) If a thing is 'relative', it has meaning in relation to something else. 'Progress' acquires its full significance only when we know to what end (or 'goal') the progress is made. That progress cannot be the goal is self-evident: *progress is relative and not the be-all and end-all.*

'Her brief was "to come up with specific goals we could ask the health service to deliver" she says.' (*The Times*) Results may be 'delivered' but goals are 'scored' or 'attained': *specific goals we could ask the health service to attain.*

Clearly the word 'goal' is thoughtlessly overused. 'President Clinton said that his visit [to Syria] was aimed at furthering the goal of an agreement.' (*Radio 4*) 'Furthering' a goal smacks of the questionable practice of moving the goal-posts: *aimed at hastening the achievement of an agreement.*

'Now that you've defined at least a temporary goal, you're ready for the next step. Doing it.' (*New Woman*) Goals can be reached or scored, but not 'done': *Achieving it.*

goodness. 'Gentle Foaming Cleanser combines the goodness of plant extracts to cleanse with water.' (*New Woman*) To speak of 'the goodness of plant extracts to cleanse' is like speaking of 'the goodness of cash to purchase things'. In each case the use of 'goodness' and of the succeeding infinitive is lax. *Gentle Foaming Cleanser combines the cleansing properties of plant extracts with those of water.*

gourmand/gourmet. It is easy to confuse these two words because both refer to a person who is very fond of food and drink, but the word 'gourmand' carries a pejorative tone, relating to one who indulges to excess, and the word 'gourmet' is positive in its connotation, referring to one who has a sophisticated taste for good food and wine.

gourmet. *See* GOURMAND.

government. This word may be followed by a singular or a plural verb according to context, but consistency must be maintained.

'The government have delayed its privatisation plans' (*Radio 4*) should be: *The government has delayed its privatisation plans. See also* COUNCIL.

grateful. One is grateful 'to' a person 'for' his help. 'I am also grateful to the introduction by a student of mine to brown madder alizarin' (*The Artist*) should be: *grateful to a student of mine for the introduction to brown madder alizarin.*

greet. 'Our arrival was greeted with an indelibly soggy scene.' (*Country Living*) An arrival might be 'greeted' with delight or with anger, but not with a soggy scene. *On arrival we were confronted by an indelibly soggy scene.*

grind. *See* GROUND.

ground (noun). 'I think that the centre ground in education has moved in the Tory direction.' (*Radio 4*) We hear too much now about the 'centre ground'. Whatever it is, it is surely not mobile: *basic thinking about education has moved in the Tory direction.*

There are even more remarkable misuses of 'ground'. 'It's no use saying there is no common ground on the table.' (*Radio 4*) The collision of metaphors is surely too violent here. *It's no use saying that there is nothing at all that we can agree about.*

ground (verb). 'In Yorkshire the river Derwent – a relatively easy restoration which had already been started – ground to a halt.' (*Waterways World*) We are here told that the river ground to a halt. A slight change in construction would remove the error. *In Yorkshire the restoration of the river Derwent – a relatively easy undertaking which had already been started – ground to a halt.*

guarantee. 'A one-way passage on the QE2 to America can cost six and a half thousand pounds, guaranteeing the ship's ultra-exclusive image.' (*Radio 4*) This is abuse of the word 'guarantee', which means to serve as assurance for something. The high price does not 'guarantee' anything. *A one-way passage on the QE2 to America can cost six and a half thousand pounds, a price in keeping with the ship's ultra-exclusive image.*

H

habitat. 'His wife is the former Heather Sneddon, an elegant Englishwoman whose natural habitat is a Surrey garden with a basket over one arm.' (*The Times*) Neither a habitat nor a garden can have a basket over one arm: *an elegant Englishwoman who would be most at home in a Surrey garden with a basket over one arm.*

hang. 'My grandfather was working here right up until he died, and he hanged his hat and coat on that particular nail.' (*Radio 4*) The past tense of the verb 'to hang', used in this sense, is 'hung': *and he hung his hat and coat on that particular nail.* If a person is suspended by the neck until he is dead, then indeed he is 'hanged'.

happen. 'It was always going to be hard to make the code happen without extra resources.' (*TheTimes*) Codes cannot 'happen'; they are not events. *It was always going to be hard to make the code effective*, or *to make the code operate*.

'The government wanted fair treatment [from the BBC] and he suggested this was not happening at the moment.' (*Radio 4*) Treatment does not 'happen': *he suggested that they were not getting it at the moment*.

'Was this an issue that was bound to happen sooner or later?' (*Radio 4*) Issues do not 'happen'. *Was this an issue that was bound to arise sooner or later?*

hardly. 'You wouldn't hardly know it was here, would you?' (*Radio 4*) For some reason 'hardly' (and sometimes 'scarcely') attracts a negative verb where the positive verb is required. *You would hardly know it was here.*

hate. This is a verb which readily leads to use of the gerciple. 'You hate it hanging around your face when you work.' (*Prima*) If directly corrected, this would be awkward ('You hate its hanging'), so it is better to change the construction. *You hate it to hang around your face.*

hatred. 'All Peel's notorious failings as a party leader are here candidly acknowledged: his contempt for backbenchers, his growing hatred to the Tory right wing . . .' (*History Today*) 'Hatred to' is poor usage: *his growing hatred of the Tory right wing.*

having. 'Having' is a dangerous word to use at the beginning of a sentence. 'Having eaten his supper, he went straight to bed' is correct because 'he' is the one who ate. 'Having eaten his supper, the telephone suddenly disturbed his peace' will not do because the telephone did not eat, and nor did his 'peace'. 'Having' must be clearly attached to a person or a thing.

'Having packed off her completed manuscript with a highly virtuous feeling, work was over.' (*Novel*) Here the novelist makes it appear that the work had packed off the manuscript. *Having packed off her completed manuscript, she had finished her work.*

'Back on board and having made short work of the poached salmon in shrimp sauce, it was time for some interviews.' (*Cumbria Life*) Here we do not learn who it was who made short work of the salmon, nor indeed who was 'back on board'. *Back on board and having made short work of the poached salmon in shrimp sauce, I was ready for some interviews.*

'The first is the world of the Royal Family. Having now met him [Lord Snowdon], the mystery of his involvement with it is even more bizarre.' (*Woman's Journal*) The grammatical sequence suggests that it is 'the mystery' that has now met him: *Having now met him, I find the mystery of his involvement with it quite bizarre.*

'Having freshly painted the kerbstones near Pomeroy police station red, white and blue overnight, the march passed off without serious incident.' (*Guardian*) But it was not the 'march' that painted the kerbstones. *Though the kerbstones near Pomeroy police station had been freshly painted red, white and blue overnight, the march passed off without serious incident.*

'Having sacked all its own National Union of Journalists office-holders and banned NUJ general-secretary John Foster from even entering *Mirror* premises, the phone line is *not* open to the hypocritical rag's own army of new short contract staff.' (*Private Eye*) According to this, it was the phone line that did the sacking and banning and the NUJ members were the phone's journalists ('its own'). It would be better here to use the passive voice: *The Mirror's own NUJ office-holders and the NUJ general secretary having been banned from entering the firm's premises, the phone line is not open.*

'Having had former successes in the Melton, Meynell and Harborough rides, and completing the Pardubice on Wells Fargo, this years's Marlborough Cup race over timber is being given some consideration.' (*Hunting*) Since the Marlborough Cup race did not ride in the Melton etc., 'having' must go: *After the trainer's former successes.*

'Having made the link between these two atrocious crimes, it is clear that Victor Farrant is a ferocious and dangerous man who must be found.' (*The Times*) Victor Farrant is not the man who has made the link, but the police whose representative is speaking. To use 'having' as an impersonal alternative to some causal expression such as 'now that' is grammatically unacceptable. *Now that the link has been made between these two atrocious crimes, it is clear.*

'Having secured the pole ends in ringlets at the six pegging points, the poles are hoisted up to form a dome.' (*Camping*) This should be: *The pole ends being secured in ringlets at the six pegging points, the poles are hoisted up.*

'Having been in the monumental and stone masonry business for most of our lives, the need for grave tending and maintenance has become more apparent.' (*Lancashire Life*) This should be: *Having been in the monumental and stone masonry business all our lives, we find that the need for grave tending and maintenance has become more apparent.*

having said that/this. 'Having said that, his father left him' is correct because his father spoke. 'Having said that, the rain was not very heavy' is incorrect because the rain did not speak.

'Having said this, many watercolourists will have to go through this "careful stage" in order to gain the experience . . .' (*The Artist*) The watercolourists did not say anything. If 'having said this' is kept, we need: *Having said this, I must add that the watercolourists will have to go through*. Much simpler would be: *That being said, the watercolourists will have to go through*, and best of all: *That said, the watercolourists will have to go through*.

'Having said that, the context is vitally important.' (*Radio 4*) Here the Chief Inspector of Schools is telling us that the context spoke. *That said, the context is vitally important.*

'That said, most of us have to wear shoes' (*Outdoors Illustrated*) is an all too rare instance of a sound usage that should be cultivated.

he. 'HE' FOR 'HIM' 'He' is used as the subject of the verb ('He likes me'), and 'him' as the object of the verb ('I like him'). Whereas there is sometimes a tendency to use 'I' where 'me' would be correct, it is rare to find 'he' used where 'him' would be correct.

'Let he who is without sin cast the first stone, they say.' (*The Times*) The journalist would be unlikely ever to have written or said 'Let he have the day off' or 'Let I go to the meeting', but that is the grammatical error here. *Let him who is without sin cast the first stone.*

OTHER MISUSES 'In Izaak Walton's book *The Compleat Angler*, published in 1654, he mentions the dun fly' (*Shooting Times*). This is a careless evasion of simple word order. The use of 'he' should not be necessary. *In his book* The Compleat Angler, *published in 1654, Izaak Walton mentions the dun fly.*

It is important to ensure that, like other personal pronouns, the word 'he' is clearly connected to something preceding it. 'Around 80% of domestic burglaries are committed by opportunists, so if you can make it look too risky or too much of an effort, he may think twice.' (*Perfect Home*) There is no singular noun here to which the word 'he' could refer: *so if you make it look too risky or too much of an effort, a potential burglar may think twice.*

heave. *See* HOVE.

help. Slackness in the use of the word 'help' is now widely prevalent.

'A huge Indian rug discovered in a Harvey Nichols sale helps balance the darker blues with the white . . .' (*Woman's Journal*) The proper construction is to use the infinitive (with 'to') here: *helps to balance*.

Similarly 'The combination of clinical white for brilliance with hand-painted green coving helps create a fresh effect' (*Ideal Home*) should be: *helps to create a fresh effect*.

Where the construction is slightly more complex the neglect of the infinitive (with 'to') is more damaging. 'Finding out about various companies also helps target your job application letters.' (*Company*) Here the help is directed at 'you' and the grammar should reckon with that: *helps you to target your job application letters*.

'Would a short assertiveness course help you be more confident?' (*Company*) Here the grammatical short cut grates on the logical ear: *help you to be more confident*.

her. This is the form of the pronoun 'she' which is used for the object of a sentence ('I liked her'). 'Her' can never form the subject of a sentence ('She liked me'). 'Mum's not naive . . . Both her and dad expect me to marry . . .' (*New Woman*) must be: *Both she and dad expect me to marry*.

'The other girls in the office were far more excited about the gift than her' (*Woman*) should be: *The other girls in the office were far more excited about the gift than she (was)*.

hers. 'Her's was a generation of mod cons' (*OK! Homes*) should be: *Hers was a generation*. The pronouns, 'mine', 'his', 'hers', 'ours', 'yours' and 'theirs', do not have the apostrophe needed by nouns. 'That book is hers, not her brother's' is correct.

hiatus. 'There's been such a hiatus over bringing women into the priesthood that I think we've got to respect that and take one step at a time.' (*Radio 4*) This lady's reply to a question about the possibility of consecrating women bishops in the Church of England seems to misuse the word 'hiatus' which means a break in continuity. Does she not mean: *There's been such a rumpus/such a to-do*?

him. **'HIM' FOR 'HE'** 'After all, it is him who receives the exciting brown paper parcels'. (*Shooting Times*) The parcels come to 'him', but 'he' receives them: *it is he who receives the parcels*.

'It was him, after all, who had agreed to hand over government documents to the parliamentary commission.' (*Radio 4*) This should be: *It was he, after all, who agreed to hand over government documents to the parliamentary commission.*

'The thrust of the report rings true – that not only him but also several other ministers would have regarded any decision to close the single currency option as unacceptable.' (*The Times*) The journalist would not have written 'Him regarded the decision as unacceptable', yet that is his error here: *that not only he but several other ministers would have regarded any decision as unacceptable.*

'HIM' FOR 'HIS' Care must be exercised not to write 'him' where 'his' is required. 'It isn't just a matter of him constantly mentioning her name.' (*Catch*) 'Him mentioning' is a corrupt construction which I have called the 'gerciple'. The issue is not 'him' but 'his' habit of mentioning something. *It isn't just a matter of his constantly mentioning her name.*

'Two weeks of defiant celebration in Iraq to mark the 56th birthday of President Saddam Hussein culminated in him riding in a golden chariot.' (*The Times*) The same applies here: *culminated in his riding in a golden chariot.*

Similarly 'the thought of him not being there' (*New Woman*) should be: *the thought of his not being there*, or, safer still: *the thought that he may not be there.*

hint. 'The police are already making the usual hints they make, that this was all part of a wider bombing campaign.' (*Radio 4*) There is perhaps no logical reason why a hint should not be 'made', but conventional usage would be: *The police are already dropping the usual hints they drop.*

his. Two different kinds of possessive connotation may be conveyed by the word 'his'. The objective use is exemplified in 'He loves his dog' and the subjective use in 'I am concerned for his welfare'. Certain nouns tolerate either the subjective or the objective possessive usage. 'I am under his protection' is objective. 'The gun is for his protection' is subjective. *See also* PORTRAYAL, SELECTION.

This freedom is not extended to many nouns. We hear talk of a sick child: 'His care is divided between home and NHS trusts' (*Radio 4*). The care of the boy is not strictly 'his care'. Nor is the care 'divided'. *Caring for him is a responsibility shared between home and NHS trusts.*

historically. 'Historically, the Dee fished from its opening day on February 1.' (*Trout & Salmon*) What is the point of the word 'historically' here? It would be absurd to say 'Historically, Shakespeare was born in 1564'. *In the past the Dee fished from its opening day on February 1.*

homeless. 'John Birt, editor of the homeless magazine, *The Big Issue*' (*Children in Focus*). This exemplifies a recent tendency to misapply words such as 'homeless' and 'disabled'. It is not the magazine that lacks a home: *magazine for the homeless.*

honorary/honourable. Where 'honourable' is applied to someone or something worthy of honour ('*For Brutus is an honourable man*'), 'honorary' is applied to things which are bestowed as an honour (*The university awarded him an honorary doctorate.*) As well as being used to describe high-minded people and noble acts, 'honourable' is also used as an official title for the children of certain peers and a courtesy title for some officials such as members of the Privy Council. 'Honorary', on the other hand, from being applied to posts and distinctions (such as higher degrees) granted purely as an honour and without normal legal requirements, has come to be applied to posts that are unpaid. Both 'honourable' and 'honorary' are abbreviated to 'hon' when used before names. Thus in parliamentery use of *The hon member for York* and in the use of 'hon' in naming certain aristocrats the word 'honourable' is intended, while in *Hon Secretary* the word 'honorary' is intended.

honourable. *See* HONORARY.

hope. 'This article hopes to help relieve this situation.' (*Midland Bank*) Increasingly such carelessness is found. The article of course does not 'hope' to do anything. The writer does. *In this article I hope to help to relieve this situation. See also* EXPECT.

hound (verb). 'The following week it was the turn of the morning dailies to hound the issue.' (*Steam World*) To hound is to pursue something relentlessly with the determination to destroy. The press do not want to finish the issue off: *it was the turn of the morning dailies to pounce on the issue.*

hove. 'The horse-drawn dray from the local Weston's Cider works hoves into view.' (*Country Lovers Magazine*) There is no verb 'to hove'. 'Hove' is the past tense of 'heave': *heaves into view.*

'He hoved into view bearing a large knobbly stick' (*TheTimes*) is like saying 'He sanged a song' or 'He threwed a stone'. It should be: *He hove into view.*

humanitarian. A recent dictionary defines this word (adjective) as 'having the interests of mankind at heart'.

'Meanwhile a delegation . . . is due in Chechen to review the humanitarian situation there.' (*Radio 4*) A situation cannot be humanitarian. The BBC's regular misuse of the word as though it meant 'having to do with welfare' threatens to destroy a useful connotation: *due in Chechen to review welfare conditions there.*

hung. *See* HANG.

hurdle. 'You have these three hurdles, as it were, to get through this week. Let me go through them sequentially, if I may.' (*Radio 4*) This interviewer thinks that hurdles are something you go 'through', and compounds his mistake by offering to go through them alongside his interviewee. Either the hurdles must be removed: *You have these three difficulties to contend with this week*, or they must be approached more gymnastically: *You have these three hurdles to get over this week. Let me consider each one in turn.*

Hyphens. Various constructions in which hyphens are required are considered below. They lock words together in compounds that function as a single unit.

NOUN + PRESENT PARTICIPLE OR GERUND 'The wheelsets [were] lowered to release the tank securing nuts' (*Steam Classic*) Nuts which secure tanks may be described as *tank-securing nuts*, but the hyphen is essential.

'. . . the 10lb (medium) weight for blanching and jam making and the 5lb (low) weight for fruit bottling.' (*Practical Gardening*) Where 'tank-securing' constituted a compound adjective qualifying 'nuts', *jam-making* and *fruit-bottling* are compound nouns but the hyphens are again essential.

NOUN + PAST PARTICIPLE This is a commoner form of compound. 'The plant derived colours have the translucency of watercolours . . .' (*The Artist*) Colours that have been derived from plants may be described as *plant-derived*, but the hyphen is essential.

'Flash fry steaks are lean cuts of beef which have been passed through knife covered rollers to tenderise the meat.' (*Prima*) The rollers covered with knives must be called *knife-covered*.

'This family run property enjoys a convenient location.' (*Aspro Holidays*) should be: *This family-run property*.

'Lister engines came much later and in all shapes and sizes, both water and air cooled.' (*Old Glory*) This is a case where two hyphens are needed: *both water- and air-cooled*.

ADJECTIVE + PAST PARTICIPLE 'So if you happen to be on Red Screes, and bump into a cheeky faced, bald headed, white fringed mountaineer . . .' (*Cumbria Life*) This adjectival construction is far too common for carelessness over hyphens to be tolerable: *cheeky-faced, bald-headed, white-fringed.*

'Patches of masking fluid were also dry brushed across the sky . . .' (*The Artist*) Here the adjective 'dry' is attached to the verb 'brush' to make a new compound verb 'to dry-brush', and the hyphen is essential: *dry-brushed across the sky.*

NOUN + ADJECTIVE 'Another misconception is that children who play, sleep, or are active after surgery are pain free.' (*Essentials*) 'Free of pain' must become *pain-free* with a hyphen.

'Child friendly too . . .' (*Woman's Journal*) must become *Child-friendly too.*

'It is written for non-insulin dependent diabetics . . .' (*Nursing Standard*) A second hyphen is required here: *non-insulin-dependent diabetics*, though one might prefer: *insulin-independent diabetics.*

NOUN + NOUN 'The tiles are tested for strength and frost resistance . . .' (*Traditional Homes*) 'Frost' and 'resistance' are both nouns which, thus tied, constitute compound nouns, and the hyphen is essential: *frost-resistance.*

'Plastic boats and plastic foot rests are not affected by sea water . . .' (*Outdoors Illustrated*) Here are two compound nouns, each separately made of two nouns: *Plastic boats and plastic foot-rests are not affected by sea-water.*

The function of the hyphen in joining two nouns can be seen by comparing a 'bin-liner' which lines a bin with an 'ocean liner' which does not in fact line an ocean.

ESTABLISHED COMPOUND ADJECTIVES 'Its staff have up to date information' (*Church Army*) must become: *up-to-date information.*

'Your brief will be to manage the day to day accounting function' (*The Times*) should be: *to manage the day-to-day accounting.* (The layman may question the need for the word 'function'.)

'Not only is *Mystic Pizza* an out and out girl's film' (*Catch*) should be: *an out-and-out girls'* [sic] *film.*

OTHER ESTABLISHED COMPOUNDS The widespread use of a compound does not justify neglect of the hyphen. 'The 15 year old who decides she's too fat . . .' (*New Woman*) should be: *The fifteen-year-old.* 'For the easiest introduction to hang gliding . . .' (*Outdoors Illustrated*) should be: *introduction to hang-gliding.*

I

I. A surprisingly common mistake is to use 'I' where 'me' would be correct.

AS OBJECT AFTER A VERB Writers are unlikely to go wrong in distinguishing the subject 'I' from the object 'me' in sentences such as 'I liked him and he liked me'. The mistake tends to occur after the word 'and'. 'You and I are good friends', we say, and conversely we should say 'They have invited you and me to dinner'. If anyone is tempted to write 'They have invited you and I to dinner', a sure test of accuracy is to separate the two parts of the sentence joined by 'and' into 'They have invited you to dinner' and 'They have invited I to dinner', which is plainly wrong.

Thus 'The next day . . . our host allowed a great friend and I to take my two daughters . . . on an expedition' (*The Field*) should be: *our host allowed a great friend and me to take my two daughters*.

The error is not rare. 'Granada Television flew Kitty and I from Bristol to Liverpool' (*The Times*) should be: *flew Kitty and me*.

'My mother then sent my sister and I to stay with our gran' (*Best of British*) should be: *sent my sister and me*.

'Last year nearly saw John and I stranded in snowbound Scotland for Christmas' (*Dalesman*) should be: *Last year nearly saw John and me stranded*.

AFTER A PREPOSITION It is correct to say 'Give it to me' not 'Give it to I' and 'The present is for me' not 'The present is for I'. This rule applies equally after the word 'and'. We say 'The present is for you and me'.

Thus 'an adventure holiday for my husband and I' (*19*) should be: *for my husband and me*.

Likewise 'To you or I the answer may be obvious' (*Radio 4*) should be: *To you or me the answer may be obvious*.

The claim 'My children were dealt with at home by Norma and I in a way that was appropriate' (*The Times*) should be: *by Norma and me*.

'Diana never managed to gather such a group, although she used to attend sessions with John and I' (*The Times*) should be: *with John and me. See also* ME.

idea. There are two current bad practices in the use of this word.

'IDEA OF' AND 'IDEA THAT' There are two alternative ways of handling constructions after 'the idea' – 'The idea of losing the race never enters his head' or 'The idea that he might lose the race never enters his head'. The latter construction in fact sometimes renders 'the idea of' unnecessary ('That he might lose the race never enters his head.')

This construction is always the better one when what follows 'the idea' is not brief ('of losing the race') but more complex as in the following sentence. 'Yet the idea of abortion needing a grieving process is anathema to some members of the pro-choice lobby.' (*Options*) All too often we see the words 'the idea of' thus luring the writer to use of the gerciple ('of abortion needing'). In any case, the phrasing must be improved: *The idea that abortion leads to a period of grief* or *that abortion causes grief*.

'Only the most diehard Unionists resent the idea of flexible cross-border institutions taking their authority from the assembly to cooperate with the South.' (*The Times*) Here 'idea of' should be replaced by 'idea that': *the idea that flexible cross-border institutions should take their authority from the assembly*.

'The Protestant Community resents the idea of Dublin interfering in the affairs of the Province' (*The Times*) should be: *the idea of Dublin's interference in the affairs of the Province*.

Where a personal pronoun follows 'the idea of' comparable dangers arise. 'I like the idea of us working together' (*Woman's Own*) should be: *I like the idea of our working together*. The safe alternative, as always, is: *I like the idea that we should work together*.

LAX USE OF 'IDEA' There is now a tendency to use 'idea' too loosely. 'But this apparently simple idea needs a bit of time and thought, and some preparation.' (*Family History*) It is not the 'idea' that needs time: *But this apparently simple plan will require a bit of time and thought*.

At its worst, habit turns 'idea' into a throwaway counter of no value. 'Panache on Main Street have some very interesting and unusual gift ideas' (*Allerdale Outlook*) could be (without loss): *have some very interesting and unusual gifts*.

identify. 'Mary, as police later identified her, fought off his assault.' (*The*

Times) They identified her 'as' Mary, but 'as' cannot do double service when what is meant is 'Mary, as the police later identified her as', which clearly needs to be improved upon. *Mary, later so identified by the police, fought off his assault.*

identity. 'The Indian authorities say they have arrested a senior member of the Harkut-ul-Ansar, the militant group they believe to be the real identity of Al Faran.' (*Radio 4*) The group cannot 'be' an identity. Either the word 'identity' must be omitted: *the militant group they believe to be Al Faran,* or the verb 'identify' should be used: *the militant group they have identified as Al Faran.*

if. A subtle grammatical error occurs when 'if' is made to hinge on a noun instead of on a verb. 'We shall stay in if it rains' is correct because 'if it rains' hangs on the verb 'stay in'. 'He stressed the importance of healthy eating if illness is to be avoided' is incorrect because 'if' does not hang on the verb 'stressed' but on the words 'importance of healthy eating'. In the first sentence the staying in is dependent on whether it rains, but in the second sentence the healthy eating is not dependent on whether he stressed something. Either a verb must be provided for 'if' to hang on: *He stressed how important healthy eating is if illness is to be avoided,* or the construction must be changed.

'Concerns have recently been voiced about a rapid series of takeovers – and disruptive transfers of savings accounts – if banks and others are allowed to make hostile bids for societies.' (*Halifax Building Society*) Here a verb must be supplied for 'if' to hang on. *Concerns have recently been voiced about the rapid series of takeovers . . . that would follow if banks and others are allowed to make hostile bids.*

'Senior doctors are threatening a campaign of non-cooperation if the government imposes a new pay structure on them.' (*Radio 4*) The threatening does not happen only 'if' something is imposed on them. The doctors are threatening that there 'will be' a campaign 'if' something is imposed. The newswriter has tried to make 'if' hang on the noun 'non-cooperation', which is grammatically unacceptable. As so often, if the noun is changed to a verb, all is well. *Doctors are threatening not to cooperate if the government imposes a new pay structure.*

'The French government has warned of catastrophic consequences if the strikes which have hit the country continue.' (*Radio 4*) Again the 'if' clause is improperly tied to the noun 'consequences'. A verb must be supplied for it: *warned that there would be catastrophic consequences if the strikes continue.*

'It is usually unnecessary to correct foot motion, even if, for instance, you very obviously over-pronate, if this has not caused problems directly related to the over-pronation.' (*Outdoors Illustrated*) Repetition of 'if' can be avoided. Here 'provided that' could be substituted for the second 'if': *provided that this has not caused problems.*

'If you burn without sun protection after 10 minutes in strong sun, an SPF12 will protect you for 12 times as long – two hours.' (*Woman*) There is no true condition here. Something which will protect you only 'if you burn' already, will not be in time to do you any good. The word 'if' must go. *People who burn without sun protection after 10 minutes in strong sun will find that SPF12 will protect them for 12 times as long – two hours.*

There is often an alternative to the use of 'if'. 'If he comes, I shall go', could equally well be 'Were he to come, I should go'.

if/whether. There is now a common use of 'if' in contexts where 'whether' would seem to be preferable. It is satisfactory to say 'I stay indoors if the weather is bad', where 'if' introduces a real condition, but less satisfactory to say 'He wants to know if it is raining' instead of 'He wants to know whether it is raining'. It may be out of date now to use the words 'correct' and 'incorrect' of this differentiation, but the following preferences should be noted.

'Though I trusted the big geese not to hurt the little ones I didn't know if they could keep them warm' (*Oldie*) should be: *I didn't know whether they could keep them warm.*

'The next Tuesday, back in London, the Cabinet Office met to decide if Tweddle was right or if he had made a fool of himself' (*Gentlemen's Quarterly*) should be: *met to decide whether Tweddle was right or (whether he) had made a fool of himself.*

The usage seems to be especially awkward when some noun such as 'question' introduces the construction. 'It is no longer a question if we will have to pay for our abuse of the Earth, but of how and when' (*Country-Side*) should be : *It is no longer a question whether we shall* [sic] *have to pay for our abuse of the Earth.*

Similarly 'all of them involved with people they love and not one of them absolutely, positively sure in their bones if they've found it' (*Company*) should be either: *whether they've found it* or: *that they've found it.*

'Members are expected to indicate today if they believe there should be any lifting of the ban on British beef' (*Radio 4*) should be: *to indicate today whether they believe there should be any lifting of the ban.*

'It's not clear if they've split up' (*Radio 4*) should be: *It's not clear whether they have split up.*

if possible. Use of this expression inevitably establishes a condition, 'If possible I shall be there'.

'If possible, last night's fighting in the area to the north of the presidential palace was even more fierce than on previous nights.' (*Radio 4*) This represents a grave instance of illogicality. Of course it was possible for the fighting to be fiercer [*sic*] last night, but by 'if possible' the speaker really means something like 'Astonishingly enough'. *Believe it or not, fighting last night was even fiercer than on previous nights.*

illusory. 'Blencowe had appeared to be responding extremely well to treatment. But this conviction has shown this improvement was illusory.' (*The Times*) In spite of what 'appeared' the 'improvement' was really non-existent. *But this conviction has shown that the appearance was illusory.*

imaginary/imaginative. The word 'imaginary' distinguishes what is manufactured by the imagination from what exists in reality and therefore may be used pejoratively of something not meriting credence: *Dismissing the case, the judge said that her grievances were purely imaginary*. The word 'imaginative' is applied to what the imagination creates, especially in works of art, and is wholly positive in connotation: *In characterisation Shakespeare's imaginative range has never been surpassed.*

imaginative. *See* IMAGINARY.

immanent/imminent. The word 'immanent' is a philosophical term meaning 'indwelling', used for instance, of *a divine presence immanent in the universe*. 'Imminent', used once of mountains or cliffs to mean physically overhanging, is applied to events that are impending, soon about to occur: *What could they know of the imminent disaster when they boarded the* Titanic *that day?*

imminent. *See* IMMANENT.

imminently. A newsreader speaks of hard-line views from the IRA 'which do nothing to suggest that a ceasefire could be restored imminently'. (*Radio 4*) Something which is 'imminent' hangs threateningly (usually) over one. To use 'imminent' as though it were a synonym for 'immediate' is at best highly insensitive: *nothing to suggest that a cease-fire could soon be restored.*

impact. 'The slogan-chanting and placard-waving as the Sunday afternoon demo reaches Hyde Park no longer carry any political impact.' (*Radio 4*) An impact is basically the force of a physical collision, and therefore the impression made on people by an idea. It is not something that can be 'carried' any more than a collision is. The broadcaster is thinking of the way an argument or theory may 'carry weight': *no longer make an impact politically.*

impinge. 'That is all the charisma that will ever matter: does a politician's nature impinge itself upon the citizens and draw their affection and sympathy?' (*Private Eye*, quoting the *Guardian*) 'Impinge' (meaning to encroach) is an intransitive verb. Nothing can impinge 'itself'. Was the journalist confusing the word with 'imprint'? *Does the politician's nature impinge on the citizens' consciousness and win their affection. See also* INFRINGE.

implement. An 'implement' (noun) is a tool for enabling a task to be performed, and the verb 'to implement' is used of carrying out some plan or scheme. It is now overused.

The minister for shipping, defending the government's arrangements for making roll-on, roll-off ferries safe, said, 'The timetable tackles the worst ships first and those that are nearer the standard have a lower priority, and it is those ships which will take longer to be implemented up to the agreed standard.' (*Radio 4*) It is not the ships that are to be 'implemented' but the plan for improving them: *it is those ships which will take longer to be brought up to the agreed standard.*

implication. 'It has implications on the peace process.' (*Radio 4*) This is an instance of improper prepositional transfer. The writer wrongly transfers a usage ('effects on the peace process'), from one noun ('effects') to another ('implications'). *It has implications for the peace process. See also* INFERENCE.

implicit. *See* EXPLICIT.

imply. *See* INFER.

importance. 'John Major's comments yesterday about the importance of EMU being a success . . .' (*The Times*) The word 'importance' lures the writer thus to the illicit gerciple ('of EMU being'). It is safer to use the adjective 'important' than the noun 'importance', even though it involves recasting the rest of the sentence in this case. *John Major said yesterday that it was important for EMU to be a success.*

important. 'It is also important having the computer in a social setting . . .' (*Computer Weekly*) We may say 'Having the computer in a social setting is important', but 'it is important' should be followed by the infinitive (or by 'that'). *It is also important to have the computer in a social setting.*

'It is important, however, that the British and Irish Governments do not overburden the document with expectation.' (*The Times*) This illustrates a now growing habit of overusing the present indicative tense. Conventional usage would require the conditional tense. *It is important that the British and Irish Governments should not overburden the document.*

'I believe it is important that significant historical buildings are protected against unsympathetic development.' (*Cottage & Castle*) Again convention would require: *I believe it is important that significant historical buildings should be protected.*

impossible. Writing which devalues words is to be avoided. The more forceful or colourful the word devalued, the more regrettable the devaluation is. 'The houses huddle higgledy-piggledy in impossible density.' (*Independent*) Loosely to fling around a powerful word like 'impossible' as though it meant no more than 'remarkable' or 'surprising' is an instance of devaluation.

improvement. This word tends to lead writers into false parallels.

'The Retail Consortium, a lobby group, acknowledged that the July sales figures were an improvement on earlier this year.' (*The Times*) This is a common form of mismatch. The figures cannot strictly be said to be an improvement on 'earlier this year'. The usage might be acceptable in conversation but the written word should avoid such laxity: *the July sales figures were an improvement on the figures earlier this year.*

'Recent research confirms that 75 per cent of Firstdirect's customers believe branchless banking to be a significant improvement over their previous conventional bank.' (*Meridian*) The 'branchless banking' is not an improvement on the previous bank but on the service provided by the previous bank: *a significant improvement over the service provided by their previous conventional bank.*

impulse-buy. *See* COINAGES.

in addition to. These words must link grammatically equivalent items.

'In addition to his gifts as a teacher, de Wet was also an able and innovative research worker.' (*The Times*) He was not a research worker 'in addition' to his gifts. Either a proper parallel must be found to match 'gifts': *In addition to his gifts as a teacher, de Wet had ability and ingenuity as a research worker*, or the construction 'as well as' should be substituted for 'in addition to': *As well as a gifted teacher, de Wet was an able and innovative research worker*. (This is often a way of escape from misuse of 'in addition to'.)

in common with. Misplacing this phrase can produce absurdity.

'The caterpillars, in common with other areas of the Scottish mainland, have devastated plantations at Garynahine and Aline on Lewis.' (*The Times*) The caterpillars must not be said to act in the same way as 'areas' of terrain. This is a matter of word order, but 'other' must go because the island plantations cannot be related to 'other' areas of the 'mainland'. *Plantations at Garynahine and Aline on Lewis, in common with areas of the Scottish mainland, have been devastated by the caterpillars.*

in keeping with. 'In keeping with not damaging the immediate environment, all of the Foundation's food is organically grown.' (*Green Magazine*) 'In keeping with' means 'in conformity with'. What is really meant here is 'in keeping with the principle' of not damaging the environment. *In accordance with the policy of not damaging the immediate environment, all the Foundation's food is organically grown.*

'One notable point is that *The Masterpiece's* wheels are unrubbered, being in keeping with the engines of the period.' (*Old Glory*) This is at best a clumsy way of saying something very straightforward: *The Masterpiece's wheels are unrubbered, like those of the engines of the period.*

in order. 'In order for the body to return to normal, it needs to break down the stress chemical.' (*She*) This construction is an awkward hybrid. Either 'in order' must be omitted: *For the body to return to normal, it needs to break down the stress chemical*, or the construction involving 'for' must go: *In order to restore the body to normal you must break down the stress chemical.*

'In order for a disciplinary charge to be proved, it has to be done on a criminal standard and beyond reasonable doubt.' (*Radio 4*) Again this would be better if either 'in order' were removed: *For a disciplinary charge to be proved*, or 'for' were removed: *In order to prove a discipli-*

nary charge. Moreover a 'criminal standard' is not a fit basis for judgment. The standard itself must be a just one. *For a disciplinary charge to be proved, criminal behaviour must be established beyond reasonable doubt.*

in order to. 'Unfortunately . . . the departure of most of its builders to other projects caused its demise in order to build something better.' (*Railway Modeller*) 'In order to' must hang on a verb ('He changed his job in order to better himself'). It cannot hang on the noun 'departure' or 'demise' as above. *Unfortunately . . . most of its builders departed to other projects and this project was abandoned in favour of a better one.*

'During the early Middle Ages, as mediaeval village life took shape, occupational names developed, in order to describe the increase in specialised skills.' (*Family History*) Names cannot describe 'an increase' in skills; nor were they developed for that purpose: *occupational names multiplied to match the increase in skills.*

in terms of. This expression means 'as expressed by' or, more loosely 'as regards'. Latterly the words have been used to mean 'in connection with' and 'with reference to'. Gradually more and more liberties are being taken with the phrase.

'I should have thought that gives clear prima facie ground for any political review to rule that action unlawful and not in terms of British law.' (*Radio 4*) Here the correct words would be: *not in accordance with British law.*

'In Dover too there are many of my constituents who would be affected in terms of losing their jobs'. (*Radio 4*) The words 'terms of' seem redundant here. *In Dover too many of my constituents would be affected in losing their jobs.*

Speaking of the case in which British soldiers raped and murdered a girl in Cyprus, an officer said 'In terms of reality I can assure you that the shame felt within the armed forces was very clear.' (*Radio 4*) Here 'in terms of reality' becomes a pretentious variant of 'as a matter of fact'. *I can assure you that the shame felt was in fact very clear.*

in the event. 'Furthermore, in the unlikely event of an error occurring, you need only contact your Midland branch.' (*Meridian*) This is one more construction that leads to a gerciple, 'an error occurring', where the issue is really the occurrence of error and where therefore the correct usage would be 'an error's occurring'. To avoid this perhaps awkward construction the writer should follow 'in the event' by 'that' instead of by 'of'. *In the unlikely event that an error occurs, you need only contact your Midland branch.*

'Critical illness cover is designed to provide a tax-free lump sum in the event of you suffering a critical illness.' (*Perfect Homes*) Similarly here either the construction must be corrected: *in the event of your suffering a critical illness*, or it must be changed: *in the event that you suffer a critical illness.*

in this case. This phrase must be used with exact reference to whatever the 'case' is.

'Finally watch out for early signs of eczema – persistent small rough patches of skin which your baby tries to scratch. In this case, keep his fingernails short and clean, and consult your doctor for advice.' (*Parents*) What the writer means here by 'in this case' is something like 'in these circumstances', but in fact the most natural thing would be to use the word 'if': *if he does so, keep his fingernails short and clean.*

in time. 'The 100 registered target competition was not allocated to the ground in time to reach the other shooting magazine press dates.' (*Shooting Times*) It was not the competition that failed to reach press dates, but notification of it: *in time for notification to reach the other magazine press dates.*

include. 'Membership also includes a monthly journal . . .' (*Cottage & Castle*) This is a common vulgarism. *Membership also entitles one to a monthly journal.*

'His career included many stage parts as well as films and television.' (*Radio 4*) It is lax to speak of a 'career' as including stage parts, films and television. Why introduce the word? *He played many parts on stage as well as in films and television.*

'So far, seventy sites in need of regeneration have been identified. These include turning a waste area into a wildlife haven, opening a canal blocked for the last fifty years . . .' (*Country Lovers Magazine*) Neither 'turning a waste area into a wildlife haven' nor 'opening a canal' can be defined as specimen 'sites', so 'these include' will not do: *The projects include turning a waste area into a wildlife haven.*

'Thus my business trips included not only my camera but my trusty recorder together with supplies of tape and batteries.' (*Steam World*) A trip might include a visit to Greece but it cannot include a camera or a tape-recorder. *Thus on my business trips I took not only my camera but my trusty recorder.*

included. 'Since Hungarian agriculture is suffering the most savage blight of all, the production of the heady wines of Tokay included . . .' (*Daily Mail*) Although this sentence can be defended grammatically, in that the production of Tokay is 'included' in Hungarian agriculture, it could easily be improved: *Since Hungarian agriculture is suffering the most savage blight of all, affecting even the production of the heady wines of Tokay.*

including. When properly used, 'including' introduces specimen items from some named group. 'We take several Sunday papers including the "Sunday Times".' Where this exactness of reference does not apply, use of the word leads to error.

'Alan Lockwood has exhibited throughout Britain including the Mall Galleries, London.' (*Artists & Illustrators Magazine*) The Mall Galleries could be 'included' in a list of exhibition sites, but 'Britain' does not include them. *Alan Lockwood has exhibited at many venues throughout Britain, including the Mall Galleries, London.*

'Major changes have been announced in the controversial Child Support Agency, including an appeals procedure.' (*Radio 4*) An 'appeals procedure' cannot be cited as a major change. The imprecision borders on inaccuracy. *Major changes have been announced in the controversial Child Support Agency, including the setting up of an appeals procedure.*

'It could affect both the short-term morale of Tory MPs, including the chances of a leadership challenge by Wednesday's deadline, and the party's prospects of saving the next election.' (*The Times*) This is non-sense. Nobody's 'morale' could ever conceivably 'include' a leadership challenge. 'Including' is totally out of place, and the simplest correction would involve taking out 'both'. *It could affect the short-term morale of Tory MPs, the chances of a leadership challenge by Wednesday's deadline, and the party's prospects of saving the next election.*

'He has been a teacher of technical design and drawing, including at Brunel University . . . ' (*Artists & Illustrators Magazine*) It would surely be generally recognised as incorrect to say 'I was a grocer, including at Hartlepool'. Even so, this should be: *He has been a teacher of technical design and drawing, for a time at Brunel University.*

'Michael Howard intervened directly in the running of the Prison Service, including ordering its Director General to make hostile statements about the Prison Officers' Association.' (*The Times*) 'Including' cannot be anchored to a verb ('intervened'). Here the word can be simply omitted.

Inconsequentiality. It happens all too often that writers allow a shuffling of terms through which sentences lose logical coherence. There are multifarious ways in which the writer's mind veers from its course in hasty thinking and pulls words askew. Sometimes the trouble occurs through transferring to paper a freedom that one might well take in conversation. Sometimes the writer's mind slides off course in such a way that what begins a sentence as the subject is displaced, perhaps quite quickly, by another word. 'Exploring the village of Turville, with its beautiful parish church, provides a worth-while stopping-point on a walk through the Chilterns.' (*The Times*) Clearly the writer forgot that the sentence began with 'Exploring', for exploring cannot provide a stopping-point. If 'exploring' is kept, 'stopping-point' must go. *Exploring the village of Turville provides a worth-while digression on a walk through the Chilterns.*

'This restful atmosphere, with its large range of products, creates the right environment for parents to browse and buy.' (*Lancashire Life*) This description of a shop shows the writer's mind skidding across the paths of strict logic. The atmosphere is said to own a large range of products and to manufacture an environment which people can purchase. *The shop has a large range of products on show in a restful atmosphere which encourages parents to browse and make purchases.*

'I have never met Simon Raven, although as a private in the Shrewsbury School JTC, we have been members of the same regiment: the King's Shropshire Light Infantry.' (*The Times*) It is incorrect to say 'As an MP, we are friends'. It would have to be 'As MPs, we are friends'. Because of the error here we do not know what the writer means. Which of the two, the writer or his friend, was a private in the JTC? Perhaps he means: *As I was a private in the Shrewsbury School JTC, we have been members of the same regiment.*

'Speed limits lower than 50 and 60mph may be set by the police, who can override the automatic system in an emergency. This makes sense but we are worried that a manually set speed limit may result in it being left on unnecessarily.' (*AA Magazine*) This is tortuous. Presumably it should read: *we are worried that if a speed limit is set manually, someone may forget to amend it.* 'You can also apply as a member of expedition staff.' (*Raleigh International Trust*) What this means is that the applicant can apply to be a member of staff. At the time of applying he or she will not be a member of staff, and therefore cannot apply 'as' one. *You can also apply to become a member of expedition staff.*

incredibly. 'Dengie have . . . developed a feeding regime which is prov-ing incredibly successful in countering the many problems involved in balancing a horse's diet.' (*Horse & Hound*) Exaggerated use of 'incredibly' ('unbelievably') is common: *which is proving remarkably successful*.

incriminate. 'In America and Scandinavia they produce the meat-and-bone meal in the same manner that was incriminated in this country.' (*Radio 4*) Only people can be 'incriminated', that is, charged with or sus-pected of crime: *in the same manner that was condemned in this coun-try*, or: *that was made illegal in this country*.

Indirect Speech. Care must be taken not to confuse indirect speech by usage proper to direct speech.

'A second concern is that given the many new minimally invasive pro-cedures that are being introduced every year, how can patients tell whether what's on offer is as good as the conventional operation?' (*Liv-ing*) The direct question 'How can patients tell?' cannot follow 'A sec-ond concern is that'. One or the other must go: *A second concern is that, given the new procedures that are being introduced every year, patients may be unable to tell whether what's on offer is as good*.

'Consumers are concerned about is fish going to be sustainable in the future?' (*Radio 4*) This is like saying 'I am concerned about how are you?' Direct questions, such as 'How are you?' or 'Is fish going to be sus-tainable?' cannot follow the construction 'concerned about': *Consumers are concerned about whether fish is going to be sustainable*.

indistinguishable. This is a word which establishes a linkage ('This is indistinguishable from that'), and there must be proper parallelism be-tween this and that.

'The performance of catalyst-equipped models is usually indistin-guishable from those which do not have catalysts.' (*Green Magazine*) The performance of one set of models must not be said to be indistin-guishable from another set of models, but from the performance of the other set. What is being matched is performance with performance, not performance with models: *The performance of catalyst-equipped models is usually indistinguishable from the performance of those which do not have catalysts*. If this is thought to be too clumsy, there is an alternative: *Catalyst-equipped models are usually indistinguishable in performance from those which do not have catalysts*.

individually. 'If a couple find themselves deadlocked over this issue, one solution could be counselling, either individually or jointly.' (*New Woman*) It would be incorrect to say 'I like rooms brightly and airily' instead of 'I like rooms bright and airy'. One may counsel 'individually' but the counselling itself is 'individual': *one solution could be counselling, either individual or joint.*

infer. To 'infer' something is to deduce it from what is said or presented.

'In suggesting that foreigners should pay double for a game licence Mr Wells infers, therefore, that people in my position [living abroad] will be treated automatically as foreigners and penalised accordingly.' (*The Field*) To 'infer' something is a matter of concluding, not of conveying. The speaker implies something, the listener infers something. *Mr Wells implies that people in my position will be treated automatically as foreigners.*

inference. This noun suffers the same misuse as the corresponding verb. 'Our home is our castle – or so the saying goes. The inference being, of course, that it is where we can rely on being safe.' (*OK! Homes*) An 'inference' is a conclusion that an auditor or reader derives from a statement. An 'implication' is a suggestion that the maker of a statement conveys: *The implication being that it is where we can rely on being safe.* See also IMPLICATION.

Infinitives. The infinitive form of the verb is what naturally follows certain verbs such as 'wish', 'help', and 'learn' ('He learned to swim'). It can also function in an explanatory way with certain nouns ('the wish to resign', 'the means to survive'), but this is not a construction that can be used with any noun one chooses.

AMPLIFICATION BY INFINITIVE The infinitive is not properly used in being attached to a noun to supply a descriptive notation. 'Nancy Walker had a talent to make people laugh' (*The Times*) should be: *Nancy Walker had a talent for making people laugh.*

'The Cadbury Committee guidelines to improve corporate governance are inadequate' (*The Times*) should be: *The Cadbury Committee guidelines for improving corporate governance.* Alternatively the infinitive could be made legitimate by being anchored to a participle: *The Cadbury Committee guidelines designed to improve corporate governance are inadequate.*

'The first report from the school-teachers' body under Sir Graham Day shows some fresh thinking to improve recruitment and retention' (*The Times*) should be: *some fresh thinking about improving recruitment.*

So far we have replaced infinitives by gerunds, but sometimes the amplification is such that a relative clause is called for. 'Courses to qualify as a speech and language therapist usually require a mixture of three science and arts subjects at A level.' (*The Times*) Here is a case in point: *Courses which qualify one as a speech and language therapist.*

'This course costs £7500 to include all lectures, extensive course manual and data sheets, two nights accommodation and all meals.' (*Dogs Monthly*) 'To include' here attaches properly neither to the verb 'costs' nor to any noun. To qualify '£7500' a relative clause is required. *This course costs £7500, which covers all lectures.*

INFINITIVES AND PURPOSE The infinitive is often attached to a noun so as to convey an element of purpose. 'Kenneth Clarke, the Chancellor, attempted to play down the threat of further interest rate rises to keep the lid on inflation'. (*The Times*) The writer here mis-attaches the infinitive directly to the noun 'rises'. Where the purposive element is as plain as that, a participle should be supplied for the infinitive to hinge upon: *attempted to play down the threat of further interest rate rises designed to keep the lid on inflation.*

The purposive element is even stronger in 'The expulsion of Britain's High Commissioner in Sri Lanka, David Gladstone, was apparently to stifle his criticism of the country's unsatisfactory human rights record.' (*Independent*) Again a participle should be added to sustain the infinitive: *The expulsion of Britain's High Commissioner was apparently intended to stifle his criticism.*

'Check that any loose cushions are reversible to even out the wear.' (*OK! Homes*) It would be proper to write 'Check that any loose cushions are reversible to save yourself trouble later on' because there the infinitive 'to save' would attach to the verb 'check', but here the infinitive 'to even out' is hung on the adjective 'reversible'. An appropriate verb must be supplied to support the infinitive. *Check than any loose cushions have been made reversible to even out the wear.*

INFINITIVES AND CONDITIONS There is another bad use of the infinitive which abuses the word 'to' even more grotesquely. 'Now, if only we could find some way of hiding satellite dishes which, unlike aerials, need consent to be placed on listed buildings.' (*Old-House Journal*) This is a crude way of avoiding a conditional clause: *some way of hiding satellite dishes which, unlike aerials, need consent if they are to be placed on listed buildings.*

'Pictures like this often have to combine information from other sources to build them up into one statement' (*The Artist*) should be: *have to combine information from other sources if they are to be built up into one statement.*

WANDERING INFINITIVES There is a loose use of the infinitive which leaves it without anchorage. 'Bedfordshire has a lovely collection to go and explore.' (*In Britain*) It sounds as though the collection will do the exploring: *a lovely collection for you to explore.*

'If the weather is too wet and windy to get out there and grapple with the seasons . . . ' (*Practical Gardening*) It is not the weather that wants to get out there. The infinitive 'to get out' must be detached from 'the weather': *too wet and windy for you to get out there.*

'She had spent six years away on duty with the WRACs and it appeared too long a gap to have any hope of reviving Coed Gwydr.' (*Best of British*). It is not the 'gap' that lacks hope. Again the infinitive must be detached from 'gap': *too long a gap for her to have any hope.*

'Abbey Well Natural Mineral Water . . . is offering three superb Peter Blake prints to win.' (*AA Magazine*) Clearly there is no sense in which the prints are 'to win': *is offering three superb prints to be won.*

In 'bottle banks are the most popular way for people to recycle' (*Allerdale Outlook*) use of the infinitive causes the notion of recycling people to intrude: *bottle banks are the most popular method of recycling.*

It is useful to distinguish the two constructions, 'John wanted a friend to join him', where 'to join him' is what the friend will do, and 'John wanted a friend to play with', where 'to play' is what John will do. The freedom allowed thus must not be misused.

'But then he reflected that she would probably not have had an attic to stow away unwanted objects at Crosshedges.' (*Novel*) She did not want an attic to stow away, nor did she want to stow away an attic. The novelist needed more words here: *She would not have had an attic in which to stow away unwanted objects.*

TRUNCATED INFINITIVE The infinitive can function as a noun. In 'To err is human, to forgive divine' two infinitives act as subjects of the verb 'to be'. In 'I hated to go', the infinitive acts as direct object of the verb 'hated'.

'The best thing I ever did was go on an Agricultural Training Board course one winter.' (*Cumbria*) Here the infinitive is needed to provide a proper complement after the verb 'was': *The best thing I ever did was to go on an Agricultural Training Board Course.*

inflict. 'Why are we inflicted with double doses of all the "soaps"?' (*Best of British*) To inflict a burden on someone is to impose it on them. 'We' cannot be 'inflicted': the burden is inflicted on us. *Why are double doses of all the 'soaps' inflicted on us?*

influence. 'He doubtless had a strong hand in influencing the citizens of Richard's rightful claims to the throne.' (*Family History*) This is rather like saying 'My father influenced me of a career in law'. It is incorrect to speak of influencing people 'of' this or that: *a strong hand in persuading the citizens of Richard's rightful claims.*

'China intends to keep pressurising Taiwan, attempting to influence the political landscape there.' (*Radio 4*) To speak of 'influencing' a landscape is incongruous. Either the noun should be changed: *attempting to influence political attitudes there*, or the verb: *attempting to re-shape the political landscape there.*

information. 'I remember watching the dancers in total amazement, not knowing what information to put on the paper first.' (*Artists & Illustrators Magazine*) The artist is painting the dancers. 'Information' is acquired knowledge and the wrong word here: *not knowing where to start.*

infringe. 'Is there any reason why carrying an Identity Card should infringe upon any of those liberties?' (*Radio 4*) 'Upon' is unnecessary (though not incorrect) in that to infringe is to violate: *should infringe any of those liberties.* There are other verbs which do require 'upon' such as 'encroach upon' and 'impinge upon'.

-ing. Nothing in current English usage so lures to error as the form of the verb ending in -ing. The fact that it can work as a noun ('Swimming is good for you') or adjectivally ('I found him swimming in his pool') seems to encourage writers to treat it with anarchic disregard for rule and regulation.

FLOATING PARTICIPLE 'Working as a district nursing sister, there was one particular patient who would have tried the patience of a saint.' (*Nursing Standard*) Uncorrected, this sentence conveys that one particular patient was working as a district nursing sister. *When I was working as a nursing sister, I had one particular patient who would have tried the patience of a saint.*

'Saying that, the 16th does present birdie possibilities.' (*Lancashire Life*) Similarly, this sentence conveys that the 16th hole was saying something. There is a simple construction for correcting this. *That said, the 16th does present birdie possibilities.*

EVADING 'WHICH' OR 'WHO' 'Bromley Hospitals Trust, which runs the hospital, has agreed to monitor staff managing confused patients and provide them with guidance.' (*Nursing Standard*) This is a case where a relative clause would be more elegant than the use of 'managing': *has agreed to monitor staff who manage confused patients.*

SUBSTITUTE FOR A NOUN 'The 35 trail boats attending was possibly a record for such an event.' (*Waterways World*) This is a grammatically awkward way of saying: *The attendance of 35 trail boats was possibly a record.*

CARELESSLY ATTACHED 'Built in the early 1930s, it was one of eleven built at Dapdune and was used carrying cargo between Guildford and the London Docks.' (*Waterways World*) 'Used carrying' is grammatically bad: *and was used for carrying cargo. See also* GERCIPLES, PRESENT PARTICIPLES.

ingenious/ingenuous. An 'ingenious' man is a man who uses his skill inventively, and an ingenious device is the product of such cleverness. From meaning honestly straightforward and candid 'ingenuous' has now come to be used for what is innocent and artless to the point of naivete: *She was ingenuous enough to take his extravagant claims literally.*

ingenuous. *See* INGENIOUS.

initiate. *See* INSTIGATE.

initiative. 'He added that . . . compulsory dog registration was an initiative which "any enlightened society would introduce without resistance".' (*Independent*) An 'initiative' is itself a commencing move. It is scarcely something to be 'introduced': *compulsory dog registration was something which any enlightened society would introduce without resistance.*

inject. 'As the Pennine Way progresses northwards from Middleton-in-Teesdale, it injects a soft pastoral interlude of riparian meadows before heading for the highest ground of all.' (*Dalesman*) The verb 'inject' is here pretentiously out of place: *it interposes a soft pastoral interlude.*

injustice. 'This is an area of injustice in which the Government should take a lead.' (*The Times*) [The issue is the claim of divorced women on their ex-husbands' pensions.] We should recognise the absurdity of 'This is criminal activity in which the Government should take a lead', yet it is no more absurd than the above. *This is an area of injustice for which the Government should legislate.*

insist. 'The sovereignty row over the Diaoyu islands (or the Senkakus, as Tokyo would insist) has emerged as a rare point of agreement.' (*Independent*) To justify this use of 'insist' a longer sentence would be required: *or the Senkakus, as Tokyo insists on calling them.* Otherwise quotation marks could be put around the name: *or the 'Senkakus', as Tokyo calls them.*

insist on. Where this expression is followed by a noun or nouns, no problem arises ('He insisted on secrecy').

'If your project is being financed by a bank it will insist on you using a professional.' (*Meridian*) There are two possible ways of correcting this. Either the gerciple ('you using') can become a true gerund: *it will insist on your using a professional*, or 'insist on' can be replaced by 'insist that', which is safer: *it will insist that you use a professional.*

instance. 'Certainly there are many recorded instances of them [cats] making their way home over very long distances.' (*Wild About Animals*) Like 'record' and 'example', this word lures the writer into erroneous use of a gerciple ('them making their way'). It should be: *instances of their making their way home.*

instead of. 'If BW had to pay out compensation for every extra week the canal was closed then the breach would have been repaired weeks ago instead of the prolonged procrastination about who is liable.' (*Waterways World*) One might say 'I shall take this book instead of that one', where there is parallelism between 'this book' and 'that one', and one might say 'I shall eat dinner instead of going to the cinema', but no one should say 'I shall eat dinner instead of the visit to the cinema' because 'the visit to the cinema' is not edible. Similarly, it is incorrect to say 'The breach would have been repaired instead of the prolonged procrastination' because a procrastination cannot be repaired: *then the breach would have been repaired months ago without the prolonged procrastination about who is liable.*

'So why didn't he give the instruction to the broker instead of Archer ringing Simon Wharmby, who last dealt for him years ago?' (*Private Eye*) This illustrates how dire can be misuse of 'instead of'. One can ask 'Why didn't he stay instead of going?' but certainly not 'Why didn't he stay instead of his brother going?' Better get rid of 'instead of'. *Why didn't he give the instruction to the broker? Why did Archer ring Simon Wharmby?*

'Instead of sable brushes, he prefers the effect created by the tip of a large round hog.' (*Artists & Illustrators Magazine*) One kind of brush may be preferred to another, or the effect it creates to the effect another one creates, but it is wrong to prefer an effect to a brush, because without the brush no effect can be created. *Instead of sable brushes he prefers the tip of a large round hog for the effect it creates. See also* RATHER THAN.

instigate. 'I did in fact instigate the first public inquiry.' (*Radio 4*) To instigate means to bring something about by incitement. It implies a stirring-up process, but is now being widely thus misused. *I did in fact initiate the first public inquiry.*

'More than 200 people were taken to six Manchester hospitals. All of them, including Manchester Royal Infirmary, instigated standard emergency proceedings.' (*Radio 4*) There is again no question of incitement here. *All of them initiated standard emergency proceedings.*

Similarly 'Mr Water joined [the AA] in 1925, instigated by a friend' (*AA Magazine*) should be: *encouraged by a friend.*

instigator. 'British Waterways were the principal instigators of the proposal for a Millennium Link across the central lowlands of Scotland.' (*Waterways World*) It is a pity thus to weaken the word 'instigator' which connotes one who moves people by exciting them: *British Waterways were the principal initiators of the proposal.*

intend. 'Far better to leave the surfaces decently painted as they were originally intended.' (*Old-House Journal*) It would be incorrect to write 'They were intended painted' instead of 'They were intended to be painted'. In the same way the above must be: *leave the surfaces decently painted as they were originally intended to be.*

intention. 'Do you think that this document lives up to its intention of using clear modern language?' (*Radio 4*) It is not a question of the document's intention but of the writer's intention. Omit 'its'. *Do you think this document lives up to the intention to use clear modern language?*

interject. 'Jack Straw fought back by taunting John Humphrys when the latter tried to interject during a discussion of regional assemblies.' (*The Times*) 'Interject' is not equivalent to 'interrupt'. To interject a remark is to interpose it; the verb requires an object: *when the latter tried to interrupt.*

interment. *See* INTERNMENT.

interminably. *See* ETERNALLY.

internment. 'For those still undeterred by the price of internment, the best solution might be to be laid to rest in the back garden.' (*The Times*) 'Internment' is imprisonment or, at least, confinement. Here it is a matter of burial – being 'interred', not 'interned': *For those still unde-terred by the price of interment.*

interpret. 'And Mr Clarke himself is neither as fatalistic nor as passive as his comments have been interpreted.' (*The Times*) His comments can-not be said to have been interpreted either 'fatalistic' or 'passive'. The verb must be changed. *And Mr Clarke himself is neither as fatalistic nor as passive as his comments have led people to assume.*

introduce. 'Fast food and family restaurants are best to introduce eating out.' (*Essentials*) It is a matter of 'introducing' children to eating out. 'Best to introduce' is awkward: *best for introducing them to eating out.*

introspection. 'The launch in 1993 of the Changing Childbirth report heralded a period of great introspection by providers of the maternity services.' (*Nursing Standard*) 'Introspection' is analysis of one's own thoughts and feelings; it is not the appropriate word for checking up on one's work: *heralded a period of reassessment/self-assessment by providers of the maternity services.*

intrusion. *See* INVASION.

invasion. 'They know that it [becoming an MP] means such a savage salary cut and such a cruel invasion on their privacy'. (*The Times*) We speak of an intrusion 'on' someone's privacy, but of an invasion 'of' their privacy: *such a cruel invasion of their privacy.*

inverted commas. *See* QUOTATION MARKS.

invest. 'General Motors is to invest 700 million pounds into its Vauxhall subsidiary.' (*Radio 4*) Money is invested 'in', not 'into' concerns: *General Motors is to invest 700 millions pounds in its Vauxhall subsidiary.*

investigation. 'This is also part of a much broader investigation into not only the bomb that went off last night in Lisle, but is also linked to the broader bombing campaign which began in France last July.' (*Radio 4*) The words 'not only' lead one to expect two matters which the investi-gation is going to probe, and they should be expressed in grammatically matching terms. 'Not only the bomb' cannot be followed by 'but is also linked'. In any case the words 'not only' are misplaced. *This is part of a much broader investigation, not only into the bomb that went off last night in Lisle, but also into the link with the broader bombing campaign.* *See also* NOT ONLY.

involve. 'I would like to tell you about a new and special kind of current account. One that does not involve you queueing up at the cashier's desk, or rushing out to the bank during your working day.' (*Midland Bank*) 'Involve' is not the best word and the gerciples, 'you queueing' and 'rushing', are bad: *One that does not require you to queue or to rush out*.

irrupt. *See* ERUPT.

is. 'That made Chris all the more determined to make the placement work, which it is.' (*Children in Focus*) This is like saying 'I work hard and so is he': *to make the placement work, which it does*.

issue (verb). As a verb, 'issue' is increasingly misused. A bad practice has developed of adding 'with' to the verb and treating it as though it meant 'supply'.

'In many parts of Wales householders have been issued with sandbags as a precaution.' (*Radio 4*) It is not the householders who have been 'issued' but the sandbags. *In many parts of Wales sandbags have been issued to householders as a precaution*.

'British Rail are issuing their staff with new uniforms'. (*Radio 4*) They are not issuing their staff. *British Rail are issuing new uniforms to their staff*.

'The England football coach, Terry Venables, has been issued with a summons.' (*Radio 4*) It is the summons that has been issued, not Terry Venables: *has been served with a summons*.

Similarly the policeman's complaint about defensive devices, 'In the UK we are not being issued with them' (*Radio 4*) should be: *In the UK they are not being issued to us*.

'I had been issued with a track permit to Waterloo' (*Steam World*) should be: *I had been given a track permit to Waterloo*.

'A spokesman for the Transport Secretary denied that franchise directors had been issued with a target date for the end of the sell-off' (*Radio 4*) should be: *denied that a target date for the end of the sell-off had been issued to franchise directors*.

it. PRECISION OF REFERENCE The word 'it' must be used in such a way that there is no doubt about what the word refers back to.

'You would probably need a car here as, although both locations are served by CSD, it is not a direct route.' (*Steam Railway*) There is no word here which 'it' can refer back to. The construction should be changed and the word removed. *You would probably need a car here as, although both locations are served by CSD, there is no direct route between them.*

The obituary of a distinguished organist tells us, of his activity in retirement, 'Though the organ was nothing out of the ordinary for a village church, it was an enjoyable experience . . .'. (*The Times*) The organ should not be said to be an 'experience'. It was playing it that was enjoyable. The sentence should read either: *Though the organ was nothing out of the ordinary, it gave him enjoyment*, or: *Though the organ was nothing out of the ordinary, the experience was enjoyable.*

'Fire investigators are still at the scene, and the cause of it has still not been established.' (*Radio 4*) Grammatically 'the cause of it' must here mean the cause of the scene. Strictly speaking, the fire has not been mentioned. If one said 'Fire insurance is costly, but you need it', 'it' would mean insurance, not fire. Similarly, after 'Fire investigators are still at the scene' any back-reference by the word 'it' can apply only to the word 'scene'. The word 'fire' must be used as a noun, if the word 'it' is to be justified. *Investigators are still at the scene of the fire, and the cause of it has still not been established.*

'Although his world was intellectual, it was expressed through his social life.' (*The Times*) What was expressed? His world? Clearly not. *His intellectual preoccupations coloured his social life.*

'IT' WITH GERUND It is always wrong to try to fuse the word 'it' with a seeming participle or gerund.

'Mark is not in the least motivated by money, apart from it enabling him to feed his birds.' (*Country Talk*) It would be grammatically correct, but stylistically awkward to write 'apart from its enabling him'. It is better to change the construction. *Mark is not much motivated by money, though he needs it for feeding his birds.*

Similarly 'There never seemed any prospect of it materialising' (*Hunting*) should be either: *prospect of its materialising*, or: *prospect that it would materialise.*

USE IN PARENTHESIS There is an accepted usage of inserting 'it seems' into a sentence to convey a degree of tentativeness. But this usage must not be carelessly extended.

'The relationship between dwelling and terrain is even more intimate, it feels, when the house or cottage is of rough-hewn stone.' (*Cottage & Castle*) Although established usage allows us to say 'It feels cold' there is no idiomatic expression 'it feels' which can be used in parenthesis: *The relationship between dwelling and terrain feels even more intimate.*

THE ANTICIPATORY 'IT' 'It was announced in the Budget last week about the increase in the childcare disregard.' (*Radio 4*) Naturally one asks, What was announced? The use of 'it' serves no purpose. *There was an announcement in the Budget last week about the increase.*

THE INTRUSIVE 'IT' 'If you don't intend trying some of the high risk activities like paragliding, it reduces the premiums by as much as 50%.' (*Adventure Travel*) Here is no word for 'it ' to refer back to. There are two better options: *you reduce the premiums*, or: *the premiums are reduced*.

'I want to make it clear that by ordering a pre-sentence report it doesn't mean you are going to receive anything other than a custodial sentence.' (*The Times*) This judge's observation represents a brand of error which seems to be, not accidentally slipped into, but laboriously manufactured by evasion of what is simple and obvious. No one surely would say 'By ordering a drink, it doesn't mean that I am thirsty'. 'By' and 'it' are equally redundant. *I want to make it clear that ordering a pre-sentence report doesn't mean you are going to receive anything other than a custodial sentence.*

it being. This combination of words is always bad. It is grammatically correct to say 'In spite of its being wet', but not 'In spite of it being wet'.

'But we recognise the reality (it being all too obvious)' (*Hunting*) should be: *we recognise the reality (it is all too obvious)* or, without the brackets: *we recognise the reality, obvious as it is.*

'Well, it being Wednesday, in just over five minutes there's Mid-Week with Libby Purves.' (*Radio 4*) Her English is so good that it's a pity to introduce her thus: *Well, as it's Wednesday.*

'It being a Sunday, however' (*The Times*) should be: *As it was Sunday.*

'Neil Ross would have liked to get on with what he was doing, it being the first evening in weeks that he had been alone with Rita.' (*My Weekly*) This should be: *since it was the first evening in weeks.*

'I would be very reluctant to advise it being used' (*Shooting Times*) should be: *to advise its use.*

it's. This form, including the apostrophe is required only when 'it's' is short for 'it is' or 'it has'. Yet it is wrongly used in the press to an astonishing extent.

'Despite it's tempo marking, the first movement is not really a fast one' (*Programme Note*) should be: *Despite its tempo marking.*

'With it's eye firmly on future generations of naturalists . . .' (*Country-Side*) should be: *With its eye firmly on future generations of naturalists.*

'We all agreed that the sheeting rain . . . was the region at it's least accommodating.' (*Cumbria Life*). Here the word 'was' should be corrected too: *the sheeting rain showed the region at its least accommodating.*

'Durango . . . reflects the New World not only in name but also in it's styling' (*Outdoors Illustrated*) should be: *in its styling.*

'Mountain Biking has it's own trails to make' (*Outdoor Illustrated*) should be: *has its own trails*; and 'known for it's protected waters' (*Outdoor Illustrated*) should be: *its protected waters.*

'*The Times* subheaded it's leader "John Redwood begins the task of Tory repair"' (*The Times*) should be: *its leader.*

'ATCO – your assurance of British engineering and craftsmanship at it's very best' (*Cumbria Life*) should be: *at its very best.*

Reference to 'the odd village clinging precariously to it's side' (*Trail*) should be: *clinging precariously to its side.*

'These witnesses were the fireman of the train, it's guard, the signalman at Lichfield' (*Steam World*) should be: *its guard.*

'The forty acre park caters for caravanner and camper alike with it's Pet and Pet free areas' (*Camping*) should be: *with its Pet and Pet-free areas.*

'It's unique design allows you to vacuum the car' (*Perfect Home*) should be: *Its unique design.*

'The filling is made from a material that is unique to the company and regains it's original shape after it has been sat on.' (*Perfect Home*) should be: *regains its original shape.*

its (subjective/objective). It is important to distinguish the subjective from the objective genitive when 'its' is used. 'The behaviour of the dog' is interchangeable with 'the dog's behaviour', or 'its behaviour', but that does not mean that 'the control of the dog' is happily interchangeable with 'the dog's control' or 'its control'.

'Asbestos kills nearly three and a half thousand people a year, mainly in the building trade. There are strict regulations about its handling, but the evidence is that they are often ignored.' (*Radio 4*) If I handle asbestos, then it is 'my handling' not the asbestos's handling that is at issue: *There are strict regulations about handling it.*

'In Dungarvon, a quiet backwater, not known for its availability of condoms . . .' (*The Times*) Here again 'its' is wrong. It is not Dungarvon's availability but the condoms' availability that is relevant: *not known for the availability of condoms.*

its. The misuse of 'its' for 'it's' is less common than the converse error.

But 'its so damn good, its difficult to fault' (*Adventure Travel*) should be: *it's so damn good it's difficult to fault.*

A new variant of error appears when an advertisement offering a post claims of Cleveland that 'Its' thriving industrial and commercial heart is surrounded by the glorious North Yorkshire Moors'. (*The Times*) The apostrophe must go.

J

Jargon. One of the most overused devices in business jargon is the hyphenated compound adjective.

COMPOUNDS WITH '-LED' AND '-LEADING' 'Pricing policies for 1992 continue to be supply-led.' (*Marketing Week*) This usage, though not grammatically offensive, is not a happy one. Supply may determine pricing policies, but it cannot strictly 'lead' them. *Pricing policies for 1992 continue to be determined by supply* is slightly wordier, but more precise.

'18 months' FMCG experience . . . will secure you an interview with this top FMCG company, to work on a market-leading grocery brand.' (*Marketing Week*) It is true that the verb 'lead' is here more accurately used, but the question arises whether, in the context, the expression 'market-leading' is not tautologous. What else can a grocery brand 'lead' except the market? Nothing is lost by writing: *to work on a leading grocery brand.* These are but mild examples of the practice we are examining.

OTHER COMPOUNDS 'Whereas the 1980s were terminal volume driven, growth in the 1990s will depend on minimising data delivery costs and maximising revenue per terminal.' (*Investors Chronicle*) The company in question provides electronic financial services. To describe a decade as 'terminal-volume-driven' (note the hyphens) presumably is to say that commercial progress made during the decade was determined by the volume of work at the terminals. And to say that growth in the 1990s will depend on 'minimising data-delivery costs' is to say that future prosperity will depend on economies in running the firm. *In the 1980s growth was due to the increasing demands on our services, but in the 1990s it will depend on the economies we can make in providing those services.*

'Candidates require . . . a successful track record of implementing change, integrating diverse management functions, and developing a customer-oriented, results-targeted organisation.' (*The Times*) This is a Tourist Board advertisement. Surely no business can survive unless it is 'customer-oriented' and 'results-targeted'? This is just word-spinning. If one could conceive of a customer-hostile and results-evasive organisation, there might be point in noting that the business in question is what it is. *See also* MOULD, NECESSITATE, NOUNS IN EXCESS, NUTRITION.

jeer. Although there have long been transitive uses of this verb, the intransitive use seems to have established itself as the more acceptable.

On that basis 'Young Croats, one wearing a Hitler mask and giving a neo-Nazi salute, jeer a group of Muslims after attacking their car' (*The Times*) would better be: *Young Croats jeer at a group of Muslims.*

jewel. 'Somerset, one of the jewels of the Exmoor National Park, could be washed off the map within 30 years unless drastic action is taken to halt the encroaching sea.' (*The Times*) The effect of the word 'jewel' is destroyed by the succeeding imagery. Jewels do not get washed off maps.

job. 'Afterwards, he held various jobs including three months in a bakery cleaning sausage roll trays.' (*The Times*) The conversational freedom illustrated here is surely out of place in a formal obituary. Various jobs cannot 'include' three months, nor can 'three months' clean sausage roll trays. As so often, the word 'including' leads to error. *Afterwards he held various jobs, even spending three months in a bakery cleaning sausage roll trays.*

joke. 'The weather used to be the dry Bank Holiday joke.' (*The Times*) The verb 'to be' is ill-used here. Various possible improvements spring to mind, for instance: *The weather gave us the dry Bank holiday joke.*

judged. Care must be taken to match this participle exactly with a noun or pronoun.

'Judged by local councils, the British Waterways and the Inland Waterways Association, the result of the architectural competition for the site was announced in mid-February.' (*Waterways World*) It was not the 'result' that was judged, but the competition itself. *After judging by local councils . . . the result of the architectural competition was an-nounced in mid-February.*

judging. This participle ought not to be converted into a kind of con-junction.

'Judging from my postbag, there are lots of people who are interested in discovering more about the history of their family.' (*Family History*) 'Judging from my postbag, I discover that there are lots of people' would be correct, because the participle 'judging' is matched by the pronoun 'I'. There is no match for the participle in the sentence in question, but there is a perfectly satisfactory alternative construction: *To judge from my postbag, there are lots of people.*

just as. 'Just as' introduces a parallelism that must be strictly main-tained.

'This year's Royal Lancashire Show looks set to be just as successful as last year.' (*Lancashire Life*) Here this year's show is compared with last year instead of with last year's show: *just as successful as last year's.*

'However, just as Balfour was ultimately undone by his deliberate am-biguity and his inability to impose his own approach, so may Mr Major.' (*The Times*) It is incorrect to say 'Just as he was imprisoned, so may I'. Grammar and common sense require 'so may I be'. If the correct wording, *so may Mr Major be*, seems inelegant, the sentence must be rewritten. *However, Balfour was ultimately undone by his deliberate am-biguity and his inability to impose his own approach: Mr Major may share his fate.*

justification. 'Some of the photographs, particularly of people, are out-standing while others, notably industrial townscapes, are so banal their only justification is for completeness.' (*Dalesman*) The preposition 'for' is wrong. No one would say 'He stole the food, but his justification was for hunger'. It is safer to use the verb 'justify': *while others are so banal that* [sic] *they can be justified only by the need for completeness.*

K

keeper. 'The estate I keeper on is typical of many.' (*Shooting Times*) We may doubt whether there is really need for this usage. It is rather like saying 'The prison I gaoler in is fine'. He is called a 'keeper' because his job is to 'keep' watch. If 'The estate I keep' will not do, it could be: *The estate where I am keeper*.

key. 'Last year the Chancellor set out a number of very key targets.' (*Radio 4*) It has become fashionable to use the noun 'key' as an adjective. It is natural to the English language to use nouns adjectivally to qualify other nouns. We speak of 'the garden shed' or 'the tool shed', using the nouns 'garden' and 'tool' to indicate what shed is meant. But the noun used thus adjectivally remains a noun, and therefore does not acquire all the features proper to an adjective. We may speak of a 'tall man', a 'very tall man', or even a 'really very tall man', but we cannot speak of a 'very garden shed', or 'a really very garden shed'. Nor can we speak of 'very key targets'. One target cannot be 'more key' than another, nor 'very key' as opposed to 'merely key'. 'Very' must go: *a number of key targets*.

The sentence does not represent a unique misuse. 'We had all expected that Sir Leon Brittan would be given this really very key job.' (*Radio 4*). It is best here to use a genuine adjective: *this really very crucial job*.

kind of/sort of. 'This kind of thing annoys me' and 'These kinds of slippers suit me best'. The singular and plural thus used do not jar.

Reporting on plans to rebuild damaged areas of Belfast, a newsreader gave us 'These kind of projects could physically still provide a buffer-zone in flashpoint areas'. (*Radio 4*) This attaches the plural 'these' to the singular 'kind' (turning the subject into a compound noun, 'kind-of-projects'). An adjustment of word order will help here. *Projects of this kind could physically still provide a buffer-zone.*

'These kind of problems are known to doctors as irritants' (*OK! Homes*) should be either: *This kind of problem is known to doctors as an irritant*, or: *Problems of this kind are known to doctors.*

'These kind of reports are closely monitored here' (*Radio 4*) should be: *Reports of this kind are closely monitored here.*

know. It has become the practice to use the verb 'to know' as though it were exactly parallel in grammatical function with the verb 'to call'.

'Dominic Taylor, who had been promoting the work of the British Invisible Export Council, as it used to be known . . .' (*The Times*) It was never 'known' the British Invisible Export Council, but it was 'called' that and it was known 'as' that: *the British Invisible Export Council, as it used to be called.*

'The principal target of the unusual broadsides is not "Sir Brittan", as he is frequently known, but the French president of the EC commission.' (*The Times*) It would be grammatically correct, but stylistically unbearable, to write '"Sir Brittan", as he is frequently known as': therefore the verb 'call' must be used: *"Sir Brittan", as he is frequently called.*

'Mount Diogenes, as it was then known' (*Options*) should be: *Mount Diogenes, as it was then called.*

'The boats, or "punts" as they are sometimes known along the Suffolk coast' (*The Field*) should be: *as they are sometimes called.*

known as. Where it is used at the beginning of a sentence, this is another construction that is often incorrectly connected to what follows it.

'Known as arrogant and amusing, his personal life was sacrificed to punishing working hours.' (*The Times*) It was not his personal life which was 'known as arrogant'. *Known as arrogant and amusing, he sacrificed his personal life to punishing working hours.*

'Already known to appear in Argentina's parliament wearing black leather mini-skirts, Maria Julia's political career was enhanced when she posed for a news magazine apparently dressed in nothing but a fox fur.' (*Tatler*) The writer makes it out that Maria Julia's political career appeared scantily dressed. *Already known to appear . . . wearing black leather mini-skirts, she enhanced her political career when she posed in nothing but a fox fur.*

L

lack. 'In compiling her book on childless couples, she discovered that far from being sterile or lacking, these partners "in fact had a very special closeness, one that is very difficult to maintain when you have children".' (*New Woman*) In 'I lack money', the verb is used transitively. In 'He is lacking in common sense' the verb is used intransitively. It is unsatisfactory to speak of someone being 'lacking' (that is, deficient) unless the deficiency is specified: *far from being sterile or deprived*.

laid. This is the past tense and also the past participle of the verb 'to lay'. The past tense of the verb 'to lie' is 'lay'. 'The woman feigned death during the attack and laid in a road near Lydden for three hours' (*The Times*) should be: *and lay in the road. See also* LAIN, LAY, LIE.

lain. 'As the duchess herself says, her troubles may well have been lain down in childhood when her home life was fractured.' (*The Times*) 'Lain' is the past participle of the verb to lie ('I have lain here asleep'). The verb required here is the verb to lay, whose past tense is 'laid': *her troubles may well have been laid down in childhood. See also* LAID, LAY, LIE.

last thing you want. 'If you're unfortunate enough to have to make a claim, the last thing you want are problems.' (*Royal Insurance*) The familiar expression works according to normal grammatical rules, so the subject 'thing' cannot be followed by the plural verb 'are': *the last thing you want is a problem*.

Latin Words. English has been assimilating Latin words for centuries. Nevertheless, in the case of some more recently acquired nouns, it is considered bad form to anglicise them completely and ignore the original Latin distinction between the singular and plural. Time brings changes in this respect. Thus the word 'focus', with its Latin plural 'foci', can now become 'focuses' in the plural. Both forms are used. *See also* FUNGUS, MEDIUM, STRATA.

latter. The proper use of 'the latter' is in succession to 'the former'. There can be no 'latter' where there has not been a former, though the word 'former' may not necessarily have been used. It is correct to say 'I brought my books and my pencil, the latter in my pocket', because 'the latter' distinguishes the pencil from the previously mentioned books.

'Stencil techniques had considerably advanced by this stage as can be seen from mid-19th century examples. The latter was applied to a ceiling of the hall and stairwell . . .' (*Old-House Journal*) There is nothing at all for the word 'latter' here to refer back to. 'Examples' cannot be applied to ceilings. The writer should take out the word 'latter' and say what it is that was so applied. Did he just mean: *There are some on the ceilings of the hall and stairwell*?

lavish. 'Fifty volunteers and ten paid assistants ensure that children at Alderman Jacobs Primary School are lavished with personal attention.' (*The Times*) To lavish is to give abundantly. It is the attention that is given in abundance, not the children: *ensure that personal attention is lavished on the children*.

'Clive had revealed himself to be charming, witty and attentive. He had lavished her with gifts, a wonderful dinner and now cocktails at Honest Ron's Hawaiian theme pub' (*Advantage*) should be: *He had lavished gifts on her, a wonderful dinner and now cocktails*.

'I lavished her with all the love in the world' (*Bella*) should be: *I lavished all the love in the world on her*.

lay. In general usage this is a transitive verb. One may 'lay' the table or 'lay' the law down.

'I can't lay on a beach and do nothing for half and hour.' (*The Times*) This confuses the verb with the verb 'to lie'. *I can't lie on a beach and do nothing for half an hour*.

'She had third degree burns on her back after laying unconscious in the sun at the quarry near Bordeaux.' (*The Times*) The same mistake is made here. *She had third degree burns on her back after lying unconscious in the sun*.

Even well-known journalists can offend. 'In his spare time he would go home, lay on his bed and be moved to tears by the music of Beethoven' (*The Times*) should be: *he would go home, lie on his bed, and be moved to tears*.

We even see the error proudly headlined: 'Shares lay low as US rate worries off investors' (*The Times*) should be: *Shares lie low*.

So too we read the caption to a photograph of 'a herb that has started growing after laying dormant for 400 years' (*The Times*) which should be: *after lying dormant*.

'"Maybe that's what's upsetting him" said her husband, laying back now with his eyes closed.' (*Woman*) should be *lying back*.

'I sat on her bed with her laying on my lap' (*Dogs Monthly*) should be: *with her lying on my lap. See also* LAID, LAIN, LIE.

lay waste. '. . . all manner of nuclear by-products will rise from the grave and lay waste to the Cumbrian countryside.' (*Cumbria Life*) In conventional usage we 'lay waste' an area; we do not lay waste 'to' it: *will rise from the grave and lay waste the Cumbrian countryside*.

lazy. 'Too lazy to walk or bicycle, the proportion of short journeys taken by car has doubled in the past 20 years.' (*The Times*) Who is 'too lazy'? The proportion of short journeys, we are told. *Too lazy to walk or bicycle, drivers have doubled the proportion of short journeys taken by car*.

lead. 'Where does this lead to?' (*Good News Magazine*) We lead someone 'to' her home, but we do not lead her 'to' there, we lead her there. Either 'where' must go or 'to' must go: *What does this lead to?* or *Where does this lead?*

'LEAD TO' AND THE GERCIPLE 'Lead' is a verb which lures writers into use of the gerciple. It is correct to say 'Ill-health led to my retirement' or 'Ill-health led to my retiring' but not 'Ill-health led to me retiring', because ill health did not lead to 'me' but to my act of retiring. The best construction is the simplest – 'Ill-health led me to retire'.

'Unfortunately, staged pay rises have led to inflation gnawing away at this advance.' (*Options*) The possible alternative corrections here are: *staged pay rises have led to the gnawing away of this advance by inflation*, or: *have led inflation to gnaw away at this advance*. Very often this recourse to the infinitive is the best usage.

'The developments led to Alan Beith adding to the calls for Mr Howard to resign' (*The Times*) should be: *The developments led Alan Beith to add to the calls for Mr Howard to resign*.

It is not always so straightforward to correct this bad usage. 'Use of the emblem led to Currie having her knuckles rapped by Madam Speaker.' (*The Times*) The correct gerund ('led to Currie's having her knuckles rapped') is awkward. It is better to change the verb from passive to active. *Use of the emblem led Madam Speaker to rap Currie's knuckles.*

'**LED TO' AND CAUSATION** Sometimes 'led to' is better changed for some other usage. 'The inadequate care at Medway hospital, Kent, led to the patient suffering extensive pressure sores that became infected.' (*Nursing Standard*) Here the use of the word 'result' would be better. *As a result of inadequate care at Medway hospital, Kent, the patient suffered extensive pressure sores.*

'It would be great if the Open led to us being able to get more jobs in the area' (*Lancashire Life*) could be: *It would be great if the Open enabled us to get more jobs in the area.*

'**LEAD' FOR 'LED'** Because in pronunciation the noun 'lead' (the metal) is the same as 'led', the past tense of the verb 'lead', there is a tendency to misspell the verb.

'The cast, lead by Françoise Pollet as Didion, is largely Francophone' (*The Times*) should be: *led by Françoise Pollet.*

And 'a high-profile campaign lead by the former Cabinet minister Barbara Castle' (*The Times*) should be: *led by the former Cabinet minister.*

'But if global warming is the hot news we are lead to believe it is' (*Shooting Times*) should be: *the hot news we are led to believe it is.*

And 'which I have always been lead to believe was the way to catch big bass' (*Sea Angler*) should be: *which I have always been led to believe.*

'Finding by the road at Pipers, our fox lead the mixed pack away' (*Horse & Hound*) should be: *our fox led the mixed pack away.*

'In East Anglia, where there is such a strong farmer-lead market' (*The Field*) should be: *a strong farmer-led market.*

leading to. These words should not be used as a link whose grammatical basis can be ignored. 'Leading' is a participle and should agree with a noun or pronoun.

'Because there are so few female-only prisons in this country many women find themselves imprisoned away from home, leading to fewer visits from friends and family.' (*Company*) In strict grammatical terms it is here 'many women' who are 'leading to fewer visits', for there is no other word for 'leading' to agree with. The construction 'leading to' should not be used here: *many women find themselves imprisoned away from home, and thus get fewer visits from friends.*

'One of the two runways had to close for most of the afternoon, leading to some flights being cancelled.' (*Radio 4*) Here the bad use of 'leading to' is followed by the bad use of 'being cancelled'. To correct the latter error ('leading to the cancellation of some flights') would still leave the former. *One of the two runways had to close for most of the afternoon, and some flights were cancelled as a result.*

leaflet. 'Anti-abortionists have already leafleted every house on the island.' (*New Woman*) To use the noun 'leaflet' as a verb is not a happy innovation. One would not say that a newsagent 'papered' houses or a dairyman 'milked' them.

least. 'Possibly the *least* best time to paint middle-distance foliage is at the height of summer.' (*The Artist*) 'Least' cannot qualify an adjective in its comparative or superlative form: *Possibly the least desirable time.*

legend. 'The last of a famous line of British legends is taking pride of place at the National Motorcycle Museum.' (*Best of British*) The metaphor would be more elegant if the 'legend' itself were not said to be taking pride of place: *The last of a legendary series of British motorcycles is taking pride of place.*

less. This word refers to bulk. It is correct to say 'I have less confidence than he has', but incorrect to say 'I have less friends than he has', because the word needed is 'fewer'.

'In other words, the more fry there are to compete for resources, the less of them will survive.' (*Sea Angler*) should be: *the more fry there are to compete for resources, the fewer will survive.* 'Of them' is redundant.

'Less foxes in spring means more food is available to those left.' (*Cumbria Life*) 'Means' is an ill-used word here. *The fewer the foxes in spring, the more food is available for those left.*

Similarly 'Less new caravans being purchased meant less new caravanners' (*Caravan Magazine*) should be: *Since fewer caravans were purchased, there were fewer caravanners.*

'The year military service ends, there'll be a lot less people in the army' (*Radio 4*) should be: *there'll be far fewer people in the army.*

This advice on parties, 'It is easier to get a good balance with more people rather than less' (*OK! Homes*), should be: *with more people rather than fewer.*

'There are also less trees around these days' (*Trail*) should be: *fewer trees.*

Sometimes the misuse gives a hint of ambiguity. 'I feel too there are less lonely people in villages compared with city life' (*Dalesman*) strictly means that village people are less lonely, though the writer seems to have meant: *there are fewer lonely people in villages.*

lesson. 'The judge said it was one of the worst cases of sexual abuse he had encountered and it raised lessons for the rest of society.' (*Radio 4*) Lessons are never 'raised', they are taught: *it raised questions for the rest of society*.

'The lessons of the previous accident had not been put into practice.' (*Radio 4*) The subject is the report on the Severn Tunnel railway accident. The 'previous accident' was the one at Clapham. It is awkward to speak of putting 'lessons into practice'. Either the verb should be changed: *the lessons of the previous accident had not been learned*, or the subject: *the recommendations that were made after the previous accident had not been acted upon/put into practice*.

let alone. This construction lines something up with something previously mentioned. 'There was no room to stand, let alone to sit down', we say, and 'to sit down' parallels 'to stand'. Such parallelism must be maintained.

'The news [of Private Clegg's return to the army] will cause anger among many in the Province who say he should have remained in prison let alone return to the army.' (*Radio 4*) This will not do. If 'let alone' is kept it must be balanced in anticipation: *who say he should not have been permitted to leave prison, let alone to return to the army*.

'It was easy enough to improve the physical environment, if you spent money on it, but it proved harder to enhance the individual child's mastery of basic skills, let alone a broadly based curriculum.' (*Times Educational Supplement*) There is ambiguity here. As it stands the text might mean: *mastery of basic skills, let alone of a broadly based curriculum*, or it might mean: *it proved harder to enhance the individual child's mastery of basic skills, let alone to develop a broadly based curriculum*.

letting. Like other such participles, this word must be properly attached to a noun or pronoun. 'It's the most amazing revolution in make-up: skin is liberated letting it breathe.' (*Company*) The skin is not letting itself breathe: *skin is liberated, enabled to breathe*.

level. 'When we have that level of problem we have to focus on it.' (*The Times*) Extending the idiomatic use of 'level' ('level of dissent', 'level of support') thus is tasteless at best. Whereas degrees of dissent or support may be represented in terms of a swelling tide or tankful of petrol, a 'problem' scarcely lends itself to that kind of quantification. The wording must be simplified. *When the problem is so great, we have to focus on it*.

'On a wider level, throughout the whole province, each subdivision now proactively encourages the local ethnic community to report any incident.' (*Radio 4*) Levels are not distinguished by varieties of width or length but by degrees of height. Neither 'on a higher level' nor 'on a lower level' would be appropriate here. And if 'wider' is kept, 'level' must go: *over a wider field*.

liberate. An enthusiast, questioned about the advantages of a folding bicycle, replied, 'It liberates the world' (*Radio 4*), yet it is not the world which is liberated when someone buys a bicycle, but the rider: *It has liberated me*, or: *It opens the world*.

lie. The verb 'to lie' is intransitive. A person can 'lie down', but no one can 'lie' anything down. The transitive verb, the verb which can take an object, is the verb 'to lay'.

'Lie everything in a heap on the ground' (*Country Life*) should be: *Lay everything in a heap on the ground*.

'Lie the kitten on its back' (*Wild About Animals*) should be: *Lay the kitten on its back*.

'I lie him on the floor on his back with a pillow for his head' (*Essentials*) should be: *I lay him on the floor on his back*. See also LAID, LAIN, LAY.

life. 'Many of our young of school-going age live lives of little parental or institutional control.' (*The Times*) A young person may live a life 'of' crime or a life 'of' service, but a life 'under' proper control is not a life 'of' control. *Many of our young of school-going age live their lives under little parental or institutional control*.

like. This is one of the most misused words in the language. The misuse takes various forms.

OMISSION OF POSSESSIVE We say 'Mary's house is like her mother's'. We do not say 'Mary's house is like her mother'. Yet this error, omitting the apostrophe from 'mother', is frequently made in the press.

'A little like Albert Barnes, Charles Saatchi's extraordinary collection was construed as a sort of revenge.' (*Harpers & Queen*) Charles Saatchi's collection must not be said to be like Albert Barnes. An apostrophe must be inserted. *A little like Albert Barnes's, Charles Saatchi's extraordinary collection was construed as a sort of revenge*.

'Like Deborah, Lynn's first thought was to try a bob' (*Prima*) should be: *Like Deborah's, Lynn's first thought was to try a bob*.

'Like P.G. Wodehouse, Herge's activities during the Second World War have long been the subject of controversy' (*The Times*) should be: *Like P.G. Wodehouse's, Herge's activities during the Second World War have long been the subject of controversy.*

'Like any castle in England, its role as a prison was incidental' (*History Today*) should be: *Like any castle's in England, its role as a prison was incidental.*

'LIKE' ATTACHED TO THE WRONG NOUN 'Like many cancer specialists, particularly those working in London, much of my practice is taken up with patients who live outside my own health district.' (*Independent*) The writer says that much of his practice is 'like many cancer specialists'. If he begins with 'Like many cancer specialists', he must afterwards introduce the word 'I': *Like many cancer specialists . . . I find that much of my practice is taken up with patients.*

Thus where 'like' properly attaches to a person, it must not be allowed to drift into a different attachment. 'Like all good modellers this was done after the models had been built.' (*Railway Modeller*) This should be either: *Like all good modellers, he did this after the models were built,* or *In accordance with the best modelling practice, this was done after the models were built.*

'Like any other violent crime, a man who beats up his partner should be arrested and charged.' (*Radio 4*) This should be: *Like any other violent criminal, a man who beats up his partner should be arrested.*

'"O dolci mani" was cooed like a turtle-dove.' (*The Times*) If someone wrote 'The boss was shunned like a leper' it would mean that as the leper is shunned so the boss was shunned. The writer above seems to say that as the turtle-dove is sung, so the aria was sung. *He cooed "O dolci mani" like a turtle-dove.*

'It is now four years on, and like the sorcerer's apprentice, it is time to consider stopping'. (*The Times*) The writer should say who is like the apprentice. *Like the sorcerer's apprentice, it is time for me to consider stopping.*

'LIKE IN' This most dangerous expression is almost always wrong. It usually needs to be replaced by 'as in'.

'However, just like in our world above the oceans, every good business attracts its seedy, disreputable imitations.' (*Wild About Animals*) This should be: *However, just as in our world above the oceans.*

Similarly, when a cabinet minister says in the house, 'Just like in "The Mikado", I've got a little list' (*Radio 4*), he means: *Just as in "The Mikado"'.*

'Do not expect short day trips like in the compact Lake district' (*Trail*) should be: *as in the compact Lake District.*

USED FOR 'AS' OR 'JUST AS' Thus 'like' is much misused where the appropriate word would be 'as' or 'just as'.

'But like Mao mustered his Red Guards, the party has its own methods of winning loyalty.' (*Radio 4*) This should be: *Just as Mao mustered his Red Guards, the party has its own methods*.

'Suzy needs to pull her life together like Tim says' (*Woman*) should be: *as Tim says*.

Writers should be especially wary of this misuse when dates are involved. 'So by then the Chancellor will face a choice; keep the economy steady, like 1986, or do what Nigel Lawson did.' (*Radio 4*) What is 'like 1986'? The economy? Of course not: *keep the economy steady, as in 1986*.

'LIKE' FOR 'AS IN' 'Like' can drift away from anchorage further still. 'But like any science which is accumulating data rapidly, the finds [fossils] do not always simplify the picture.' (*The Times*) The 'finds' must not be said to be 'like any science': *As in any science which is accumulating data*.

'But rather like asking Liz Taylor on a date, they should bear in mind what they are taking on' (*Artists & Illustrators Magazine*) should be: *Just as in asking Liz Taylor for a date*.

'But rather like musical variations, there are slight key changes' (*Artists & Illustrators Magazine*) should be: *rather as in musical variations*.

'Tricia loves Anna French and Osborne and Little fabrics – both are used to great effect throughout the house, like quilting the diamonds on the main bedroom's bedspread.' (*Perfect Home*) This should be: *used to great effect throughout the house, as in quilting*.

'Like the board game of our youth, the snakes are still far longer than the ladders' (*Money Observer*) should be: *As in the board game of our youth*.

USED FOR 'AS THOUGH' Especially offensive is the misuse of 'like' where 'as though' is needed.

'It seemed like greed, accumulation and pursuit of all things pecuniary was still driving the western world' (*Complete Traveller*) should be: *It seemed as though greed, accumulation and pursuit of all things pecuniary were still driving the western world*.

'He looked at me like he hated me' (*Marie Claire*) should be: *He looked at me as though he hated me*.

'Consequently it may still look to the public like the Duchess of York does no work' (*Majesty*) should be: *it may still look to the public as though the Duchess of York does no work*.

TOTALLY AT SEA 'Written by Angus Deayton (who also starred) and

Geoffrey Perkins this was as funny as the Paul Merton show was not – although like Merton there were moments of over-gruesome bad taste.' (*Oldie*) And here we have a moment of gruesome bad grammar. Nothing is cited which is 'like Merton': *although, as in Merton's show, there were moments of over-gruesome bad taste.*

'He slyly notes that the ancient notion that you could love prepubescent boys before moving on to women is like Eton today.' (*The Times*) There is no resemblance between the notion and the school. The only way to rescue the sentence is to get rid of 'like': *The ancient notion . . . is still alive at Eton today.*

'The Referendum Party should do better than other fringe groups because of Sir James curiosity value, like Ross Perot or Stephen Forbes.' (*The Times*) To rescue this sentence as it stands involves some recasting. *The Referendum Party should do better than other fringe groups because Sir James has the curiosity value that Ross Perot and Steve Forbes have.*

limit. 'Examination of your horse's problem will not be limited by a technique not being familiar to the veterinary surgeon.' (*Horse & Hound*) 'To limit by' readily attracts the gerciple. It is incorrect to say 'We were limited by the weather not being sunny', clumsy (though correct) to say 'We were limited by the weather's not being sunny', but natural to say 'We were limited by the lack of sunny weather'. The above must be corrected similarly. *Examination of your horse's problem will not be limited by the veterinary surgeon's lack of familiarity with a given technique.*

link (noun). Although, in material matters, one may speak of, say, a telephone link 'to' the exchange, 'link' as a noun is generally better followed by 'with'.

A news report speaks of the demand for an investigation into the loss of the bulk carrier 'Derbyshire', 'because of the direct link to losses of bulk carriers generally.' (*Radio 4*) The question involved here is whether one loss is linked 'with' another, a matter of association rather than of direct connection: *because of the direct link with losses of bulk carriers generally.*

link (verb). There is a tendency to confuse two usages. Whereas we connect a house 'to' the electricity supply, we connect a suspicious character 'with' a certain crime. The verb 'link' works with the same two prepositions.

'The results of the examination do not link his death to the CS spray'

(*Radio 4*) should be: *The results of the examination do not link his death with the CS spray.*

'He was concerned by rumours linking the disappearance of the Bishop of Argyll and the Isles to a woman.' (*Radio 4*) Again it would be better to speak of: *linking the disappearance of the Bishop with a woman.*

'The report about violent crime being linked to birth complications' (*Independent*) errs also in the use of the passive gerciple ('crime being linked'). It would better be: *The report that violent crime may be linked with birth complications.*

'The local ones [quangos] are profoundly undemocratic in the sense that they have no clear links to the people they are meant to serve.' (*Radio 4*) Here again the issue is one of association: *they have no clear links with the people they are meant to serve.*

To speak of someone being under investigation over 'links to cocaine smugglers' (*Radio 4*) should be: *links with cocaine smugglers.*

list. 'The money you make is up to you, how hard you work at it and using the information in our packet correctly figure quite high in the list.' (*Money-Maker*) What 'list'? To treat 'high in the list' as the equivalent of 'very important' is thoughtless. The sentence is extremely lax. *How much money you make is up to you; hard work together with correct use of the information in our packet will certainly help a lot.*

litany. A litany is strictly a form of prayer with a highly repetitive pattern. The word is therefore used of any tediously repetitive recital.

'Sub-Saharan Africa hosts a depressing litany of inter-ethnic bloodshed and civil wars.' (*Adventure Travel*) There is no question here of a recital or of a list so that the word is totally out of place. So too is the verb 'hosts' which implies welcome reception and entertainment. *Sub-Saharan Africa has had a depressing sequence of bloodshed and civil wars.*

literally. 'One alternative is to literally step back in time to see for yourself what life was like.' (*Camping*) The location is a museum. If words are taken 'literally', their exact meanings are accepted. No museum can allow you actually to step back in time. The converse is the case. *One alternative is, as it were, to step back in time.*

'I've been literally knocking my head against a brick wall with the Ministry of Transport.' (*Radio 4*) This is a more possible, if also more horrific process. To correct it: *I've been figuratively knocking my head against a brick wall*, seems over-pedantic since no one is likely to misunderstand: *I've been knocking my head against a brick wall.*

little. As well as its obvious use as an adjective ('a little boy') we have such expressions as 'a little tired'.

A leader-writer stretches this usage into 'There is a strong sense, no little fostered by the Prime Minister himself, that changes in British governance can be made.' (*The Times*) This use of 'no' is quite ungrammatical. The sentence should read: *not a little fostered by the Prime Minister himself*, or better still: *definitely fostered by the Prime Minister himself*.

live (verb). 'London is considered on a par with Hong Kong, New York and other major centres as a good place to live.' (*The Times*) To be strict, we should point out that nobody lives a place, but lives 'in' it: *as a good place to live in*.

live (adjective). There is an acceptable usage of this adjective in the expression 'live broadcast', as opposed to something recorded. But for the announcer to say 'Mr Needham and Labour's Brian Wilson are with me live' (*Radio 4*) seems to overstate the obvious.

living. This is one of a group of participles which, when used at the beginning of a sentence, can fail to be properly matched in what follows.

'Living abroad as a child, his introduction to humour was from his parents' records of "Beyond the Fringe".' (*The Times*) This tells us that Ian Hislop's introduction to humour lived abroad as a child. *Living abroad as a child, he was introduced to humour by his parents' record of 'Beyond the Fringe'*.

loathe/loth (loath). To 'loathe' is to hate intensely, to detest. The adjective 'loth' means reluctant or unwilling: *She was loth to part with the family silver*. It is a pity that recently the spelling 'loath' has become more common than 'loth' since it encourages confusion with the verb 'loathe'.

lobby. 'Badgers are his special favourite and he champions their conservation against the increasing farming lobby to cull them again.' (*Country Talk*) The infinitive 'to cull' cannot hang on 'lobby'. Supply a word for it to attach to: *against the increasing pressure of the farm lobby to cull them again*.

long may it remain so. 'Although it is a not a National Park, and long may it remain so, the New Forest . . . is a model of how to cope with walkers and their cars.' (*Country Walking*) It would be correct to say 'It is clean, and long may it remain so' but not 'It is not dirty, and long may it remain so'. The words 'remain so' must refer back to a positive condition of things: *Although it is outside the National Parks, and long may it remain so.*

longer. When the word 'longer' is used, not of a dimension ('The table is longer than six feet') but with reference to a period of time, it is easy to slip up.

'It is obvious that those businesses . . . will be set to flourish and grow dramatically when the upturn comes in the economy, though that will, I think, be longer than most commentators estimate.' (*Money-Maker*) This sentence conveys that the 'upturn' will be 'longer' than most people expect, when in fact what was intended is that the period before the upturn will be longer than anticipated. 'Longer' must be changed to 'later': *though that will, I think, be later than most commentators estimate.*

looking. 'Looking' is a participle which must hang on a noun or a pronoun. It cannot function independently.

'Looking to the future, work has just started in earnest on Bagnall "Austerity".' (*Steam Classic*) This is wrong because 'work' is not 'looking to the future' and the reader wants to know who is. *Looking to the future, I see that work has just started in earnest on Bagnall 'Austerity'.* In fact, of course, 'looking to the future' is here redundant, as indeed it often is.

'She changed all that; and looking back, there is a striking symmetry to the way that she did it.' (*Daily Mail*) This comment on Mrs Thatcher misuses 'looking back' as 'looking to the future' was misused above. We are not told who is looking back. Either the sentence must say who is looking back: *and looking back, we can see a striking symmetry in the way that she did it*, or the construction must be changed: *and to hindsight there is a striking symmetry in the way that she did it.*

The expression 'to hindsight' or 'retrospectively' can often rescue a writer from error in the use of 'looking back'. Thus 'But looking back on it, it wasn't childhood that was the worst, it was being 21' (*Company*) should be: *But to hindsight, it wasn't childhood that was the worst.*

It is possible to err with 'looking back' even when a proper subject is provided for the word 'looking'.

'Looking back now, I was pretty slow to piece together her non-specific symptoms.' (*The Times*) The 'I' who is 'now' looking back cannot be the subject of 'I was' in the past. It's like saying 'Looking back today, I fell yesterday'. Either a verb should be added: *Looking back, I can see that I was pretty slow*, or 'looking back' should go: *I can see now that I was pretty slow.*

'Looking round at the expressions of amazement and delight on my companions' faces, everyone else seems just as excited.' (*Country Lovers Magazine*) The longer the sentence, the easier it is to mismatch 'looking'. Here 'everyone else' is said to be looking round. The participle 'looking' should go: *As I look round.*

lose. It is possible to 'lose' something only if it is already possessed.

'Recently refurbished, it provides a unique atmosphere with subtle lighting and imaginative decor which complements the sculptures perfectly without losing any of the building's original charm.' (*Cumbria*) The building's original charm is something which only the building could 'lose', but the 'it' above is a new gallery housed in a former gunpowder factory. It would be better not to use the verb 'lose': *which complements the sculptures perfectly without detracting from the building's original charm.*

'Traditional open fires are too often inefficient and draughty, losing most of their heat into the surrounding masonry up the chimney.' (*Traditional Homes*) One may speak of losing an employee 'to' a rival firm, but more often 'losing' things implies inability any longer to locate them. It is satisfactory to say that the fire 'loses' heat, but not to say that it loses heat 'into the masonry'. *Traditional open fires are too often inefficient and draughty, wastefully directing most of their heat into the surrounding masonry.*

loss. 'Mr Rabin's dramatic loss could deal a damaging blow to the peace process.' (*Radio 4*) The assassination cannot be described as 'Mr Rabin's loss': *The dramatic loss of Mr Rabin.*

loth. *See* LOATHE.

Loss of Verbal Control. We may identify a few brands of carelessness which lead to verbal anarchy.

HIGHBROW PRETENTIOUSNESS We ought not to find lack of verbal control in highbrow reviewing, but we do.

'Svetlanov and the orchestra summoned a bravado of their own to match the pianist, and surpassed it at times in an account of Tchaikovsky's Fourth Symphony no less revelatory than Hilary Finch wrote of their Sixth Symphony on this page last Monday.' (*The Times*) The words 'no less revelatory than Hilary Finch wrote' will not do. After 'no less revelatory than' there must be a noun or noun-substitute ('This was no less revelatory than that'). It is not permissible to say 'This book is no less dull than the parson preached': it would have to be 'than the parson's sermon'. But if the above were corrected to that extent ('an account of Tchaikovsky's fourth symphony no less revelatory than Hilary Finch's account') it would still be wrong because it was not her account that was revelatory, but the performance of the sixth symphony as she described it. The writer must either start again (the better advice) or go in for complexity: *an account of Tchaikovsky's Fourth Symphony no less revelatory than their account of the Sixth Symphony as described by Hilary Finch.*

BUSINESS JARGON Articles on finance and commerce can be rich in run-away syntax. 'Some of our businesses require skills of different orders, some from systems developments – even if it's only putting information into the hands of the public; some require the old traditional banking skills, like being able to lend money and put together a proposal, and others in the very sophisticated areas of acquisitions and mergers and the markets department of Midland Montagu.' (*Meridian*) The construction, 'some are/do this, others are/do that' requires grammatical consistency, clause by clause. The sequence 'some from . . . some require . . . others in the very sophisticated areas' has no syntactical consistency.

UNCHECKED ORAL FLOW Sometimes a writer gives way to what might be a sustainable flow of words in oral utterance but which leaves the reader floundering. 'Emma Pearce, in her article 'Mediums for Oil Painting', says that each successive layer of paint should contain a higher proportion of oil or Liquin to obey this rule, seemingly applying the word "fat" to the medium and not to the thickness of the paint, as in your definition "thicker paint over thinner", which I take to mean paint containing less medium used over earlier layers which contain more.' (*Artists & Illustrators Magazine*) This passage does not seem susceptible to correction.

M

made. When a sentence begins with 'made' the writer must be careful to match the word exactly in what follows.

'Made from a huge bole of Lincoln oak, the design incorporates an exquisite setting of fish in gilded copper.' (*Trout & Salmon*) It is not 'the design' that is made of oak, as here stated. *Made from a huge bole of Lincoln oak, the altar has an exquisite setting of fish in gilded copper incorporated in its design.*

majority. It is correct to speak of the 'majority' of the audience because the audience is a collection of individuals. Where there is no such collectivity the word is out of place.

'Nevertheless, if you were to find yourself in sub-zero conditions for the majority of the time then I would recommend Ventile.' (*The Great Outdoors*) Time cannot be divided into a majority and a minority: *if you were to find yourself in sub-zero conditions for most of the time.*

'There have been accusations of bias aimed at the Arts Council, who have awarded the majority of their funds to Sadlers Wells and the Shakespeare Globe theatres.' (*Radio 4*) Again funds cannot be divided into a majority and a minority. This should be: *who have awarded the larger part/most of their funds to Sadlers Wells.*

'There was no proper road into Caithness and the majority of trade was carried out by sea.' (*Country Talk*) The word 'majority' is out of place once more, and trade is not carried 'out', though merchandise may be: *and most of the trade was carried on by sea.*

make. 'Make' is a versatile verb and the versatility should not be abused.

'Together, they hope to make a lasting legacy in the shape of a new world-class business school.' (*The Times*) A legacy is not something to be manufactured: *Together, they hope to leave a lasting legacy.*

It is the fashion among some journalists to manufacture nouns out of verbs. Thus we find the heading 'Creative Makes' (*Home Style*) for an article on manufacturing decorative articles. It should be *Things to make.* ('Creative' is a trendy word of approval that adds nothing.) *See also* SPEND.

make a statement. In vulgar journalism, especially in relation to the arts, this expression has been grossly overused to the point of absurdity.

'Step-over apples . . . form a novel edging, while the fastigiate Ballerina and Minuette apples make a statement in confined situations.' (*Practical Gardening*) The usage here is unintentionally parodic: *the fastigiate Ballerina and Minuette apples look nice.*

making. The correct use of this participle keeps it firmly tied to a noun or pronoun. In the sentence 'He worked on the stock market, making a fortune there', the word serves the function of a present participle correctly, introducing a qualification of the pronoun 'he'.

'So Lord Lichfield's mother was a niece of the Queen Mother, making him a great-nephew.' (*Majesty*) Who is 'making' what? This is a careless use of the verb 'to make'. The participle has no grammatical anchorage. *So Lord Lichfield's mother was a niece of the Queen Mother and he therefore her great nephew.*

'New Zealand lamb is delicate and versatile, making it a popular choice for busy cooks.' (*Woman's Journal*) Again use of the verb 'make' is misplaced. What the writer means is: *New Zealand lamb is delicate and versatile, and in consequence a popular choice.*

The participle 'making' cannot serve as an alternative to 'in consequence' or 'thus'. 'This means that the protective filters in NIVEA Sun's products aren't reduced or affected by the sun's energy, making them more reliable.' (*Woman*) Here again the participle 'making' is grammatically at sea: *aren't reduced or affected by the sun's energy, and are thus more reliable.* See also FORCING, PROMPTING.

manage. 'It will bring the railway network to a halt far more effectively than the signal workers managed last summer.' (*Radio 4*) The signal workers did not manage last summer. Either the verb 'manage' must be replaced: *far more effectively than the signal workers did last summer*, or 'to do' must be added: *more effectively than the signal workers managed to do last summer.*

mantel/mantle. A 'mantle' is a cloak. Care must be taken not to use that spelling for the 'mantel', which is the frame around the fireplace and gives us the word 'mantelpiece'.

mantle. *See* MANTEL.

mask. 'George Walden MP, a former higher education minister, gave warning yesterday that such steep "grade inflation" masked real improvements and threatened to damage the value of a British degree.' (*The Times*) The verb 'to mask' means to conceal or disguise. An appearance of spectacular progress ought not to be said to 'mask' what real progress there is: *such steep "grade inflation" exaggerated/misrepresented real improvements.* Better still, perhaps, would be: *behind the steep 'grade inflation' there were real improvements.*

match. 'B M & P has perfected the art of matching finely blended programmes to carefully chosen venues.' (*Radio 4*) One thing is matched 'with' another, not 'to' another: *matching finely blended programmes with carefully chosen venues.*

materialise. To materialise is to take material form, to become tangible. It is a pity to use the verb to mean nothing more than to happen or to appear.

'We don't know how much talent there is in this country, because the talent materialises from the group of people who ride at the moment.' (*Horse & Hound*) Here the verb appears to mean something like 'becomes evident' or perhaps 'develops'. The use of 'materialises' is made worse by being combined with 'from', which almost hints at spiritualistic manifestations: *because talent is always coming freshly to light among those who ride at the moment.*

matter. 'Its editor is Hilary Gray (to whom all editorial matters should be addressed).' (*Country Lovers Magazine*) We can address a letter or a communication to someone, but not a 'matter': *who will deal with all editorial matters.*

maximum. Keeping one's head in the use of the words 'maximum' and 'minimum' is not always as easy as it sounds. We so readily think of 'maximum' as indicating the limit of possibility that we tend to forget whether that limit is a ceiling or a threshold.

'Halve your age and add seven years. The result should be the maximum age of the child-woman in your life.' (*Gentlemen's Quarterly*) This is from a light-hearted piece on older men who fall for younger women. *Halve your age and add seven years. The result should be the minimum age of the child-woman in your life.*

may for **might**. 'May' belongs with present and future tenses, 'might' with past tenses.

'Police in Paris at first considered the possibility that a Mafia gang from Russia may well have played a role in the murder.' (*Radio 4*) The newswriter makes a common error here. *Police at first considered that a Mafia gang might well have played a part in the murder.* ('Role' is surely pretentious.)

'They had heard through the St Bernard Trust, of which I was a member (£7) that I may be interested.' (*Dogs Monthly*) The bracketed '£7' cannot function as a punctuation mark. A comma is needed as well as the correction of the verb 'may'. *They had heard through the St Bernard Trust, of which I was a member, that I might be interested.*

'If the international community had been tougher in its response years ago, some of today's problems may have been avoided' (*Radio 4*) should be: *some of today's problems might have been avoided.*

'Days later I had my tonsils taken out as there was a risk that I may have got an abscess behind my tonsils' (*Woman*) should be: *as there was a risk that I might have got an abscess*.

'So I gave a week's notice . . . and went to see my two-year-old son at the children's home, telling the housemother there that I may not see him again for two weeks' (*Best of British*) should be: *telling the housemother there that I might not see him again for two weeks*.

me. Two forms of error need to be noted.

'ME' FOR 'I' The mistake of using 'me' where 'I' is required is less common than the converse use of 'I' where 'me' is required.

'I realise that neither me nor the cause has the pulling power of other more glamorous charities and their supporters.' (*The Times*) The journalist would not have written 'I realise that me is tired', yet that same mistake is made here. *I realise that neither I nor the cause has the pulling power*.

Worse still perhaps we have a senior MP declaring of his voting intentions, 'Me and colleagues who think like me are not making our total final position clear until Monday night' (*Radio 4*). The MP would not have said 'Me will not make my position clear'. The error is just as bad as that. *I and colleagues who think like me are not making our position clear*.

'I couldn't stand it any longer, so I went to the police. They were very sympathetic, and my boss, not me, was arrested.' (*Mail on Sunday*) The letter-writer here would not have said 'Me was not arrested', yet that is her mistake. *My boss, not I, was arrested*.

'ME' FOLLOWED BY '-ING' Following 'me' with an '-ing' form of the verb is dangerous. 'He saw me dancing' is correct because he did indeed see 'me'. 'He's too used to me being on TV' (*Woman's Own*) is incorrect because he is not used to 'me'. *He is too used to my being on TV*.

'There's no point me telling Pete' (*Sun*) should be: *There's no point in my telling Pete*.

mean. The verb 'to mean' establishes a relationship of significance. It has been used repeatedly in this book for that purpose. '"Oblivious" means forgetful'. From this strict literal usage there is a natural development to such usages as 'Money means power', where the speaker wishes to assert a relationship between money and power that is virtually a common effectiveness. Unfortunately, this quite proper imaginative use of the verb 'to mean' has bred usages so careless that the true connotation of the verb is being dissipated. In these usages the function of the verb as indicating a relationship of significance is forgotten, and it is used for relationships of enablement, cause, or result, for which there are far better constructions.

ENABLEMENT 'The on-site pharmacy means that the GP can put a prescription on computer, send it through to the pharmacist and the patient collects his tablets on the way out.' (*Independent*) This use offends because the issue is not one of significance but of enablement: *The on-site pharmacy enables the GP to put a prescription on computer . . ..* The alternative is to make the causal relationship explicit: *Because he has an on-site pharmacy, the GP can put a prescription on computer.*

We find such misuse in many contexts. 'A companion may mean an easier labour' (*Family Circle*) again misrepresents what is really a relationship of enablement. *A companion's presence may make labour easier.*

'The opening of Braunston Tunnel meant the opening of a 9 mile stretch of the Grand Junction Canal between Braunston and Weedon.' (*Waterways World*) This should be: *The opening of Braunston Tunnel made possible the opening of a 9-mile stretch.*

'This special supplement means you can easily keep it to hand to plan those days out.' (*Waterways World*) This is like saying 'The hot sun means it can warm you' instead of 'The hot sun can warm you'. The word 'means' must go. *This special supplement can easily be kept to hand for you to plan your days out.*

CAUSATION We have seen above that the relationship of enablement implicit in slack use of 'mean' can be expressed by use of the word 'because'. There are many instances where this would be appropriate.

'A fire [on the M25] means there's only one lane open' (*Radio 4*) should be: *Because of a fire on the M25, there's only one lane open.*

'Less expansion than PVCu means the door fits more tightly into the frame' (*Perfect Home*) should become: *Because there is less expansion than is the case with PVCu, the door fits more tightly* and 'Layers also mean less expansion so doors can fit in the frame more closely' (*Perfect Home*) should become: *Because layers reduce expansion, doors can fit in the frames more easily.*

'The cricket coverage will mean that Radio 4's regular programmes will be on FM only' (*Radio 4*) should be: *Because of the cricket coverage, Radio 4's regular programmes will be on FM only.*

'Because' is not the only word that can rescue such sentences. 'Developments for the zoo meant moving on to a showground at Wrea Green' (*Lancashire Life*) could well be: *Developments at the zoo involved moving on to a showground.*

RESULT We see the usage of 'mean' drifting further and further away from what logic requires. 'The new rules issued to magistrates are expected to mean more and more people going to gaol.' (*Radio 4*) Here the question is again not one of significance, but this time of act and result. *The new rules issued to magistrates are expected to result in more gaol-sentences.*

Sometimes the emphasis on result is even more clearly demanded. 'There are no exits wide enough at checkout points in supermarkets, meaning we have to go all round the shop again to get out.' The simplest correction here would be to replace 'meaning' by 'so that': *There are no exits wide enough at checkout points in supermarkets, so that we have to go all round the shop again.*

The change to a proper 'result' construction is not always as easy as that. 'Recent disappointing figures from computer monitor maker Microvitec means a forecast of a strong profit recovery by broker Henry Cooke Lumsden is cutting little ice in the market.' (*Investors Chronicle*) This should be: *As a result of recent disappointing figures from computer monitor maker Microvitz, a forecast of a strong profit recovery by broker Henry Cooke Lumsden is cutting little ice.*

'Blackburn Diocese wants to combine the parish with that of St Helen's a few miles away. It means that St Michael's will not have a resident vicar.' (*Lancashire Life*) Although this is again a matter of result: *As a result, St Michael's will not have a resident vicar*, there is also perhaps a conditional aspect which ought to be brought out: *Were this to happen, St Michael's would not have a resident vicar.*

A double error occurs when the misuse of 'mean' is followed by a gerciple. 'Such an outcome could mean Mr Major losing by three votes.' (*The Times*) This should be: *In that event Mr Major could lose by three votes.*

meaningless. 'Time often appeared meaningless, as dinner ordered for eight was often not eaten until midnight.' (*Hunting*) This illustrates lax abuse of what should be a useful word: *Timing was often haphazard.*

means. In the sentence 'I have the means *to live* comfortably' there is an 'enabling' element in the connotation ('I have resources which enable me to live comfortably'). But in the sentence 'The press is not the ideal means of getting publicity', 'means' is the equivalent of 'method', and whereas 'way' can be followed by the infinitive ('That's the best way to go'), 'means' (meaning 'method') requires 'of' and the gerund.

'Couture may not be the source of invention it was during the late eighties, but it is still a useful means for designers to refine ideas they introduced at the ready-to-wear shows.' (*Vogue*). Here the infinitive 'to refine' should go and the word order be adjusted: *but for designers it is still a useful method (means) of refining ideas.*

medium. This Latin derivative still keeps its Latin plural form 'media'.

'Her skills extend to almost all mediums.' (*Homes & Gardens*) On the whole *media* would be preferable here. But where the word is used in a different sense the word is fully anglicised: *Both sisters were spiritualist mediums.*

melange. Even though words are used with attention to their meaning and with strict grammatical accuracy, there may be some incongruity in the way they are put together in the context.

'The melange of Hindus and Muslims, Creoles and a sprinkling of Chinese is not universally enthused by the change in constitutional status.' (*The Times*) 'Melange' is a colourful word, used properly here of the mixture of races in Mauritius, but because it is a vivid word, there is a faint absurdity about making it the subject of the verb 'enthused'. The notion of enthusing a melange cannot be treated seriously. The subject of the verb 'enthused' should be the people, not the mixture of people: *The mixed populace of Hindus and Muslims, Creoles and a sprinkling of Chinese are not all enthusiastic about the change in constitutional status.*

memorial. 'His principal memorial was the creation of a fine academic school.' (*The Times*) The 'memorial' was the school, not its 'creation'.

memories. 'You will eventually emerge from the grieving process cherishing your father's memories.' (*The Times*) The father's memories are lost with him in the grave. Clearly this should be: *cherishing your memories of your father.*

memory. 'It is obvious that Josephine has a clear memory about the attack.' (*Independent*) Normal usage would change the preposition: *Josephine has a clear memory of the attack.*

merge. 'The design ethic of the 1980's merged with the environmentally conscious 1990's to produce a greater understanding for the need to re-capture and re-invigorate the traditional skills.' (*Lancashire Life*) There are three errors here. (i) If one speaks of something 'merging' with something else, the two items must match each other grammatically and substantially. The 'ethic' of the 1980s cannot be merged with the 1990s but with some aspect of the 1990s. (ii) The apostrophes (1980's) are not needed. (iii) The word 'understanding' is followed by 'of', not 'for': *The design ethic of the 1980s merged with the environmental consciousness of the 1990s to produce a greater understanding of the need.*

merit. 'It is not a way of behaviour that merits Sinn Fein's entry to talks.' (*Radio 4*) This ministerial statement misuses the verb 'merit': *It is not behaviour that would justify Sinn Fein's entry*, or: *that would merit Sinn Fein's admission to talks.*

Metaphors. Metaphors are figures of speech by which imaginative resemblances are identified without strict literal justification. Thus if one calls a man a 'pillar of rectitude', the word 'pillar', with its connotation of uprightness, strength and reliability, enhances the description vividly. There are many metaphors that have become part of our day-to-day conversation, expressions such as 'a pig in a poke', 'a square peg in a round hole', 'a chip off the old block' or 'barking up the wrong tree'. Language is soaked in metaphor. Even some of the most scientific terms can be shown to have metaphorical origin. 'Focus' is the Latin word for hearth – the thing that people gathered round and centered upon. The description 'dead metaphor' is used of expressions which have thus acquired their own independence of the metaphorical process that created them.

Where words are used metaphorically, care must be taken to preserve metaphorical consistency in what follows. Overused metaphors tend especially to lure writers into error. *See also* FUEL, HURDLE, JEWEL, MILESTONE, PATH, SOOTHE, TAIL, TRAP, UMBRELLA.

might for **may**. 'May' belongs with the present tense, 'might' with the past tense. Perhaps 'may' is more frequently misused than 'might'.

'But try as they might, ministers cannot plausibly explain away all the bad news.' (*The Times*) This should be: *But try as they may, ministers cannot plausibly explain away all the bad news.*

milestone. 'Another milestone in South Africa's progress . . . takes place today.' (*Radio 4*) A milestone cannot 'take place'. *Another milestone in South Africa's progress is reached today.*

militate. *See* MITIGATE.

minimum. *See* MAXIMUM.

Misconnections. A perfectly unexceptional expression can make nonsense if it is wrongly attached to its context.

'At nine, her parents had an amicable divorce.' (*The Times*) Clearly the parents were older than that. *When she was nine, her parents had an am-icable divorce.* Similarly 'His mother died at the age of eight' (*The Times*) should be: *when he was eight.*

'Once dry, I paint in the tree trunks.' (*Artists & Illustrators Magazine*) It is not 'I' who have to be dry, but the paint. *Once the paint is dry, I put in the tree trunks.*

'As part of my job as a Pet Health Counsellor, owners often ask if they should breed from their bitch.' (*Wild About Animals*) The owners do not do anything as part of the speaker's job. 'As part of my job' is wrongly linked with what the owners do. *As part of my job as a Pet Health Coun-sellor, I have to advise owners who ask whether they should breed.*

'As the nights draw in, keep your eyes looking summer bright with our simple tips.' (*Living*) Here the 'tips' are made to sound like cosmetic appliances. The word 'with' establishes a false connection: *keep your eyes looking summer bright by following our simple tips.*

'A cotton screen attached to the top can be dropped down when not in use.' (*Living*) This is self-contradictory: *when the unit is not in use.*

'Startled at the sight of me, the chicken was dropped.' (*Country Lovers Magazine*) But the chicken was not startled. *Startled at the sight of me, the vixen dropped the chicken.*

'Whether it be sitting or standing, this easel is so versatile it will manoeuvre into any position.' (*Artists & Illustrators Magazine*) It is not the easel that sometimes sits: *Whether you are sitting or standing this easel is so versatile.*

'I get my ideas and inspiration and my imagination opens up more as a director than as an actor.' (*Guardian*) The imagination cannot do any-thing as a director or as an actor. Only the speaker can direct or act. *I work more imaginatively as a director than as an actor.*

'Tony Blair's jibes about Britain's "isolation" on this issue unites the latent preacher in the Labour leader with ill-judged opportunism.' (*The Times*) This sentence from a leader unites a grammatical error ('jibes . . . unites') with a subsequent ill-judged mismatch: *Tony Blair's jibes unite the latent preacher with the thoughtless opportunist.*

'The news came as a double blow to the team, firstly because their hopes had been raised by being asked detailed questions about the finances of their planned HQ.' (*The Great Outdoors*) Hopes cannot be raised by being asked questions because no one asks questions of hopes: *their hopes had been raised when they were asked detailed questions.*

misnomer. 'That is a misnomer of an argument.' (*Radio 4*) A 'misnomer' is an incorrect name applied to something. The word cannot be used as an alternative to 'mistake' or 'error' except where the blunder is a matter of nomenclature. *That is a faulty argument.*

miss out on. 'It's too good an opportunity for any knitter to miss out on.' (*Family Circle*) The subject is an offer of cheap wool. As I understand this rather barbarous expression, you might 'miss out on a party', that is, fail unfortunately to experience it. An 'opportunity' is not such an experience, but merely the chance of it, and therefore 'out on' is redundant: *too good an opportunity for any knitter to miss.*

mitigate. Confusion between 'mitigate' (meaning to make less harsh) and 'militate' (meaning to oppose) is now an established feature of journalism.

'Today, the pressures of running the Dashwood Estate mitigate against any such *louche* activities.' (*The Field*) This should be: *Today, the pressures of running the Dashwood Estate militate against any such* louche *activities.*

mixed. 'On the foreign exchanges the pound was mixed.' (*Radio 4*) This is an inexcusable shorthand for 'the fortunes of the pound were mixed'. Why not something really simple and direct: *the pound had its ups and downs*?

mobile. To say that something is mobile is to say that it has freedom of movement. A 'mobile' attitude would be a quickly changing one. Thus to call a phone a 'mobile phone' is inexact. It is like speaking of a 'mobile suitcase'. The thing has to be carried, being of itself totally immobile. We should call it a *portable phone.*

mobilise. 'A big effort is being mobilised to bring it [an epidemic] to an end as soon as possible.' (*Radio 4*) 'Mobilise' is a powerful word used of organising vast military or other national resources in an emergency. It is ill-used here in relation to the vague word 'effort'. *A big effort is being made to bring it to an end.*

modus vivendi. *See* STATUS QUO.

momentary/momentous. In addition to referring to a brief point of time (i), the noun 'moment' is used to mean significance or importance (ii), giving us the expression 'a man of moment' or 'an occasion of great moment'. The adjective 'momentary' derives from sense (i) and means brief: *She had a momentary feeling that she had seen this person before.*

The adjective 'momentous' derives from sense (ii) and means of great import: *Emigrating to Australia proved to be the most momentous act of his life.*

momentous. *See* MOMENTARY.

more. 'More than twenty schools in Kent won't be opening today.' (*Radio* 4) Except in a few instances, we do not follow 'more' with a negative. *More than twenty schools in Kent will be closed today.*

'Water conducts heat from your body 26 times more efficiently as air.' (*Trail*) It is incorrect to say 'He is more greedy as me', when one means 'than me': *26 times more efficiently than water.*

more likely. 'Patients admitted for surgery after fracturing a hip are seven times more likely to die in some hospitals than others.' (*The Times*) There is no patient of whom this statement is true; i.e. that he or she is seven times more likely to die in Glasgow, say, than in Bournemouth. Where the intended comparison is between hospital records, it should not be twisted into a comparison between patients' destinies. *The death-rate from surgery after fractures of the hip is seven times higher in some hospitals than in others.*

more . . . than. The use of the word 'more' in making comparisons has to be so disciplined that what precedes it matches what follows it in grammatical construction.

'Perhaps the reviewers were more impressed by Bogarde's courage than really revelling in the book, but they spoke with a united voice.' (*The Times*) The words 'more impressed by courage' require to be followed by something parallel, 'than by this or that'. What the writer requires here is not the word 'more' but the word 'rather': *Perhaps the reviewers were rather impressed by Bogarde's courage than delighted by his book.*

'Scottish politics and society are deeply divided. They have more parties offering rival panaceas than down South.' (*The Times*) 'They' appears to relate back to 'Scottish politics and society', but surely the subject of the second sentence should be 'The Scots'. Moreover, the comparison between 'They' (whoever they are) and 'down South' will not do. *The Scots have more parties than the English or Welsh* would do. So would *There are more parties here than down South.* The writer must not balance 'They' against 'down South'.

'But in real life Kelly belongs to Tina's 14-year-old daughter Danielle – who's more impressed by her dog being on telly than her mum.'

(*Woman's Own*) This would appear to mean that Danielle is more impressed than her mum is, but the context indicates otherwise: *who is more impressed by her dog's appearance on television than by her mum's.*

most. Neither 'more' nor 'most' should be used where an adjective or adverb has its own comparative and superlative forms ('good, better, best').

'Perhaps the most well-known techniques' (*Steam Railway*) should be: *Perhaps the best-known techniques.*

'Some of the most poorest countries are very sparsely populated.' (*The Times*) This is grammatical overkill. The word 'most' cannot add anything to the word 'poorest' and should go.

'Seattle may be the most rowing city in the nation.' (*Outdoors Illustrated*) Whatever a 'most rowing city' might be, it would not be the same as: *the city with more rowing than any other.*

'Modern engines are heavily researched and tuned to fine limits so very little improvement could be made using most of these [fuel-saving] devices.' (*AA Magazine*) The writer does not really mean that little improvement could result from using 'most of' the devices: *so use of any one of them would, in most cases, bring little improvement.*

motive. 'At times, however, names' motives are elusive.' (*Woman's Journal*) What the writer means is that she cannot explain why parents choose certain names. It is not the names' motives that is in question, but the parents' motives: *what governed the parents' choice is obscure.*

mould. 'Much of the achievements are due to a combination of medication, physical input by the child and an enormous amount of trust that created a two-way confidence mould. The child accepted my trust and this in turn has given rise to development of a lateral confidence structure, a team effort.' (*Good News Magazine*) No one would say 'Much of the races were run'. Even so here it should be: *Most of the achievements are due.* That is only the beginning. Why need the child's response be described as an 'input'? What is a 'two-way mould' even if it is made of confidence? When you are talking about trust between human beings neither moulds nor 'lateral structures' need enter into it: *Most of the achievements are due to a combination of medication, the child's responsiveness and a lot of mutual trust.* The second sentence is redundant.

mount. The verb 'to mount' is used transitively of going up a hill, climbing on to a horse, putting a picture in its setting, or (with male animals) of copulating.

'A case that goes on as long as this one does mount up the costs.' (*Radio 4*) Costs can 'mount' intransitively; but cases cannot 'mount up' them: *does increase the costs*, or *does send the costs up*.

move. 'But the Department for Education stopped short of statutory controls, a move that's drawn much attention.' (*Radio 4*) Stopping short of a certain action does not constitute 'a move'. It is rather a failure to move: *The DoE stopped short of statutory controls and thereby attracted much attention.*

much less. Care must be taken in inserting these words parenthetically. 'If they lose over 1000, much less over 1500 or even up to 2000, they are in deep, deep trouble.' (*Radio 4*) The pollster's comment on Tory prospects in local authority elections is self-contradictory. They are in more, not less, trouble if the loss is greater: *If they lose over 1000, much more so over 1500.*

muffle. 'A successful painting should pull the rug from under you. In Elizabeth Scott's case the pull is muffled, enough to make you stagger about but not enough to remove the carpet.' (*Artists & Illustrators Magazine*) To muffle is to wrap up, and thus to deaden sound: *the pull is too weak*.

N

name. It is important not to confuse the name of a person or place with that person or place.

'Sferia, which is the name of the smaller island, takes about forty-five minutes to circumnavigate on foot.' (*Go Greek*) The 'name' cannot be circumnavigated. *The smaller island called 'Sferia' takes about forty-five minutes to circumnavigate.* Moreover, to 'circumnavigate' is to sail around. A certain freedom can be allowed in stretching the word to cover journeys that are not made by sea, but where the subject is an island the mention of sailing round it is to be avoided. *The smaller island,*

Sferia, takes about forty-five minutes to circumambulate, and if that is too pretentious, make it: *takes about forty-five minutes to walk round.*

'We have 20 books to give away to the first readers' names drawn' (*Wild About Animals*) should be: *to the first readers whose names are drawn*, or: *to the readers whose names are first drawn.*

'Most British accounts of the execution omitted the name of the drug, possibly thinking that it was a new preparation which would mean little to a lay readership.' (*The Times*) Here the writer mixes up the name and the drug. In 'it was a new preparation' he is talking about the drug' but 'which would mean little' refers to the name. 'Which' must go: *possibly thinking that the name of a new preparation would mean little.*

'A number of their leaders have received threatening phone calls from the Al Faran, the name the kidnappers have given themselves.' (*Radio 4*) This is like saying, 'I was born in Sheffield, a two-syllable word'. The Al Faran, which made the phone calls, is not 'the name'. The two must be distinguished. Although: *threatening phone calls from Al Faran (that is what the kidnappers call themselves)* would be correct, it would be better to reshape the sentence: *threatening phone calls from the kidnappers, calling themselves 'Al Faran'.*

'The city's name is derived from the Old English "eel island" and was where Hereward the Wake made his last stand against William the Conqueror.' (*Best of British*) The city's name was not, as this declares, the site of Hereward's last stand. *The city derives its name from the Old English "eel island", and it was where Hereward made his last stand.*

name but a few, to. 'Take Erica, a 27-year-old nurse who is interested in sculpture, mountain climbing and banking, to name but a few.' (*New Woman*) To name but a few what? This is like saying 'We went out shopping and sight-seeing, to name but a few. The word 'few' must be given an anchorage. *Take Erica, a 27-year-old nurse whose interests include sculpture, mountain climbing and banking, to name but a few* (i.e. 'interests').

'Larger openings are for sheep and have attracted some intriguing local terminology, "cripple holes", "thawls", "sheep smooses" and "hunky holes" to name but a few.' (*Country Lovers Magazine*) One cannot speak of 'a few terminology'; 'few' cannot be anchored to 'terminology': *attracted some intriguing local names, 'cripple holes', 'thawls', 'sheep smooses' and 'hunky holes', to cite but a few.*

nationalise / naturalise. To 'nationalise' an industry or an institution is to take it from private hands and bring it under control of the state, under 'public ownership'. The verb to 'naturalise' means what one might have expected the verb 'nationalise' to mean, that is to grant a foreigner the rights of citizenship in their adopted country.

naturalise. *See* NATIONALISE.

nauseous. 'Inhale too much of the gases and you begin to feel light-headed and nauseous'. (*Complete Traveller*) It is what causes nausea that is 'nauseous'. Its effect is nauseating: *and you begin to feel light-headed and nauseated.*

necessary. *See* ESSENTIAL.

necessitate. 'Two major influences on the nurses' communication were the level of consciousness and the amount of physical care being given, necessitating more explanation.' (*Nursing Standard*) This accumulation of unnecessary words provides an object lesson in how not to write. *Nurses find it more demanding to talk to patients who are not fully conscious and to patients very dependent on them physically.*

need. This is a vogue word. People are contradicting themselves in misusing it. Thus a broadcaster, speaking of a 'parent's right to have special educational needs' (*Radio 4*) apparently meant that schools should make *special provisions*, which are the very things which eliminate 'needs'.

'If a child has a special needs requirement' (*Radio 4*) apparently means: *if a child has special needs.*

Negatives. There are some subjects which are normally not followed by verbs in the negative: *see* ALL, ANY, ANYONE. For other misuses of negatives *see* BETTER, CONTRADICTION, SCARCELY. *See also* NEITHER, NO, NOR, NOT, NOT BEING etc.

neither. 'Neither', like 'either', applies to one person or thing. Two people apply for a job, and either of them 'is' suitable, or neither of them 'is' suitable.

'Secondly neither of us were mechanically-minded' (*Complete Traveller*) should be: *neither of us was mechanically-minded.*

'By now, neither are passive, both have a gnawing need to control' (*Sunday Times*) should be: *neither is passive.*

The caption 'Mandy Allwood and her boyfriend, neither of whom countenance abortion' (*The Times*) should be: *neither of whom countenances abortion.*

'Neither of us were involved in any arguments with Baroness Thatcher over the contents of the speech. Neither of us were part of her speech-writing team.' (*The Times*) Perhaps it's as well that these (rather distinguished) correspondents were not so employed. They should have written: *Neither of us was involved . . . Neither of us was part.*

nemesis. 'For decades Professor Colin Blakemore has been the Nemesis of anti-vivisectionists.' (*Radio 4*) Nemesis was the goddess of vengeance and retribution. To meet with her was to get one's final comeuppance. The word seems to be out of place here. *Professor Colin Blakemore has been the scourge of anti-vivisectionists.*

news. 'It would not be bad news for the Conservative prospects at the next election.' (*The Times*) It is permissible to use 'good news' and 'bad news' as expressions of general satisfaction for human beings. But Conservative election prospects cannot receive either good news or bad news. *It would not detract from Conservative prospects at the next election.*

'National Power disclosed that one of its directors . . . has made more than half a million pounds today by cashing his options. The Shadow Chancellor, Gordon Brown, condemned the news.' (*Radio 4*) He did not condemn the 'news'; presumably he was happy to learn the facts of the case; he condemned the events the news recorded: *condemned the action.*

This error is not uncommon. 'The news has been criticised by chemists' organisations' (*Radio 4*) should be: *The action/decision has been criticised by chemists' organisations.*

'He had been given the news of his illness just over a year ago and faced it with considerable courage.' (*Waterways World*) It was probably not the 'news' of his illness that he received as he is likely to have already known he was ill. It was the character of the illness that was disclosed. *He had been given the diagnosis of his illness just over a year ago.*

next. 'He/she must have the vision and energy to work with purchasers and providers to ensure appropriately qualified professionals for the next century.' (*Guardian*) If someone said 'My mother is going to look after baby for the next three weeks', we should understand that the task covered that period. If the person required in the advertisement is going to ensure a suitable supply of staff 'for the next century', he/she is going to have to stay in the job for another hundred years. The words 'for the next century' must be replaced by: *for the future.*

no. Care must be taken in using 'No' as an adjective. 'If anything there

may be a case for tightening fiscal policy now, and definitely no premature tax cuts . . .' (*The Times*) 'There may be a case for' cannot introduce
'no tax cuts'. The sentence should read: *If anything there may be a case
for tightening fiscal policy now: but definitely not for premature tax
cuts.*

'But some of the insecurity . . . reflects the short-term impact of the reduction in inflation and the adjustment to low increases, or no increases,
in nominal earnings.' (*The Times*) It is at best infelicitous to speak of adjustment to 'no increases': *impact of the reduction in inflation and the adjustment to low increases or to the lack of increases in nominal earnings.*

'The study of 9704 ambulatory women aged 63 years or older points
to a link between osteopenia and death from stroke, which is stronger
when risk factors, including previous stroke, hypertension, diabetes,
smoking or no post-menopausal oestrogen use, are taken into account.'
(*Nursing Standard*) The same misuse of 'no' calls for the same correction
here: *when risk factors, including hypertension, diabetes, smoking or the
lack/absence of post-menopausal oestrogen use are taken into account.*

no exception. These words should be used only after some generalisation which is exemplified by what the writer has to say. 'English people
like roast beef: John Bull is no exception.'

Increasingly the words are being used simply as a means of affirmative
emphasis. 'It would be hard to find anyone who could fail to fall in love
with the lush beauty of Barbados and the two lovers were no exception.'
(*OK! News*) The rule which the lovers exemplify must be clearly cited.
*People easily fall in love with the lush beauty of Barbados and the two
lovers were no exception.*

The expression must be clearly attached to the generalisation it refers
to. 'In inner city areas like this officers say criminals are increasingly willing not just to carry but to use weapons. PC Morgan is no exception.'
(*Radio 4*) It almost sounds as though PC Morgan shares the criminals'
interest in weapons. *PC Morgan agrees that this is so.*

The expression must not be used as a mere alternative to 'This applies here'. 'Life is more fun when interests are shared, and painting
holidays are no exception' (*Artists & Illustrators Magazine*) should be:
*Life is more fun when interests are shared, and this applies to painting
holidays.*

no question of. 'There can be no question of Salamat and Rehmat now
returning to their village.' (*The Times*) The gerciple ('of Salamat returning') should be a gerund ('of Salamat's returning'). The awkwardness can

easily be avoided by using 'no question that', followed by a negative. *There can be no question that Salamat and Rehmat cannot now return to their village.*

no stranger to. 'Yadav is no stranger to being charged at by the beasts he does his best to protect.' (*Hello!*) Yadav is a rhinoceros. It is surely pretentious to introduce the cliché 'no stranger to' here. *Yadav is quite used to being charged at by the beasts he does his best to protect.*

nominee. 'British nominees surprise Oscar pundits.' (*The Times*) This headline misrepresents what follows where it is made clear that it was not the nominees who surprised anyone but their nomination. *British nominations surprise Oscar pundits.*

none. 'None', like 'either' and 'neither', applies to one person or thing. Several people apply for a post, but none 'is' suitable.

'None of the tall medieval towers were cut down to serve as artillery emplacements' (*History Today*) should be: *None of the tall medieval towers was cut down.*

'None of the ministers in charge of big spending departments are likely to be willing cutters' (*The Times*) should be: *None of the ministers in charge of big spending departments is likely to be a willing cutter.*

'As none of them are financial high-flyers it is not easy for them' (*Money Observer*) should be: *as none of them is a financial high-flyer.*

nor. 'Just as someone doesn't want to carry around all their money when they go out, nor do they necessarily want to keep large amounts on their Mondex card.' (*Meridian*) 'Nor' is the equivalent of 'and not', and the words cannot balance 'just as'. It would be incorrect to say 'Just as I don't like tomatoes, nor do I like cabbage'. 'Nor' must be replaced by 'so'. *Just as someone doesn't want to carry around all their money when they go out, so they do not necessarily want to keep large amounts on their Mondex card.*

not. 'If a relationship is, on balance, giving you more than it's not, then it's probably worth staying.' (*New Woman*) It would be absurd to say 'If we have more money than we haven't, then we're solvent'. What we don't have is not measurable. If we have anything at all then we have more than we haven't. *If a relationship is, on balance, giving you something, then it's probably worth staying.*

not being. 'We disliked the house being built there' and 'We disliked the house not being built there' are equally inelegant and, to the pedant, incorrect (passive gerciples). 'The final value of the car . . . is dependent on an agreed mileage limit not being exceeded and return-ing the car in good condition.' (*Meridian*) It appears here that it is the mileage limit that returns the car in good condition. Into such difficul-ties does use of the passive gerciple lead. *The final value of the car de-pends on keeping within an agreed mileage limit and returning the car in good condition.*

not just. This expression (like 'not only') serves as a hinge on which a parallel construction hangs. We say 'She campaigns not just against alcohol but also against tobacco', and the words 'not just' function prop-erly because there is parallelism between 'against alcohol' and 'against tobacco'.

'Always clean your clothes before putting them away, not just in the wardrobe, but also when storing clothes for the end of the season.' (*OK! Homes*) 'Not just in the wardrobe' logically demands a parallel, such as 'but also in the dust-bin'. What the writer means is rather: *Always clean your clothes, not only when you put them away briefly in the wardrobe, but also when you store them at* [not 'for'] *the end of the season.*

'Workmanship is not just good, its quality is effortless and achieved without ostentatious joinery detailing.' (*Waterways World*) 'Workman-ship is not just good' demands to be followed by a further parallel com-ment on the workmanship ('not just good, but beautiful'). Here the workmanship is forgotten and the subject becomes 'its quality', but whether the two descriptions that follow ('effortless and achieved with-out ostentatious joinery detailing') can equally well define that 'quality' is questionable. Re-writing is required. *Workmanship is good: it has an effortless quality achieved without any ostentatious detail in the joinery.*

not least. 'He disappointed many people, not least his parents' illus-trates the proper use of 'not least'.

'But, as it was, his participation in the South Dorset by-election left an indelible black mark against his name, not least in Conservative Central office.' (*The Times*) There are degrees of being disappointed, but indeli-ble black marks do not lend themselves to being scaled. 'Not least' is not a ready alternative to 'especially': *left an indelible black mark against his name, notably/especially in Conservative Central office.*

not only. Like 'not just', this expression serves as a hinge on which parallel constructions hang. We say 'She campaigns not only against abortion but also against euthanasia', and the words 'not only' function properly because there is parallelism between 'against abortion' and 'against euthanasia'.

'Here is a place where you'll not only find his heart but somewhere he retreats to.' (*OK! Homes*) The parallelism between 'his heart' and 'somewhere' is awkward. Moreover the words 'not only' are misplaced against the verb 'find'. *Here is a place where you'll find not only his heart but his favourite retreat.*

'It seems appropriate that 1992, the designated annus mirabilis for European unity, not only seems to have more continental travel offering a historic theme than before but also more concerned (and able) to make the connections between East and West.' (*History Today*) 'Not only seems to have this' must logically be followed by something like 'but also seems to have that'. Since 'not only' precedes 'seems', 'but also' must precede the same or a parallel verb. It is incorrect to write 'James not only seems to have more potatoes but also more hungry', which is virtually the error our writer makes. *It seems appropriate that 1992 . . . not only seems to have more continental travel offering a historic theme than before, but also gives evidence of a greater concern (and ability) to make the connections between East and West.*

'Careless use of the dampers could not only cause the fire to burn too vigorously, wasting fuel, but the intense heat wore out parts more rapidly and which were costly to repair.' (*Old-House Journal*) The words 'not only cause' should be followed by a parallel, 'but also cause' (or some other verb). The words 'but the intense heat wore out parts' thus belong to a different sentence from what precedes them. The words 'and which' introduce a further incongruous construction. *Careless use of the dampers could cause the fire to burn too vigorously, wasting fuel, and could also produce a heat intense enough to wear out costly parts too rapidly.*

'These recommendations have already been used as a pre-emptive argument against not only public demands for wider access, but even against the extension of existing access arrangements.' (*The Great Outdoors*) The placing of 'not only' is crucial. If it follows 'against' and precedes 'public demands' then the word 'against' must not be repeated. Here it should precede 'against': *argument not only against public demands for wider access, but even against the existing access arrangements.*

'Kindersley not only designed spacing systems but also half a dozen typefaces.' (*The Times*) 'Not only' is misplaced before 'designed'. *Kindersley designed not only spacing systems but also half a dozen typefaces.*

not so much. 'The damage was done not so much by inadequate growth, but rather by a mysterious change in economic behaviour.' (*The Times*) Correct usage here would follow the pattern 'He was beaten not so much by superior force as by superior know-how'. 'Not so much' cannot be followed by 'but rather'. The first construction must be completed. *The damage was done not so much by inadequate growth as by a mysterious change in economic behaviour.*

The grammatical construction of a sentence must not suggest a contrast or antithesis which does not exist. This is one of the expressions (like 'although') which naturally introduce contrasts: 'He was not so much weary as disappointed'. The two states, weariness and disappointment, must not be confused even though they may have manifestations in common.

'An appeal for "King" parts . . . was not so much hopeful as a matter of plain financial commonsense.' (*Steam Railway*) There is no relationship of contrast between being hopeful and exercising financial common sense. In fact the word 'hopeful' is the wrong one and must go. *An appeal for 'King' parts . . . was not so much a matter of pious aspiration as of sheer financial common sense.*

nothing can beat. 'Nothing can beat a C of E boarding education for knowing your Old Testament quotes.' (*Private Eye*) The boarding school is here said to be good at knowing quotes. *Nothing can beat a C of E boarding education for teaching you Old Testament quotes.*

notwithstanding. This word is most often a preposition. 'I took my walk, notwithstanding the rain.' Sometimes it is used as an adverb. 'I took my walk notwithstanding.' It is rarely used as a conjunction.

'Its mellow limestone makes it appear a place almost unchanged by the 20th century, notwithstanding double yellow lines and the M4 missing it by a whisker.' (*Heritage*) Here the preposition introduces 'double yellow lines', which should be paralleled in construction after 'and': *notwithstanding double yellow lines and the close proximity of the M4.*

Nouns. Nouns, the words by which we refer to persons, objects and places, present few difficulties to us because in English they are uninflected, that is to say, a noun does not change its form according to its grammatical function. (There is a relic of former Anglo-Saxon inflexion in the apostrophe 's' of the genitive case: 'the dog's dinner'.) The only change is from singular to plural. Most plurals are formed by simply adding '-s' ('book', 'books') or, in the case of nouns ending in '-y', changing the '-y' to '-ies' ('difficulty', 'difficulties'). A few nouns (but some of them much used) are irregular in this respect ('man', 'men'; 'woman', 'women'; 'mouse', 'mice'; 'sheep', 'sheep'). For the difference between 'common' and 'proper' nouns *see* CAPITAL LETTERS. *See also* NOUNS IN EXCESS, NOUNS USED AS ADJECTIVES.

Nouns in Excess. The tendency to overuse nouns (to the neglect of verbs) is to be deplored because of its weakening effect on utterance. Avoidance of verbs destroys the vigour of language. Similarly the tendency to turn nouns into pseudo-adjectives rigidifies utterance.

'This challenging position offers career development potential coupled with industry exposure at the highest levels.' (*The Times*) The words 'career', 'development' and 'potential' are all nouns. So are the words 'industry' and 'exposure'. Let us translate the sentence into English. *In this post you will have the chance to rise and to work with senior management in industry.*

'The Association of Waterways Cruising Clubs is also opposing the speed of introduction of the requirement for existing craft to comply with BW standards.' (*Waterways World*) 'Speed . . . of introduction . . . of requirement': the accumulation of nouns is a dead weight on the utterance. *The Association of Waterways Cruising Clubs does not want the move to require existing craft to comply with BW standards to be hastily implemented.*

'It is Peter's view of re-establishment of a number of interdependent forestry-based crafts that is at the heart of what he is doing.' (*Cumbria Life*) The good thing here is that the writer wrote 'that is at the heart of what he is doing' instead of using some noun ('that is at the heart of his activities'). The bad thing is that he did not begin his sentence in the same vein, avoiding 'view of re-establishment'. *It is Peter's desire to reestablish a number of interdependent forestry-based crafts that is at the heart of what he is doing.*

Nouns too readily spring to the mind when what is required is a construction involving a verb. *See* OCCURRENCE.

Nouns used as Adjectives. If a noun is used as an adjective, it must not be referred back to as though it were a noun. 'Betty's latest project is a book on Essex ghosts, a county renowned for its goblins and fairies.' (*Country Talk*) In 'Essex ghosts' the word 'Essex' is used adjectivally. Grammatically speaking, there is no mention of Essex to which the words 'a county renowned' could be applied. There is a simple way of correcting this. *Betty's latest project is a book on* *the ghosts of Essex, a county renowned for its goblins and fairies.*

'The Trafalgar price has plunged from the 70p level since it first made its aborted bid for Northern Electric.' (*The Times*) But the price did not make a bid. 'Trafalgar', qualifying 'price' adjectivally, cannot be referred back to as 'it' and then govern a verb. *The price of Trafalgar has plunged from the 70p level since it first made its aborted bid.*

nuance. This is a useful noun meaning a subtle distinction.

'The aim was to show that the differences between the Chancellor and the Governor were generally nuanced.' (*Guardian*) This is not a happy innovation. There is no verb 'to nuance', and if there were it would surely not work thus: *the differences between the Chancellor and the Governor were generally a matter of nuance.*

number. 'The hunt is on, then, for a policy that relieves the pain of negative equity without infuriating an equal or greater number of voters.' (*The Times*) Equal or greater number than what? There is no such thing as a greater number of voters than the pain of negative equity: *a policy that relieves the pain of those suffering from negative equity without infuriating an equal or greater number of voters.*

nutrition. 'They developed a conceptual model for communicating nutrition, with the focus on the "audience" or "receiver" of information.' (*Nursing Standard*) Can nutrition be communicated? It appears that 'they' wanted to improve the eating habits of patients, and it would be better if they had left it at that.

O

objective. 'Of the three objectives Ron set for the festival, the first two were demonstrably successful.' (*Waterways World*) An objective is a goal or aim. It can be successfully achieved but it is not itself thereby 'successful'. *Of the three objectives the first two were clearly attained.*

objectivity. 'An article about the Queen . . . should warn the reader of the author's objectivity.' (*The Times*) If an author is 'objective', his views are undistorted by personal prejudice. No warning is needed where there is objectivity. The writer seemingly means the opposite of what he has said: *should warn the reader about the author's possible lack of objectivity.*

oblivious. 'By dinnertime in Pali official Bosnian Serb radio was seemingly oblivious to the news known to the rest of the world.' (*Radio 4*) Strictly 'oblivious' means forgetful and is followed by 'of' not by 'to', but to say 'oblivious of the news' would highlight the unsuitability of using here a word that connotes forgetfulness. *By dinnertime in Pali official Bosnian Serb radio was seemingly unaware of the news known to the rest of the world.*

obsess. 'When you're not obsessing about whether he'll still adore you when you put on weight . . .' (*Company*) To obsess is to preoccupy with intensity: *When you're not obsessed about whether he'll still adore you.*

obstacle. 'These two men are the obstacle to Mr Major setting out a sensible position for a fifth term.' (*The Times*) The word 'obstacle' lures the writer to use the illicit gerciple ('to Mr Major setting out'). Abstract nouns such as 'obstacle' can often be better replaced by verbs: *These two men prevent Mr Major from setting out a sensible position.*

obtuse. 'An IRA statement about yesterday's murder was pointedly obtuse. It neither condoned nor condemned the killing.' (*Radio 4*) An 'obtuse' person is a mentally slow one, not one who prevaricates or is non-committal. *An IRA statement about yesterday's murder was intentionally (notably?) ambiguous (obscure?).*

occasioned by. 'This historical anomaly was occasioned by the Coventry Canal Company running short of money.' (*Waterways World*) The expression 'occasioned by' (as an alternative to 'caused by') is clumsy at the best of times. If it is used it must not be followed by a gerciple ('Company running short'). Correct but crude would be: *occasioned by the Coventry Canal's running short of money.* It is best to change the construction. *This historical anomaly arose when the Coventry Canal Company ran short of money.*

occurrence. 'Few people have ever seen a live mole but their occurrence along a canal bank can easily be confirmed by the presence of earthen mounds heaved up during their excavations.' (*Waterways World*) Here the writer seizes on the noun 'occurrence' when he really means 'the fact that they occur'; but the two expressions are not synonymous. In any case do animals 'occur'? Surely they live, they inhabit an area, they appear, but they do not 'occur'. Again, to talk about 'presence' being 'confirmed' is to talk like an old-fashioned stage policeman. Moreover, 'their' in the plural cannot refer back to 'a live mole'. *Few people have ever seen a live mole, but that moles live along canal banks is proved by the earthen mounds left over from their excavations.*

of. See FOR.

official / officious. The adjective 'official' is used of what relates to an office and its administration, and therefore of what is sanctioned by authority: *They received from the local authority an official notice to quit.* The adjective 'officious' is used of people who are quite unnecessarily forward in offering advice or assistance: *My new neighbour was somewhat officious in instructing me where I should keep my dust bin and how often I should mow my lawn.*

officious. See OFFICIAL.

often. 'Often' should not too readily be used as the equivalent of 'in many cases'. Its strict temporal connotation ought not to be lost sight of.

'Moreover, as they are often sited in some of our most beautiful countryside, holiday parks must blend in with their surroundings.' (*Caravan Magazine*) There is really no question of frequency here. If it is 'often the case' that holiday parks are sited in beautiful areas, that does not mean that the parks are 'often sited' there. A park is sited here or there once and for all. *However, as they tend to be sited in some of our most beautiful countryside, holiday parks must blend in with their surroundings.*

'I prefer the scented sharpness of the small alpine strawberry to the only too often blandness of the large-fruited kind.' (*The Field*) 'Often' is an adverb, not an adjective like 'frequent'. One can say 'It is often stated', but one cannot refer to 'the often statement': *the only too frequent blandness.*

omnipresent. This word means what it appears to mean, 'present everywhere'.

'I managed a cold shower (just), helped chop some logs for the omnipresent woodburning stove and marvelled at the toilet.' (*Complete Traveller*) The writer does not mean that a woodburning stove has the supernatural capacity to be present everywhere at once, but that is what he conveys. He is purposely using hyperbole, of course. Nevertheless what he means is, presumably, that the model of stove is found everywhere: *the ubiquitous woodburning stove.*

on. There is a useful construction involving 'on': 'On hearing the bad news, we decided to leave'. This usage gives to 'on hearing' the significance of 'when we heard'. There is also in the connotation a slight implicit causal element: hearing the news caused us to make the decision we did. This slight causal element ought not to be separated from the mainly temporal connotation involved in such usages as 'on hearing the first cuckoo in spring'.

'Many European and north American paper producers actually incurred substantial losses in 1991 as paper grade prices fell on weakening demand and new capacity.' (*Investors Chronicle*) Something can fall on the floor, or can just fall, but nothing can fall on a demand: *as paper grade prices fell because of weakening demand.*

on a par with. 'Some underwriters virtually double the premium [for a boat that is lived in], while others will keep premiums on a par with pleasure craft, but refuse to insure the contents.' (*Waterways World*) The premiums are not 'on a par' with pleasure craft but with the premiums for pleasure craft: *while others will keep premiums on a par with those for pleasure craft.*

on entering. It is correct to say 'On entering the room, the stranger was baffled by what he saw' because 'on entering' is related to 'the stranger'. It is incorrect to say 'On entering the room, the vivid wallpaper exuded brightness' because the wallpaper did not enter the room.

'The Staplehurst is the four-bedroom executive home on Shires meadow, with many special features, not least the inglenook fireplace, which makes an impressive focal point on entering the room.' (*Perfect Home*) The fireplace does not enter the room and therefore this is incorrect: *which makes an impressive focal point as one enters the room.*

once. There is a useful idiom that allows us to say 'Once back home, we laughed with relief.' Its justification depends on the connection established by 'once' between 'back home' and 'we'. This connection must be clear and sure.

'Once a well-known poet, Martyn Skinner's fame had faded with the years.' (*The Times*) His 'fame' was never a well-known poet. *Once a well-known poet, Martyn Skinner had seen his fame fade with the years.* (The error exemplifies the POSSESSIVE TRAP.)

'Once there, breathless and red-faced, it was all worthwhile for again the birds came speeding over.' (*Shooting Times*) Who arrived 'there, breathless and red-faced'? According to the grammatical construction 'it' did. An appropriate subject is needed: *Once there, breathless and red-faced, we found it all worthwhile.*

'And, he warns, once inside your garden, the house itself may look more promising.' (*Perfect Home*) The passage is about the way thieves get into property. As the wording stands, it is the house that finds itself 'once inside the garden'. The reader needs to know who is. *Once inside the garden, the thief will find the house more promising.*

once bitten, twice shy. This expression illustrates a convenient usage of 'once'. It is an abbreviated way of saying 'Once a person is bitten, he will be doubly cautious'. The person who is 'bitten' is of course the person who is 'shy'.

one. 'Step inside a New York theatre this season, and one finds an array of divas whose like Manhattan has not seen in an age.' (*The Times*) The pronoun 'one' cannot be used indiscriminately as an alternative to 'you', 'I', or 'me'. All imperative forms of the verb function as the second person of the verb functions. It would be correct to say 'Inside a New York theatre one finds an array' but the order 'Step inside' is the equivalent of 'You step inside': *Step inside a New York theatre and you find an array of divas.*

one in six. The singular verb is used after this construction. 'Only one in six women get the full state pension' (*Prima*) should be: *Only one in six women gets the full state pension.*

one of. 'At one time people would regard museums as being dull. In recent years things have changed and they have become one of the most popular places to visit.' (*Camping*) 'They . . . have become one of the most' is grammatically awkward. 'They' requires a plural equivalent: *they have become some of the most popular places to visit.*

only. 'Only' is a word which has to be carefully placed. 'I only came here yesterday' is slack for 'I came here only yesterday'.

'The slates have helped to date the house: the shallow pitch of the roof shows that they are the original roofing material, and such slates were only brought to Cirencester after the opening of the canal linking the Severn and the Thames in 1789.' (*Traditional Homes*) Here is a clear case. The slates were not 'only brought after' the date defined, they were *brought only after the opening of the canal in 1789.*

'Although it was used regularly in the cooking of Spain and Italy, the rest of Europe thought of sweetcorn as only fit for animals.' (*Hello!*) The corn was not 'only fit', it was *fit only for animals*.

'The responsibility lies with the mediators. . . who have so far only come up with a plan acceptable to the Bosnians' (*Radio 4*) should be: *have so far come up with a plan acceptable only to the Bosnians*.

Sometimes misplacing 'only' seriously affects the meaning. 'Although only chairman of the company for two years' (*The Times*) implies that all he managed to be was chairman, which is not what was intended: *Although chairman of the company for only two years*.

onwards. 'From the Prime Minister and the Leader of the Opposition onwards, politics will immediately subsume the decision.' (*The Times*) One could understand the words 'From tomorrow onwards', or perhaps even 'From the Prime Minister and the Leader of the Opposition downwards', if their political followers are being referred to. As it is, the word 'onwards' is incomprehensible.

opinion. 'Expert opinion in Moscow and London give us their views.' (*Radio 4*) This use of 'opinion' to mean a body of people requires a singular verb ('Expert opinion is against the idea'). Here the word is followed by 'give' and is anyway not needed. *Experts in Moscow and London give us their views*.

opt out. The verb 'to opt' is now overused. Whereas 'to choose' can have an object ('We choose freedom'), 'to opt' is intransitive ('We opt *for* the alternative proposal').

'A further 450,000 had been encouraged to opt out their present company [pension] schemes.' (*The Times*) As one cannot 'opt' anything, so one cannot 'opt out' anything. *A further 450,000 had been encouraged to opt out of their present company schemes*.

'Others are totally confused and opt straight out of the fashion/style equation.' (*Options*) The notion of opting out of an equation is bizarre. The verb or the noun must be changed. *Others are totally confused and reject the fashion/style equation*.

or. It is surprising that the word 'or' can be so variously misused as it is.

'OR' AND NEGATIVE 'Rape or buggery are not shown on the videos.' (*The Times*) It is incorrect to say 'My wife or I will not attend' when what is meant is 'Neither my wife nor I will attend'. A negative verb cannot be used after 'or'. *Neither rape nor buggery is shown on the videos*.

'MORI or Gallup do not even bother to test the electorate.' (*The*

Times) 'Or' is again totally out of place in this leader. *Neither MORI nor Gallup bothers even to test the electorate.*

'OR' FOR 'AND' 'Why not music? After all, I know who really wrote the *St Louis Blues* or Purcell's *Trumpet Voluntary.*' (*New Statesman*) The writer good-humouredly wants to know why he is never given music as a topic in Trivial Pursuit. We do not say 'I know this or that' when what we mean is that we know both. Here 'or' should be replaced by: *and.* 'Or' could be kept only if the main verb were changed: *I could tell them who wrote the* St Louis Blues *or Purcell's* Trumpet Voluntary.

Similarly 'Although we know that penicillin can cure pneumonia or that a hip replacement will greatly improve an arthritic patient's quality of life' (*Living*) should be: *that penicillin can cure pneumonia and that a hip replacement will greatly improve the quality of life.*

PRESERVING PARALLELISM Parallelism must be preserved before and after 'or'. 'Some of these senses are relatively easy for us to comprehend, such as the heightened hearing of a cat . . . or the wheeling hawk with eyesight so keen that it can spot a mouse . . .' (*Wild About Animals*) Bring the alternative after 'or' into balance with what precedes it: *the heightened hearing of a cat or the keen eyesight of the wheeling hawk.*

THE CONDITIONAL 'OR' 'More large demonstrations are expected tomorrow . . . and today's explosion is being seen as a warning to the population not to take part or to face more violent consequences.' (*Radio 4*) In 'I order you not to take part or to lend support' the meaning of 'or' is clear. You are warned not to do either of two things. In the sentence quoted 'or' does not introduce any such parallel alternative. A conditional construction is required: *today's explosion is being seen as a warning to the population that if they take part they will face more violent consequences.*

oral. *See* AURAL.

ordain. 'The Type 2 diesel specification as envisaged and ordained as a result of BR Modernisation Plan of 1995 . . .' (*Railway Modeller*) To 'ordain' is to consecrate or establish and the word carries a flavour of dignity. It is improperly applied to the plan for a diesel locomotive: *The Type 2 diesel specification as envisaged and approved under the BR Modernisation Plan.*

order. 'An unprecedented attack on credit cards fraud has been ordered to fight the "crime of the Nineties".' (*Daily Mail*) One might order a person to fight, but one would not 'order' an attack to fight. *An* *unprecedented attack on credit card fraud has been launched in order to fight the 'crime of the Nineties'.*

origin. 'The origin of why chapels were built on bridges is obscure.' (*Waterways World*) The word 'origin' is out of place. What is meant is: *The reason why chapels were first built on bridges is obscure*, or better still: *Why chapels were first built on bridges is obscure.*

originating. 'The "summer" hosts numerous rides starting with the 26 mile "Chilly Hilly" that tours the islands of Puget Sound utilising the Seattle originating public ferry system.' (*Outdoors Illustrated*) It is bad to pile other parts of speech together to constitute a kind of compound adjective. The words 'Seattle originating public ferry' function together thus in relation to the noun 'system'. The abuse of the word 'originating' is particularly gross: *utilising the public ferries that start from Seattle.*

other. The word 'other' reflects back on something already mentioned and must do so accurately.

'There has long been concern about the vetting of people employed to care for children and other vulnerable adults.' (*Radio 4*) It is incorrect to speak of children 'and other adults' because children are not adults. Either 'other' must be omitted or adults' must be changed: *children and other vulnerable people.*

'They rescued a 28-year-old man from a lift. He was taken to the Manchester Royal Infirmary and later transferred to the Intensive Care Unit at Withington Hospital. Two other women were taken to hospital with minor burns.' (*Radio 4*) Only a man has been mentioned when 'other' women are referred to, so the word 'other' must go. *Two women also were taken to hospital.*

'Although a Sudbury Vale Group meeting, other enthusiasts will be welcome as this should prove a worthwhile meeting.' (*Old Glory*) One might say 'Although a working man, he was very rich' because 'Although a working man' attaches itself to 'he'. But one would not say 'Although a working man, other relations were rich', where 'although a working man' is left hanging in the air' and 'other relations' makes nonsense because 'relations' have not been mentioned. Likewise 'Although a Sudbury Vale Group meeting' has no connection with 'other enthusiasts', words which could be used only if there had already been mention of some enthusiasts. *Although it is a Sudbury Vale Group meeting, enthusiasts who are not members of the group will be welcome.*

other than. 'Other than get married and having kids this is the finest thing a man can ever do, to build his own house.' (*The Times*) The three constructions after 'other than' must match. *Other than to get married and to have kids, this is the finest thing a man can ever do, to build his own house.*

'Nowadays, as a number of well-regarded manufacturers are proving, there are other materials worth considering other than Gore-Tex.' (*Outdoors Illustrated*) The repetition of 'other' is bad. It is best to change the order here: *there are materials other than Gore-Tex worth considering.*

otherwise. In 'Take an umbrella; otherwise you will get wet', the word is equivalent to 'or else'. In 'I myself would have acted otherwise', it means 'in a different way'.

'Vested interest should always have a question mark raised over it, not least when it seeks to stamp on the efforts of scientists who sincerely believe otherwise.' (*The Times*) Otherwise than what? The sentence appears to say that vested interest should be questioned, especially by scientists who sincerely believe that vested interest should not be questioned. That is self-contradictory. *Vested interest should always have a question mark raised over it, not least when it seeks to stamp on the efforts of scientists who challenge it.*

ours. *See* HERS.

out of all recognition. This is an expression which acts as an intensifier in relation to certain verbs: 'He was changed out of all recognition'. But it cannot act thus in relation to any verb one chooses.

'Certainly Ulrika's respect for her husband increased out of all recognition over his handling of the crisis in their marriage.' (*OK! Magazine*) The expression is out of place: *Ulrika's respect for her husband increased immensely.*

out of sorts. This expression is used of someone who is not in normal health. A party politician, commenting on a bad by-election result said, 'It's silly to try to find a scapegoat for the fact that our natural supporters are out of sorts with us, or we are out of sorts with our natural supporters.' (*Radio 4*) She used the wrong phrase: *the fact that our natural supporters are out of sympathy/step with us.*

outshop. *See* COINAGES.

overcome. 'In an effort to overcome lingering territorial disputes senior American officials have been meeting the presidents of the countries involved.' (*Radio 4*) A dispute is not something that has to be conquered ('overcome'): *In an effort to resolve the lingering territorial disputes.*

overdue. 'Askja's last eruption was in 1961, and it is now overdue.' (*Outdoors Illustrated*) It is true that the next eruption will be able to be called the 'last' once it has occurred, but not until. In any case the eruption that occurred in 1961 is not the eruption that is overdue: *and the next is now overdue.*

overpower. To overpower someone is to render them ineffective by superior force.

'He could overpower the most hostile situation.' (*Independent*) Situations are not like people: they cannot be 'overpowered'. A better word would be 'master' or 'cope with', or better still, perhaps: *He could handle the most hostile situation.*

overreach. 'But I think in this case he [Saddam Hussein] may have overreached his hand.' (*Radio 4*) On the spur of the moment the speaker seems to have mixed up two expressions. To overplay one's hand is to overestimate the strength of one's position. To overreach (oneself) is to thwart oneself by biting off more than one can chew: *But I think in this case he may have overreached himself.*

overspent. 'A survey shows that one in three self-governing trusts are already overspent.' (*The Times*) To 'be' overspent is to be exhausted. If a trust has spent too much it will not necessarily 'be' overspent; it may be quite fresh. *A survey shows that one in three trusts has already overspent.*

overstay. 'The Home Office says X and Y have overstayed their permission to be in Britain.' (*Radio 4*) It is not the 'permission' that has been overstayed but the permitted period: *overstayed their permitted period in Britain.*

owing to. *See* DUE TO.

P

paint. 'He is unrepentant, shrugging off the bad boy image the Democrats have painted him with.' (*Radio 4*) One may paint with a paint brush but scarcely with a bad boy image. The metaphor does not come off here. *He is unrepentant, shrugging off the bad boy image the Democrats have attributed to him.* If an alternative metaphor is required it could be: *pinned on him*, or: *clothed him with*.

'Leaded glass was prohibitively expensive, so one building in North Carolina painted its simple panes in lozenge patterns.' (*World of Interiors*) Buildings cannot paint: *so one building had its simple panes painted in lozenge patterns.*

pander. 'It is not merely pandering for Irish-American votes.' (*Radio 4*) To pander to someone is to play up to their taste or weakness, 'Pander' is never followed by 'for'. *It is not merely pandering to the Irish-American electorate.*

Parallels that Fail to Match. If two items are linked in 'apposition', as in 'John Smith, the butcher, lives here', it is important that the second ('the butcher') should fully match the first ('John Smith'). In its crudest form, failure to match produces absurdity.

'A keen fisherman, the peace of the River Test was an antidote to a stormy marriage.' (*Hunting*) This turns the peace of the River Test into a keen fisherman. There must be a word to parallel 'keen fisherman'. *A keen fisherman, he found in the peace of the River Test an antidote to a stormy marriage.*

Similarly 'A Yorkshireman and a professional, time off from work is not to be wasted' (*Hunting*) turns time off into a Yorkshireman. *A Yorkshireman and a professional, he does not waste what time he has off from work.*

Sometimes the failure in parallelism is a grammatical failure. 'Even today, 50-year-old double-deckers are still in jeopardy from the elements, both weather and human.' (*Best of British*) The noun 'weather' cannot parallel the adjective 'human'. Two adjectives must be used: *still in jeopardy from the elements, both natural and human.*

More complex errors are less easily detected. 'Nowhere has the preoccupation with monetary union been more pervasive than in France, a once dynamic economy that has been transformed.' (*The Times*) France is not 'an economy' but a country. *Nowhere has the preoccupation with monetary union been more pervasive than in France, whose once dynamic economy has been transformed.*

Sometimes the word 'as', in opening a sentence, introduces a mismatch. 'As a newly wed it was the Queen Mother's favourite holiday home.' (*OK! Homes*) This speaks of 'it' [Birkhall on the Balmoral Estate] as being a newly wed, for the description cannot attach to anything else mentioned. *As a newly wed, the Queen Mother made it her favourite holiday home.*

'The South African sections [of a novel] are utterly convincing: a country he has never visited.' (*The Times*) The 'country' has not been mentioned. It is incorrect to say 'I like South African oranges, a country I have never visited' because oranges are not a country. *The sections on South Africa, a country he has never visited, are utterly convincing.*

part. This word is used for a portion of a whole. It is an impersonal term that is not very happily used when the whole in question is a body of people, although one might say 'Part of the army was deployed at home' where 'army' is a collective and readily divisible into official sections.

'Down on the street everything got a little scruffier, but the great part of the passengers using it knew little of the Seven Sisters Road and its long decline.' (*British Railways Illustrated*) Here the writer is speaking of attitudes held by a number of people, and 'part' is quite inappropriate: *but most of the passengers using it knew little of the Seven Sisters Road.*

'Murray Stewart and Jonathon Gould, and an unidentified person inside British Aerospace, were part of a plot to channel funds from the company into an off-shore account.' (*The Times*) An assassination might be 'part of a plot' but not human beings. There is an obvious construction available. *Murray Stewart and Jonathon Gould, and an unidentified person inside British Aerospace, took part in a plot.*

'I've often heard it said that the acquisition of adult pleasures is one of the more comforting parts of growing old.' (*Daily Telegraph*) Growing old cannot be divided into 'parts'. It's a process, not a machine: *the acquisition of adult pleasures is one of the more comforting aspects of growing old.*

'For many of us, the most wonderful part of Christmas Day is the children.' (*NSPCC*) A day can be divided into hours and minutes, but it cannot be divided into children: *what gives us most delight on Christmas Day is the children.*

'UN officials said he had been seized because of a local dispute and not part of the hostage-taking.' (*Radio 4*) 'He' could scarcely be 'part' of the hostage-taking: *He had been seized because of a local dispute and not as one of the hostages.*

'As part of its return from the West Highland line to its base in Carnforth, Stanier "Black 5" No5407 headed a Scottish Railway Society special over the Forth Bridge on January 4.' (*Steam Classic*) What is 'part' of the return? 'Return journey' might be better, but the word 'part' is not worth rescuing: *While returning from the West Highland line to its base in Carnforth.*

Participles. Current usage is plagued by mishandled participles.

'Sitting in cinemas, my knees are usually knocking the seat in front.' (*The Times*) The knees are not 'sitting' and must not be so described. Either the present participle 'sitting' must have something to agree with: *Sitting in the cinema, I find my knees knocking the seat in front*, or it must be scrapped: *When I sit in the cinema, my knees knock the seat in front.*

The past participle is similarly misused. 'Educated until 17 at Sherborne School, his archaeological experience was developed in that part of the Wessex chalklands whose prehistory was to draw him throughout his life.' (*The Times*) The obituarist tells us that someone's archaeological experience was educated at Sherborne School. A noun or pronoun must be provided for 'educated' to agree with: *Educated until 17 at Sherborne School, he developed his archaeological experience in that part of the Wessex chalklands.* See also PRESENT PARTICIPLES, PAST PARTICIPLES.

particularly. 'The developing network of canals and particularly the railways made low-cost coal available.' (*Old-House Journal*) It would be correct to write 'The developing network of transport and particularly the railways' because the railways are a particular specimen of the transport referred to. But railways are not a particular specimen of canal. *The developing network of canals, and even more of railways made low-cost coal available.*

partly. It is correct to say 'The house is partly finished', where 'partly' does not require to be followed up. It is also correct to say 'The idea was partly his and partly mine', where the first 'partly' calls for a second.

'The price you pay is based partly on performance but also on the number of attachments and accessories included.'(*Moneywise*) This exemplifies the usage where a second 'partly' is required. To replace it by 'but also' is to change construction in mid-stream. *The price you pay is based partly on performance and partly on the number of attachments and accessories included.*

Past Participles. Like the present participle, the past participle is now often used incorrectly. When opening a statement with a past participle, a writer must take care to match it correctly with what follows.

'Pocket-sized, well-researched and good value for money, the range of areas is unusually broad and their definitive nature rarely challenged.' (*Outdoors Illustrated*) In recommending guide books, the writer tells us that the range of areas covered is pocket-sized and well-researched. *Pocket-sized, well-researched and good value for money, the guides cover an unusually broad range of areas.*

'Recently named Artistic Director of the Moscow State Symphony Orchestra, his performance in May 1989 of Beethoven's Concerto No. 5 was recorded live by Melodiya/RCA records.' (*Programme Note*) This tells us that 'his performance' of a concerto has recently been named Artistic Director of an orchestra. *Recently named Artistic Director . . . he gave a performance in May 1989 . . . which was recorded live.* It will be observed that the introductory adverb 'recently' somehow makes it easier to forget that 'named' must have its appropriate subject.

Even a fine novelist can be led astray by this construction. 'Originally designed to occupy two full evenings in the theatre, this adaptation runs for a little over three hours.' (*Oldie*) The play is Schiller's *Wallenstein*, and it is this play, not the 'adaptation', which was 'originally designed to occupy two full evenings'. The adaptation apparently changed all that. *The play was originally designed to occupy two full evenings in the theatre, but this adaptation runs for a little over three hours.*

If to begin a sentence with a participle is often risky, to begin with two participles may be to court disaster. 'Led by John Lennon in white and followed by Ringo Starr in black, a barefooted McCartney and George Harrison in jeans, the four Beatles were seen to represent a priest, an undertaker, a corpse and a gravedigger in a funeral procession.' (*The Times*) Idiomatic usage would allow us to say 'Led by John

Lennon, the four Beatles crossed the road', even though, strictly speaking, only three of the Beatles were 'led' by John Lennon. Lennon did the leading. But in the sentence above we are told that 'four Beatles' were led by Lennon and followed by Starr, McCartney and Harrison. That makes at least seven of them. The sentence runs itself into confusion. A very simple alteration could correct this. The first 'and' should be replaced by 'who was': *Led by John Lennon in white, who was followed by Ringo Starr.* It is then clear that it is Lennon alone who was 'followed' and not the four of them. *See* STARTING A SENTENCE for more examples.

path. 'The path to peace in the Middle East has once again been dealt a terrible blow.' (*Radio 4*) A path cannot receive blows. The word 'path' must go. *Progress towards peace in the Middle East has once again been set back.* And the message continued, 'So is the Oslo Accord, which began the path to peace, still threatened?' An accord cannot 'begin' a path. *So is the Oslo Accord, which started the peace process, still threatened?*

pay. 'Old people living in private residential homes are to have their nursing costs paid for by the Government.' (*The Times*) Nursing can be 'paid for', but we 'pay' costs, we do not pay 'for' them: *are to have their nursing costs paid by the Government.*

There are various accepted idiomatic usages of the verb 'to pay'. As well as paying bills one may 'pay homage' to a person, or 'pay tribute' to a person. In these cases 'pay' is appropriate because homage and tribute are properly 'owed'.

'The people of Tyneside paid an emotional farewell to the last ship to be built on the Tyne.' (*Radio 4*) A farewell is not something that is owed and can be 'paid'. *The people of Tyneside bade farewell with great emotion to the last ship to be built on the Tyne.*

'The PLO leader, Yasser Arafat, has visited Israel to pay his condolences to Mr Rabin's widow.' (*Radio 4*) Condolence is an expression of sympathy. Here again therefore the notion of payment is inappropriate: *has visited Israel to offer his condolences.*

penalty. 'Customs officials are reluctant to lay down the penalties for a holidaymaker not declaring goods.' (*Meridian*) This is one more word which attracts gerciples ('a holiday maker not declaring'). *Customs officials are reluctant to lay down the penalties for a holidaymaker's failure to declare goods.* The same writer used the gerund correctly in the previous sentence ('when items are shipped there is always the possibility of their [*sic*] going astray').

peremptory/perfunctory. The adjective 'peremptory' is applied to demands and commands that are decisive and seemingly preclude possible contradiction. The adjective 'perfunctory' is applied to acts which are performed with a minimum of attention and half-heartedly as a matter of routine.

perfectly. 'Though neither ingenious nor complicated, this Budget was not perfectly unsound.' (*The Times*) This is a contradiction in terms. A thing can be perfectly good but not 'perfectly' bad, perfectly sound but not 'perfectly' unsound: *this Budget was not wholly unsound.*

perform. 'Their departures from the £2.7bn retail combine were accompanied by far less playing to the gallery than that performed by the Saatchi refuseniks.' (*Marketing Week*) Playing to the gallery cannot be 'performed'. The verb must be changed: *far less playing to the gallery than the Saatchi refuseniks went in for.*

'The architects fully performed their obligations.' (*The Times*) An obligation is not something to be 'performed' like a piano sonata or a part in a play. *The architects fulfilled all their obligations.*

'The judge was clearly impressed with that argument, agreeing that Gilmour should perform 240 hours community service rather than a custodial sentence.' (*Radio 4*) Where a verb is followed by two distinct objects, it is important that it should make sense in relation to both. A person can 'perform' community service, but no one can 'perform' a custodial sentence. Two verbs are needed: *agreeing that Gilmour should do 240 hours community service rather than serve a custodial sentence.*

performance. 'More fundamentally, is our unsatisfactory performance with the average pupil and the disadvantaged falling or improving?' (*The Times*) The former Chairman of the National Curriculum Council is asking this question. There is firstly a question whether a 'performance' can be said to 'fall'. There is secondly a question whether an 'unsatisfactory performance' can 'improve', for if it does, then presumably it ceases to be unsatisfactory. A performance which is at present unsatisfactory can of course 'improve'. Logic requires the writer, either to stick to falling and rising, or to go for improving and deteriorating. The question should be either: *is our at present low level of performance falling or rising?* or: *is our at present unsatisfactory performance improving or deteriorating?*

'The greatest challenge any manufacturer faces is to be taken seriously at the performance end of the market.' (*Outdoors Illustrated*) The 'performance end of the market' appears to be the point at which the product is tested in doing what it is designed to do. *The greatest challenge any manufacturer faces is to make his products work.*

In modern advertising the word 'performance' is often redundant. 'The lasting legend in performance walking and climbing boots for women.' (*The Great Outdoors*) Walking boots that did not perform as such would not be walking boots. The word should be omitted.

perfunctory. *See* PEREMPTORY.

perpetrate. To perpetrate a crime is to commit a crime and the verb is generally used of what is offensive.

'What the Conservative party has done, I think very differently from the views which socialist governments perpetrated between the war and now . . . .' (*Radio 4*) All kinds of horrible deeds can be perpetrated, but 'views' cannot be perpetrated: *What the Conservative party has done, in contrast to what socialist governments recommended.*

perpetuate. 'These descendants of the great Nkosi Dhlamini of three centuries ago perpetuate some splendid public occasions.' (*Independent*) To perpetuate something is to make it go on and on. The 'occasions' are not perpetuated thus. Either 'perpetuate' must be changed: *these descendants of the great Nkosi of three centuries ago celebrate some splendid public occasions*, or 'occasions': *perpetuate some splendid public traditions.*

perquisite/prerequisite. These two terms, superficially similar in form, have no relationship. A 'perquisite' is a benefit additional to the accepted wage or salary received from one's employment. The word is commonly abbreviated ('perk'). A company car or free travel to work would be a 'perk'. A 'prerequisite' is a 'requisite' made in advance, in other words, a prior condition: *A prerequisite of the post I applied for was residence in London.*

persuasive. 'Just as persuasive, housewives were told that whereas the entire cooking for a middle class family might cost as much as a shilling a day on a coal range, using gas it would be as little as 2½ d.' (*Old-House Journal*) What is 'persuasive'? Not the housewives, as the grammar would suggest. The adjective must be replaced by the adverb: *Just as persuasively, housewives were told.*

pervade. 'The odour pervaded throughout the bar.' (*The Times*) To pervade is to spread through and, like 'permeate', it is transitive. *The odour pervaded the whole bar.*

pessimistic. 'Mr A acknowledged that events and developments [in Bosnia] were what he called overwhelmingly pessimistic.' (*Radio 4*) To be 'pessimistic' is to expect the worst. Events themselves cannot be 'pessimistic'. Only human beings can expect the worst: *he was overwhelmingly pessimistic about events and developments.* Otherwise use a different adjective: *events and developments were wholly ominous.*

petrify. 'Sandra Stone . . . said a little boy who had had heart surgery was too petrified of pain to move.' (*Nursing Standard*) To petrify is to turn to stone. To transfer the 'of' ('terrified of') to the verb 'petrify' will not do. The boy is either: *too terrified of pain* or: *too petrified by pain.*

photograph. 'The photograph of the tree in Berkeley Square is not an oak; it is a plane.' (*The Times*) The photograph is neither of course. *The tree photographed in Berkeley Square is not an oak; it is a plane.*

Phrases. A 'phrase' is a group of related words in a sentence which may include a participle but do not include a finite verb, and must therefore have a firm grammatical connection with the sentence as a whole.

'Photograph album in hand, Helensburgh was our first stop.' (*The People's Friend*) Helensburgh is a town and it could not hold a photograph album in its hand. The phrase 'photograph album in hand' must be properly attached to some person or persons. *Photograph album in hand, we made Helensburgh our first stop.*

'While by no means his finest novel, Banks yet again makes complex SF utterly compelling.' (*Focus*) 'While by no means his finest novel' is likewise unattached to anything that would make sense of the phrase. A strict grammatical reading of the words as they stand would suggest that Banks is by no means his finest novel. *While by no means his finest novel, Banks's new one yet again makes SF utterly compelling.*

'The menu is packed with notes on provenance and the origin of each main course ingredient. Carried to faintly absurd lengths one can't help but conjecture if Perthshire pigeon refers to its resting place or where it was shot!' (*Lancashire Life*) What is 'carried to absurd lengths'? It appears that 'one' is. To make sense the phrase must be anchored. *Carried to faintly absurd lengths, this practice makes one wonder whether Perthshire pigeon refers to its resting place.*

'Not to be outdone by the characters in her novels, Edmonds's home life, her financial problems, is the stuff of *Hello* magazine.' (*Daily*

Express) Who is not to be outdone? We are not told. It appears that someone's home life is not to be outdone. *Not to be outdone by the characters in her novels, Edmonds makes her home life . . . the stuff of* Hello *magazine. See also* PARALLELS THAT FAIL TO MATCH.

place. 'Most places know very little about vitamins, much less the science of nutrition.' (*Options*) 'Places' cannot 'know' things. From the context it is clear that the writer means: *Most shop-keepers know very little about vitamins.*

'It shouldn't be anybody's place to take a picture of them just because they are wearing a low top.' (*The Times*) 'It's my place to look after the children' means 'It's my duty' to do so. But duty does not seem to be the concept involved here. *It shouldn't be anybody's right to take a picture of them just because they are wearing a low top.*

plan. 'Postal workers are staging a one-day strike today and another is planned on Monday.' (*Radio 4*) The day 'on' which a strike is staged is not the day 'on' which it is planned: *another is planned for Monday.*

'Inflation . . . Interest Rates . . . Tax . . . All these factors are beyond your control: the secret is to plan them into your investing strategy.' (*Moneywise*) If they are beyond your control, how can you possibly 'plan' them? A different verb is needed: *the secret is to allow for them in planning your investments.*

platform. 'Earlier work by Touche-Ross, the accountant, in connection with the refinancing provided a platform for further essential enquiries.' (*The Times*) A platform is a station from which people make announcements or state beliefs. They do not press 'enquiries' from the platform but from the auditorium. The 'platform' is an aid to publicity, not to investigation. *Earlier work by Touche Ross provided a starting-point for further enquiries.*

plight. 'Our products (which include casual clothing, low energy lighting, bags and holdalls, tee shirts and many other items) supports groups striving to educate us in the ways we can help the many plights threatening man, beast and our land the world over.' (*Advertisement*) This is full of errors. The subject 'products' cannot be followed by the singular verb 'supports'. In any case, it is not the 'products' themselves that give support but, presumably, their sale. A 'plight' is a condition of hardship. We do not speak of 'helping' such hardship, but of removing it: *The sale of our products will benefit groups striving to reduce the damage done to men, animals and the earth.*

plunge. 'He is convinced that the publication of biography and letters have plunged Larkin in contemporary esteem.' (*The Times*) We know what it means to 'plunge' into water, or to be 'plunged' in despair. The water or the despair swallows up the plunged one. But the writer does not here mean that Larkin is immersed in contemporary esteem. He has used the wrong verb. Moreover, the single noun 'publication', as subject, cannot be followed by the plural verb 'have plunged'. *He is convinced that the publication of biography and letters has lowered Larkin in contemporary esteem.*

point. 'The point to be said is that we're not labelling anything.' (*Radio 4*) In English usage we do not 'say' points. *The point to be made is that we're not labelling anything.*

pore. *See* POUR.

portrait. 'Studied with a psychological insight and intensity of expression, his people, whether portraits or participants in one of the biblical stories, draw the spectator into the artist's world.' (*Vivid*) The subject is Rembrandt. One cannot 'study' a work with intensity of expression, though one might write about it with intensity of expression. People are not 'portraits', and to balance 'portraits' against 'participants' in something or other is illogical. *Studied with psychological insight and intensity of concentration, his figures, whether living portraits or studies of characters in biblical stories, draw the spectator into the artist's world.*

portrayal. 'He is very much hurt by his portrayal in Channel 4's documentary opera-soap, *The House*.' (*Private Eye*) We speak of Dickens's portrayal of Mr Micawber, not of Mr Micawber's portrayal by Dickens. It is best to restrict the possessive of 'portrayal' to the former (objective) usage. *He is very much hurt by the way he is portrayed in Channel 4's documentary opera-soap, 'The House'.* See also HIS.

position. 'The position requires a young enthusiastic television journalist to take responsibility for the production aspects of the business.' (*Guardian*) It is not the position that 'requires' this, but the employer. *A young enthusiastic television journalist is required to take responsibility for production aspects of the business.*

'I have been concerned over the position that has occurred at the Whittington Hospital.' (*Radio 4*) A position cannot 'occur'. *I have been concerned about the situation (that has obtained) at the Whittington Hospital.*

possession. 'There could be a number of other contaminated tablets apparently in possession of persons at this time.' (*Radio 4*) The tablets are not in possession of persons: the persons are in possession of the tablets: *contaminated tablets in people's possession.*

Possessive Trap. A common error is to use a noun in the possessive case and in the same sentence to refer forward or backward to the noun as though the case were not possessive.

POSSESSIVE WRONGLY PRECEDED 'A familiar customer at the Berkeley Hotel in Mayfair and an occasional visitor to the Savoy, Sanderson's easy manner made him friends at the highest level in the City.' (*The Times*) The obituarist tells us that Sanderson's easy manner was in the habit of visiting expensive hotels. If the opening of the sentence is kept, then 'Sanderson' must be used without the possessive. *A familiar customer at the Berkeley Hotel in Mayfair and an occasional visitor to the Savoy, Sanderson had an easy manner which made him friends at the highest level in the City.*

'Shy and retiring, modest and hard-working, this man's knowledge and experience is quite clearly immense.' (*Country Lovers Magazine*) Here we are told that this man's knowledge is 'shy and retiring'. *Shy and retiring, modest and hard-working, this man clearly has immense knowledge and experience.*

'Famous for their made-to-measure furniture covers, Plumbs' new cotton and linen range, called Monogram, offers over 40 different designs.' (*Home Style*) Here the word 'famous' attaches itself to the new range, because 'Plumbs'' is in the possessive case. *Famous for their made-to-measure furniture covers, Plumbs have a new cotton and linen range which offers over 40 different designs.*

'With responsibility for making sure everything runs smoothly on Britain's number one breakfast show, Toby's past credits include *The Word*'. (*Company*) Here we are told that Toby's past credits hold responsibility for ensuring that things go well. *Responsible for making sure everything runs smoothly, Toby has past credits that include* The Word.

Sometimes the same error is made although there is no noun in the possessive case. 'The son of a carpenter, his skills as a painter, draughtsman and printmaker were developed in the studios of Francesco Squarcione.' (*Artists & Illustrators Magazine*) The writer seemingly begins the sentence intending to make Andrea Mantegna the subject, then switches to make his 'skills' the subject, and proclaims them to be the son of a carpenter. *The son of a carpenter, he developed his skills as a painter, draughtsman and printmaker in the studios of Francesco Squarcione.*

POSSESSIVE WRONGLY FOLLOWED Perhaps the error is easier to spot when the possessive precedes the misuse. 'But the ferret's image has changed and now it is as likely to be found cosseted in a palatial coop in Kensington as caged behind a keeper's cottage.' (*The Field*) Here the ferret's image, instead of the ferret, is said to be cosseted in a palatial coop. *The ferret now has a new image and is as likely to be found cosseted in a palatial coop in Kensington as caged behind a keeper's cottage.*

'Emma's commitment hasn't faltered, despite being gaoled for two weeks.' (*Company*) The commitment must not be said to have been gaoled. *Emma hasn't faltered in her commitment, despite being gaoled for two weeks.*

'Originally a cattle drovers' inn, the waters of Loch Awe come right up to Taychreggan's gardens.' (*AA Magazine*) Neither the waters of Loch Awe nor the gardens were originally an inn. *Originally a cattle drovers' inn, Taychreggan Hotel has the waters of Loch Awe at the bottom of its gardens.*

'It [the Kirkstone Pass] also measures a driver's patience if stuck behind a coach.' (*AA Magazine*) But it is the driver, not his patience, that gets 'stuck behind a coach'. The driver must be mentioned, without an apostrophe. *It also tests the patience of a driver, if stuck behind a coach.*

'However, on a summer morning when the streets are quiet, there is nothing better than mooching round Hem's patch (as his mates called him).' (*The Times*) The reference is to Ernest Hemingway. His mates did not call him 'Hem's patch', as is said here. Either the construction must be changed: *nothing better than mooching around Hem's patch (his mates called him 'Hem')*, or possibly the pronoun: *Hem's patch (as his mates called it)*. *See also* SWITCH-START.

Possessives. We use the possessive of nouns and pronouns in two different ways. Between 'John's essay was the best' and 'John's mark was the highest' there is a slight difference. The essay is in all senses 'John's'. The mark is awarded to the essay and one might equally justifiably call it the 'teacher's mark'. In 'I admire his persistence, but I disapprove of his promotion' the persistence is fully 'his', but the promotion is someone else's doing. 'The explorer's discovery of the cave' is better English than 'the cave's discovery by the explorer'. The 'discovery' does not belong to the cave in the way it belongs to the explorer. There is carelessness in this respect.

'It is worth looking out for the very high toxic plants and avoiding their use.' (*Dog's Monthly*) It would be correct, but awkward to write 'avoiding use of them' or 'avoiding using them'. It would be better to take out 'avoid'. *It is worth looking out for the very high toxic plants and rejecting them.* Alternatively one could simply say: *and not using them.* See also DESCRIPTION, MEMORIES, PORTRAYAL.

possibility. This is a word which attracts gerciples. To speak of the 'possibility of drowning' is correct, but to speak of the 'possibility of the baby drowning' is incorrect ('the baby's drowning' would be correct but awkward). Unless 'possibility' is followed by a single word (such as 'drowning' above) the safe thing to do is to follow it by 'that' (*possibility that the baby will drown*).

Thus 'Even giving the dog a bath presents the possibility of the dog scrabbling to get out of an unfamiliar situation and injuring himself' (*Dog's Monthly*) should be: *presents the possibility that the dog will scrabble to get out and injure himself.*

'The possibility of it [a debate] being on Friday will be up to the government.' (*Radio 4*) Again we have the ungrammatical gerciple ('of it being'). But worse still, what does it mean to say that a possibility is 'up to the government'? It seems to be a clear case of illicit constructional transfer. One can say 'The decision is up to the government', and the newswriter transfers this usage from the word 'decision' to the word 'possibility'. The announcement should be: *Whether a debate will be held on Friday will be decided by the government.*

post. 'This post will be responsible for providing the administrative back up and support for over 80 Sporting Clubs and Non Sporting Societies.' (*Guardian*) It is not the post that will be thus 'responsible' but the appointee. The words 'back up' and 'support' duplicate each other, and they do not need the definite article before them. *The new appointee will be responsible for providing administrative support for over 80 Clubs and Non-Sporting Societies.*

postponement. 'The postponement appeared to be because the fighting had made it difficult to deploy monitors in Iraq rather than an attempt to punish Saddam.' (*The Times*) We see here the danger of beginning with the noun 'postponement' and avoiding use of the verb 'postpone'. To follow a noun by 'appeared to be because' is incorrect. Use of the verb 'postpone' is necessary: *The scheme appeared to have been postponed because the fighting had made it difficult.* The rest of the sentence is grammatically unsatisfactory. It is like saying 'The meal appeared to be because people were hungry rather than an effort to be sociable'. What follows 'rather than' must balance what precedes it. The construction would be better avoided here. *The scheme appeared to have been postponed because the fighting had made it difficult to deploy monitors in Iraq, and not in any attempt to punish Saddam. See* BECAUSE.

potential. 'There were calls from several western capitals today for restraint by the newly victorious Croatian forces as the potential for a major conflict with Serbia over Eastern Slavonia continued.' (*Radio 4*) This is BBC newspeak at its most turgid. Attachment to abstract nouns like 'potential' is always a threat to good English. To speak of potential continuing is absurd. 'Remained' would be better than 'continued'. It would be better still to get rid of 'potential': *as a major conflict with Serbia still threatened.*

pour. 'When ministers have had eight days to pour over the report' (*The Times*) says a leader, referring to the Scott report, as though days could be released from a jug: *When ministers have had eight days to pore over the Scott report.*

practice/practise. The noun is 'practice', and the verb is 'practise'.

Thus 'familiar to those that practice this exhilarating pastime' (*Outdoors Illustrated*) should be: *familiar to those who practise this exhilarating pastime.*

Similarly 'The societies that practice it as a life-style' (*Complete Traveller*) should be: *that practise it as a life-style.*

Conversely 'and get you your certificate by a concentrated theory and practise programme' (*Outdoors Illustrated*) should be: *by a concentrated theory and practice programme.*

And 'this is not a good practise' (*Cumbria Life*) should be: *this is not a good practice.*

The Americans have got rid of 'practise' and use 'practice' for both noun and verb. But English does not have many verbs ending in '-ice' (though 'suffice' comes to mind). Although pronunciation conceals the fact, 'practise' as a verb goes with dozens of others such as 'realise', 'advertise', and 'compromise'. And some of those verbs, like 'compromise', can be used as nouns too.

practise. *See* PRACTICE.

pragmatic. 'It is important that a pragmatic way is found to repair the lock gates.' (*Waterways World*) 'Pragmatic' is a philosophical term descriptive of arguments that concentrate on practical consequences rather than on theoretical positions. It is clear that to repair lock gates in any other way than with concentration on the practical results of the operation would be nonsensical. The word should be either omitted or replaced. And 'is found' must become 'should be found'. *It is important that a satisfactory way should be found to repair the lock gates.*

praise. 'US Secretary of State, Warren Christopher, praised the success of the peace deal.' (*Radio 4*) Surely what he 'praised' was the successful peace deal. The 'success' requires a different verb: *Warren Christopher acclaimed the success of the peace deal.*

prayer. 'Finally the Dean led the congregation in a prayer to Izaak Walton composed by the Rev David Scott.' (*Trout & Salmon*) The scene is Winchester Cathedral where, presumably, prayers are offered only to God. It must have been either: *a prayer for Izaak Walton*, or: *a prayer about Izaak Walton.*

precedent. 'Your report on the successful claim for damages to a walker injured by cows creates an alarming precedent.' (*The Times*) It is not the 'report' that creates the precedent, but the successful claim. *The successful claim you report, for damages to a walker injured by cows, creates an alarming precedent.*

precipitate. 'The ridge strikes northward . . . the main path . . . avoiding numerous granite tors and the brink of the plunging crags that precipitate the viewpoints along this rim over Coire a'Bhradain with potential danger.' (*The Great Outdoors*) Sometimes verbal errors defy analysis. How can crags precipitate a viewpoint? And not only precipitate it but precipitate it 'with danger'? 'Precipitate' as an adjective means 'over-hasty'. 'Precipitous' means 'very steep'. When something 'precipitates' an event, the event is brought on prematurely.

preclude. *See* EXCLUDE.

predict. 'By arranging a CAT scan of the medial temporal lobe of the brain . . . they have been able to predict with 95 per cent accuracy which of their patients have Alzheimers.' (*The Times*) It is possible to predict that it will rain tomorrow, but not to predict from inside a shuttered room that it is now raining. Prediction refers to the future: *they have been able to detect with 95 per cent accuracy which of their patients have Alzheimers.*

prediction. 'The door to your home is crucial. If it opens directly out onto the street, children leaving home early might not be too fanciful a prediction.' (*Meridian*) We are in the world of feng-shui doctrine. Children leaving home could never be a prediction. It is an act which, perhaps, fulfils a prediction. Wet weather is itself never a forecast. It fulfils a forecast. *If it opens directly on to the street, it might not be too fanciful to predict that the children will leave home early.*

preempt. To preempt is to acquire or appropriate in advance.

'Is any kind of regulation going to preempt the kind of thing that has happened at Barclays?' (*Radio 4*) The questioner appears to think that 'preempt' is an alternative to 'prevent'. To 'preempt' an action or development would be to get in with it before anyone else, the very opposite of what is intended here. *Is any kind of regulation going to forestall the kind of thing that has happened at Barclays?*

'Today's judgment said the outcome of the case should not preempt the result of any future claims.' (*Radio 4*) Again, in this comment on an asbestos-related case, there is no question of acquisition or appropriation. *Today's judgment said the outcome of the case should not prejudice the result of any future claims.*

'*The Times* understands that yesterday's statement by solicitors was issued to preempt a Sunday newspaper, which intended to publish details of the couple's marriage breakdown this weekend.' (*The Times*) It was not the Sunday newspaper that was 'preempted' but that paper's expected scoop: *yesterday's statement by solicitors was issued to forestall a Sunday newspaper.*

'I can't preempt what the Safety Authority will say' should be: *I can't anticipate what the Safety Authority will say.*

preference. 'With reference to the planned deportation of a Saudi diplomat, do you think that national commercial considerations should take preference over human rights?' (*Radio 4*) One can 'give' preference to one thing or person over another, but nothing can 'take' preference. The wrong word has been used: *do you think that national commercial considerations should take precedence over human rights?*

preoccupation. 'The Supplement on Adventure Travel will now be an annual event to coincide with your preoccupation on where to travel.' (*Outdoors Illustrated*) A person is not preoccupied 'on' things, but 'with' them: *your preoccupation with where to travel.*

Prepositions. Prepositions are words used, generally before a noun or a pronoun, to link it with its grammatical context. Some prepositions, such as 'of', 'for', 'by', 'with', 'before' and 'after', are among the most used words in the language. A much quoted rule, that a sentence should not end with a preposition, has no real validity. Churchill mocked it by tortuously writing 'This is the sort of English up with which I will not put', instead of the more natural 'This is the sort of English I will not put up with', a sentence which ends with two prepositions.

There is a prevalent tendency to break the accepted conventions in the use of prepositions. It is perhaps not too strong to speak of an epidemic of prepositional anarchy in the media, especially on the radio. Illicit constructional transfers are made. Accustomed to saying 'tired of', someone presumes to say 'bored of'. Accustomed to saying 'destructive of', another says 'devastating of'. Because one can speak of 'concentration on', a third presumes to speak of 'preoccupation on'. Thus we find 'hatred to' instead of 'hatred of', 'pander for' instead of 'pander to' and 'rebel from' instead of 'rebel against'.

A few of the numerous instances accumulated in this book can be found under: ACCOUNT, CONNECT, CONNIVE, DEDICATION, DISSOCI-ATE, DISTASTE, ELABORATE, ENAMOURED, EQUATE, EXAMINATION, EXPAND, EXPOUND, FASCINATION, FORBID, INVESTIGATION, PETRIFY, PREOCCUPATION, PROVIDE, RECAPITULATE, RENOWNED.

Prepositions, Omission of. Neglect of appropriate prepositions can produce confusions which a very small change could rectify. 'Stagecoach, which is based in Perth, said profit at the units could be raised by investing in new vehicles and cost economies in fuel, spare parts and insurance resulting from being a part of a larger group.' (*The Times*) A firm might invest in new vehicles and other equipment, but not in new vehicles and cost economies. Insert 'by': *by investing in new vehicles and by cost economies in fuel, spare parts and insurance.*

'There's more sea kayakers here than any other city in the States.' (*Outdoors Illustrated*) To make this logically sound, the preposition 'in' must be repeated. *There's more sea kayakers here than in any other city in the States.*

'Not only had I caused a great deal of anxiety to my family and Don in particular, but also the rescue service individuals who put their own lives at risk to rescue me.' (*The Great Outdoors*) Here the preposition 'to' must be repeated: *Not only had I caused a great deal of anxiety to my family and Don in particular, but also to the rescue service individuals.* The purist would also want to shift the words 'not only': *I had caused a great deal of anxiety not only to my family and Don in particular, but also to the rescue service.*

prerequisite. *See* PERQUISITE.

prescribe. 'Women who may be taking these medicines are being advised to visit their doctors to see if they need to be prescribed something else.' (*Radio 4*) Medicines are prescribed: people are never prescribed: *are being advised to visit their doctors to see if something else needs to be prescribed for them.*

'On his tour he heard calls for nurse prescribing to be extended to all community nurses.' (*Nursing Standard*) 'Nurse prescribing' would mean prescribing a nurse instead of some other medicine. Nevertheless the expression is repeatedly misused in this context. *On his tour he heard calls for the right to prescribe to be extended to all community nurses.*

prescribe/proscribe. The verb to 'prescribe' is used of laying down rules or, medically, of defining what medications are to be taken and what regimen followed. The verb to 'proscribe' is used of officially prohibiting certain courses of action and of publicly outlawing someone.

Present Participles. The writing tends to slide off course sometimes when present participles are used.

PARTICIPLE PRECEDING SUBJECT Starting a sentence with a present participle often leads to error through failure to match the participle correctly in what follows.

'Pulling back the heather, an intricate design of concentric circles and small cup-shaped depressions was revealed.' (*Country Talk*) The writer tells us that an intricate design pulled back the heather. A subject must be supplied for 'pulling back' to agree with. *Pulling back the heather, I saw an intricate design of concentric circles and small cup-shaped depressions.*

'Clipping them [box and yew] into the same dome shapes, they would rise over the next 20 years like puddings in an oven.' (*The Times*) Who is 'clipping' them? They are said here to clip themselves. *Clipped into the same dome shapes, they would rise like puddings.*

Gardening seems to encourage such failures of parallelism. 'Rising as they do to about 2ft above the grassy leaves, the effect is charming.' (*Practical Gardening*) 'They' are cited, but then the subject becomes 'the effect'. The correction is simple. *Rising as they do to about 2ft above the grassy leaves, they make a charming effect.*

'Catching sight of herself in the mirror tweaking her own breast, the silly lost expression left her face instantly.' (*New Woman*) Here, similarly, the silly lost expression is said to have caught sight of herself in the mirror. Again a proper subject must be supplied for 'catching sight' to attach to. *Catching sight of herself in the mirror tweaking her own breast, she lost the silly expression on her face immediately.*

'Chugging higher onto the body of Krafla now, still on road, the scene turns desolate.' (*Outdoors Illustrated*) The scene does not chug. *As we chug higher on to the body of Krafla now, still on road, the scene turns desolate.*

SUBJECT/OBJECT PRECEDING PARTICIPLE A comparable error is often made when the present participle follows the subject but still fails in agreement. A syntactical shift is made by which what begins as the subject of the sentence seemingly ceases to be so.

'Our Thomas Cook "Escorted Journey" began in Cairo, staying in comfort at the Semiramis InterContinental Hotel.' (*Meridian*) The 'journey' did not stay at the hotel. *We began our 'Escorted Journey' in Cairo, staying in comfort at the Semiramis InterContinental Hotel.*

'Any that seem content can be repotted, teasing a little soil for the surface of the root ball.' (*Homes & Gardens*) In this advice about re-potting plants, the plants themselves are said to tease soil. The real subject is 'Any' (plants), but the seeming subject then becomes the unnamed gardener. If 'teasing' is kept, the subject must be changed. *You can repot any that seem content, teasing a little soil for the surface of the root ball.*

'We glimpse Gombrich's early years in Vienna, growing up in a Jewish middle-class family connected with Mahler and friendly with Schonberg.' (*Oldie*) Here it is not the subject of the main verb ('We') that is faultily attached to the participle 'growing', but the object ('Gombrich's early years'). The 'early years' are said to have grown up in Vienna. *We glimpse Gombrich in his early years in Vienna, growing up in a Jewish middle-class family.* See also STARTING A SENTENCE.

Present Tense Misused. 'A tribunal ruled that Jonathan Wolf, 21, had done what many of his predecessors had got away with, help their friends up the greasy pole and sabotage the opposition.' (*The Times*) We may say 'He had done what he wanted, climbed Mount Everest', but not 'He had done what he wanted, climb Mount Everest'. So here it must be: *Jonathan Wolf had done what many of his predecessors had got away with, helped their friends up the greasy pole and sabotaged the opposition.*

'Helping to make the interior seem more spacious perhaps than it really was, the window area is large for this size of caravan.' (*Caravan Magazine*) If 'it really was' is kept here, then the past tense 'was' is required after it: *Helping the interior seem more spacious perhaps than it really was, the window area was large.* See also IMPORTANT.

preserve. 'His life and loves have been preserved at Shaw's Corner, Ayot St Lawrence.' (*Family History*) The facts of Shaw's life should be distinguished from the record of it here. *The record of his life and loves has been preserved at Shaw's Corner.*

presumptive / presumptuous. A 'presumptuous' person boldly 'presumes' too much for himself or herself: *It was highly presumptuous of the man, as a new member of the society, to propose himself for office.* Something that is 'presumptive' is presumed to be highly probable and can be reliably inferred. The word has a special use in relation to royal succession. The 'heir apparent' to a throne is the heir who will definitely succeed if he or she survives. The 'heir presumptive' will succeed provided that no heir with a stronger claim appears. Thus if a British monarch had a daughter and no son, that daughter would be 'heir presumptive' until a son were born. The eldest son would be 'heir apparent' from birth.

presumptuous. *See* PRESUMPTIVE.

pretty. '*Braveheart* was pretty slated by the critics.' (*Radio 4*) There is an adverbial use of this adjective, meaning 'rather' or 'fairly' ('The weather is pretty dismal'), but only before an adjective, not before a verb. '*Braveheart' was rather slated by the critics.*

prevaricate / procrastinate. The verb to 'prevaricate', deriving from a Latin verb which means to walk crookedly, is used of acting or speaking evasively or falsely in order to deceive. To 'procrastinate' is to delay, to put something off to the future. There is a certain common element between the two verbs in that prevarication, like procrastination, is often a matter of 'playing for time'.

prevent. 'Have lots of long, cool drinks to quench your thirst and prevent you dehydrating.' (*Woman*) This should be: *prevent you from dehydrating.* The verb 'prevent' very often needs to be followed by 'from'.

'He claims that Britain will be powerless to prevent thousands of illegal immigrants because it has agreed to a "Europe without frontiers"'. (*The Times*) What the writer means is: *powerless to prevent the entry of thousands of immigrants*, or: *powerless to prevent thousands of immigrants from entering.*

price. 'The price of £75 is quite high but it does replace both windshirt and base layer.' (*The Great Outdoors*) The 'price' does not replace other garments. The tendency to slide from speaking of the cost of an item to speaking of the item itself must be resisted. *The price of £75 is quite high but the garment does replace both windshirt and base layer.*

principal. This word is used as an adjective, meaning first in rank ('principal boy'), and also as a noun, meaning chief ('principal of the college'). It can be confused with 'principle', meaning a standard or rule.

'There are no such puritan principals for our Boxing Day heroes.' (*Shooting Times*) This is a case in point. It should be: *There are no such no such puritan principles for our Boxing Day heroes.*

principle. This is a noun, meaning a standard or rule.

To write of the 'principle characters' in a novel (*The Times*) is to confuse the word with 'principal', meaning (as an adjective) first in rank and (as a noun) the person in such a position: *principal characters.*

Thus 'Alex was Principle of Bournville College of Art' (*Artists & Illustrators Magazine*) should be: *Principal.*

Similarly 'Principle interest centred on the 1924 dining car set' (*Steam World*) should be: *Principal interest.*

prior to. 'It is possible that the car could have spent some time in the Belgian Congo . . . "K" would indicate Katanga as the registering authority but it seems that little information is available on this prior to 1920.' (*Automobile*) The writer implies that we shall have to wait patiently for the year 1920 for information to be available: *little information is available on the period prior to 1920.*

prise. *See* PRY.

problem. Usage of this word often raises problems.

'I have no problem with footballers wearing ear-rings.' (*The Times*) This usage produces the ungrammatical 'footballers wearing ear-rings' where *the wearing of ear-rings by footballers* would be correct. It would be better perhaps to get rid of 'the problem'. *I have no objection to footballers who wear ear-rings.*

'For example, minor alterations on the first floor include the construction of a passage-way, to solve the problem of bedrooms leading directly into each other.' (*Traditional Homes*) It would be correct to write 'He constructed [verb] a passage-way to solve the problem', but not to write of 'the construction [noun] to solve the problem'. It would be necessary to write of 'the construction of a passage-way designed to solve the problem'. But is rescuing the words 'solve the problem' worth the effort? The word 'problem' introduces an ungrammatical gerciple ('of bedrooms leading'). One issue here is the preference for nouns ('construction' and 'problem') over verbs. *For example, among minor alterations on the first floor, a passage-way has been constructed to allow separate access to communicating bedrooms.*

'The hot weather created real problems to fish in the canalised part of the estuary, because the high temperatures caused high algae levels to develop.' (*Trout & Salmon*) Problems are not created 'to' people or 'to' fish either: *The hot weather created real problems for fish.*

process. This is another vogue word. 'We're only part of the information process' (*Radio 4*) appears to mean: *There are other sources of information.*

procrastinate. 'Settle unfinished business, the small things you have been procrastinating.' (*Artists & Illustrators Magazine*) This verb is now usually intransitive: *the small things you have been postponing. See also* PREVARICATE.

prodigy. 'It was a leisured, extravagant age and she became a prodigy of the Duchess of Rutland.' (*The Times*) A prodigy is a youngster of remarkable talent. It is the wrong word here: *she became a protégée of the Duchess of Rutland.*

produce (noun). 'Carlebach was the talented produce of an illustrious rabbinic family rooted in the German-Jewish tradition.' (*The Times*) We use 'produce' especially of agricultural products. Accepted usage would find the word out of place here: *Carlebach was the talented product of an illustrious rabbinic family.*

produce (verb). 'Mr Stagg was arrested . . . after a complaint that a man had produced what appeared to be an axe at a 30-year-old man and his son.' (*The Times*) A man might produce a play 'at' the Aldwych or even a gun 'at' a party, but he could not produce an axe 'at' a man: *had seemingly produced an axe before a 30-year-old man and his son.*

product. 'But how much of the blurb on food labels is marketing rather than useful product details?' (*Good Housekeeping*) This illustrates the regrettable tendency to try to make other forms of speech do the work of adjectives. The concept of a 'marketing detail' is tenable, but a 'useful product detail' is a grammatical monstrosity. *How much of the blurb on food labels is intended to help sales rather than to give information about the product?*

profession. 'He's most likely to be a lawyer or an art dealer, professions that mean he has an excuse not only to walk on the wild side but to set up an office there.' (*Company*) The law is a profession, but a 'lawyer' is not. Nor is an art dealer. *He's most likely to be a lawyer or an art dealer, and thus to have an excuse.*

programme. 'Tonight's programme sits round the table with the extended family and gets its teeth into something very dear to Yiddish culture, food.' (*Radio 4*) A programme cannot sit round a table: *In tonight's programme we sit round the table with the extended family and get our teeth into something very dear to Yiddish culture.*

'The BBC 2's interiors programme "The Home Front" has asked *Cottage & Castle* readers for help making its next series.' (*Cottage & Castle*) Programmes cannot ask for help: *The director of the BBC 2's programme has asked* Cottage & Castle *readers for help*.

progression. 'There is often much pain related to movements of dysfunction but it should be measurable and progression into the painfree range should be achieved gradually.' (*Good News Magazine*) If pain can be gradually reduced, one should say so instead of introducing a 'progression' and a 'range': *it should be measurable and gradually eliminated*.

projection. 'The traffic projections for the UK as a whole are becoming unsustainable.' (*Radio 4*) What this means is that it will not be possible to tolerate the amount of traffic anticipated in the forecasts. But that does not make the forecasts, or the projections, 'unsustainable'. On the contrary, it will confirm them. *The UK as a whole will not be able to sustain the level of traffic projected.*

prominent. 'He played a fairly prominent part though very much in the background behind the scenes.' (*Radio 4*) This is self-contradictory. 'Prominent' means 'standing out from its surroundings' or 'noticeable'. No one can be prominent 'behind the scenes'. *He played a leading part, though very much behind the scenes.*

promote. Politicians overuse this word. 'How can we hope to promote ties between the two heartlands of democracy?' (*Radio 4*) Surely only a gentlemen's outfitter would want to 'promote' ties. What is wrong with the obvious verb: *How can we strengthen ties?*

prompting. 'A leading human rights activist has been arrested by the Palestinian Security Forces in East Jerusalem, prompting new criticism of the PLO leader Yasser Arafat.' (*Radio 4*) In the sentence, 'I sat in the wings, prompting the performers', the participle of the verb 'to prompt' is correctly used. There is no excuse for the journalistic habit of using it as a shorthand way of expressing causal connections. The activist has not 'prompted' anything: his arrest has. *The arrest of a leading human rights activist by the Palestinian Security Forces in East Jerusalem has sparked off new criticism of the PLO leader Yasser Arafat.*

prone. 'Mrs Karr was much prone to grand fur coats and silk dresses.' (*The Times*) 'Prone', meaning 'having an inclination towards', needs to be followed by a verb: *prone to purchase grand fur coats*. Otherwise it should be: *was much attached to grand fur coats*.

'This area is prone to an awful lot of crime.' (*Radio 4*) A person is 'prone' who is flat on the ground, prostrate. Hence the word is used of people's tendencies. It is lax to use the word other than of human (or animal) inclinations. *This area suffers from an awful lot of crime.*

Pronouns. Pronouns are words which can be used in place of nouns. There are 'personal' pronouns, 'demonstrative' pronouns, 'relative' and 'interrogative' pronouns, and 'indefinite' pronouns. The personal pronouns ('I' and 'me', 'you', 'he' and 'him', 'she' and 'her', 'we', 'they' and 'them') and the demonstrative pronouns ('this' and 'these', 'that' and 'those') must always be used in such a way that it is clear what noun it is that they stand for. What results from careless use of these words, and of some related terms ('my' and 'mine', 'your' and 'yours', 'his', 'her' and 'hers', 'their' and 'theirs') can be seen in entries under their respective headings as well as incidentally in other entries. *See* especially: I, HER, HERS, HIM, HIS, ME, THAT, THEIR, THEM, THESE, THEY, THIS, THOSE. For difficulties with relative and interrogative pronouns ('who', 'which', 'what' and 'that') *see* especially: THAT, WHO, WHOM. *See also* BOTH, EACH.

proportion. 'At the moment we are subsidising every visitor by about £1 – a large proportion of which are children.' (*Lake District Guardian*) Children cannot be a proportion of £1. *We spend £1 in subsidy for each of the visitors – a large proportion of whom are children.*

proposal. 'His proposals include a weekend in gaol for young offenders.' (*The Times*) A weekend in gaol is not a proposal. 'Proposal' and comparable words such as 'suggestion' are commonly thus misused. The trouble arises from evasion of verbs in favour of nouns like 'proposal'. *He proposed sending young offenders to gaol for a weekend.*

proscribe. *See* PRESCRIBE.

prosecution. 'Where sufficient evidence is available, prosecution will be taken.' (*The Times*) Prosecutions are not 'taken'. They may be 'initiated' or 'undertaken', but it would be better to say: *Where sufficient evidence is available, there will be prosecutions.*

prospect. 'Senior civil servants are having talks with unions representing health service staff in a bid to avert the prospect of industrial action.' (*Radio 4*) The expectation ('prospect') of industrial action is not what they are trying to avert, but industrial action itself. It is too late to remove the 'prospect': *in a bid to avert the proposed industrial action.*

'Those who stand accused of serious sexual offences face the prospect of their lives dragged into the public domain.' (*Radio 4*) Unless the word 'prospect' is to be followed by something simple ('prospect of victory'), 'prospect that' is safer than 'prospect of': *face the prospect that their lives will be dragged into the public domain.*

'It also increases the prospect of this country forming alliances with others to delay or derail EMU.' (*The Times*) The word 'prospect' tempts writers thus to use the illicit gerciple ('of this country forming'). Again one should substitute 'that': *It also increases the prospect that this country will form alliances with others.*

prospective. A spokesman from the teaching profession complained of new government proposals that they would 'lead to disappointed parents and to soured relationships between schools and prospective parents.' (*Radio 4*) A pregnant woman and her husband are 'prospective parents'; that is, parents-to-be. People contacting schools about the children they already have are not 'prospective' parents: *soured relationships between schools and parents of prospective pupils.*

protect. 'The Home Office was not going to lift a finger to protect the taxpayers' money being grabbed in this way.' (*Oldie*) A teacher would surely correct a child who wrote 'I wore it to protect my money being pinched'. One cannot protect things 'being done': *to prevent the taxpayers' money from being grabbed,* or *to safeguard the taxpayers' money against this kind of rapacity.*

We are told that in a certain model of car, 'front seatbacks protect front occupants from those in the back'. (*AA Magazine*) We ought to be told in what circumstances front-seat riders require protection from those behind.

proverbial. 'Prince is the jewel in this summer's proverbial pop concert crown, providing by far the most imaginative and extravagant show.'

(*Daily Mail*) A 'proverbial' cat would be a cat displaying the qualities noted in the proverb, having nine lives. There is no 'proverb' about a jewel in a crown. The word 'proverbial' here adds nothing to the familiar image and should be omitted.

provide. A reporter speaks of a 'summit that has cost enough to provide livestock, water and education to more than one million Sudanese'. (*Radio 4*) But we do not provide things 'to' people. We provide people 'with' things: *cost enough to provide one million Sudanese with livestock, water and education.*

providing. 'By the time a young dog is a year old, providing that it has been bred and reared correctly, all manner of "nice moves" have been developed.' (*Country Talk*) 'Providing' is now thus widely misused where 'provided' is intended. Thus *provided that it has been bred and reared correctly* would satisfy all but the purists. Fowler insisted that 'provided that' should be used only where there is a stipulation ('a demand for prior fulfilment of a conditions' as in 'You may have the cottage provided that you pay in advance'). In other contexts the proper (and obvious) word is 'if': *if it has been bred and reared correctly.*

proximity. 'In 1992 *Skiing Magazine* voted Seattle the Best Ski Town in America. Part of the reason is proximity.' (*Outdoors Illustrated*) 'Proximity' is nearness or closeness. To be near one area is to be distant from another. 'Part' and 'reason' are also inadequate words here. *One cause of this is its accessibility.*

pry. 'Marilyn fusses over her hero, prying him out of his wet clothes'. (*Woman's Own*) This is an American usage for what in English should be: *prising him out of his wet clothes.*

Pseudo-Possessives. The possessive form of nouns is sometimes improperly used.

'The Chairman of the Prison Officers' Association told this programme that West's supervision had been reduced because he'd fitted into the prison routine.' (*Radio 4*) The authority's supervision of a prisoner cannot happily be called the 'prisoner's' supervision: *The Chairman of the Prison Officers' Association told this programme that the supervision of West had been reduced.*

publicity. 'Since then publicity surrounding the virus [HIV] has been raised enormously.' (*Radio 4*) We do not 'raise' publicity. *Since then publicity about* [not 'surrounding'] *the virus has been intensified.*

'Publicity' is a word which tempts to inaccurate short-circuiting. 'The charge that the armed forces are indifferent to publicity such as the conviction of three British soldiers in Cyprus for rape . . .' (*Radio 4*) This wording cites the conviction for rape as a specimen of publicity. Unless the construction is changed there is no escape from some such expansion as: *indifferent to publicity such as that given to the conviction of three British soldiers.*

pyrrhic victory. Pyrrhus defeated the Romans with such losses on his side that he said 'One more such victory and we are lost'.

'Any business they "win" will be a pyrrhic victory.' (*Precision Marketing*) It is not any given 'business' that will be a pyrrhic victory, but 'winning' it. *Any business takeover they achieve will be a pyrrhic victory.*

Q

quality. 'It looks snazzy, original, and alluring, all of which qualities it amply demonstrates in drive mode too.' (*Lancashire Life*) Strictly no 'quality' has been mentioned here. It is incorrect to write 'He is courageous, a quality I admire', instead of 'He has courage, a quality I admire'. If 'qualities' is kept the adjectives must be replaced by nouns, but it would be better to let the word 'qualities' go. *It looks snazzy, original, and alluring, and feels so too when one drives it.*

Quotation Marks. Quotation marks, or 'inverted commas', are used at the beginning and end of direct speech. They are used to separate quoted material from unquoted material.

Current practice is to use single quotation marks. '*The news is bad,*' he *said*. Although 'The news is bad' forms a complete sentence in itself, it is not ended with a full stop because it is here part of the larger sentence ending with 'said'. Commas are thus used to separate verbs of saying from the material said. '*Whenever I have a problem,*' she *said*, '*I still consult my mother.*' In the quoted sentence here, *Whenever I have a problem,*

I still consult my mother, a comma is needed after 'problem', and therefore the comma remains so placed when the words 'she said' are added. But if the quoted sentence needs no such punctuation in its course (*I refuse to accept their decision*), then it is correct to insert the comma *after* the quotation mark: 'I refuse', she declared, 'to accept their decision.'

Question marks and exclamation marks should be placed according to sense. *'What is the point', he asked, 'of all this fuss?'* There the question mark attaches to the quoted question. *Why does he keep repeating 'I don't know'?* There the question mark attaches to the unquoted question, the sentence as a whole.

Where there is a quotation within a quotation, double quotation marks should be used. *'I can only tell you', replied defending counsel, 'that the prisoner repeatedly said "Not guilty".'*

Quotation marks are also placed around the titles of poems: *Shelley's 'Ode to a Skylark'.*

Modern practice is to use quotation marks to draw attention, sometimes ironically, to a given word or phrase: *We hear a bit too much about 'market forces'.* The device enables writers to distance themselves, disapprovingly or perhaps comically, from the expressions they use.

R

raft. 'There has been such a raft of change over a very short time people feel there's no opportunity to draw breath and consolidate.' (*Nursing Standard*) Recently the word 'raft' has been used as a convenient metaphor for an accumulation of decisions or developments bound together. It would be a pity if the word lost all metaphorical vividness, as it does here. Moreover 'that' is needed after the word 'such' (or the words 'so many'). *There have been so many changes over a very short time that people feel there's no opportunity to draw breath.*

raise. 'It will slowly start to overheat and its respiration rate and its temperature will start to raise.' (*Radio 4*) 'Raise' is a transitive verb which requires an object. When we raise the temperature, the temperature rises: *its temperature will start to rise.*

'At a time of raising environmental awareness' (*AA Magazine*) should be: *At a time of rising environmental awareness.*

range (noun). When used as a collective noun, 'range' must have a verb in the singular. 'A vast range of courses are available' (*Artists & Illustrators Magazine*) should be: *A vast range of courses is available.*

'The Hotjo range of mugs are great for people on the move. The range includes the Hotjo Shuttle.' (*Home Style*) Here the writer gets it wrong first time ('are') and right the second time ('includes'). *The Hotjo range of mugs is great.*

'Less than nine miles due north from the centre of Sarajevo are a range of hills' (*The Times*) should be: *is a range of hills.*

range (verb). 'Prices range from £2.50 to in the hundreds.' (*Period Living*) The construction 'to in' will not do. *Prices range from £2.50 to figures in the hundreds.*

ranging from. The items which are listed after these words must match one another grammatically.

'There are businesses with products ranging from cosmetics, motorcycle restoration and ceramics to farm diversification and food processing.' (*Country Lovers Magazine*) Only two items in this sequence ('cosmetics' and 'ceramics') are 'products'. The others are processes. *There are businesses ranging from the manufacture of cosmetics or ceramics to motor cycle restoration, farm diversification and food processing.*

'He [Sir Anthony Eden] was prone to severe personal judgments ranging from Mussolini to Nasser.' (*The Times*) Here Mussolini and Nasser are cited as examples of Eden's personal judgments. That is not what the writer meant. *He was prone to make severe personal judgments on people ranging from Mussolini to Nasser.*

rare. 'An 8-year-old boy has died of flu. The Argyle and Clyde Health Board said that his death was a tragic but rare event.' (*Radio 4*) The particular boy's death was not 'rare'. Everyone contributes one death to the sum total. The word 'his' must be changed. *The Argyle and Clyde Health Board said that such a death was a tragic but rare event.*

rate. 'Restaurants are rated by knives and forks.' (*AA Magazine*) This explanation of the system of classification is misleading. It suggests that a cutlery-count is the rating criterion. *The rating of restaurants is represented by knives and forks.*

rather than. This construction has to do with preference: 'He chose to go rather than to stay'. What follows 'rather than' must parallel what precedes it ('to go' . . . 'to stay').

THE MISPLACED GERUND 'Rather than' somehow lures writers to follow it by a gerund, although that is correct only where 'rather than' is preceded by a gerund, as in 'He usually goes hunting rather than fishing'.

'Many's the time he's been unquestionably right to drive by and size up the reality of the situation, rather than relying purely on the estate agent's photofit.' (*Annabel*) The infinitive 'to drive by' is improperly matched by the gerund 'relying'. *Many's the time he's been unquestionably right to drive by and size up the situation rather than to rely purely on the estate agent's photofit.*

'Some delegates said that pensioners' incomes should be increased rather than giving them the concessions.' (*The Times*) The mismatch between 'be increased' and the gerund 'giving' should be corrected. *Some delegates said that pensioners should be given increased pensions rather than the concessions.*

'But the ABI chose to present this as statistically insignificant rather than being concerned at the finding' (*The Times*) should be: *rather than to be concerned at the finding.*

'The more subtle response to Mr Blair is to take him on his own terms, rather than creating imaginary bogeys' (*The Times*) should be: *to take him on his own terms rather than to create imaginary bogeys.* This simple correction is called for a dozen times a day in the press.

'At present, ministers wish to make only limited changes to the rules, rather than establishing a new system' (*The Times*) should be: *to make only limited changes to the rules, rather than to establish a new system.*

'Therefore it is important to start with a notion of the complete design rather than regarding the background as secondary' (*The Artist*) should be: *to start with a notion of the complete design rather than to regard the background as secondary.*

'RATHER THAN BEING' There is a temptation to reach mentally for the word 'being' to follow 'rather than'.

'The result should be that historic buildings are converted for civilian use, retaining their outward appearance, rather than being bulldozed.' (*The Times*) Here 'being' is redundant and should go: *converted for civilian use rather than bulldozed.*

OTHER LAPSES When this kind of laxity is combined with other grammatical lapses, stylistic horrors accumulate.

'She crossed first barefoot, before we illogically decided that, rather than me carry her boots across and risk getting them wet when I duly fell in, I should lob them over instead.' (*The Great Outdoors*) The final 'instead' is not needed to supplement 'rather than'. 'Instead' can be used initially and the crude 'me carry' cut out: *we illogically decided that, instead of carrying her boots across and probably getting them wet, I should lob them over.*

Since the introduction of a gerund is so often the cause of error after 'rather than', it is odd to find a case where the error is failure to use a gerund, 'I limited myself to using brushes and pigment only even to the extent of using clear water to place initial marks rather than get involved with pencil.' (*The Artist*) Clearly this should be: *using clear water to place initial remarks rather than getting involved with pencil.*

'RATHER THAN' OR 'INSTEAD OF' 'Rather than' is concerned with what is preferred to what; 'instead of' is concerned with what is substituted for what. These two connotations often overlap, so that sometimes either construction might serve. It is worth remembering that 'instead of' allows greater grammatical freedom to the writer.

'Scottish law allows police officers to take drunken offenders to designated places rather than arresting them' (*Nursing Standard*) can be corrected to either: *allows police to take drunken offenders to designated places rather than to arrest them*, or: *allows police to take drunken offenders to designated places instead of arresting them.*

'We all sit down together rather than grabbing food on the run' (*Options*) should be: *We all sit down together instead of grabbing food on the run.*

'Farmers who trap a cheetah call the CCF rather than shooting the big cat' (*Wild About Animals*) should be: *instead of shooting the big cat. See also* INSTEAD OF.

THE PLACING OF 'RATHER THAN' The effect of misuse is worse when 'rather than' precedes the two alternatives. 'The other bonus of cooperative competition is that rather than life becoming a winner-take-all fight, this kind of healthy competition can actually make the whole experience fun.' (*Company*) Here 'rather than' should be replaced by 'instead of' and a common subject found for the alternatives. *The other bonus is that, instead of turning life into a winner-take-all fight, this kind of cooperative competition can make the whole experience fun.* It is always risky to begin a sentence with 'rather than'.

'Rather than jockey us along the WWT is in danger of just making enemies in the shooting world.' (*Shooting Times*) This is one of those rare occasions when the gerund after 'rather than' (to match 'making') would be correct. *Rather than jockeying us along the WWT is in danger of just making enemies in the shooting world*. However 'Instead of' would be better still: *Instead of jockeying us along*.

'Rather than returning home after touring with India in 1946, he took his family name of Kardar and went up to Oxford.' (*The Times*) Again 'instead of' is required: *Instead of returning home*.

OVERKILL There is a tendency to combine 'more' (or some other comparative) with 'rather than' in such a way as to upset the grammar.

'The square sitting-room with its single window looked to him more typical of a London suburb rather than these deep country woods.' (*Novel*) This exemplifies ungrammatical overkill. Either 'rather' should be omitted: *looked to him more typical of a London suburb than of these deep country woods*, or 'more' should be omitted: *seemed to him typical of a London suburb rather than of these deep country woods*. Note that 'of' is needed before 'these . . . woods': otherwise the square sitting room is said to be more typical of London than the country woods are.

'His concluding comment that he thought Sarajevo will eventually be liberated suggests considerably more faith in a military solution rather than internationally sponsored peace initiatives' (*Radio 4*) should be: *suggests considerably more faith in a military solution than in peace initiatives*.

'If you have elderly parents/grandparents staying over, they may find it easier to step into a shower rather than climbing into a bath' (*Perfect Home*) should be: *they may find it easier to step into a shower than to climb into a bath*.

'The German appeal for an armistice was put to President Woodrow Wilson in the hope that it would get a better deal from him rather than from Britain or France.' (*The Times*) Here again the word 'rather' should be omitted.

ration. 'I spend my time trying to ration how much TV my children watch.' (*The Times*) To ration a commodity is to restrict its distribution. It is correct to speak of 'rationing TV' but not of 'rationing how much'. *I spend my time trying to control how much TV my children watch*.

reaction. 'Yes, I can understand people taking that reaction.' (*Radio 4*) This exemplifies a growing habit of mistakenly transferring a usage from one construction to another. One can 'take' a certain attitude, but a reaction is not something that can be 'taken'. It may indeed be involuntary. *Yes, I can understand that people may react like that.*

read. 'The great strength is the text: every route is a classic and a delight to read.' (*The Great Outdoors*) The thing which is 'a classic', that is the route described, may be a delight to walk, but one cannot 'read' it: *every route is a classic and delightfully described.*

reading. 'Reading *Paintings in Progress*, it all came together' (*Artists & Illustrators Magazine*) illustrates the danger of opening a sentence with 'reading'. The participle must be matched by the subject. The reader needs to know who is 'reading'. *Reading* Paintings in Progress, *I found that it all came together.* Alternatively the participle could be dropped in favour of a separate clause. *When I read* Paintings in Progress *it all came together.* See *also* PRESENT PARTICIPLES.

ready. 'American officials hope that a deal may be ready to initial on Sunday.' (*Radio 4*) The pedant might well object to this as lax. In strict terms, the deal is not going to be ready to initial anything. *American officials hope that a deal may be ready to be initialled on Sunday.*

reality. 'Each of the films bears witness to the reality of when it was made.' (*The Times*) 'Reality' is a favourite word for manufacturers of high-sounding vacuity, as this sentence illustrates. It adds nothing. *Each of the films bears witness to when it was made.*

reappraisal. 'There has been some Department of Health money for these initial projects; others have been undertaken by a reappraisal of existing resources.' (*Nursing Standard*) We know what this means, but it remains ill-expressed: *others have been funded by redistributing existing resources.*

reason. There are various usages of this word. The one that concerns us here is its use for a human motive for action.

    REASON AND CAUSE 'He had good reason to change his job.' This connotation (involving human motive) should be distinguished from purely causal connotations. The 'reason' why he was hurrying to the post office was his wish to catch the post; but if he fell over a stone en route, the stone was the 'cause' of his fall, and not the 'reason' for his fall.

    'The reason for the crash is not clear.' (*Radio 4*) This sentence typifies the slack use of 'reason'. The air crash was an 'accident' which (probably) no one wanted. It is a question of 'cause', not 'reason'. *The cause of the crash is not known.*

    'The sudden exposure to unaccustomed hot sun that millions of us get every year on foreign holidays is probably the reason for the recent big increase in skin cancer.' (*Essentials*) This too should be: *is probably the cause of the recent big increase in skin cancer*.

Similarly talk of the Bank of England doing this or that 'in an attempt to ascertain the reasons behind sterling's weakness' (*The Times*) should be: *in an attempt to ascertain the causes behind sterling's weakness*, or better still: *to ascertain why sterling is weak*.

'Some problems [speech and language difficulties in children] are hereditary, others are caused by a head injury or are due to non-specific reasons.' (*The Times*) Here causality is again the issue, as the use of the verb 'caused' correctly indicates, for there can be no question of 'reasons' (human motivation) behind the difficulties. To avoid repeating the word 'cause' the correction could be: *others are due to a head injury or have non-specific causes*.

'There is no doubt that exercises and retrieval strategies can improve memory . . . But there is a whole range of reasons which interfere with the process, including depression, ill-health, lack of interest and attention.' (*Daily Mail*) These are not 'reasons'. They are certainly 'causes', but there is no need for the word 'cause' since the verb 'interfere' would make it redundant. *But there is a whole range of conditions which interfere with the process, including depression, ill-health, lack of interest and attention*.

THE REASON WHY Care must be taken in choosing the construction to follow 'the reason why'. It is correct to say 'The reason why I stayed at home was that I was tired', where the words could be reversed, 'That I was tired was the reason why I stayed at home'. 'The reason why' must be followed by 'that', not by 'because'.

'Wasn't the reason why grunge looked so out of sorts on the runway because the clients of designers who aped its holey sweaters and unwashed locks weren't living the lifestyle it paraded?' (*Vogue*) There are two alternative corrections. If 'because' is removed the corrected sentence will be clumsy: *Wasn't the reason why grunge looked so out of place on the runway (the fact) that the clients weren't living the lifestyle it paraded?* Therefore it is better to remove 'reason': *Wasn't it because the clients of designers . . . weren't living the lifestyle it paraded that grunge looked so out of place on the runway?*

rebel. 'She was born in Egypt with a severe and scornful father from whom she was to spend her life rebelling.' (*The Times*) We rebel 'against' people or institutions, not 'from' them. Moreover, someone might be born with a birthmark or even with a twin sister, but no one can be born 'with' a father. *She was born in Egypt to a severe and scornful father against whom she was to spend her life rebelling.*

rebuke. A government minister wrote a letter to *The Times* criticising Baroness Thatcher, and received a reprimand. 'Alistair Burt's rebuke was widely rumoured at Westminster.' (*Radio 4*) But the rebuke administered by Mr Major could not become the possession of the rebuked ('Alistair Burt's'). Nor was the rebuke 'rumoured', but the act of rebuking. *That Alistair Burt had been rebuked was widely rumoured at Westminster.*

recapitulate. 'The report does not recapitulate on the DTI report published in 1990.' (*The Times*) To recapitulate an argument is to restate it. Just as we do not 'restate "on"' a matter, so we do not 'recapitulate "on"' it. The preposition 'on' must go. *The report does not recapitulate the substance of the DTI report published in 1990.*

receive. 'In view of the enthusiasm received from owners of all makes and types of historic motor vehicles, it has been decided to include them in the event.' (*Old Glory*) Enthusiasm cannot be 'received'. It may be aroused, registered, or communicated: *In view of the enthusiasm registered by owners of all makes and types.*

recent. 'The government and opposition parties in the republic agreed to hold talks with Russia about ending the recent fighting.' (*Radio 4*) A recent happening belongs to the past. It is no more possible to end 'recent' fighting than to prevent a recent accident. The fighting and the accident have happened. It is too late to 'end' them: *talks with Russia about ending the fighting which has recently broken out.*

reception. 'The contrast between the reception to Norman Lamont's preelection budget five years ago and that given to Kenneth Clarke's budget 10 days ago is striking.' (*Daily Telegraph*) Convention allows two options: 'the reception "of" the budget' and 'the reception "given to" the budget'. Either 'given' must be inserted in the first part of the sentence: *The contrast between the reception given to Norman Lamont's preelection budget five years ago and that given to Kenneth Clarke's*, or 'given' removed in the second part of the sentence, and 'of' used instead of 'to': *The contrast between the reception of Norman Lamont's budget five years ago and that of Kenneth Clarke's budget 10 days ago.*

record. 'Only five or six records of them being seen in the country in February exist.' (*Wild About Animals*) Like 'example' and 'instance', 'record' tends to lead to this error: *only five or six records of their being seen. See also* GERCIPLES.

recoup. 'The region is . . . a country of great charm and tranquillity, a place to recoup from the pressure of modern city life.' (*The Great Outdoors*) 'Recoup' is a transitive verb, used especially of recovering financial losses. It is not used intransitively of recovering from stress or ill-health: *a place to recover from the pressure of modern city life.*

recourse/resort. The connection between these two words can be seen in the dictionary definition of 'recourse' as 'the act of resorting to a course of action'. Where 'resort' can be a noun or a verb, 'recourse' is a noun only. It occurs most often after the verb 'to have' ('to have recourse to'). Thus *When all else failed, her last resort was to call the police* could equally well be *When all else failed she finally had recourse to calling the police* or even *When all else failed she finally resorted to calling the police.*

recrimination. 'Mr Major is said to bear no recriminations on the visit of Gerry Adams' [to the USA]. (*Radio 4*) A 'recrimination' is a counter-accusation. It is not something that people 'bear'. *Mr Major is said not to resent the visit of Gerry Adams.*

rectify. 'Should Eurotunnel ever have been as confident as it was that a disaster of that type could be prevented, contained or, at worst, easily rectified?' (*Radio 4*) Disasters cannot be corrected or 'rectified'. Strictly speaking they cannot even be remedied, though their effects might be. It is difficult to find the right word without changing the construction. Possibly it could be: *prevented, contained or, at least, easily offset.*

reek/wreak. 'The recent cold spell has reeked havoc on homes and businesses alike.' (*Kes Mail*) To reek is to stink. The required word is the verb 'to wreak'. *The recent cold spell has wreaked havoc.*

'The place wreaked of disinfectant, greasy food, sweat and ash.' (*The Times*) The verb to 'wreak' means to cause, generally used of doing damage ('wreaking havoc'). So the correct wording is: *The place reeked of disinfectant.*

refer to. 'In the underwater world, or "inner space", as Jacques Cousteau refers to it, divers can explore the secrets of sunken cities or shipwrecks.' (*Outdoors Illustrated*) Jacques Cousteau can 'refer to the underwater world as "inner space"', but that construction cannot be put into reverse ('the "inner space" as Jacques Cousteau refers to it as') because of the grammatical necessity for the second 'as'. In all such usages ('known as', 'described as' etc.) the reverse cannot be used ('very wicked, as he was described as'). This is no loss because the verb 'call' is always available: *or "inner space", as Jacques Cousteau calls it. See* KNOWN AS.

reference. '"Shaw", meaning "thicket", was once almost as common as the word "wood" itself, and in Chaucer there are several references to the word.' (*Family History*) There is here confusion between word and thing, name and item, between use of a word ('The wood is a lonely place') and reference to a word ('"Wood" is a monosyllable'). Chaucer does not contain 'references' to the word: *and Chaucer uses the word several times.*

reference to. This expression lures to the use of the gerciple. 'But the sceptics want a more specific reference to Britain not being affected.' (*The Times*) To correct this as it stands would be clumsy ('to Britain's not being affected'). It is better to change the construction. *But the sceptics want it specifically stated that Britain will not be affected.*

refurnish. 'The interior of the chapel was re-furnished including a new altar, the work of artist Peter Ball.' (*Trout & Salmon*) This sentence wrongly includes the 'new' altar among the items 'refurnished'. *The interior of the chapel was refurnished and a new altar, the work of artist Peter Ball, was installed.*

regard. When used in the expressions 'with regard to' or 'as regards', there is almost always a better word.

'Ofgas have certain powers to determine disputes between British Gas and any person claiming compensation with regard to whether compensation is payable under the scheme or whether the amount of such compensation is appropriate.' (*British Gas*) The writer should start again. *Where disputes arise between British Gas and persons claiming compensation, Ofgas have the power to determine whether compensation is payable under the scheme and what the amount of such compensation should be.*

'He was years ahead of his colleagues in this regard' (*The Times*) is an awkward way of saying: *He was years ahead of his colleagues in this respect.*

regarded. This participle must be not be allowed to drift from proper anchorage.

'Generally regarded as a highly competent and efficient Secretary General [of NATO], his successor will inherit a variety of urgent problems.'

(*Radio* 4) This tells us that 'his successor' was regarded as highly competent. *He was generally regarded as a highly competent and efficient General Secretary, but his successor will inherit certain problems.*

'Regarded as "Multi-Fuel", meaning it can burn just about anything that can be compressed and lit, you will have little trouble finding a suitable propellant.' (*Adventure Travel*) We are here told that we are regarded as Multi-Fuel. Moreover, the word 'meaning' is ill-used. *Since it is regarded as "Multi-Fuel", and can therefore burn just about anything that can be compressed and lit, you will have little difficulty in finding a suitable propellant.*

'Regarded as a close friend of Mian Nawaz Sharif, the prime minister, his appointment will help to end existing mistrust.' (*The Times*) Here someone's appointment is said to be regarded as a close friend of a prime minister. Either the first part of the sentence must be changed: *As he is regarded as a close friend of the prime minister, his appointment will help to end existing mistrust*, or the second part: *Regarded as a close friend, he will by his appointment help to end existing mistrust.*

regarding. Overuse of this word to mean 'in connection with' or even 'as for' is now common. Worse still it is used where a simple preposition would be better.

'REGARDING' FOR 'IN' 'Timing is of the essence regarding obtaining the correct moves from a dog.' (*Country Talk*) Here the word required is 'in' and 'of the essence' is pretentious. *Timing is essential in obtaining the correct moves from a dog.*

'REGARDING' FOR 'ABOUT' 'The Belgian Justice Minister is due to give an emergency statement shortly regarding the series of child murders.' (*Radio* 4) Why 'regarding'? What is wrong with the simple English word 'about'? And is 'give' the right word? *The Belgian Justice Minister is due to make an emergency statement shortly about the series of child murders.*

'REGARDING' FOR 'ON' 'In Tailback, issue 16, you summarised the law regarding wheel clamping' (*AA Magazine*) should be: *you summarised the law on wheel clamping.*

regime. 'Pharmacists can organise your medicines if you have a complicated regime.' (*New Woman*) It is a pity that the word 'regime', with its political and social connotations, should now be ousting the more specific term in medical matters: *if you have a complicated regimen.*

reinforce. 'The new findings reinforce how much we have to learn.' (*Radio* 4) To reinforce something is to give it added support. Either the construction must be changed: *These new findings reinforce the view that we have much to learn*, or the verb: *emphasise how much we have to learn*.

reintroduction. 'But SNH has no plans to look at either wolf or bear reintroduction at present.' (*The Great Outdoors*) The issue is a proposal to bring back wolves to Scotland. Such absurd usages as 'wolf reintroduction' arise from fondness for nouns instead of verbs. *But SNH has no plans to reintroduce either the bear or the wolf.*

related. When writers begin sentences with this word, they must remember to match it in what follows.

'Related in a sequence of self-contained episodes that oscillate between past and present, McCrary Boyd's vivid prose follows firmly in the Southern footsteps of writers like Ellen Gilchrist, Florence King and Rita Mae Brown.' (*Woman's Journal*) What is 'related in self-contained episodes'? The writer tells us that the vivid prose is. That is not what was meant. However accomplished the writing may seem on the surface, the error is really an elementary one. *Relating a sequence of self-contained episodes that oscillate between past and present, McCrary Boyd's vivid prose follows firmly in the Southern footsteps of writers like Ellen Gilchrist, Florence King and Rita Mae Brown.*

relieve. 'We share the shopping, the cooking and the washing up, which has certainly relieved the domestic burden.' (*She*) If a man carries his wife's shopping bag he does not relieve the shopping bag; he relieves his wife of it. One cannot 'relieve' a burden. *We share the shopping, the cooking and the washing up, which has certainly reduced the domestic burden.*

relinquish. 'He failed to relinquish an incompetent colleague of his duties despite a number of warnings from senior operating department assistants.' (*Private Eye*) To relinquish something is to give it up, to let it go. It is incorrect to speak of relinquishing someone else of something: *He failed to relieve an incompetent colleague of his duties.* One hopes that the editor of *Private Eye* proves equally indulgent.

rely. 'But overall safety with pets relies very much in the hands of the pet-owner.' (*OK! Homes*) We rely 'on' something, not 'in' it. Either the preposition must be changed: *relies very much on the pet-owner*, or the verb: *lies very much in the hands of the pet-owner.*

remember. 'Do you remember me telling you a while back about Anne catching me out when I was in the bathroom?' (*The People's Friend*) The verb 'remember' lures to this error: *Do you remember my telling you,* or: *Do you remember how I told you. See* GERCIPLES.

remission / remittance. Though they are commonly connected with the verb 'to remit', these two words are very different in their meanings. The noun 'remission' is used of releasing someone from a penalty, or forgiving them: *The record of good conduct earned him remission of three months imprisonment*. The noun 'remittance' is used of a payment, usually one sent through the post: *Send your order, along with the appropriate remittance, to the firm's headquarters*.

remittance. *See* REMISSION.

remote. 'The remote site hampered search and rescue operations.' (*Radio 4*) The use of the adjective 'remote' here is open to question. We may say 'A thick wall impeded our progress', because the wall did indeed 'impede'. But in the sentence here the spokesman did not really mean that the 'site' hampered anyone. The remoteness did. *The remoteness of the site hampered search and rescue operations*.

renowned. 'Renowned not just throughout Britain but by railway enthusiasts the world over as one of the greatest feats of Victorian railway engineering, the Settle to Carlisle line is now safe from the threat of closure.' (*Cumbria Life*) Enthusiasts cannot 'renown' things, not even a railway, so the line is not renowned 'by' enthusiasts but 'among' them: *Renowned not just throughout Britain but among railway enthusiasts the world over*. Alternatively the verb could be changed to one which can be followed by the preposition 'by': *Acclaimed not just throughout Britain but by railway enthusiasts the world over as one of the greatest feats*.

Care must be taken to connect the word properly in its context. 'Internationally renowned for its collections and associated research, The Natural History Museum's aim is to be relevant and accessible.' (*The Times*) Here the 'aim', instead of the museum, is said to be internationally renowned: *Internationally renowned for its collections and associated research, the Museum aims to be relevant*.

replace. 'Actually, they've replaced my imagination – for someone else's – yours, in fact, dear sister. Now I know all your intimate thoughts.' (*The Times*) Usage allows us to 'exchange' one thing for another, or 'substitute' one thing for another, but one cannot 'replace' something 'for' another. We replace one thing 'by' another: *Actually they've replaced my imagination by someone else's*.

require. 'To provide Fully Comprehensive cover for a boat fabricated by a reputable builder, underwriters require simply the type of craft and its value.' (*Waterways World*) The underwriters do not 'require' anything except information. Avoid here the fancy word 'fabricated'. *To provide Fully Comprehensive cover for a boat built by a reputable builder, underwriters need only to know the type of craft and its value.*

research. 'I am currently involved in an in-depth research upon Single Women Travellers, both for those involved in travel for personal and business purposes.' (*Complete Traveller*) We do not research 'upon' subjects, the word 'both' is misplaced, and the word 'for' is redundant. *I am currently involved in research into Single Women Travellers, whether travelling for personal or for business purposes.*

resilient. 'At any age, women today expect to have luminous skin, that is resilient to ageing.' (*Company*) Something which is resilient bounces back when put out of shape. Human beings can be resilient in response to difficulties or shocks. The advertiser seems to assume that 'resilient to' is an alternative to 'resistant to'. A woman might be said to be 'resilient' in combating the effects of ageing, but not her skin. In any case, if 're-silient' is used it cannot be followed by 'to ageing'. It is better not to use the word here: *luminous skin that is unaffected by ageing.*

resolve. 'A new arrears processing system has enabled the Society to contact almost all borrowers in arrears. . . in order to discuss how their financial position can be resolved.' (*Britannia Building Society*) There are things (like 'doubts') that can be resolved, and things that can't. A financial position is not something that can be resolved: *how their financial position might be improved/restored.*

resort. *See* RECOURSE.

responsible for. This expression can easily lead to use of the gerciple. 'It was largely his hard talking that was responsible in 1976 for the first non-white South African being elected to a scholarship.' (*The Times*) Technically it would be correct to write 'responsible for the first non-white South African's being elected to a scholarship', but the construction is unnecessary: *responsible for the election of the first non-white South African to a scholarship.*

restive/restless. Both adjectives mean what the word 'restless' obviously conveys, unable to be still, and both imply uneasiness, but 'restless' is the more generally used because 'restive' has the additional, faintly pejorative connotation of impatience with some authority: *He was restive under the new regime.*

restless. *See* RESTIVE.

result (noun). Someone might say 'He worked hard on the picture and the result was beautiful', but this free conversational use of the construction (calling a 'result' beautiful) should not be over-elaborated.

'More work has gone into this novel, and the result, while losing none of her characteristic lambency, is the best that Isabel Colegate has written.' (*Independent*) A 'result' cannot be said to lose or not lose lambency. *More work has gone into this book: as a consequence the novel lacks none of her characteristic lambency and is the best Isabel Colegate has written.*

'The gentle non-drip formula smooths long hair with no mess, leaving a completely natural result.' (*Essentials*) It is not the 'result' that is natural, but the condition that results. In any case the word 'result' is unnecessary, merely repeating what the word 'leaving' conveys: *leaving it completely natural. See also* FORMULA.

result (verb). Where 'result' is used as a verb, it lures the writer into gerciples. 'And that resulted in us being separated' (*Best of British*) should be: *in our being separated.*

'He must have felt tired and that tiredness may have resulted in him falling asleep.' (*The Times*) Better here than the direct correction ('in his falling asleep') would be to change the verb: *and that tiredness may have caused him to fall asleep.*

'The low level bridge would prevent yachts from navigating the Ribble and there is concern that this could result in the marina no longer remaining economically viable, leading to closure.' (*Waterways World*) Direct correction would be: *result in the marina's no longer remaining viable.* But it might be better to scrap the verb 'result' and use the phrase 'as a result' instead: *and there is concern that as a result the marina would no longer remain economically viable and would have to close.*

'His rugged but light designs resulted in him towing in remote areas and in such hostile terrain as Morocco.' (*Caravan Magazine*) It is illogical to suggest that the ruggedness and lightness of the caravan 'resulted' in the owner's trips abroad. It is best to change the verb: *The rugged but light design enabled him to tow in remote areas.*

'The location of the engine results in a total prop shaft length of 33ft in 3 sections' (*Waterways World*) should be: *The engine is so placed that the total prop shaft length is 33ft in 3 sections.*

'He got into a fight with a 34-year-old gas-fitter which resulted in both suffering cuts and bruises.' (*The Times*) Again the word 'resulted' is not worth keeping. *He got into a fight with a 34-year-old gas-fitter which left both with cuts and bruises.*

retrace. 'T S Eliot's *Murder in the Cathedral* tells the story of his [Becket's] death, a tale which is retraced today by thousands of visitors to Canterbury Cathedral and which Canon Dr Ingram Hill knows step by step.' (*Radio 4*) The visitors do not 'retrace' a tale but a certain sequence of events which the tale records. People do not know tales 'step by step'. Murder in the Cathedral *tells the story of Becket's death, events which are recalled today by thousands of visitors to Canterbury Cathedral, and which Canon Dr Ingram Hill can retrace step by step.*

retract. 'They stand by their story. They don't retract from the broad thrust.' (*Radio 4*) Though there is archaic use of 'retract' as an intransitive verb, in modern usage the verb is transitive. *They don't retract the broad thrust.*

reverence. '. . . Greek orthodox adherents who take special reverence in their language being the word of Christ . . .' (*The Times*) People may 'feel' reverence, but they do not 'take' it. If 'take' is kept, 'reverence' must go: *who take special pride in their language as the word of Christ.* If 'reverence' is kept, 'take' must go: *who feel special reverence for their language as the word of Christ.*

reversal/reversion. If a policy is 'reversed', that constitutes a 'reversal', a change from going in one direction to going in the opposite direction. Where, in a man's will, income is left to his widow during her lifetime, but will 'revert' to his son and heir after her death, that constitutes a 'reversion'.

reversion. *See* REVERSAL.

reward. 'Mr Blair has rewarded innovators and high-fliers rather than the traditional patronage given to trade unionists.' (*The Times*) This is like saying 'I eat meat rather than the fashionable vegetarianism'. Parallelism after 'rather than' must be preserved. *Mr Blair has rewarded innovators and high-fliers rather than the trade unionists traditionally honoured.*

rifle. 'You may be given piles of old junk to take away and rifle through in your own time.' (*Family History*) To 'rifle' is to ransack or steal, and the verb is transitive. (It would not require to be followed by 'through'.)

The verb meaning to flick through pages and thus to make a quick examination of things is 'riffle', followed by 'through': *piles of old junk to take away and riffle through in your own time.*

'She rifled through the leaflets, marvelling at the choice there seemed to be in terms of where to stay.' (*Woman*) Although to 'rifle' can be to search (transitively), again the verb looks out of place: *She riffled through the leaflets.*

rigorous. 'Sir Ron [Dearing] said his objective was to bring another fifth of young people into successful education and training whilst ensuring the qualifications are rigorous.' (*Radio 4*) A qualification such as a diploma or a degree cannot be strict or harsh ('rigorous'). Only the programme of studies or the required examination can be so: *whilst ensuring that the courses are rigorous.*

ring. 'His duty was to see that all their snouts were properly rung.' (*Family History*) The verb to 'ring' (a bell etc.) has the past tense 'rung', but not so the verb used here. *His duty was to see that all their snouts were properly ringed.*

rise. *See* RAISE.

risk (noun). This is another word that attracts gerciples.

'One way to spread the risk of changes in inflation and interest rates affecting your equity-based holdings is to invest part of your portfolio overseas.' (*Moneywise*) The best way to avoid the bad construction ('of changes affecting') is to get into the habit of following the word 'risk' by 'that' instead of by 'of': *One way to spread the risk that changes in inflation and interest rates will affect your equity-based holdings.*

'There's far higher risk of a child being killed' (*Woman's Own*) should be: *a far higher risk that a child will be killed.*

'The idea of super glueing well-formed knots enabling tag ends to be clipped off near the knot without risk of the knot slipping' (*Sea Angler*) should become: *without risk that the knot will slip.*

'Japanese have been thinking seriously about how to cope with the ever greater risks of earthquakes destroying their cities' (*The Times*) should be: *how to cope with the ever greater risks that earthquakes will destroy their cities.*

'It can help reduce the risk of the baby being born with spina bifida' (*Living*) should be: *It can help reduce the risk that the baby might be born with spina bifida.*

'Get rid of the debris from rhubarb patches and asparagus beds to lessen the risk of disease and rot getting in during the winter' (*Cumbria Life*) should be: *to lessen the risk that disease and rot will get in during the winter.*

risk (verb). The verb 'to risk' lures to the same error as the noun. The same remedy is recommended. Acquire the habit of following 'risk' by 'that'.

Thus 'You must be prepared to risk the romantic relationships ending' (*New Woman*) would become: *You must be prepared to risk that the romantic relationship will end.*

'Unless you're prepared to risk the rate on your savings becoming uncompetitive' (*Woman's Own*) would be: *risk that your savings will become uncompetitive.*

risky. As one should remember to follow 'risk' by 'that' rather than by 'of', so one must remember to follow 'risky' by 'to' (the infinitive) rather than by a gerund.

'It is too risky being linked to accountants' (*The Times*) should be: *It is too risky to be linked to accountants.*

role. 'It seems inevitable that the role of endowment policies in their current form will continue to decline.' (*Moneywise*) Overuse of the word 'role' is common. It means the part played by a person or the function performed. The connotation is such that it is better not used except of living beings. *It seems inevitable that the use of endowment policies in their present form will decrease.*

'Peter Baring, 59, the chairman, reputedly earns about £1.2 million a year, including his role as deputy chairman of the Provident Mutual Life Assurance Association.' (*The Times*) But his role is not part of his earnings: *reputedly earns about £1.2 million a year, including what he makes as chairman of the Provident Mutual Life Assurance Association.*

romanticise. 'Local legend romanticises on what lies beneath the tor.' (*Caravan Magazine*) The verb 'to romanticise' is transitive. We can romanticise a situation, but we cannot romanticise 'on' it. *Local legend has romantic theories about what lies beneath the tor.*

Routes. Giving directions for routes readily produces error often involving grammatical misconnections.

'Travelling south after arriving at Orlando, the first stop is Sea World of Florida.' (*New Woman*) This conveys that the first stop was travelling south. It is safest to avoid beginning a sentence with a participle. *As you travel south after arriving at Orlando, the first stop is Sea World of Florida.*

'Passing the site of one of the first radar stations, there is an option of turning downhill for Ventnor.' (*Country Walking*) Here an option is said to be passing the site. *Passing the site of one of the first radar stations, the walker has the option of turning downhill for Ventnor.*

'From Martindale the walk heads back down to Howtown by taking the path from behind the church.' (*Trail*) But the the walk does not take the path; the walker does: *From Martindale the walker heads back down to Howtown by taking the path.*

'This curving arête, with fine views across Llanberis Pass to the Gliders, is soon left on the left (west) side, down red screes at the end of the sharp section and across rough slabs towards Llyn Glas, conscious all the time of the superb setting of the Clogwyn y Parson arête.' (*The Great Outdoors*) Who is 'conscious'? We are told that the 'arête' is 'conscious' of the superb setting. If 'conscious' is kept, a subject must be found for it: *and we are conscious all the time of the superb setting.*

rub. 'John Major said he could not rub away all the bruises.' (*Radio 4*) Surely rubbing is not the appropriate treatment for bruises. *John Major said he could not heal all the bruises.*

S

safeguard. 'We believe this is an essential safeguard not only against illegal immigration, but also to combat transnational crime and terrorism.' (*The Times*) My double-glazed windows may be a safeguard against crime but they cannot be a safeguard 'to combat thieves'. Safeguards are not implements of combat. Moreover, the words 'not only' . . . 'but also' must be followed by matching grammatical constructions. 'not only against' cannot be followed by 'but also to'. *We believe this is an essential safeguard not only against illegal immigration but also against transnational crime and terrorism.* The alternative is to change the construction. *We believe that this will not only prevent illegal immigration but also impede transnational crime and terrorism.*

salacious. 'He also denied rumours of other possible defections, saying "They are just salacious stories".' (*The Times*) 'Salacious' means bawdy or erotic. It would seem that the minister here quoted was feeling for some word that means spiteful and malicious. *They are just mischievous gossip.*

same. 'Strictly speaking they should be called glass container banks . . . but this descriptive name doesn't trip off the tongue the same as "Bottle Banks".' (*Allerdale Outlook*) 'Same' is generally an adjective and cannot be turned into a kind of conjunction: *this descriptive name doesn't trip off the tongue as does 'Bottle Banks'.*

'Competition between breeders for a coveted prize and the top prices commanded by a champion animal were the motives behind the effort to ensure that whatever the quality of this year's stock, next year's would be better. The same is still true.' (*The Field*) This is like saying, 'They believed in hard work: the same is still true' instead of 'They believed in hard work, and they still do'. The word 'same', the notion of similarity, is not relevant. The writer seems to mean: *That is still the case*, or perhaps better: *That will always be the case.*

same as. Parallels must be placed ('This' is the same as 'that') so that there can be no mistake about what is being compared to what.

'He [Tagliavini] also made his North American debut with the Chicago Lyric Opera, by way of Mexico City, in the same season as Rodolfo'. (*The Times*) The uninitiated are going to assume that Rodolfo is another opera singer with a parallel career, though he is the leading tenor character in *La Bohème*. The word order should be changed: *In the same season he also made his North American debut as Rodolfo with the Chicago Lyric Opera.*

There is nothing to be said for substituting 'same that' for 'same as'. 'Deep planting can actually kill trees, so plant them at the same level that they were planted at the nursery.' (*Country Living*) This should be: *plant them at the same level as they were planted at in the nursery.*

sanguine. 'Joanna Cox, who has lobbied at the UN for many years for a Swiss Women's Charity, is sanguine about such textual discussions.' (*Radio 4*) From the context it was clear that here was a misunderstanding of the word 'sanguine', which means cheerful and confident: *Joanna Cox is lukewarm/sceptical about such textual discussions.*

sat. 'Sat silently at the next table, we soaked up every moment.' (*Go Greek*) No one can be described as 'sat'. It is like saying 'Lived next door, she was my best friend' instead of 'Living next door, she was my best friend'. *Sitting silently at the next table, we soaked up every moment.*

save. There is a lax use of 'save', where 'prevent' would be better.

'My four-year-old daughter would like to know what colour spider blood is. Do please answer, to save any more experiments being carried out.' (*BBC Wildlife*) 'Save' is not the best word here. *Do please answer, to prevent any more experiments from being carried out.* But better still would be to economise in words by using the neglected verb 'forestall', which would obviate the need for the last four words of the sentence: *to forestall any more experiments.*

say. 'The pages held a long list of names, and one name seemed to crop up regularly, in the same form each time. It unmistakably said "Smith".' (*Family History*) The name did not 'say' Smith: *one name seemed to crop up regularly in the same form each time. It was 'Smith'*. The verb 'say' can be followed by a quoted statement in direct speech ('He said "Get off"') or indirect speech ('She said it was time to go'). It can also be followed by certain general terms ('She said a lot' or 'She said little'), but we cannot 'say' a speech or a statement.

'A director general must be prepared to voice in public the criticisms of government policy which most bosses will say only in private.' (*The Times*) Usage allows us to 'make' or 'utter' a criticism, but not to 'say' it: *the criticisms of government policy which most bosses will make only in private.*

'Everything the scientists have said to us to do we have done.' (*Radio 4*) The verb 'say' is not thus followed by the infinitive 'to do'. Either the verb must be changed: *Everything the scientists have advised us to do we have done*, or the construction that follows it: *Everything the scientists have said that we should do, we have done.*

'We haven't particularly said in those warnings about the bomber.' (*Radio 4*) Usage allows us to 'speak' about a bomber, but not to 'say' about him. *We haven't particularly spoken in those warnings about the bomber.* An alternative would be: *We didn't specifically mention the bomber in those warnings.*

scarcely. 'Scarcely a single name among the most prominent of younger British composers could not be associated with his teaching.' (*The Times*) Sentences introduced thus by 'scarcely' require a verb in the affirmative. *Scarcely a single name among the most prominent of younger British composers lacked association with his teaching.*

scratchbuilt. This innovatory compound – 'Scratchbuilt wagons' (*Railway Modeller*) meaning 'wagons built from scratch' – has seemingly established itself in the world of modelling. We also find 'kitbuilt' (built from a kit), presumably on the model of 'stone-built'. Whereas the material of construction may be stone or a kit, scratch does not get used thus. The innovation is more ingenious than felicitous.

scrawl. To scrawl is to write or scribble carelessly and untidily.

'Little notebooks with ivory pages survive, some of them scrawled with love letters.' (*Country Living*) Letters can be 'scrawled' but pages cannot. *Little notebooks with ivory pages survive, some with love letters scrawled on them.*

seasonable. *See* SEASONAL.

seasonal/seasonable. The adjective 'seasonal' stands in relation to the noun 'season' as the adjective 'daily' stands in relation to the noun 'day': *In tourist areas there is plenty of seasonal employment in the hotel trade.* The adjective 'seasonable' means appropriate to the given season: *In England a snowfall may be seasonable in January, but it is certainly not in June.*

secret. 'The secret to getting it right is knowing your undertone.' (*Company*) This is an instance of improper constructional transfer. The preposition 'to' is transferred from the usage 'the clue to success' to the noun 'secret' to which it cannot be properly linked: *The secret of getting it right.*

'The secret to carving a chicken is to use a sharp knife' (*Essentials*) should be: *The secret of carving a chicken.*

section (noun). 'The emphasis is on things Scottish, including jewellery, paintings, pottery, drawings and, most importantly, modern and vintage sporting guns and rifles. This section came in the evening.' (*Shooting Times*) The fact that a show contains many displays does not justify calling any one of them a 'section', nor should one say that a section 'came'. *This display took place in the evening.*

section (verb). 'But why are GPs so reluctant to get involved in the sectioning of clients with mental health problems?' (*Nursing Times*) This curious usage derives from reference to the section of the Mental Health Act which governs the detention of patients in institutions. If the verb is strictly understood, 'sectioning' a patient would be a gruesome surgical process. For this reason one may question whether the new usage is an improvement on the old. *But why are GPs so reluctant to get involved in certifying clients with mental health problems?*

see. We have a legitimate use of this verb in 'I have lived to see better times', which has been extended into 'Investors have seen the stockmarket fall heavily', and then into 'The stockmarket has seen a heavy fall', where the literal meaning of 'see' is lost. It is lax to extend this usage further.

'Tesco's ratings have been harshly treated partly because it may see marginally lower same-store sales growth than its rivals.' (*Investors Chronicle*) What is 'it'? Presumably the firm. The metaphor of 'seeing' is out of place: *partly because the firm may record marginally lower same-store sales.*

seep. 'As the impact of this budget seeps through' (*Radio 4*) represents an unfortunate mixture of idioms. No 'impact' could possibly leak through the ground: *As the impact of this budget makes itself felt.*

segment. 'There are also segments of our population who don't work after the age of 50 or 55.' (*The Scots Magazine*) This is an inappropriate and pretentious evasion of what should be simple and direct. *Some people don't work after the age of 50 or 55.*

selection. This collective noun generally takes a singular verb.

'However, this selection of his achievements, both national and international, serve only to illustrate Geoffrey Slack's rare quality of inspired leadership' (*Independent*) should be: *this selection of his achievements, both national and international, serves only to illustrate Geoffrey Slack's rare quality.*

'Later he told the BBC his selection would help end the rift in his local Tory association.' (*Radio 4*) If Jane selects John as her bridge partner, he is 'her' selection, and it is not the best usage to speak of 'his' selection (by Jane) in that context. The noun 'selection' would be better avoided here in favour of the verb 'select': *he told the BBC that selecting him would help end the rift in his local Tory party*, or: *that if he were selected it would help to end the rift.*

self-. As a prefix 'self-' is well established in compounds such as 'self-service' and 'self-control', which have to do with serving the self and controlling the self.

'The Open University has developed a wide range of popular self-study packs' (*Midland Choice*) misuses the prefix. 'Self-study' would be study of the self: *has developed a wide range of private study packs*.

Semicolon. The semicolon is used to mark a slightly more definite break than the comma indicates. Generally speaking, it separates clauses which are too closely related to justify use of a colon or a full stop between them (*My father paid for the reception; my mother gave us our honeymoon*). The semicolon is also useful in such sequences of related items as *We were too tired to walk further; moreover it was getting dark*. See also COMMA: WHERE COMMAS ARE INADEQUATE.

sense. 'The deck is high-sided, adding significantly to the interior's sense of space.' (*Waterways World*) A human being may experience a 'sense of space' but an 'interior' cannot have one: *adding significantly to the interior's seeming spaciousness*, or: *adding significantly to one's sense of space inside*.

sensible. 'Where there's a great similarity between a movie and a crime there might be a sensible connection.' (*New Woman*) The quoted speaker does not say what he means here. It is not the 'connection' that might be 'sensible', but making it. *Where there's a great similarity between a movie and a crime, it might be sensible to make a connection*.

sensitivity. 'Allegations of wrong-doing in school opt-out ballots are nothing new, but when they are made in the Labour leader's own backyard, they achieve even greater sensitivity.' (*Radio 4*) Even greater sensitivity than what? We have just been told that such allegations are common. What logic leads us to expect after 'but' is some kind of contrast. As it is the sentence is a pure non-sequitur. It is like saying 'Road accidents are common, but when they happen in the your own street they achieve greater publicity', which clearly does not make sense. The word 'greater' must go from both sentences: *but when they are made in the Labour leader's own backyard they become sensitive political matters*.

sensual/sensuous. Both these adjectives have to do with the pleasures of the senses, but 'sensual' has a pejorative connotation, and 'sensuous' does not. To speak of a man as given over to 'sensual' delights is to imply that he is a slave to the body's appetites, over-indulgent in food or wine or sexual pleasure. By contrast 'sensuous' has a positive connotation. It is used in praising what is physically beautiful: *Ruben's nudes have a rich, sensuous appeal*.

sensuous. *See* SENSUAL.

Sentences. A sentence should make an articulate whole. Failures in sentence structure take various forms.

FAILURE IN STRUCTURAL CONTINUITY To switch construction in the middle of a sentence ought to be impossible to the good writer. 'Mr George has openly acknowledged that he would like consumer demand to slacken and for the economy's firepower to be redirected towards exports and investment.' (*The Times*) The sentence, 'I would like you to sing and (to) dance', maintains a consistent construction. The sentence, 'I would like you to sing and for dancing to be done', does not. The word 'for' leads the writer astray. *Mr George has openly acknowledged that he would like consumer demand to slacken and the economy's firepower to be redirected.*

'Being pilot involved Viv joining (or leaving) ships in the river Mersey adjacent to Canning Dock and to safely navigate through the narrow channel up the river to Widnes dock.' (*Waterways World*) Here 'involved Viv' is followed first by 'joining' and then by 'to safely navigate' as though the two constructions were the same. *Being pilot involved Viv in joining (or leaving) ships in the river Mersey adjacent to Canning Dock and in safely navigating through the narrow channel.*

'As a tranquilliser Largactil has an obvious use in the treatment of schizophrenia, manic depressive psychosis and when dealing with garrulous, obstreperous and dangerous psychopaths.' (*The Times*) The sequential listing here again breaks down after 'and'. A list such as 'the consumption of potatoes, beans, and when having a picnic' will not do. The word 'when' must go: *the treatment of schizophrenia, manic depressive psychosis and dangerous psychopaths.*

'Operators of these holidays have a number of duties to clients including dealing promptly and fairly with justifiable complaints, not seeking to blame third parties for the problems, and to ensure they are sufficiently protected to provide consumer funds in the event of company failure.' (*Lancashire Life*) In the list of three items that follow the word 'including', the construction changes between the second and the third so that 'dealing promptly' and 'not seeking' are followed by 'to ensure': *not seeking to blame third parties, and ensuring that they are sufficiently protected.*

'Many of the products are ideal as starters such as boned quail and smoked Irish mussels rolled in seasalt and black pepper and of course the distinctive taste of Scottish salmon.' (*Country Talk*) Here the list of products breaks down when 'quail' and 'mussels' are followed by the 'taste' of salmon: *such as boned quails and smoked Irish mussels rolled in seasalt and black pepper, and of course the distinctively tasty Scottish salmon.*

FAULTY FUSION Errors arise when two constructions are improperly fused together in the same sentence. 'Firstdirect was launched. Its highly visible and rather eccentric advertising was designed to, and succeeded in making it famous quickly and at an affordable cost.' (*Meridian*) The words 'designed to' must be followed by 'make'; they cannot be followed by 'in making'; nor could 'succeeded' be followed by 'to make'. The two constructions cannot be fused. *Its highly visible and rather eccentric advertising was designed to make it famous quickly at an affordable cost, and succeeded in doing so.*

'It's super because unlike many ordinary cod liver oils it contains about fifty per cent more EPA and DHA.' (*Woman's Journal*) The writer here fuses two incompatible constructions. One may say 'John has more sense than his brothers' or 'Unlike his brother, John has plenty of sense', but the two constructions cannot be combined in 'Unlike his brother, John has more sense' because the two brothers could not possibly resemble each other in both having 'more' sense than the other. Nor could the various cod liver oils be like each other in all having fifty per cent more this or that. So 'unlike' must go. *It's super because it contains fifty per cent more EPA and DHA than many ordinary cod liver oils.*

series. 'President Milosovitch from Serbia has been trying to influence both people within the SDS and a series of other parties.' (*Radio 4*) Surely the various parties consulted are not really a 'series', a group of related things in successive order. It is a pity to weaken the word's connotation. And why President Milosovitch 'from' Serbia. One would not speak of 'Queen Elizabeth from England'. *President Milosovitch of Serbia has been trying to influence people both within the SDS and in a number of other parties.*

serious. 'What unites us is much more serious than the enormous division between us and the Labour party.' (*Radio 4*) What is meant here? The Tory speaker implies that the division between Tory and Labour is not after all the most 'serious' thing. *What divides us is trivial compared to the enormous division between us and Labour.*

'If it continues to follow such an unpopular and self-destruct policy, then it will bring the whole European Union into serious disrepute.'

(*Radio* 4) This use of 'serious' as a catch-all term of emphasis weakens a useful word. It is here redundant. It should be omitted, and a proper adjective should be put in place of the grammatically unclassifiable 'self-destruct'. *If it continues to follow such an unpopular and fruitless policy, it will bring the whole European Union into disrepute.*

service. 'The accident happened when an Amtrack long-distance train hit the back of a commuter service during a snow storm.' (*Radio* 4) A newswriter should distinguish between a train and a train service. It was the train that was hit, not the service: *when an Amtrack long-distance train hit the back of a commuter train.*

settle. 'Inevitably there are organisations and individuals who have other objectives which will eventually be settled.' (*Automobile*) 'Objectives' are goals to be aimed at; they are not disputes or disturbances that can be 'settled'. *Inevitably there are organisations and individuals who have other objectives which will eventually be served.*

sexuality. 'The wife . . . discovered her husband's true sexuality only after a family row prompted her to hire a private detective who found his birth certificate.' (*The Times*) The birth certificate revealed the 'husband' to be a female. In short it established the sex. The word 'sexuality' is out of place: *discovered her husband's true sex.*

shackles. 'The shackles of shuttle diplomacy are clattering in ever more complicated patterns across the Middle East.' (*Radio* 4) Alliteration seems to have lured the commentator into excess here. The movements of a shuttle may be mechanical, but the thing would not work at all if it were shackled. As for clattering here and there in complicated patterns, this is not the way shackles function. *There are ever more complex movements of shuttle diplomacy across the Middle East.*

she. *See* HER.

shore. 'What he's doing is shoring up all sorts of trouble for the future.' (*Radio* 4) To 'shore' something up is to give it support and make it safe. It is the wrong verb to use here. *What he's doing is storing up all sorts of trouble.*

show. Although this is usually a transitive verb, it is sometimes used intransitively ('The new film is showing in London'). The usage is not elegant, and should not be extended.

'An exhibition of the building of eighteenth-century Bath is showing at the Royal Institute of British Architects Heinz Gallery' (*Independent*) would better be: *An exhibition is on show*, and better still, since an exhibition is itself a show: *An exhibition is being held*.

side. An idiomatic use of this word allows us to say 'There was another side to his life', even though we are not picturing a 'side', but rather using the word loosely of an 'aspect' or 'department' of something. That usage would not justify the following.

'Another side of his life was as a Freeman of the Goldsmiths Company.' (*Independent*) The 'side' cannot 'be' 'as a Freeman': the word is out of place. *He also served as a Freeman of the Goldsmiths Company*.

'The industry has spent a fortune in pursuit of the conservation side.' (*Shooting Times*) There is no such 'side'. The word is unnecessary anyway: *spent a fortune in pursuit of conservation*.

significance. 'The paintings collected from all over the country hold special significance to the exhibition.' (*Cumbria Life*) 'To' is here the wrong preposition after 'hold'. The paintings either: *have a special significance for the exhibition*, or *give a special significance to the exhibition*.

signify. '21st June saw the bicentennial of Braunston Tunnel being opened. This was commemorated on the 15th June when Tim Boswell MP unveiled a plaque signifying the event.' (*Waterways World*) The passive gerciple ('of Braunston Tunnel being opened') is not good and 'signifying' is not the appropriate verb. It is not a matter of indicating something but of recalling it. *21st June saw the bicentennial of the opening of Braunston Tunnel. This was commemorated on 15th June when Tim Boswell MP unveiled a plaque celebrating the event*.

similar. This is one of those adjectives which link items together in parallel, and the parallelism must be maintained. 'He has a "realised eschatology" similar to Albert Schweitzer.' (*Independent*) The eschatology is not similar to Schweitzer but to Schweitzer's eschatology. *He has a 'realised eschatology' similar to Schweitzer's*.

'The drizzling rain on the windscreen was similar to the night on which he'd been killed.' (*Woman*) Rain cannot be 'similar' to a night. Since it would be clumsy to correct this directly to 'similar to that on the night on which he was killed', it would be better to scrap 'similar': *The drizzling rain on the windscreen reminded her of the night on which he was killed*.

It is not unusual to find this error of comparing something to a past time instead of to what happened at that time. 'As in previous years, the vast majority have been in the topmost reaches of the estuary, upstream of Newburn, but we have recovered about 15 from further upstream, similar to previous years.' (*Trout & Salmon*) The first comparison with the past ('As in previous years') is satisfactory, but in the second, 'similar' does not connect either backwards or forwards: *but we have recovered about 15 from further upstream, as in previous years.*

similarities. 'Similarities include both connecting a number of lakes by artificial channels, and military reasons for their construction.' (*Waterways World*) The subject is the 'twinning of the Caledonian and Rideau canals'. The sentence excellently illustrates the awkwardness of using nouns, such as 'similarities' and 'construction', instead of verbs. *The two are similar in that both connect a number of lakes by artificial channels and both were constructed for military purposes.*

similarity. What applies to 'similar' applies to 'similarity'. Due parallelism must be preserved between items linked together by resemblance.

'We are very concerned at the similarity between our client and the name proposed for the half-hour programme.' (*The Times*) The parallel is misrepresented here. *We are very concerned at the similarity between our client's name and the name proposed for the programme.*

since. The most natural use of this word is in statements such as 'We haven't seen her since Christmas', where 'since' places the act of seeing her.

'Colleagues believe that the 3.5 per cent reduction since last October has not made sufficient political impact.' (*The Times*) Here 'since' is awkwardly attached to the noun 'reduction'. There should be a verb which functions as 'haven't seen' functions above. *Colleagues believe that the 3.5 per cent reduction made since last October has not had sufficient political impact.*

'Sheffield Polytechnic yesterday announced the biggest building and reconstruction programme in higher education since the new universities.' (*The Times*) 'New universities' does not place events as 'last October' placed them above. Either a suitable word should be inserted: *the biggest building and reconstruction programme . . . since the foundation of the new universities,* or a verb added: *since the new universities were founded.*

Singular and Plural. A singular subject should generally be followed by a singular verb and a plural subject by a plural verb. There are circumstances in which writers slip up in this respect seemingly through sheer forgetfulness.

MISUSE OF SINGULAR VERB It is less common (but perhaps cruder) for writers to forget that their subject is plural and to follow it by a singular verb than to lapse conversely after a singular subject.

'Ancient connections between dark things and evil and witchcraft ensures we think dark or black hair has a slightly sinister but erotic appeal.' (*Company*) The singular verb grates badly: *Ancient connections . . . ensure that we think.*

'Some 187 courses, as well as many conferences and training sessions brings in some 3,700 residential guests.' (*Country Lovers Magazine*) This should be: *courses as well as many conferences bring in guests.* There is more excuse for this error when the sentence is longer. 'The coating is so thin that its protective properties under exposure, say on the chassis of a car, is almost negligible.' (*Automobile*) The parenthesis ('say on the chassis of a car') lengthens the sentence and allows the writer to forget the plurality of 'protective properties': *its protective properties . . . are almost negligible.*

MISUSE OF SINGULAR NOUN No less awkward is the kind of forgetfulness which affects what should be a plural noun. 'Most of the stewards at the Royal Show would be insulted to be considered a yuppy' (*The Field*) would better be: *Most of the stewards . . . would be insulted to be considered yuppies.*

'Often patients deemed suitable are allowed home at the weekends with their beds being filled by an emergency admission' (*Radio 4*) should be: *their beds being filled by emergency admissions.* ('With' must go. *See* WITH.)

MISUSE OF PLURAL VERB There is little temptation to slip up over singular and plural where the singular subject is directly followed by the verb. No one would write (of a picture) 'The final richness are added', but we read 'The final richness of colour and tone are added' (*Artists & Illustrators Magazine*). Having written 'colour and tone', the writer forgets that his subject is the singular word 'richness', but no number of elaborations can affect what accuracy requires: *The final richness of colour and tone is added.* This is a common cause of error. In 'The high tide of the free market and trade union reforms have passed.' (*The Times*) the listing of 'free market and trade union reforms' causes the writer to forget that the subject of his sentence was the singular 'high tide'. *The high tide of the free market and trade union reforms has passed.*

'A fall in investment returns on the world's share and bond markets mean that today's policies may no longer grow enough to repay a home loan.' (*The Times*) The plurals 'returns', 'markets', and 'policies' lure the writer to forget that his subject 'fall' was singular and should be followed by *means*.

'Now they are having to admit that the continued liberty of people like Karadic and the fifty or so other war criminals are posing a threat to these elections.' (*Radio 4*) It is the singular 'continued liberty' that *is posing a threat*.

On the subject of potted palms we read 'Their distinctly structural appearance fits the essence of Art Deco style yet are also a good complement for contemporary design.' (*Perfect Home*) The writer's mind is on 'palms' (mentioned in the previous sentence) when it ought to be on 'appearance': *Their distinctly structural appearance fits the essence of Art Deco style yet is also a good complement*.

'The EU, with the support of trade unions, argues that working long hours are a threat to health and safety' (*The Times*) should be: *working long hours is a threat to health and safety*.

'The price of large houses, particularly in central London, are rising sharply' (*The Times*) should be: *The price of large houses . . . is rising sharply*.

THE UNIVERSAL SINGULAR The universal singular has traditionally been used in such statements as Shakespeare's 'What a piece of work is man!' where the word 'man', singular in form, covers the whole human race. 'Although men like having a blonde on their arm for fun, when it comes to settling down they prefer a brunette, who they reckon are more trustworthy.' (*19*) 'Men like having a blonde' acceptably moves from the plural to the generalised singular 'blonde', but the generalised singular 'brunette' cannot be followed by 'who are more trustworthy'. It is best to stick to the plural: *when it comes to settling down they prefer brunettes*.

'Create a focal point – these are invaluable for adding interest and structure'. (*Home Style*) Again the generalised singular ('a focal point') would be better avoided in view of what follows: *Create focal points, these are invaluable*.

In descriptive writing the artificial singular noun can be attractive but easily leads to grammatical inconsistency. 'At night the birch can take on a magical air as the light of the moon is held on their silver surface' (*Dalesman*) should be: *as the light of the moon is held on its silver surface*.

'When the coil, the IUD, was first introduced, it seemed an ideal method of contraception. Initially, when they are fitted, there is a danger of the perforation of the uterus.' (*The Times*) Although there are two sentences here, the transition from 'it seemed' to 'they are fitted' is slip-shod: *Initially, when it is fitted there is a danger.*

site. 'The site at Shires Meadow, Warfield, near Bracknell, is among a consortium of builders all vying for trade.' (*Perfect Home*) A 'consortium' is an association usually of businessmen or companies. The site cannot be involved in a consortium. Nor, presumably, would members of a consortium all 'vie' with each other for trade. We have to guess what is meant. *On the site at Shires Meadow, Warfield, near Bracknell, various builders are vying for trade.*

sitting. Where a sentence begins with this participle, an appropriate word must follow in agreement with it.

'Sitting with the guide open at the appropriate page, there seemed to be no difficulties.' (*Best of British*) We need to know who is 'sitting'. *Sitting with the guide open at the appropriate page, I found no difficulties.*

'Sitting by the fire, thoughts go back to friends and relations no longer with us.' (*Dalesman*) The thoughts are not sitting by the fire. *Sitting by the fire, I think of friends and relations no longer with us.*

situation. This word became a vogue word two decades ago. It was no longer the thing to speak of 'the man in business' or 'the person on holiday'; one had to say 'the man in a business situation' or 'the person in a holiday situation'. The worst excesses of this practice may have gone, but traces remain.

'Husbands staying away from their families for prolonged periods in hotels or rented accommodation is a situation best avoided.' (*Me*) The word is redundant. *The absence of husbands from their families for prolonged periods in hotels or rented accommodation is best avoided.*

There is also a tendency to use the word 'situation' inexactly. 'She [a government minister] decided that the situation should now go ahead.' (*Radio 4*) The concept of a situation 'going ahead' exemplifies how usage of the word has degenerated. Probably the most satisfactory paraphrase would be: *She decided to let things stand*, or possibly: *She decided to let the scheme go forward.*

small. The word 'small' has a flavour of formality which 'little' lacks. 'In a small piece of luck the Trust withdrew £150,000 [from Barings Bank] just last Thursday.' (*Radio 4*) The idiomatic 'piece' of luck cannot happily be subjected to measurement. And anyway the Trust is not 'in' it. *By a stroke of luck the Trust withdrew £150,000 just last Thursday.*

small print. 'As the UK's largest animal insurer we have the best claims settlement in the market, fewer exclusions than anyone else and no hidden small print.' (*Horse & Hound*) 'Small print' may not be easily read, but it is surely not 'hidden'. (Why bother to make it small if it is hidden anyway?) This should be either: *no hidden conditions*, or just: *no small print*.

so. In conversation we use this word with a freedom which would be inappropriate in print. Sometimes all that is necessary to correct the usage is to turn 'so' into 'so that'.

'But now your child certainly needs to build up his own life outside the family so he has something to fall back on as your pregnancy advances.' (*Parents*) This would become: *so that he has something to fall back on*.

Correction is not always so simple as that. 'Duggie Jooste has designed and built a beautiful new winery with vaulted ceilings, a gallery so visitors can walk round and watch it at work . . .' (*Decanter*) The clause beginning with 'so' applies only to the gallery and thus performs a pseudo-adjectival function. It should be replaced by a genuine adjectival clause: *a gallery which enables people to walk round*.

so does. 'As the diplomatic initiatives continue, so does the military exchanges across the border between Israel and Lebanon.' (*Radio 4*) The familiar expression 'so does' slips too easily into the mind of the newswriter. *As the diplomatic initiatives continue, so do the military exchanges across the border*.

so that. Used to introduce a result, 'so that' must hinge on a verb ('She saved up so that she could go abroad').

'Despite surgery so that the ear drained, an abscess formed.' (*The Times*) 'So that' cannot hinge thus on the noun 'surgery'. In one way or another the construction must be changed. *Despite surgery, undertaken to drain the ear, an abscess formed*. Alternatively a relative clause could be used. *Despite surgery, which drained the ear, an abscess formed*.

solution. 'It is about finding the right solutions to a myriad of opportunities.' (*Precision Marketing*) 'It' is expert marketing. But opportunities do not demand solutions. On the contrary, they open up possibilities. *It is about making the most of a myriad of opportunities*.

solve. Like 'solution' (above), this word ought not to be used in relation to matters that are in no sense soluble.

'The fate of the Russian Czars may be solved today.' (*Radio 4*) This news item was about the identification of remains supposed to be those of the murdered Czar and his family. Identification could not solve their fate, because a fate is not soluble. Either an appropriate subject for 'solved' must be introduced: *The mystery about the murder of the Czar may be solved*, or the word 'solved' must go: *The fate of the Russian Czars may become known*. Best of all would be to get rid of 'fate' too: *What happened to the Russian Czars may become known today*.

some . . . others. There must be strict parallelism in the two constructions following these two words when used together.

'The main aims and objectives of the Strategy will be achieved in a variety of ways, some through already accepted methods, others which are completely new ideas require a totally different approach.' (*Country-Side*) The construction after 'others' must balance the construction after 'some'. Either the construction after 'some' must be changed: *some can be dealt with by already accepted methods, others, which are completely new ideas, require a totally different approach*, or the construction after 'others': *some through already accepted methods, others, which are completely new ideas, through a totally different approach*.

sometimes. 'Sometimes' means 'now and then'. It should not be used without this temporal connotation. 'Old deeds, unfortunately, now often languish hidden in financial institutions and are sometimes never seen by the houses owners.' (*Old-House Journal*) The juxtaposition of 'sometimes never' is unfortunate: *and in some cases are never seen by the houses' owners*.

somewhere. 'Do ensure that you are registered with the National House Building Council, the Master Builders Federation, or some similar professional body, so that you have somewhere to appeal to if the work goes horribly wrong.' (*Meridian*) These bodies are not locations, so 'somewhere' is slipshod English, but the misuse is not rare: *so that you have some body to appeal to*.

soothe. 'Sentiments like these have done nothing to soothe old wounds in the Tory party.' (*Radio 4*) One may soothe someone by curing their complaint but it is not the complaint that is 'soothed': *have done nothing to heal old wounds in the Tory party*.

'Soothe and smooth one of the latest body creams, lotions or oils on to damp skin.' (*Company*) Why tell the reader to soothe a body cream? This is using the verb 'soothe' meaninglessly for the sake of the nice noise it makes. *Smooth one of the creams soothingly on to damp skin*.

sort of. *See* KIND OF.

sound. 'Bullfinches are a typical sound on hot July days.' (*Times*) A bird cannot be a sound. And one should discourage this insensitive use of the word 'typical' as a kind of synonym for 'frequent'. *The song of the bullfinch is often heard on hot July days.*

speak. 'Mr Hanley of course is a member of the . . . committee set up to try to spot ministerial gaffes before they are spoken.' (*Radio 4*) We do not 'speak' gaffes: *to try to spot ministerial gaffes before they are made.*

speaking. 'Speaking' is a participle which must agree with a noun or pronoun ('Speaking as a judge, I condemn the act').

'Speaking as someone who's involved in business, we've got to stop this hysteria about Europe.' (*Radio 4*) But 'we' are not speaking. *Speaking as someone who's involved in business, I think we must stop this hysteria.*

specify. To 'specify' something is to refer to it specifically. It is a pity to weaken the word by careless use.

'If specifying a passenger lift has become difficult you may like to try a Stannah.' (*The Times*) The issue is not one of specifying, but of selecting. *If choosing a passenger lift has become difficult, you may like to try a Stannah.*

speed. 'The thefts [after an earthquake] are being seen as a further sign of frustration over the speed of the rescue effort.' (*Radio 4*) 'Speed' is not frustrating anyone: it is the lack of speed that is the trouble. *The thefts are being seen as a further sign of frustration over the slowness/tardiness of the rescue effort.*

spend. The business world has a tendency to turn verbs into nouns and nouns into verbs. 'It can increase the average spend of customers.' (*Marketing Week*) There is no noun 'spend'. The gerund of the verb can be used: *increase the average spending.* Otherwise the corresponding noun can be used. *It can increase the average expenditure of customers. See also* MAKE.

spiritual. 'The chapel is still a place of worship with services held every Tuesday, although its previous five hundred years have not all been spiritual.' (*Waterways World*) A 'year' cannot be spiritual: *although its use over the last five hundred years has not been exclusively spiritual.*

Split Infinitives. To split an infinitive is to insert an adverb between two elements of the infinitive, that is, to write (i) *She was determined to proudly rebuff him* instead of either (ii) *She was determined proudly to rebuff him* or (iii) *She was determined to rebuff him proudly*. From this example it should be clear that the split infinitive often provides a more satisfactory sentence than does evasion of the construction. Version (ii) is unsatisfactory because the adverb 'proudly', so placed, attaches itself to the verb 'determined' instead of to the verb 'rebuff'. Version (iii) is unsatisfactory because the word order sounds unnatural. There areindeed occasions when the split infinitive sounds awkward, but these occasions are not numerous enough to justify a general judgment against the split infinitive. Sensitivity to what is natural in word order is a better guide in this matter than any rule. In *Modern English Usage* Fowler has great fun with the contortions that the anti-split-infinitive brigade sometimes resort to. And indeed the most foolish of those contortions is the misapplication of the rule to sentences involving the verb 'to be'. Thus to change (i) *The rescuer ought to be most generously rewarded* into (ii) *The rescuer ought most generously to be rewarded* is unsound because there is no split infinitive in (i). The verb is 'to be' in English grammar. Only in Latin grammar could 'to be rewarded' be regarded as a unit.

square the circle. Because it is impossible to construct a square which has the same area as a given circle, the expression is used of attempting the impossible.

Speaking of the situation in Haiti after the landing of American troops there, a newsreader spoke of 'Washington trying to square a difficult circle'. (*Radio 4*) This is linguistic overkill. No circle can be easier or more difficult than another when it comes to the attempt to square it: *Washington trying to square the circle.*

stage. 'The dun stage of a fly is that highly edible one when the nymph, which has lived in the water, emerges as the immature flying insect.' (*Shooting Times*) No 'stage' can be edible. Only the insect can. *The dun stage of a fly, at which it is highly edible, is reached when the nymph, which has lived in the water, emerges as the immature flying insect.*

stamina. 'This [the loose construction of the work] perhaps contributed to the ensuing neglect of the concerto over the ensuing years, along with the stamina required for the heroic solo part.' (*Programme Note*) The concerto in question is Rachmaninov's 3rd piano concerto. Plainly it was not the required 'stamina' that contributed to its neglect but the need for it and the rarity of it: *along with the demand for stamina made by the heroic solo part.*

standstill. 'Large areas of France are at a standstill today.' (*Radio 4*) This comment on industrial action suggests that the areas are normally mobile. *In large areas of France business is at a standstill today.*

start (noun). 'Michael Saunders noted that an abrupt plunge in housing starts in 1989–90 was one of the first clues to the severity of the subsequent recession, and the continued refusal of starts to pick up in 1991 and early 1992 signalled that the overall economy would remain sluggish.' (*The Times*) 'Housing starts' are credited here with 'refusal' to act. Sometimes verbal economy is purchased at too high a cost in smoothness and elegance: *Michael Saunders noted that a sharp drop in the number of houses started in 1989–90 was one of the first clues . . . and the continued failure to reverse this trend in 1991 and early 1992 signalled that the overall economy would remain sluggish.*

start (verb). 'The number of houses that started construction in the final three months of 1995 slumped 20 per cent from a year earlier.' (*The Times*) Surely houses do not 'start' construction. Builders do that: *The number of houses that began to be built in the final three months.*

Starting a Sentence. There are several constructions which, when used at the beginning of a sentence, can easily lead to error. Starting from any of these constructions requires special care.

FROM PAST PARTICIPLE Making a risky start to a sentence often involves what is called a 'hanging participle' or a 'detached participle'. In the sentence 'We found him drenched to the skin', it is clear that 'drenched to the skin' describes 'him'. In the sentence 'Drenched to the skin, he rushed indoors to change his clothes', it is again clear that 'drenched to the skin' applies to 'he'. But beginning with 'Drenched to the skin' has its risks. The careless writer gives us 'Drenched to the skin, the hot bath was pure delight'. And what is wrong with that is that it describes the 'hot bath' as 'drenched to the skin'. The writer has made a false start. He begins by writing a sentence with the subject 'he' in mind, and switches to a sentence with the subject 'bath'. It is easily done.

'Made as part of the Rivers of France series, the artist appears to have discovered a natural empathy with the mighty River Seine.' (*Oxford Today*) This is an advertisement for Turner prints. It tells us that the artist was made as part of a series, the writer having switched from a sentence intended to be about the prints to a sentence about the artist.

Made as part of the Rivers of France series, they show the artist to have discovered a natural empathy.

Describing books, works of art or their makers seems to tempt writers into this kind of difficulty.

'Illustrated with colour photographs and plans, and with concise plant profiles, you will be able to group plants of each particular season together.' (*Independent*) This time 'you', the reader, are said to be illustrated with colour photographs. *Illustrated with colour photographs and plans, the book will enable you to group plants of each particular season together.*

'Custom-made for a perfect fit, prices start at £39.' (*OK! Homes*) Here the prices are said to be 'custom-made'. *Custom-made for a perfect fit, the roller blind is priced from £39.*

There are one or two words which seem especially to tempt the writer into risky starts of this kind. *See* FACED, KNOWN AS, REGARDED, RENOWNED.

FROM PRESENT PARTICIPLE Just as starting with a past participle often leads astray, so does opening with a present participle. 'Working closely with Mrs Royston, the mural quickly evolved from early sketches.' (*The Times*) When the writer began with 'Working closely . . .' she plainly intended to make the subject of her sentence the artist, Seth Royston. She forgot. So her sentence tells us instead that the mural worked with Mrs Royston. *Working closely with Mrs Royston, he quickly created the mural from early sketches.*

This degree of grammatical forgetfulness is far from rare. 'Requiring small bulbs for my car, the local motor accessory shop quoted 55p each.' (*The Times*) But it was not the 'local motor shop' which required the bulbs, as here stated. *When I required small bulbs for my car, the local motor accessory shop quoted 55p.* It will be seen that when the participle opening ('Requiring') is abandoned in favour of 'When', the danger of error is diminished.

The more complicated the sentence, the easier it is to go astray from initial construction. 'Presiding over cod and apple-pie dinners at her Queen Square salon, a mesmerisingly eccentric spirit shone out.' (*Vogue*) It was not this mesmerising spirit that presided at the table but the hostess in whom it dwelt. Again it is better to drop the participle. *As she presided over . . . dinners at her Queen Square salon, her mesmerisingly eccentric spirit shone out.*

'Striking deep into the rural heartland, his interest in the ever-changing landscape never flagged.' (*Home & Country*) It was not his interest that struck deep into the heartland, as here indicated. The possessive 'his' cannot stand for 'he'. *As he struck deep into the rural heartland, his interest never flagged. See also* POSSESSIVE TRAP.

FROM PAST & PRESENT PARTICIPLES Even in sophisticated writing this bad usage frequently slips in. 'Forced prematurely into contemplative and well-mannered adulthood, teetering and uncertain on her red suede high heels, the seeds of Rego's phobia-driven imaginative talents sprang up thick and strong.' (*The Times*) This writer tells us that the seeds of the artist's imaginative talents wore red suede high heels and were forced prematurely into adulthood. If the participles ('forced' and 'teetering') are to be kept, then 'Rego' (not her 'talents' or their 'seeds') must become the subject of what follows. *Forced prematurely into contemplative and well-mannered adulthood, Rego felt the seeds of her phobia-driven imaginative talents springing up thick and strong.*

FROM A GERUND There is a risky kind of start which does not involve a participle but a gerund, 'In going away, we lost our bearings' is satisfactory because 'we' are the ones who are 'going away'. 'In losing an identifiable adversary after the Cold War, Nato's role has been called into question by elected politicians and planners alike.' (*The Times*) This second leader implies that Nato's role has lost its adversary. The writer has been caught by the possessive trap. *In losing an identifiable adversary after the Cold War, Nato has found its role called into question.*

FROM AN APPOSITIONAL PHRASE 'An honest tradesman, John Smith prospered' is correct because John Smith is the 'honest tradesman' already described. 'An honest tradesman, John Smith's shop was well patronised' is faulty because the shop was not an honest tradesman. In complex sentences, this error is easily hidden and therefore common. 'A member of the London Group who came to notice as a "kitchen sink painter" inspired by ordinary domestic surroundings, the late John Bratby's vigorous realism made him a key figure in 20th-century British painting.' (*Artists & Illustrators Magazine*) This tells us that John Bratby's realism was a member of the London Group. It represents again the possessive trap. John Bratby must be distinguished from his 'realism'. *A member of the London Group who came to notice as a 'kitchen sink painter', the late John Bratby became a key figure in 20th-century British painting through his vigorous realism.*

starting from. When giving directions, it can be risky to begin a sentence with 'Starting from'.

'Starting from the laybys in Llanberis Pass, Clogwyn y Person can be approached up footpaths that climb steeply up Cwm Glas Mawr.' (*The Great Outdoors*) This tells us that Clogwyn y Person starts from the laybys. The participle is best avoided. *If one starts from the laybys in Llanberis Pass, Clogwyn y Person can be approached up footpaths. See also* ROUTES.

status quo. This Latin expression means the existing state of things.

'A source within the United Nations protection forces said a status quo had been reached in the enclave.' (*Radio 4*) People cannot in discussion 'reach' a status quo. The wrong Latin expression appears to have been used. *A source within the UN said a modus vivendi had been reached.* A 'modus vivendi' is a working compromise between conflicting parties.

stay. 'I cannot think of a place I would prefer to stay.' (*Saga Magazine*) One does not stay a place. One stays 'at' it. *I cannot think of a place I would prefer to stay at.*

stay-clean. *See* COINAGES.

staying. 'Staying with the frames, they are tied together by cross stays or stretchers . . .' (*Steam Classic*) This is a curious idiom. 'Staying with the Browns, we went fishing' would be an appropriate usage. Above 'they' are the frames, but they are not 'staying'. It should be either: *While on the subject of the frames, they are tied together*, or better still: *As for the frames, they are tied together.*

step. 'When we contacted the Department of Health, it acknowledged there simply aren't enough [psychiatric beds], pointing out that urgent steps are under way to address the shortfall.' (*Radio 4*) If we 'take' steps to improve matters, it is not the steps that are then 'under way', but the improvement: *pointing out that steps are being taken to deal with the shortfall.*

'The first positive step has been taken in the form of the excellent Mill Arts Centre beside the lock.' (*Waterways World*) But the first step in the development of the old canal area at Banbury was not 'in the form' of the Centre. *The first positive step has been taken in the construction of the excellent Mill Arts Centre beside the lock.*

stepping-stone. 'Suddenly the stepping stone has tilted the wrong way.' (*Radio 4*) Is the newswriter, commenting on developments in Labour party politics about clause 4, thinking of a see-saw? The usefulness of a stepping-stone is not primarily determined by the direction of its tilt. A weathercock or a barometer might provide a safer metaphor.

stereotype. 'We live in an extremely complex society and we need to categorise things to simplify them. Stereotypes are going too far, but they do help other people understand the basic messages we're sending by our actions.' (*Company*) The stereotypes are not 'going too far'. Presumably what is meant is: *Stereotyping can go too far, but it does help other people.*

stimulant/stimulus. These two nouns are both concerned with what 'stimulates'. The more generally used is 'stimulus'. Anything that stimulates, whether it be a physical goad, a psychological incentive to action, or a drug, can be called a 'stimulus'. But 'stimulant' is used chiefly of drugs and in particular of alcohol.

stimulus. *See* STIMULANT.

stipulate. In making deals or agreements we may 'stipulate' that this or that is a necessary condition. The word is not synonymous with 'specify', which is used without reference to the making of demands.

'It did not stipulate which station the bomb had been left at.' (*Radio 4*) This refers to a coded warning from the IRA about an incident at a railway station. There is no question of a deal here. The message from the IRA is purely informative. *It did not specify which station the bomb had been left at.*

stoop. 'As he [the Pope] was met by President Chirac and his wife, he looked stooped and he shuffled as he walked.' (*Radio 4*) In general use the verb is intransitive, like 'to sleep' and one would not say 'He looked slept'. *As he was met he seemed to stoop.*

stop. If you 'stop' a ball on the field, you halt its progress. Unless there is movement or action, there is nothing to stop.

' . . . solid rubber or "sucker" feet will stop your machine bouncing off the table at high speeds.' (*Moneywise*) One cannot stop the thing bouncing unless it has started to bounce: *solid rubber or 'sucker' feet will prevent your machine from bouncing off the table.*

This confusion between 'stop' and 'prevent' is all too common. 'And it didn't stop the shares in both companies falling' (*Investors Chronicle*) should be: *And it didn't prevent the shares in both companies from falling.*

store. *See* SHORE.

straight. 'A straight garden path can be improved if it curves gently.'

(*Meridian*) If a garden path is straight, then it does not curve. What 'can be improved' is not the straight path, but the path. As long as it is straight, there will be no improvement. *A garden path which is straight can be improved by a gentle curve.*

strata. 'But for a certain youngish strata of musicians and rock fans . . .' (*The Times*) A 'stratum' is a layer. The word keeps its Latin plural 'strata', which cannot be singular: *But for a certain youngish stratum of musicians.*

Even a government minister can slip up too. 'He had also identified himself . . . as coming from a particular strata of English educational history' (*The Times*) should be: *coming from a particular stratum of English educational history.*

study. 'Routine sreening for breast cancer is to be extended to older women in a study announced by the Government yesterday.' (*The Times*) The screening is not going to be extended in a study. This is like saying 'The battle of Waterloo will be fought in chapter 3'. *Routine screening for breast cancer is to be extended to older women, according to a Government study.*

subject. A subject acts while an object suffers the action. If you subject me to ridicule, I become the object of your ridicule.

'The Rev Lynne Mayers, from Liverpool, said all the women ministers she had spoken to had at some time been the subject of sexual misconduct.' (*Independent*) The wrong word has been used here. Either 'subject' must be changed to 'object': *all the women ministers had at some time been the object of sexual harrassment,* or 'subject' must become a verb: *had at some time been subjected to sexual harrassment.*

'Sweaters, pullovers, waistcoats and jackets are her main subjects.' (*Cumbria Life*) She makes fashionable knitwear, but the sweaters and pullovers are not her 'subjects': *are her main products.*

Subjunctives. We make statements in the 'indicative' mood, but where doubts, suggestions or suppositions are being expressed the mood which 'indicates' has been considered inappropriate. *If they were to be defeated, the manager would resign.* In this instance 'were to be' is a subjunctive. However, in current usage, one would be more likely to get: *If they are defeated, the manager will resign.* Thus the subjunctive is disappearing from the language. In expressing hypotheses we still make use of the subjunctive: *I dearly wish it were all over and done with.* And the form is useful where conditions are being proposed which the speaker thinks unlikely to be fulfilled: *If someone were to turn up unexpectedly,*

I could always open a can of beans. But for most expressions of condition and possibility we use the auxiliary forms 'may' and 'might', 'would' and 'should'. Indeed nowadays awareness of the subjunctive mood is necessary chiefly for purposes of translation.

subscribe. 'Can I write about these images of American churches with the same detachment that Walter Evans, their photographer, subscribed to?' (*World of Interiors*) To subscribe to a cause is to give it support and approval. A person can reveal, achieve, or even value detachment, but to speak of 'subscribing to it' is misplaced: *the same pure detachment that Walker Evans, their photographer, achieved*.

substance. 'Patients with a substance misuse and a mental health problem . . .' (*Nursing Standard*) Expressions such as 'a substance misuse problem' indicate an acute vocabulary misuse problem. What is wrong with: *patients who take drugs and are mentally unstable*?

substantially. The adjective 'substantial' means of a considerable size, value, or importance.

'An initial prospectus reveals the government intends to sell substantially all of its holding in the company.' (*Radio 4*) The company in question is Railtrack. The word 'substantially' appears here to be meaningless. The government is selling either 'all' its holding or 'most of its holding'.

substantiate. 'The packaged produce now went direct from the manufacturer to the kitchen "untouched by human hand". To substantiate these newly wrapped and branded goods the firms added messages of credibility – medals awarded for excellence or guarantees of quality.' (*Best of British*) We 'substantiate' a claim when we support it with evidence. It was not the 'goods' that were substantiated, but the claims made for those goods. Moreover, medals are not 'messages of credibility': *To substantiate the claim made for these newly wrapped and branded goods the firm added evidence of their reliability*.

substitute. A manager may substitute a reserve player for an injured player. Therefore the reserve player is 'substituted', not the injured one, who is 'replaced'. The tendency now, as often as not, is to get this clear distinction wrong.

Thus 'The Department of Health has now ordered that wooden spatulas be withdrawn and substituted by sterile plastic splints' (*Radio 4*) should be either: *should be withdrawn and replaced by sterile plastic splints,* or: *should be withdrawn and sterile plastic splints substituted.*

'Biography has attained great significance – it sometimes seems as if life-as-reported has started to substitute for life-as-lived.' (*Independent*) This leader should read: *it sometimes seems as if life-as-reported has started to replace life-as lived.*

The advice to walkers, 'you can terminate the full horseshoe and substitute it with a shorter yet still useful round' (*The Great Outdoors*) should be: *you can terminate the full horseshoe and substitute for it a shorter yet still useful round.*

'On the "Thatcherite Revolutionary" T-shirt, Che Guevara is substituted with Mrs T' (*Elle*) should be either: *Mrs T is substituted for Che Guevara,* or *Che Guevara is replaced by Mrs T.*

'He was always prepared to substitute as organist in chapel on Sunday in the absence of the regular organist.' (*The Times*) The best usage does not allow this intransitive form of 'substitute'. There is no need to use the word at all when one can say: *He was always prepared to stand in as organist in chapel on Sunday.*

Similarly 'President Leonid Kravchuk . . . who let xenophobic nationalism substitute for economic sense' (*The Times*) should be either: *who substituted xenophobic nationalism for economic sense,* or: *who allowed xenophobic nationalism to replace economic sense.*

substitution. This noun is misused in the same way as the verb 'substitute'. In a game of football the substitution 'of' a new player constitutes the replacement of the departing one.

'Substitution of hazardous materials with safer ones that do the same job is the most effective form of protection.' (*Artists & Illustrators Magazine*) Hazardous materials must not be 'substituted': *Replacement of hazardous materials by safer ones.*

subtitle. 'Grey also includes a chapter on his approach to kitchens . . . before he gets down to the subtitle of the book "planning for comfort and style".' (*Country Living*) This is like saying 'Smith has a chapter of travel advice before he visits the title of the book which is "Greece"'. Smith does not visit the title, he visits Greece. And Grey does not get down to the subtitle, he gets down to planning for comfort and style: *before he gets down to the 'planning for comfort and style' promised in the subtitle. See also* NAME.

succeed. 'I think he has succeeded to make sure that magazines do have a responsible attitude.' (*Radio 4*) If it is a matter of succession then one may succeed 'to' the throne. But if it is a matter of success one does not succeed 'to' do anything. *I think he has succeeded in making sure that magazines do have a responsible attitude.*

successful. 'A successful soundtrack needs more time, effort and money than producers are usually willing to allow.' (*New Woman*) If a soundtrack is successful it does not need any of these things. The writer means something different. *To be successful a soundtrack needs more time, effort and money than producers are usually willing to allow.*

such. 'Such' is one of those words with a backward reference which must be exactly definable.

'Anthony Aloysius St John Hancock of 23 Railway Cuttings, East Cheam, touched a nerve which is still tender. The actor Alfred Molina is one such fan.' (*Sunday Times*) 'Such' as what or who? One has to go back a paragraph to discover a reference to 'scores of people' who felt affection for the comedian. It is too far off. 'Such' must be omitted.

The error can be found in supposedly highbrow criticism. '. . . an underlying symbolism runs through *Konigskinder* . . . The falling star that sets the Goose-girl free may suggest her awakening sexuality. And is her life with the Witch prison . . . or a sanctuary? Another such is the bond between the Witch and the Fiddler . . .' (*Opera Now*) Another such what? That is the question. The writer ought to start again. By arduous detective work one may conclude that 'such' refers to words the writer has never used. Instead of 'underlying symbolism' he needed something like 'a series of symbolic themes'. Then there would be something for 'another such' to refer back to.

'The frog needs to be positioned such that a car taking the left hand route will be pulling its pole to the left as it runs through the frog.' (*Railway Modeller*) This is like saying 'He behaved such that he offended us all'. 'Such' cannot be thus overworked: *The frog needs to be positioned in such a way that.*

such as. It is correct to say 'We celebrate occasions such as birthdays', because a birthday is indeed a specimen occasion. It is incorrect to say 'The Prime Minister has had previous confrontations with Mr Paisley, such as last December' (*The Times*) because December is not a specimen confrontation. *The Prime Minister has had previous confrontations with Mr Paisley, such as the one last December.*

such like. The accepted idiom, 'Dogs and such like pets' (meaning 'pets of that kind') represents the only usage in which 'like' can follow 'such'.

'[The judge] told Smith there would have to be the most serious consideration before such a dangerous man like him could be released' (*Radio 4*) should be: *there would have to be the most serious consideration before such a dangerous man as he could be released.*

suggest. 'Suggest at sexiness but don't flaunt it: wear a pushup bra.' (*Options*) 'To suggest' is to convey an impression or idea and is a transitive verb. The word 'at' is therefore out of place: *Suggest sexiness.*

suggestion. 'The only thing that can kill germs is sterilisation, so that means lashings of hot water plus our cleaning suggestions.' (*Essentials*) Mixing suggestions with hot water is no recipe for cleaning anything. *The only thing that can kill germs is sterilisation, so use lashings of hot water and follow the suggestions below.*

suit. A silly habit has arisen of inverting the usage of the verb 'suit'.
'I'm going for dark and dramatic eyes and lips which Maureen suits as she has great colouring – not everyone would suit this.' (*Catch*) These aspects of beauty treatment may or may not suit Maureen and the rest, but Maureen and company are the fixed subjects to which the beauty treatment must be adapted, and not vice versa. *I'm going for dark and dramatic eyes and lips which will suit Maureen . . . they would not suit everyone.*
'Over the past 15 years it [Chenin Blanc] has been losing ground in eastern Touraine, especially on sand and gravel soils where it is ill-suited.' (*Decanter*) A thing is well- or ill-suited 'to' a given terrain. The use of 'where' is wrong: *especially on sand and gravel soils to which it is ill-suited.*

superior. 'This may have something to do with his understanding of colour which is superior than many of his contemporaries.' (*Cumbria*) We speak of something being superior 'to' (not 'than') something else. And his understanding of colour must be said, not to be superior to his contemporaries, but to their own understanding of colour. *This may have something to do with his understanding of colour by which he excels many of his contemporaries.*

This erroneous usage is not as hard to find as it should be, as the following recommendation for a boat reveals. '. . . the MI 380 seems to be far superior than the Dancer . . .' (*Outdoors Illustrated*) This should read: *far superior to the Dancer.*

Superlatives. *See* COMPARATIVES AND SUPERLATIVES.

supervision. For an eminent statesman to speak of 'supervision for schools' (*Radio 4*) shows how far prepositional anarchy prevails: *supervision of schools.*

survive. 'He has promised that the modesty of women will be strictly enforced should his views survive.' (*Radio 4*) Views can 'survive' and yet have no influence at all. The wrong verb has been used: *the modesty of women will be strictly enforced should his views prevail.*

survivor. To survive, applied to living beings, is to continue to live. The survivors of any event live after it has transpired.

'Randy Shilts leaves no survivors.' (*The Times*) This conclusion to a touching obituary seemingly conveys that the human race came to an end on the death of the deceased. *Randy Shilts leaves no surviving relatives.*

A *Times* obituarist makes the same claim of Albert Goldman. 'He leaves no survivors' should be: *He leaves no surviving relatives.*

suspect. 'She could not have hoped to hide her condition indefinitely, and at the date of this discussion she must at least have suspected her pregnancy.' (*The Times*) She did not regard her pregnancy as suspicious: *at the date of this discussion she must at least have suspected that she was pregnant.*

sustainable. 'That means that where it's caught and how it's caught is sustainable.' (*Radio 4*) The subject is fish stocks. The supply of fish may or may not be 'sustainable', but to say that 'where's it's caught' is sustainable will not do. *That means that we can go on catching fish as we do and where we do.*

sympathetic/unsympathetic. To feel or show sympathy or understanding is to be 'sympathetic'. I can be sympathetic to your demands, but that does not make your demands 'sympathetic'.

'Though poorly, he reassures the Marquess that he does not have that beastly homosexual disease that we Tories find so unsympathetic.' (*Private Eye*) The irony misfires. It is the Tories, not the disease, which may or may not lack sympathy: *that beastly homosexual disease to which we Tories are so unsympathetic.* It is perhaps justifiable to speak of a congenial environment providing a 'sympathetic' atmosphere, but this idiomatic freedom ought not to be extended.

sympathy. Distinction must be made between sympathy 'for' a person who is in some kind of trouble or distress, and sympathy 'with' a person, who is taking some action which one supports.

Here a leader is commenting on strike action threatened by teachers in resistance to having to deal with a trouble-maker. 'Teachers have been threatened and felt their lives in danger. It is impossible not to have sympathy for them.' (*Independent*) Though the sentence makes perfect sense, the intended meaning was surely: *It is impossible not to have sympathy with them.*

'His role is one requiring a sympathy of the natural elements.' (*Country Talk*) He is a fish-farmer and he needs sympathy *for* (or *with*) the natural elements.

syndrome. 'Running shoes rarely prevent running injuries, because these are almost invariably overuse syndromes caused by overtraining.' (*Outdoors Illustrated*) A syndrome is a combination of symptoms or characteristics. Running injuries are not 'syndromes'. Pretentious overuse of the word is now the fashion. Here it is better omitted: *running injuries, which are usually due to over-training.*

synonymous. A word is 'synonymous' with another word when the two have the same meaning. Only a word can be synonymous 'with' another. The word will lose its usefulness if it is abused to mean nothing more than 'associated with'.

'Our client Reebok International is synonymous throughout the world for quality sports footwear and apparel.' (*The Times*) Nothing can be synonymous 'for' anything. *Our client Reebok International is well-known throughout the world for quality sports footwear and apparel.*

'Cordings' classic country clothes bear the unmistakable mark of distinction . . . and the Cordings name has always been synonymous with outdoor life' (*Shooting Times*) should be: *the Cordings name has always been associated with outdoor life.*

'Liberace was synonymous with vulgarity . . .' (*Marie Claire*) should be: *Liberace represented the acme of vulgarity.*

T

tail. The word is used often and justifiably of the end section of some matter.

'Meanwhile, the older tail of losses [at Lloyds] should be crystallised when syndicates are offered a final reinsurance premium.' (*The Times*) How does one crystallise a tail? It is doubtful whether either metaphor can be effectively rescued.

take. 'The government has taken action to suspend the Royal Mail's monopoly on delivering letters costing less than £1 because of the strike currently being taken by postal workers.' (*Radio 4*) Workers do not 'take' a strike. This is an instance of constructional transfer. Because people 'take' industrial action, the mind improperly transfers the usage to the verb 'strike'. No verb is needed anyway: *because of the current strike by postal workers.*

take place. When an event takes place, it 'occurs'. No sense of human agency attaches to this usage.

'It's the first comprehensive White Paper on rural England that has ever taken place.' (*Radio 4*) A White Paper cannot 'take place'. Someone has to devise it. *It's the first comprehensive White Paper on rural England ever presented.*

'The rabbi's prayer that began the remembrance ceremony took place at the very edge of the wooded ravine.' (*Radio 4*) A prayer needs to be uttered; it cannot just occur. *The remembrance ceremony, which began with the rabbi's prayer, took place at the very edge of the wooded ravine.*

'I could obtain information from targeted individuals and indeed cultivate them if the opportunity took place.' (*Radio 4*) An opportunity is not an event and cannot 'take place'. *I could cultivate them if the opportunity arose.*

'The chief executive of the NHS Trust says changes have already taken place and local people need not worry about the standard.' (*Radio 4*) Changes in the climate might 'take place', but changes in hospital management require human action. *The chief executive of the NHS Trust says that changes have already been made.*

tales. 'His company is a major exception to tales of woe in time of recession.' (*Vivid*) The company itself is not an exception to 'tales' of any kind. One should say what is. *His company's report is a major exception to tales of woe.*

talk about. 'Dr Owen talks about us making the voluntary ban work.' (*Shooting Times*) He can talk about us, but not about us 'doing' anything. *Dr Owen talks about our making the voluntary ban work. See also* GERCIPLES.

tally. 'A generation of women has been told that to be sexually provocative is to be strong, but to be sexually active is to be weak, to be potentially a victim. The argument doesn't tally.' (*The Times*) When two things 'tally' they correspond one with the other. This usage of the verb does not allow of a singular subject. *The two arguments don't tally.*

tapestry. 'The rich tapestry of life does include ups and downs.' (*Radio 4*) Tapestries are not mobile. The visual image requires visual elaboration. *The rich tapestry of life does include the bright and the dark.*

target. This word, used metaphorically, has become a favourite with politicians and economists. Unfortunately some who use it forget that a target is something to be aimed at and to hit or miss.

Of the Criminal Justice Bill an opposition spokesman declared 'It will fail to tackle the real target of reducing crime'. (*Radio 4*) We do not 'tackle' targets. Either the noun 'target' should be changed: *It will fail to tackle the real problem*, or the verb 'tackle': *It will fail to hit the desired target.*

'Judging schools against these targets is the only true indicator of their performance.' (*Independent*) We do not judge people or their achievements 'against targets'. *Judging schools by these criteria is the only true indicator of their performance.*

task. 'Because of the low volume of production, spare parts are even more of a task to obtain.' (*Old Glory*) This is an unnecessary evasion of simplicity: *spare parts are even harder to obtain.*

teach. 'It is the only centre in Britain . . . employing Hungarian staff to teach spastic children intense physical exercises.' (*Daily Telegraph*) Subjects such as Latin or geography can be 'taught'. 'Exercises' cannot be 'taught' because they are the mode by which teaching is accomplished: *employing Hungarian staff to train spastic children with intense physical exercises.*

'Parents must teach this issue [the abuse of alcohol] to their children.' (*Radio 4*) 'Issues' may be 'explored' but they cannot be 'taught', any more than a 'question' or a 'problem' can be 'taught'. It is customary to speak of teaching children something, not of teaching something 'to' children. *Parents must raise this issue with their children.*

tease. 'The Corbetts, by definition, tend to be more solitary, isolated summits so are by no means "old Men's Munros" as someone once teased a friend.' (*The Great Outdoors*) The writer means 'as someone once called them, teasing a friend' but the words 'as teased' cannot carry the burden of all that: *'old Men's Munros', as someone once teasingly defined them to a friend.*

tell. 'The boast about cycling from Paris to London was going to be something to tell his folks back home.' (*Independent*) A boast is not something that can be 'told', though one might tell someone 'about' a boast: *was going to be something to report to his folks back home.*

'Matthews tried to teach the boys cricket without much success, an experience he told in one of his early books.' (*The Times*) Nor can one 'tell' an experience: *an experience he recounted in one of his early books.*

'Told through contemporary letters and personal papers, this book gives a unique insight into the men and women who sought to influence the future of the country.' (*Majesty*) One cannot 'tell' a book. No book is 'told': *Using contemporary letters and personal papers, this book gives a unique insight into the men and women.*

'To help visitors find their way while telling the story of evolution, illustrated information boards are dotted about the maze.' (*Wild About Animals*) The visitors are not 'telling the story of evolution', they are taking it in: *To help visitors find their way while learning the story of evolution.*

temptation. This is one of those nouns which calls for an infinitive after it.

'He warns that the temptation of using the drawing power of the cathedral to finance its work can result in decision-making being controlled by the need for money.' (*The Times*) Here is a case where the first gerund ('of using') is misplaced after 'temptation' and the subsequent false passive gerciple ('decision-making being controlled') is equally awkward. An infinitive should be substituted in each case. *He warns that the temptation to use the drawing power of the cathedral to finance its work could cause decision-making to be controlled by the need for money.* But it would really be far better to start again. *He warns that if the cathedral relies on the drawing power of money to finance its work, policy may be determined by the need for money.*

tendency. There is a tendency to refer back to a 'tendency' where no tendency has been cited. 'Useful facts and tips were appreciated by the East Germans, and this tendency is still growing.' (*Marketing Week*) We are dealing with the magazine market. Appreciation of facts and tips does not necessarily constitute a 'tendency'. *Useful facts and tips were appreciated by the East Germans, and the appetite for them is still growing.*

tension. 'The flysheet is attached by quick-release snap buckles which can be tensioned to assure a tight pitch.' (*The Great Outdoors*) There is no verb 'to tension': *quick-release snap buckles which can be tightened to assure a firm/taut pitch.*

testament. In law a testament is a will. In general use it signifies some kind of attestation. The word is increasingly being used where a better word would be testimony ('witness').

We hear it announced that a government minister's speech 'bore testament' to his conviction' (*Radio 4*) and later that 'countless Russian soldiers bore testament to the fierce street battles'. 'Bearing testimony' is giving evidence and the verb 'bear' thus goes better with 'testimony' than with 'testament': *bore testimony.*

than. 'British women are twice as likely to get divorced than in any other of the countries.' (*The Times*) There is a tangle of error here. In the first place we do not say 'This is twice as big than that' but 'as that'. In the second place British women must be compared with foreign women. If what happens 'in' other countries is the issue, then what happens 'in Britain' must balance it. *British women are twice as likely to get divorced as the women in any other of the countries.*

'Than' is a word which often introduces a false comparison. 'The pale beige seats feel softer and more luxurious than the 6 series.' (*Tatler*) This piece, on testing a BMW, compares the seats of one model with another model instead of with that model's seats. Where an apostrophe cannot neatly be used, 'that of' or 'those of' must be introduced. *The pale beige*

seats feel softer and more luxurious than those of the 6 series. See also
COMPARISONS.

that (pronoun and adverb). **CLARITY OF REFERENCE** Where 'that' is used
as a demonstrative pronoun to refer back to something already
mentioned, there must be no doubt about what it refers to. In 'He insulted his mother: that is inexcusable' 'that' clearly refers back to what
'he' did. 'It's almost impossible to believe that Paul Newman will be 70
on January 26th, 1995. Mind you, we said that when he reached 60, and
50 too.' (*OK! Magazine*) What was said on these previous occasions was
certainly not that it was impossible to believe that he was 70. The words
'we said that' should be changed. *Mind you, we talked like that when he
reached 60.*

'THAT' AS AN ADVERB 'To dispose of the weed push the plunger in; it's
that simple.' (*The Times*) It is increasingly common to use 'that' thus. In
the past the usage has been considered vulgar. Conventional usage requires: *it's as simple as that.*

that (conjunction). **REPETITION OF 'THAT'** There is in conversation a tendency to repeat 'that' in complex sentences. The repetition is never good,
but it is particularly bad in print. 'It is only fair that where additional
costs arise, from customers who make high usage of certain services,
that these customers should make a contribution towards those costs
rather than spreading the expense over all accounts.' (*The Times*) Here
the second 'that' must go, and 'rather than' must become 'instead of'.
Moreover, as the sentence is worded, it sounds as though the customers
are responsible for 'spreading the expense over all accounts'. *It is only
fair that, where additional costs arise from customers who make high
usage of certain services, these customers should make a contribution towards those costs instead of their being spread over all accounts.*

OMISSION OF 'THAT' AFTER 'SO' AND 'SUCH' Omission of 'that', like repetition of 'that', may be acceptable in conversation, 'I was so busy I forgot
to phone,' we say. In print the omission can look inelegant. 'The cult
took up so much of John's time he had little left for her' (*Company*)
should be: *The cult took up so much of John's time that he had little left
for her.*

'At the moment the NHS is such a rat race trusts just try to concentrate the majority of their efforts on keeping their own house in order'
(*Nursing Standard*) should be: *such a rat race that trusts just try to concentrate most* [not 'the majority'] *of their efforts on keeping their own
house in order.*

'Such is its potential popularity this year, trade stands had already been filled by April' (*Lancashire Life*) should be: *Such is its popularity this year that trade stands had already been filled by April.*

OMISSION OF 'THAT' AFTER CERTAIN VERBS Here again the freedom acceptable in conversation, when adopted in print, can sometimes make for lack of clarity as well as of elegance.

'They also suggested they should be exposed earlier to practice' (*Nursing Standard*) should be: *suggested that they should be exposed earlier to practice.*

'The legislation is aimed at ensuring these threatened animals are not taken from the wild' (*Practical Gardening*) should be: *ensuring that these threatened animals are not taken from the wild.*

'Elaine was setting up her cassette recorder and checking she had her tape ready' (*Woman*) should be: *checking that she had her tape ready.*

The longer the sentence and the more complex the construction, the worse the laxity seems. 'He told the National Association of Health Authorities and Trusts annual conference in Harrogate last week a reassessment of the roles of professionals was needed' (*Nursing Standard*) should be: *that a reassessment of the roles of professionals was needed.*

In the construction 'It is true that she likes antiques' 'that she likes antiques' is the equivalent of 'it'. In conversation 'that' might be omitted ('It's true she likes antiques') but in writing it is better retained. 'It's in everybody's interest we proceed with caution' (*Nursing Standard*) should be: *It's in everybody's interest that we proceed with caution.*

the thing to do. These words must always refer back to something that can be 'done'.

'Soon she bought more sheep. They were ordinary commercial animals from the marketplace which, as she now remarks, was absolutely not the thing to do.' (*Country Living*) 'She bought' must be clearly connected with 'the thing to do'. *Soon she bought more sheep. She bought ordinary commercial sheep from the marketplace which, as she now remarks, was not the thing to do.*

their. When 'their' refers back to persons already mentioned, the reference must be exact. '*Queen Victoria's Children (1980)* continued the good work by demonstrating that their home life was happy and cheerful.' (*The Times*) Strictly speaking, the children have not been mentioned, only the title of a book, and therefore 'their' is misplaced. One would not say 'I have just read *The Last Days of Pompeii* which I visited last summer'. So here: *continued the good work by demonstrating* *that the home life was happy and cheerful. See also* NAME, SUBTITLE.

In the most common usage of 'their' ('Their home is in London') the word indicates personal ownership. In another, less common, usage ('We approved their election to the committee') 'their' concerns what has happened to them and there is no note of ownership. This usage must be handled with care. 'These links would make North Africa a central focus for Nato's strategic arrangements. Their proposal stems from Mr Claes's belief that Muslim fundamentalism is now as big a threat to the alliance as communism once was.' (*The Times*) 'Their proposal' could only mean the proposal 'they' (whoever 'they' are) have made, when what is needed is something that means 'the proposal of them' ('them' being the material proposed). The gerund, which is so often used where it should not be, is here required: *Proposing them stems from Mr Claes's belief that Muslim fundamentalism is now as big a threat to the alliance.*

theirs. *See* HERS, YOURS.

them. Beware of following 'them' by what appears to be a gerund or a participle: it will probably be an inadmissible gerciple.

'This could therefore lead to them feeling that their partner is unreliable.' (*New Woman*) Better than merely to correct the construction: *lead to their feeling that their partner is unreliable*, would be to use the infinitive: *lead them to feel that their partner is unreliable*.

Very often, of course, the error is most effectively corrected by changing 'them' to 'their'. 'Women often feel wary at work, as though they're on trial in some way, which is reflected in them being given the job but not the pay rise.' (*Vogue*): *which is reflected in their being given the job but not the pay rise.*

This error frequently arises through using the expression 'result in' instead of 'cause'. 'Make sure that the chimney stacks look stable and that there are no cracks in the pots that might result in them falling off.' (*Me*) To correct directly: *there are no cracks that might result in their falling off*, is probably less satisfactory than to change the verb and the construction: *there are no cracks that might cause them to fall off. See also* RESULT.

there's. 'There's', being an abbreviation of 'there is', must be followed by a singular noun. 'There's also several classes of sheep to be judged' (*Country Lovers Magazine*) should be: *There are also several classes of sheep to be judged.*

these. Where 'these' is used to refer back to something already mentioned, there must be no confusion over exactly what it refers to.

'The Citizens Charter Department has . . . worked out a plan under which British Gas can pull up its standards of service. If these are not done by the end of the year . . .' (*Radio 4*) It is not the standards ('these') that have to be 'done': *If this is not done by the end of the year.*

they. When 'they' is used, care must be taken to prevent uncertainty about what it refers to.

'Public participation in "rural decision-making" is fine – as long as they pick the same solution as council planners.' (*The Field*) 'They' cannot refer back to 'public', which is here used adjectivally. A noun must be provided for 'they' to refer back to. *Participation by the public is fine as long as they pick the same solution as council planners do.*

'The Tory answer is flawed. There are many merits in the restructuring of public services. But because of their own past actions, they are hardly suitable advocates of institutional renewal.' (*The Times*) Grammatically, 'they' can refer back only to one of the two plural nouns of the previous sentence – 'merits' or 'public services'. In fact the writer means neither. He is vainly trying to attach 'they' to Tories, who have not been mentioned. The adjectival use of 'Tory' in 'Tory answer' has made him think that he has mentioned Tories. He should do so. *But because of their own past actions, the Tories are hardly suitable advocates.*

Political polemic seems to foster this bad practice. 'Michael Portillo is rather too continental for the Tory taste. They are descended from beery Saxon warriors.' (*The Times*) This should be: *Michael Portillo is rather too continental for the taste of the Tories. They are descended.*

think. 'The results [of an investigation into treatment of the aged] indicate a far wider occurrence of abuse than was previously thought.' (*Radio 4*) One cannot 'think' a wider occurrence. If the verb 'think' is kept here, clumsy expansion will be needed: *a far wider occurrence of abuse than was previously thought to obtain.* It would be better to change the verb: *a far wider occurrence of abuse than was previously reckoned with.*

third. 'It is also a puzzle why, in the case of identical twins, one twin can have diabetes while only one third of the other twins goes on to develop it.' (*Sunday Times*) This taxing comparison could be better expressed. *It is also a puzzle why, in the case of identical twins,*

*where one has diabetes, the chances that the other will develop it
are only one in three.*

this. The habit of using 'this' where 'so' or 'as' would be more appropriate is still regarded as crude.

'It is rare to find houses this early which have not had radical alterations' should be: *It is rare to find houses as old as this which have not had radical alterations.*

'No radio this small ever sounded so big' (*The Times*) should be: *No radio as small as this ever sounded so big.*

those. There must be clear reference when this word is used.

'Great literary works have been written in remote cottages, in imposing mansions, in manor houses and in tiny terraced houses. What inspired those authors to create tales and characters that influence readers generations later?' (*Home & Country*) Who are 'those' authors? No authors have been mentioned, only literary works and various kinds of domicile. If 'those' is to be kept, the first sentence must be rewritten. *Men and women have written great literary works in remote cottages . . . What inspired them?* Alternatively 'those' can be omitted. *Great literary works have been written in remote cottages . . . What inspired authors to create tales and characters?*

threaten. 'The Prime Minister issued a statement accusing the IRA of callously threatening the desire for peace.' (*Radio 4*) To threaten someone or something is to put them or it at risk. The IRA could not be said to be putting the 'desire' for peace at risk. On the contrary, if they pursued hostilities the 'desire' for peace would presumably only increase. What is put at risk is peace itself: *The Prime Minister issued a statement accusing the IRA of callously threatening the possibility of peace*, or: *callously flouting the desire for peace.*

through. Prepositions must not be required to do a job beyond their capacity. 'This has been seen in the endless stream of bills through parliament that have taken powers away from local government.' (*New Statesman*) There is no such thing as a 'bill through parliament'. Either a verb must be used: *This has been seen in the endless stream of bills passing through parliament*, or the wording simplified: *This has been seen in the endless stream of parliamentary bills.*

thus. 'Sometimes in the last month of the year the weather can surprise us and make Christmas preparations unseasonable, though of course the commercial world would have us thus involved in October or earlier.' (*Dalesman*) To be involved 'thus' is to be involved in this or that manner, and the word cannot refer back to the noun 'preparations'. A verb must be supplied: *make it unseasonable to be preparing for Christmas, though of course the commercial world would have us thus involved in October or earlier.*

time. We say 'This is the first time I have been here', but this conversational usage should not be extended, especially in print.

'Future fund raising may prove to be an easier time to pick up stock.' (*Investors Chronicle*) Even though the fund raising is temporally placed, it cannot be a 'time' to do anything. This use of the word should be avoided. *Future fund raising may provide a better opportunity to pick up stock.*

'The coup, mounted by many in his immediate presidential government and party circles, was the first time he had been thrown.' (*The Times*) The coup must not be said to be a 'time'. *The coup . . . gave him his first experience of being thrown.*

'Research aimed to establish whether the wide range of illnesses suffered by veterans is caused by the time they spent in the Gulf.' (*Radio 4*) The 'time' could not conceivably be a cause of illness: *whether the wide range of illnesses suffered by veterans is caused by their experience in the Gulf.*

tip. 'There are few tips for would be Wayfarers, other than the obvious, such as wearing good boots and waterproofs.' (*Dalesman*) Wearing good boots is not a tip. A tip is a piece of advice 'to' do something or other. *There are few tips for would be wayfarers, other than the obvious ones, such as to wear good boots.*

'Trudie Chalder gave us these tips to chilling out.' (*Options*) The preposition 'to' is out of place. What is needed is: *tips for chilling out.*

tire. Where a verb has both a transitive and an intransitive form, care should be taken not to confuse the two.

'All quite teasingly sexy and funny – but such fantasy tires rather quickly.' (*The Times*) A person may tire of a given activity or the given activity can tire them, but in the latter case the verb 'tire' requires an object: *but such fantasy tires one rather quickly.*

titillate/titivate. To 'titillate' is to tickle, to excite pleasurably: *She made the most succulent puddings to titillate his palate.* To 'titivate' is to spruce up, to smarten, especially in the sense of adding the finishing touch. *The ladies titivated themselves with the aid of the hall mirror before entering the dining room.*

titivate. *See* TITILLATE.

to. There is a tendency to use 'to' where a different preposition is required.

'From that moment he set about creating an Italian style to both the original Georgian house and gardens.' (*Best of British*) This should be: *Italian style for the house and gardens.*

'Of course, the reason for disliking your best friend's man can seem uncomfortably petty to mention to her.' (*Essentials*) To justify the use of 'to mention' insert 'too': *can seem too uncomfortably petty to mention to her. See also* PREPOSITIONS.

to mark. In 'We gave him a present to mark his retirement' (Usage A), 'to mark' hangs grammatically on the verb 'gave'. In the (less felicitous) sentence 'A present to mark his retirement would be a good idea' (Usage B), 'to mark' hangs directly on the noun 'present'. It is the present that is thus characterised.

'Thirty-seven people have been arrested at celebrations at Stonehenge to mark the summer solstice.' (*Radio 4*) Read with grammatical strictness (Usage A), this means that the people were arrested to mark the summer solstice. Avoiding Usage B by linking 'to mark' to a verb would remove the ambiguity. *Thirty-seven people have been arrested at celebrations held at Stonehenge to mark the summer solstice.*

to name but a few. *See* NAME BUT A FEW.

to the extent that. This is a clumsy expression at best. 'I am seldom satisfied with my work to the extent that my friends think I am a pessimist.' (*The Artist*) Nothing at all is gained here by use of the expression instead of the simple word 'so'. *I am so seldom satisfied with my work that my friends think I am a pessimist.*

toilet. 'Rats are very intelligent and usually try to get off you and back to their cage when they want to go to the toilet.' (*Wild About Animals*) Human beings naturally have recourse to euphemisms when referring to certain physical functions. To apply these to animals and speak of rats as going to the toilet is delicacy gone mad: *when they want to defecate.*

toll. A 'toll' is a levy formerly exacted for use of a road. The word is now often used metaphorically.

'Massive oil spills and blazing oil fields have taken a severe toll on the Gulf environment.' (*Meridian*) We do not take toll 'on' things but 'of' them: *have taken a severe toll of the Gulf environment.*

transcend. 'Being at the top of the food chain and transcending between land and water . . .' (*Country Lovers Magazine*) This description of the otter misuses the verb 'transcend', which means to be superior to. It is erroneous to speak of transcending 'between' things: *Being at the top of the food chain and at home on land or in water . . .*

trap. 'The unemployment trap, the overlap between benefit levels and unskilled wage levels, defies simple solutions.' (*The Times*) There is no way to 'solve' a trap. If it is set for you, you either fall into it or evade it. But what is at issue here is the problem of getting rid of the 'trap': *The unemployment trap, the overlap between benefit levels and unskilled wage levels, cannot be easily removed.*

trappings. 'Is he [the new Israeli Prime Minister] already, do you think, regretting some of the trappings of power?' (*Radio 4*) The questioner clearly did not understand that the 'trappings' are the external adornments and protocols going with an office. *Is he already regretting some of the responsibilities of his position?*

trend. 'You can see the trend that is happening.' (*Radio 4*) A trend is not an event that can 'happen'. It is a tendency. Why not: *You can see what is the present trend?*

trial. 'Up until then, the company had tested a small in-house campaign but decided that it needed to trial the medium comprehensively.' (*Precision Marketing*) Is the verb 'trial' invented to forestall repetition of the verb 'test'? It is unnecessary. *Up until then the company had tried a small in-house campaign but decided that it needed to test the medium comprehensively.*

'The process, named "Magneta Flake" has been trialed by several police forces.' (*Focus*) Nothing is gained by turning 'trial' into a verb. *The process has been tested/tried out by several police forces.*

trouble. There is a growing habit of making short cuts in use of this word.

'The Conservatives . . . have in practice had trouble stopping expenditure in fields such as health and education from rising.' (*Independent*) A preposition is required after 'trouble': *have had trouble in preventing expenditure . . . from rising.*

true. 'The Pentagon said that the Iraqi move would be wise if true.'

(*Radio 4*) The 'move' itself cannot be either true or false. It is a question of the reporting of the move. *The Pentagon said that the Iraqi move would be wise, if correctly reported.* Strictly speaking, however, the move would be wise whether truly or falsely reported, so the use of the conditional 'if' is not precise.

A correspondent suggests that we need a new national anthem. 'What about Purcell's *Fairest Isle*, perhaps no longer true but something decent and attainable to aim at and a lovely tune.' (*The Times*) The confusion here between title and substance is complete. How can a song be true or false, – or 'attainable'? *Purcell's 'Fairest Isle', – whose title perhaps no longer describes our country accurately, though it represents a worthwhile ideal – but which has a lovely tune.*

'Given the volume of the record of the British Empire, and a historical past which includes much more medieval paper than is true of other countries . . .' (*The Times*) No one would say 'I want more pudding than is true of my guests'. The construction 'than is true of' is out of place. And the word 'includes' applied to the past is awkward: *a historical past which has left us with much more medieval paper than other countries have.*

'The spread between buying and selling prices of the Top 100 shares is much narrower than is true of shares in general.' (*Money Observer*) It would be clumsy to say 'He is taller than is true of teenagers in general'. The words 'than is true' should be taken out. *The gap between buying and selling prices of the Top 100 shares is much narrower than the corresponding gap for shares in general.*

'They have revealed a glimpse of the Labour Party which is increasingly true and increasingly unattractive.' (*Radio 4*) What the Tory propagandist means is, presumably: *a glimpse of the Labour Party which is increasingly representative of its increasing unattractiveness.*

truth. Sometimes we find the word 'truth' used as though it were a synonym of some vague word such as 'fact'.

'The cult of individualism will be a continuing truth.' (*The Times*) The word is totally out of place here. The writer does not mean 'truth': *The cult of individualism will be a continuing trend*, or better still: *The cult of individualism will continue.*

There is a tendency in careless reporting to misapply the word. 'Whatever the truth of the incident, it has already aggravated tensions between Israel and the Palestinians.' (*Radio 4*) It is not the incident that may be true or false, but the report of it. And truth does not vary in quantity. *However reliable the report of the incident may be, it has already aggravated tensions between Israel and the Palestinians.*

'That, at least, is the theory; for some it is also the passion. But the early truth, as our correspondent reports today from Jerusalem, has disappointed those anxious for genuine democracy in the Gaza strip.' (*The Times*) This leader similarly misuses the word 'truth'. Falsehood is balanced by truth, theory by fact. *But the events to date, as our correspondent reports from Jerusalem, have disappointed those anxious for genuine democracy in the Gaza strip.*

'Another car trail takes the hardy explorer back further in time to the Dark Age Kingdom of Powys and the alleged truth of the legendary King Arthur.' (*In Britain*) The car trail does not take anyone back to a truth, let alone an alleged one. *Another car trail takes the hardy explorer back further in time to the Dark Age Kingdom of Powys and to the world of the legendary, perhaps historical, King Arthur.*

'If we are actively seeking imitative truth, our searches should take us through a wide range of material.' (*Trout & Salmon*) The topic is the manufacture of bait. 'Truth' is the wrong word: *If we are actively seeking imitative accuracy.*

Twinning. Certain twinned nouns together may take a singular verb. 'Bread and butter was his sole diet' we say, using the singular verb 'was'. Care must be taken in extending this freedom.

'Quality and performance has also been improved' (*Shooting Times*) should be: *have also been improved.*

type. 'They will provide funds for these type of developments.' (*Radio 4*) Singular and plural cannot be thus confused: *for this type of development*, or: *these types of development. See also* KIND OF.

'Those type of things really ought by government ministers to be sorted out in private.' (*Radio 4*) There seems to be widespread confusion over singular and plural in this usage. In fact there is no need for plural or even for the word 'type': *This kind of thing really ought to be sorted out in private.*

'The type of shed that you choose depends on its proposed use and the amount of space it will be allocated.' (*Perfect Home*) What 'depends' on these matters is not the actual 'type' chosen but 'which' type is chosen: *Which type of shed you choose depends on its proposed use.*

'The men who built the great cathedrals were probably responsible for the substantial type of early bridges.' (*Waterways World*) Does this mean: *responsible for the more substantial of the early bridges*, or *responsible for the substantial quality of the early bridges?*

U

ultimatum. 'The ultimatum to the Bosnian Serbs draws nearer.' (*Radio 4*) The ultimatum had already been issued when this announcement was made; it was not approaching. *The deadline set by the ultimatum draws nearer.*

umbrella. 'The KLF invented the phrase "ambient house" when pushed to describe their music. Within this umbrella, the dance beat is always there, but other features are added.' (*Vivid*) People do not generally operate 'within' an umbrella: *Under this umbrella.*

unable. 'To maintain anonymity, we are unable to respond to comments made on the questionnaire.' (*AA Magazine*) 'Unable' is the wrong word and makes nonsense of the rest of the sentence. We have been told that the motive for the decision is 'to maintain anonymity'. Inability is not an issue. The point is that the AA has voluntarily decided not to respond to comments. *To maintain anonymity, we have decided not to respond to comments made on the questionnaire.*

uncommon. 'There are open sewers with people excreting in the street not uncommon.' (*Cumbria Life*) 'With' is inelegant and 'uncommon' ill-placed. *There are open sewers and it is not uncommon to see people excreting in the street.*

undecided. We say a matter or a person is undecided when some future decision hangs in the balance.

'It is wary of the Environmental Protection Agency, the Government's proposed, but as yet undecided body which will harmonise the work.' (*The Field*) Presumably the writer here means that the body, though proposed, has not yet been established. Since it does not yet exist, it cannot be 'undecided' about anything. *It is wary of the Environmental Protection Agency, the Government's proposed but not yet established body which will harmonise the work.*

underestimate. 'We cannot underestimate that he is a very serious man.' (*The Times*) We may 'underestimate' a person, a quality, or a quantity, but 'underestimate' cannot be followed thus by 'that'. Either a proper object for the verb 'underestimate' must be provided: *We cannot underestimate his seriousness*, or the verb must be changed: *We cannot doubt that he is a very serious man.*

undermine. 'Scientists weren't given the full facts about the chemicals that soldiers were exposed to, so undermining many results.' (*Radio 4*) 'Undermining' is a participle and must agree with a noun or noun-equivalent. If the sentence had read 'The authorities did not give the full facts to the scientists, so undermining their research', the usage would be correct because the word 'undermining' would attach itself to the word 'authorities'. As it is, there is no word for 'undermining' to qualify. Moreover, it was not the 'results' that were 'undermined' but the work that led to them. *The scientists weren't given the full facts about the chemicals the soldiers were exposed to, and thus their efforts to get at the truth were undermined.*

understanding. 'Therefore when international cooperation regarding older vehicles gained momentum it was felt there was a need for delineations that would have better understanding.' (*Automobile*) The issue here is the classification of old cars. Delineations are incapable of understanding and cannot be granted better understanding: *it was felt there was a need for delineations that would be more broadly understood.*

uninterested. *See* DISINTERESTED.

unique. 'Our attention to detail is what makes us unique and one of Britain's leading conservatory companies.' (*Perfect Home*) There is an element of contradiction here. If something is 'unique' it is the only one of its kind. Whatever makes us 'unique' certainly cannot also make us 'one of' a group. *What makes us special and one of Britain's leading conservatory companies.*

unless. This conjunction must hinge on a verb ('I shall be there unless it rains'). 'The note warned of more deaths unless the Indian government responded to the demand within two days.' (*Radio 4*) 'Unless' cannot thus hinge on the noun 'deaths'. *The note warned that more would die unless the Indian government responded.*

unlike. 'Unlike' is an adjective which works in two directions. In 'Jane is unlike her mother' the word does its work by linking the two nouns 'Jane' and 'mother'. If there is any failure thus to match two parallel items, 'unlike' will be misused. Misuse is now common.

COMPARING PERIOD WITH PERIOD The error is all too common when comparisons are made between one period and another.

'Unlike 1914, the Balkans is not part of a wider struggle.' (*The Times*) The Balkans must not be said to be unlike 1914. The most satisfactory correction is often to scrap 'unlike' and use a construction involving 'as'. *The Balkan crisis today is not part of a wider struggle as it was in 1914.*

'Unlike last year, however, the only practical obstruction is the rubble of the planned economy.' (*The Times*) An obstruction must not be said to be unlike a year. A proper parallel must be supplied, and the only thing that can be compared with 'last year' is 'this year'. *This year, unlike last year, however, the only practical obstruction is the rubble of the planned economy.*

This error is one which turns up with alarming regularity in the supposed quality press. 'Unlike the past two years, Euro-sceptic ministers have been scrupulously loyal about Mr Major.' (*The Times*) We do not need to be told that Euro-sceptic ministers are unlike the past two years, but we do need to be told what is 'unlike' those years if the word is used at all. It is better not used. *Despite their conduct over the past two years, Euro-sceptic ministers have been scrupulously loyal about Mr Major.*

'Unlike last week, the President of the Board of Trade, Michael Heseltine, made no comment on the role of his cabinet colleague, Jonathan Aitken.' (*Radio 4*) Michael Heseltine must not be compared with last week. *The President of the Board of Trade made no comment such as he made last week.*

'Unlike five years ago, Mr Major cannot present his Government as new.' (*The Times*) This should be: *Mr Major cannot present his government as new, as he did five years ago.*

Sometimes the mismatch in comparing period with period is slightly more complicated. 'Unlike its behaviour in the 1970s, the ultraleft is still on the defensive.' (*The Times*) There is no proper parallel to the word 'behaviour' here. *By contrast with the 1970s, the ultraleft is today on the defensive.*

'Unlike previous periods of Tory unpopularity, there has been substantial switching by former supporters directly to Labour.' (*The Times*) Since there is nothing here for 'unlike' to agree with, the word must go. *What is unprecedented in periods of Tory unpopularity is the substantial switching by former Tory supporters directly to Labour.*

COMPARISONS INVOLVING PEOPLE Comparison involving people must be carefully framed.

'Unlike his German prison cell, Nick Leeson won't be free to give television interviews.' (*BBC TV*) To tell us that Nick Leeson does not resemble a prison cell is absurd. 'Unlike' must go. *Nick Leeson won't be free to give television interviews, as he was in his German prison cell.*

'Unlike some other strikes, where Labour have intervened much earlier and called for arbitration, Tony Blair and the party leadership have publicly expressed sympathy with the postal workers.' (*Radio 4*) As Nick Leeson was compared with a prison cell, so now we find Tony Blair compared with strikes. He and the party leadership are said to be unlike some other strikes. This illustrates the extent to which the error has taken hold of BBC newscasters. The best escape is perhaps through 'whereas'. *Whereas in other strikes Labour have intervened much earlier and called for arbitration, Tony Blair and the party leadership have publicly expressed sympathy with the postal workers.*

'Unlike an Old Master or a Van Gogh, an auctioneer cannot always guess what will tickle the fancy.' (*The Times*) This time we have an auctioneer compared with an Old Master. It was not what the writer intended. *Unless he is dealing with an Old Master or a Van Gogh, an auctioneer cannot always guess what will tickle the fancy.*

'Unlike the collapse in the flotation market during the recession, fund managers still have the cash to back the companies they like.' (*The Times*) Similarly the fund managers ought not to be contrasted with the collapse in the market: *By contrast with their position when the flotation market collapsed, the fund managers still have the cash.*

It will be seen that 'unlike' is a dangerous word with which to begin a sentence. Even a judge in a literary competition (for the Whitbread Prize) can slip up. 'Unlike the Booker Prize. . . . we Whitbreaders are each sent a civilised third of a vetting list.' (*The Times*). *Unlike the judges for the Booker Prize, we Whitbreaders are each sent a civilised third of a vetting list.*

OTHER FALSE PARALLELS 'Unlike shops who simply act as salesmen on commission, all Thomas Lloyd leather furniture is hand crafted by ourselves.' (*Perfect Home*) Here Thomas Lloyd furniture is said to be unlike other firm's shops, which scarcely needs saying. *Unlike what is sold in shops where retailers simply act as salesmen on commission, all Thomas Lloyd leather furniture is hand-crafted by ourselves.*

'Unlike British institutions, where directors are directly involved with every major activity, the Louvre's seven department heads each have almost complete control of their area.' (*The Times*) The department heads of the Louvre are compared with British institutions, instead of with their directors. *Unlike British institutions, where directors are directly involved with every major activity, the Louvre gives its seven department heads almost complete control of their respective areas.*

THE POSSESSIVE TRAP False parallels after 'unlike' often result from neglect or misuse of the possessive case.

'Unlike Prince Charles, who hated Salem's sister school, Gordonstoun, Sofia's spirit was not crushed by the regime.' (*Majesty*) Prince Charles must be matched with Sofia, not with her 'spirit'. *Unlike Prince Charles, who hated Salem's sister school, Gordonstoun, Sofia was not dispirited by the regime.*

'Unlike some other members of the Royal Family, it was Princess Michael of Kent's looks that were making the headlines in 1994, not her behaviour.' (*Majesty*) This compares the Princess's looks, instead of the Princess herself, with other members of the royal family. *Unlike some other members of the Royal Family, Princess Michael made headlines in 1994 with her looks, not her behaviour.*

DOUBLE ERROR 'Unlike her brother, who tended to surround himself with palace officials and courtiers, her circle was much wider.' (*The Times*) Here 'the circle' is mismatched with 'her brother', so that one is tempted to correct it to 'Unlike her brother . . . she had a much wider circle', but this would still be wrong. The comparison 'much wider' cannot be combined with what follows 'unlike'. We need either: *Unlike her brother she had a wide circle*, or: *By comparison with her brother she had a wider circle*.

'UNLIKE IN' It is always dangerous to follow 'unlike' by 'in'.

'It could be argued that here in Britain, unlike in the United States . . .' (*The Times*) The two items in contrast are 'Britain' and 'the United States'. The intrusive second 'in' manufactures error: *It could be argued that here in Britain, unlike the United States . . .*

'Moreover, schools which have managed to retain loyal and experienced staff have to spend more on salaries which, unlike in a private company, cannot be recouped in higher profits.' (*The Times*) Again 'in' leads to error. Like must be compared with like. *Moreover, schools which have managed to retain loyal and experienced staff have to spend more on salaries and, unlike private companies, cannot recoup them in higher profits.*

'Unlike in Mrs Simpson's day, when she had to be hustled off to Ipswich in the vain hope that the hearing would remain unnoticed, the legal act of divorce is painless, clinical and brief.' (*The Times*) Nothing can be said to be 'unlike in Mrs Simpson's day'. The words 'unlike in' must go: *Whereas in her day Mrs Simpson had to be hustled off to Ipswich.*

'All the gears are constantly meshed together, unlike in a car gearbox, where changing gears involves sliding gearwheels into engagement with each other.' (*Waterways World*) It is not difficult to correct this: *All the gears are constantly meshed together, unlike those in a car gearbox.*

WILD COMPARISONS The wider the divergence in the false contrast, the more absurd the error will seem.

' . . . unlike most sex and shopping books, the mechanics and exotic mores of the fashion industry are deliciously accurate.' (*Options*) The mechanics and mores of the sex industry are here contrasted with sex and shopping books. The logical breakdown is complete. The writer is reviewing a novel. *Unlike most sex and shopping books, the novel gives a deliciously accurate account of the mechanics and exotic mores of the fashion industry.*

'Another aspect of the French style of eating is that mealtimes are strictly observed, unlike our tendency to have haphazard meals, snacks, or a quick sandwich in front of the TV.' (*Company*) The French mealtimes cannot be contrasted with our 'tendency'. Again 'unlike' must go: *mealtimes are strictly observed, whereas we tend to have haphazard snacks.*

'So you decide how much to spend, unlike most theme parks which charge a whacking entrance fee.' (*Bella*) You are here compared with theme parks. 'Unlike' must go. *So you decide here how much to spend, whereas most theme parks charge a whacking entrance fee.*

'Unlike the help which Jeffrey Archer's novel received over 16 drafts, Hardy was always hounded and hampered by inferior prurient editors.' (*The Times*) Why tell us that Hardy did not resemble the help given to Jeffrey Archer's book? We never suspect such a likeness. The word 'unlike' should go. *Whereas Jeffrey Archer's novel received help over 16 drafts, Hardy was always hounded and hampered by inferior prurient editors.*

'Unlike the recent amnesty for knives, these weapons will have to be handed over to a police officer.' (*Radio 4*) Either amnesty must be compared with amnesty: *Unlike the recent amnesty for knives, this amnesty for guns will require the weapons to be handed over to a police officer,* or weapons with weapons: *Unlike the knives collected in the recent amnesty, these guns will have to be handed over.*

'Unlike that event tickets for today cost as much as £200.' (*Radio 4*) The tickets must not be compared with the event. To add an apostrophe would correct the error: *Unlike that event tickets for today's (event) cost as much as £200.*

unsympathetic. *See* SYMPATHETIC.

until. 'Until' is a conjunction which connects a verb to some sequel, as in 'She laughed until she cried'. It is not good style to hang 'until' on to a noun instead of a verb.

'Labour's passionate support for the European exchange rate mechanism, until Britain came out of it, does not augur well.' (*The Times*) 'Until' cannot thus hang on the noun 'support'. It must be attached to a verb. *Labour's passionate support for the European exchange rate mechanism, maintained until Britain came out of it, does not augur well.*

unusual. 'There are thought to be no more than fifteen males left, and a sighting of this large heron-sized marsh-wanderer is an even more unusual event.' (*Country Lovers Magazine*) More unusual than what? No other 'event' has been mentioned: *a sighting of this large heron-sized marsh-wanderer is a rare event.*

up. This word must not be given any job beyond its capacity. 'Up until about 8.45am on the morning of the first day of term can only be described as hell on earth.' (*Woman*) The writer means: *The period up to 8.45am. . . can only be described as hell on earth.*

Notice that we change 'Up until' to 'Up to'. Prefacing 'until' by 'up' smacks of redundancy. 'Up until the early 20th century, perfume was sold in large pharmaceutical jars to be decanted on request.' (*Period Living*) This should be simply: *Until the 20th century.*

'Pregnancy gives plenty of time for planning and you can change your mind right up until you are in labour.' (*Parents*) Here a more appropriate usage could be found: *and you can change your mind at any time until you are in labour.*

urge. To urge someone to do something is to encourage or stimulate them to do it. 'More than 1,000 hunting folk gathered . . . carrying placards urging the Labour motion to be rejected.' (*Horse & Hound*) No one can 'urge' a motion to do anything or to be subject to anything: *urging that the Labour motion be rejected.*

us. Two misuses of 'us' are current.

'US' FOR 'WE' 'Us' is the form of the pronoun 'we' when it is the object and not the subject of a verb ('We like them', 'They like us').

'And whereas women have role models like Madonna and Janet Jackson, us poor men can't claim any red-blooded hoofing legends.' (*New Woman*) The writer probably would not say 'Us like to live in the country', but the mistake here is just as bad: *we poor men can't claim any red-blooded hoofing legends.*

'It was a coincidence that certain gamefarms also imported American stock at the same time as us' (*Shooting Times*) means that we were imported along with American stock. It should be: *imported American stock at the same time as we did.*

There is a certain freedom in usage after the verb 'to be'. Although 'It is I' is strictly correct, 'It's me' is the accepted idiom. In the same way 'It's not just us who do the work' (*The Scots Magazine*) is perhaps an acceptable variant of: *It's not just we who do the work.*

'US' FOR 'OUR' Before writing 'us' care must be taken to check whether what is really needed is the word 'our'.

'There wasn't much chance of us staying friends after that' (*Catch*) should be: *There wasn't much chance of our staying friends after that.*

Similarly 'If you agree to us contacting you by phone, give a day-time phone-number' (*Inland Revenue*) should be: *If you agree to our contacting you by phone . . .*

There is a special danger in phrases beginning with 'without'. 'But why are all these mysterious signals flying around without us even realising it' (*19*) should be: *without our even realising it.*

use. 'Over the years the use of jackets and other items of clothing in disruptive or camouflage patterns has become accepted gear among woodland stalkers.' (*Shooting Times*) It is not the 'use' of these items that has become accepted gear, but the items themselves. The words 'the use of' should be removed. *Over the years jackets and other items of clothing in disruptive or camouflage patterns have become accepted gear.*

using. 'Using' is a participle and should agree with a noun or pronoun.

'The exhibition aims to reveal how objects are identified using visual clues.' (*Period Living*) The objects do not use visual clues. It is the unmentioned investigators who use them. *The exhibition also aims to reveal how objects are identified by the use of visual clues.* One could hazard the guess that in half the appearances of 'using' in the press, this error is made and could be corrected by the use of 'by the use of'.

'It looks stunning, yet this realistic balcony scene is easy to copy as it is created using five different stencils.' (*OK! Homes*) The scene must not be said to use stencils. It is the unmentioned designer who does: *it is created by the use of five different stencils.*

'Whole neighbourhoods can be psychologically summed up at a glance using the latest consumer profiling system.' (*Marketing Week*) The neighbourhoods do not 'use' the system. *Whole neighbourhoods can be summed up at a glance by use of the latest consumer profiling system.*

Sometimes a slightly different correction is required. 'There are no side effects using PILI ointments.' (*Dogs Monthly*) If one said 'There are no children using this playground' the meaning would be obvious, but one does not expect side effects to use ointment. *There are no side effects from the use of PILI ointments.*

usually. It is easy to slip up with this word. 'What's more, these ladies have brains as well as beauty. Most speak English and are usually well-educated and work in high professions.' (*Esquire*) If one said of the ladies 'Most are usually polite' it would imply that sometimes they are not polite. To say that they are 'usually' well-educated implies that there are occasions when they are not. The word 'usually' is misplaced. *Most speak English; most are well-educated.*

uxorious. 'He renounced, as Gandhi had done, all uxorious pleasures.' (*The Times*) A man who is 'uxorious' is excessively or obsessively attached to his wife. A 'pleasure' cannot be so attached. *He renounced, as Gandhi had done, all the pleasures of marriage.*

V

valuation. 'The problem is that the valuation is not being done correctly.' (*Radio 4*) People do not 'do' valuations, they make them: *the valuation is not being made correctly.*

value. 'National Power has consistently demonstrated its ability to deliver value since privatisation. We are confident that our plans for the future will continue to deliver excellent value for our shareholders.' (*National Power*) The debasement of the word 'value' in business-speak is regrettable. The business of National Power is to deliver power, not 'value', whatever that is. As for 'excellent value', it might be attributed to a given purchase, but it surely cannot be distributed far and wide. *Since privatisation National Power has shown that it can do well. We are sure that we shall be able to go on doing well for the benefit of our shareholders.*

vanish. 'You can vanish unemployment by removing the Employment Department.' (*Radio 4*) 'Vanish' is an intransitive verb (like 'disappear'). A thing can vanish, but one cannot 'vanish' it. *You can make unemployment vanish by removing the Employment Department.*

variety. This is a singular noun. When it is used collectively it remains singular. 'A variety of other drying places were devised' (*Traditional Homes*) should be: *A variety of other drying places was devised.*

vary. 'Your stride can vary from the next person in a myriad different ways.' (*Outdoors Illustrated*) Your stride does not vary from the next person but from the next person's stride: *Your stride can vary from the next person's.*

veer. To veer is to change direction, used often of shifting from one plan or opinion to another.

'There is some truth in the comments that she veers vertiginously from idolising and deriding her late husband.' (*The Times*) The word 'vertiginously', meaning in a dizzying fashion, indicates that the journalist has used the wrong verb ('veer') and the wrong preposition ('from'). Presumably, what she means is that the woman in question: *oscillates vertiginiously between idolising and deriding her late husband.*

Verbs. Verbs are those parts of speech which indicate the occurrence of an action (*She 'pressed' the button*) or the existence of a certain state (*The atmosphere 'is' invigorating*). A *transitive* verb requires a direct object to complete its meaning: *They slaughtered a herd of cows.* An *intransitive* verb makes complete sense on its own: *The Smiths are coming.* Many verbs are used both transitively (*He keeps chickens*) and intransitively (*The cheese will keep*). Transitive verbs have both an active and a passive voice. In the active voice, the subject is active (*She makes delightful meals*) and in the passive voice the subject 'suffers' the action (*She was made an honorary member*). Intransitive verbs do not have a passive voice. A being can 'sleep', but nothing can 'be slept'.

The verb 'to be' does not link a subject to an object; what follows the verb 'complements' what precedes it (*She is an actress; she is beautiful*).

The same applies to such verbs as 'become' and 'seem'. What follows them matches what precedes them (*He became an MP; he seems happy*).

The various 'tenses' of the verb allow us to place actions in time: present (*I read the paper in the mornings*, or *I am reading the paper*), future (*I shall take a walk*, or *I shall be taking a walk*), and past (*I walked home*, or *I have walked home* and *I had walked home* or *I had been walking home*).

In the above examples we see the verb 'to be' used in 'I am reading' and the verb 'to have' used in 'I have walked'. In the same way various auxiliary verbs are brought into use: *I 'do' love potatoes, She 'can' never leave the house, You 'must' try again, We 'may' come tomorrow*.

There is a great deal of evidence in this book that poor writing often results from overuse of nouns and underuse of verbs. *See* NOUNS IN EXCESS.

very. 'The astronomer Patrick Moore is very against this activity. The RAS are also very against it.' (*Radio 4*) This is like saying 'The thermometer is very up'. 'Against' is a preposition and neither adverbs nor adjectives can be applied to prepositions. If the RAS are very against, then it sounds as though some people are very for. *The astronomer Patrick Moore is very much against this activity*.

via. This useful word for 'by way of' is best reserved for use in describing routes ('You can go via Newcastle or via Carlisle'). It is not a satisfactory alternative to 'by means of'.

'And the U-shaped front pole attaches via clips' (*The Great Outdoors*) should be: *attaches by means of clips*.

vice versa. 'I did my best for her, and vice versa' conveys that she did the best for me, exactly matching what I did for her.

'Secondly, it [a home office] would separate work from household activities and vice versa.' (*Meridian*) This is tautologous. If you separate the sheep from the goats, you cannot avoid separating the goats from the sheep. 'Vice versa' is redundant: *it would separate work from household activities*.

viewpoint. 'There's an entirely different viewpoint between the astronomical and the astrological.' (*The Times*) A viewpoint does not exist 'between' people; a 'difference' may. *There's a great difference of viewpoint between the astronomical and the astrological*.

vindicate. 'Mr King has claimed the report vindicates him of any wrongdoing.' (*Radio* 4) To vindicate someone is to clear them in the face of any imputation. *Mr King has claimed that the report vindicates him.* If anything more is added, conventional usage requires 'from', not 'of': *vindicates him from any charge of wrongdoing.*

violate. 'Sir, I received recently a polite and helpful letter from a lady at the Royal Mail in which she described herself as Violated Mail Manager.' (*The Times*) This letter illustrates a problem that can arise when two nouns are joined ('Mail Manager') and an adjective or participle precedes them. In the phrase 'enterprising antiques dealer' the word 'enterprising' describes the dealer, but in 'rare antiques dealer' the word 'rare' describes the antiques. Where ambiguity might arise ('oriental antiques dealer'), the context usually indicates what is meant. In the sentence above commonsense will recognise that it is the mail that is violated and not the female, but the careful writer will always avoid giving room for alternative readings.

visit. 'These receptionists have to send doctors to 35,000 home visits each year.' (*Radio* 4) A visit is not something a doctor goes 'to'. *These receptionists have to send doctors on 35,000 home visits each year.*

'A visit to the Parc Naturel Regional des Volcans de l'Auvergne near Clermont-Ferrand in Puy de Dome, makes a fitting place to begin your exploration.' (*Camping*) It is the Parc, not the 'visit' that makes a fitting 'place' to start. *A visit to the Parc Naturel makes a fitting start to your exploration.*

W

watch. 'Members of the cabinet will be watching with interest a speech which the new President of the European Commission, Jacques Santer, is making.' (*Radio* 4) It is acceptable to use the verb 'watch' of paying attention to something or someone even where eyesight is not strictly involved ('We must watch how the situation develops'). But when it is a matter of paying close attention to the spoken word, the verb 'watch' is out of place. *Members of the cabinet will be attentively weighing a speech which the new President is making.*

water down. Once-vivid metaphorical expressions can lose their sharpness. We speak of watering down, or diluting a programme or a document. When a speaker says 'The government has watered down its stance' (*Radio 4*), the listener winces because a 'stance' is so firmly and solidly resistant to dilution. *The government has modified its stance.*

way. 'Cold ceramic paints are an ideal way to apply instant colour and pattern to nonporous ceramics.' (*Artists & Illustrators Magazine*) The paints are not a 'way'. *Cold ceramic paints are ideal for applying colour and pattern to nonporous ceramics.*

'There are few better ways to enjoy a country walk than when you are in the company of a real expert.' (*Country Talk*) It would be logical to say 'There are few better times for walking than when the weather is cool', following 'times' by 'when', but there is no need for 'when you are' after 'ways'. *There are few better ways to enjoy a country walk than in the company of a real expert.*

The word 'way' is often used too loosely. 'Alex pointed out that the begonia, with its large, brightly-coloured blooms, is a good example of the way that flowers have been selected and cultivated since they were taken from the wild.' (*The Scots Magazine*) The begonia is not itself an example of the method ('way') of selection and cultivation: *the begonia, with its large, brightly-coloured blooms, exemplifies how flowers have been selected and cultivated.*

'The researchers think this may provide more evidence that the way a baby is fed is important to growth and development.' (*Living*) As often, it would be better to eliminate 'way': *this may provide more evidence that how a baby is fed affects growth and development.*

we. 'We' is used as the subject of a verb, 'us' as its object. 'Let we of the older generation be thankful.' (*The Scots Magazine*) This is like saying 'Let I go' instead of 'Let me go'. *Let us of the older generation be thankful.* See also US.

what is the point? This construction lures writers to use the gerciple. 'What is the point of him carrying on?' (*The Times*) should be: *What is the point of his carrying on?*

whatever. This word has its own special usefulness, but has lately been abused. 'Whatever, the dilemma of being the piggy-in-the-middle party involves sending some mixed signals to voters in both main camps.' (*Gentlemen's Quarterly*) Here the word should be: *However*.

when. Most misuses of 'when' arise from hanging the word on to the wrong kind of noun. Although you can speak of 'the day when my father died' (because 'day' is a noun of time), it is not good to speak of 'the train journey when the engine broke down', making the 'when' clause descriptive of the train journey (*on which the engine broke down*).

'WHEN' FOR 'WHICH' 'If your child does have a hearing defect . . . it could be a perforated ear drum or glue ear; or a nerve loss when the inner ear fails to function.' (*Prima*) Here 'when the inner ear fails to function', a clause which should hang on a verb, is used to qualify 'nerve loss'. The construction demanded involves the word 'which': *or a nerve loss by which the inner ear fails to function.*

'Given as a free service, this puts an end to those costly mistakes when a product looks wonderful at the counter but awful at home.' (*Daily Mail*) To hang a 'when' clause on the word 'mistakes' is clearly illogical: *those costly mistakes by which a product looks wonderful at the counter but awful at home.*

'Satellite activities include three weekend tutorials per year, when members can reap the benefits of classes by professional teachers.' (*Artists & Illustrators Magazine*) There is some excuse for the use 'when' here because the tutorials are in fact 'occasions'. Nevertheless the relative pronoun 'which' would be better: *three weekend tutorials per year, at which members can reap the benefits of classes by professional teachers.*

'The strength of feeling among NHS staff will be seen this Thursday when a national protest has been called.' (*Radio 4*) Thursday is not the day 'when' the protest has been called, but the day 'for which' the protest has been called. If 'when' is kept, the verb must be changed. *The strength of feeling will be seen on Thursday when a national protest will be held.*

'WHEN' FOR 'WHERE' 'The Prime Minister of Pakistan has accused Indian Intelligence agents of carrying out two recent bomb attacks, one on a bus and the second in a hospital when six people died.' (*Radio 4*) The word 'when' as used here must hang on the word 'second' (attack), but the emphasis on the 'bus' and the 'hospital' seems to drag it towards the word 'hospital' for which it is not appropriate: *the second in a hospital where six people died.*

WILDER MISUSES OF 'WHEN' The worst misuses of 'when' occur when the mind takes a wild leap over all grammatical awareness. 'Bradbury Star has only one blot on his record, when unseating his rider at the first Ascot in November.' (*Horse & Hound*) It is improper to speak of a blot 'when' something happened. In fact 'when' can be scrapped: *has only one blot on his record – unseating his rider at the first Ascot in November.*

'One of my favourite quotes from Nancy Mitford is when she takes her nephew out to tea.' (*Oldie*) Clearly the favourite quote is nothing of the kind. *One of my favourite quotes from Nancy Mitford derives from an occasion when she took her nephew out to tea.*

'These accounts culminate, perhaps, when Vera Brittain describes the sight and smell of the bloodstained clothes caked with mud, of her beloved Roland Leighton.' (*Guardian*) The accounts do not culminate at that point 'when' the description is penned, or even read. They culminate in the description itself. *These accounts culminate, perhaps, in Vera Brittain's description of the sight and smell of the bloodstained clothes.*

AMBIGUITY AFTER 'WHEN' There is a temptation to over-compress the wording after 'when' and so to produce ambiguity. 'Peeling chestnuts is easier when hot' (*Woman's Journal*) suggests that the peeler ought to warm up for the task. *Peeling chestnuts is easier when they are hot.*

'No two days are the same when juggling all the different roles that modern life entails.' (*Woman's Journal*) The grammatical construction here might suggest that days juggle roles. It would be better to write: *No two days are the same when you are juggling all the different rules.*

where. There are mistakes common to the use of 'when' and of 'where'.

'WHERE' FOR 'WHICH' It is correct to speak of the 'place where I fell ill' (because a place is a locality) but not of the 'picnic where I fell ill'.

Thus 'Note that it is not the WI where menfolk are barred' (*Money-Maker*) should be: *not the WI from which menfolk are barred.*

'His onsite meetings where craftsmen contributed from their practical experience' (*Old-House Journal*) would be better as: *His onsite meetings at which craftsmen contributed from their practical experience.*

The error can easily be hidden in a more complex sentence. 'Moreover, his interests included the history of the later Roman imperial period, where his magisterial article *De Rebus Bellicis* . . . is especially note-worthy.' (*The Times*) His magisterial article is certainly not located in the later Roman imperial period. This should be: *His interests included the history of the later Roman imperial period, on which his magisterial article is especially noteworthy.*

'They will discuss Northern Ireland, where American patience with the republicans is beginning to wear thin.' (*Radio 4*) The topic of Northern Ireland, which Bill Clinton and John Major will discuss, is not the place 'where' American patience is wearing thin. It is wearing thin in the US. *They will discuss Northern Ireland, over which American patience with the republicans is beginning to wear thin.*

'WHERE' OVERDONE It is now acceptable to use 'where' to mean 'in circumstances such that'. One may say 'The courts may take action where debts remain unpaid'. It is important not to stretch this idiomatic freedom too far.

'Fishing is clearly an industry where the doctrine of subsidiarity allows the Community to act where member government's individual policies must be coordinated.' (*The Times*) The double use of 'where' is unfortunate here. It is probably best to change the first one. *Fishing is clearly an industry for which the doctrine of subsidiarity allows the Community to act where member governments' individual policies have to be coordinated.*

whether. *See* IF.

while. The most common use of 'while' is in relation to duration, but it is also used as an alternative to 'although'. But the two words, 'although' and 'while' are not interchangeable.

'While Paul's telling of the tale makes it sound easy, Roscoff [a Belfast restaurant] opened just as the recession began.' (*Weekend Telegraph*) Surely 'although' is called for here. *Although Paul's telling of the tale makes it sound easy, Roscoff opened just as the recession began.*

'But Yugoslavia's ethnic geography requires some pragmatic dilution of the principle of self-determination, while respecting existing borders.' (*The Times*) This shows us how not to use 'while'. It introduces a participle 'respecting' which appears to be meant to qualify 'dilution'. It would be proper to say 'dilute while respecting' but there is no such usage as 'dilution . . . while respecting'. 'While' must go. *Yugoslavia's ethnic geography requires some pragmatic dilution of the principle of self-determination which respects existing borders.*

Care must be taken when 'while' is followed by a gerund. 'Goya's Sorting the Bulls is one of a series of 12 small-scale cabinet pictures painted while convalescing after a serious illness in 1793.' (*The Field*) Since the subject here is the picture and not Goya, 'painted while convalescing' represents the pictures as convalescent. As it stands, the phrase requires back-reference to 'Goya' (without the apostrophe). But insertion of the word 'he' is all that is required: *one of a series of 12 small-scale cabinet pictures he painted while convalescing.*

whilst. 'Whilst relatively few find a priest hole or even magnificent fireplaces hidden behind wallpaper but more mundane but equally interesting discoveries may be there still waiting to be found.' (*Old-House Journal*) One might say 'Whilst he stayed at home, I went out' or 'He stayed at home but I went out', but the two constructions could not be combined in 'Whilst he stayed at home but I went out.' Either 'whilst' must go to make sense of 'but', or 'but' must go to make sense of 'whilst': *Whilst few find a priesthole or even a magnificent fireplace hidden behind wallpaper, more mundane discoveries may be waiting.*

whittle. 'Tony Blair . . . has whittled away at the unions' power within the party.' (*Newsweek*) To 'whittle' is to pare a stick or some other item and thus gradually to reduce it. It is usual to speak of 'whittling down' or 'whittling away' and 'at' is quite out of place. *Tony Blair has whittled away the unions' power within the party.*

who. We have few relics in modern English of the old Anglo-Saxon inflexions, but the pronoun 'who' still keeps its forms 'whom' and 'whose'. There is convenience in being able to distinguish between a girl 'who dislikes me' and a girl 'whom I dislike', where we see the two forms 'I/me' as well as 'who/whom' in use.

Some popular journals seem to be trying to remove 'whom' from use. 'As a working mother of two children – who I love dearly' (*Woman*) should be: *whom I love dearly.*

'I realised I was falling for the head of our faculty (who I'll call David)' (*New Woman*) should be: *whom I'll call David.*

Reference to 'a six-year-old girl hiding behind a tree who he then shot at point-blank range' (*The Times*) should be: *whom he then shot at point-blank range.*

'The two million people who we serve every day' (*Radio 4*) should be: *whom we serve every day.*

'We now have a thriving community of goldfish who we feed each morning' (*Living*) should be: *whom/which we feed each morning.*

'They are the patients who other doctors have referred to Cathy' (*New Woman*) should be: *whom other doctors have referred to Cathy.*

Reference to 'a photograph of an ancestor who nobody seems to know' (*Family History*) should be: *whom nobody seems to know.*

Even a book-reviewer can speak of 'an account of the egregious Duffill, a fellow passenger who the author, to say nothing of the reader, found annoying beyond measure.' (*Complete Traveller*). This should be corrected to: *a fellow passenger whom the author . . . found annoying beyond measure.*

'I got to know the artist Adrian George – who I ended up modelling for' (*Woman's Journal*) should be: *for whom I ended up modelling.*

'Sadly the same is not true of Petronella Wyatt who he hired as a columnnist' (*Private Eye*) should be: *whom he hired as a columnist.*

And 'I served my apprenticeship with a guy called Jeremy Hindley, who I worked with for eight years' (*Majesty*) should be: *with whom I worked for eight years.*

'It was the usual crowd . . . and a few other women who Jane knew well enough to smile at' (*Woman*) should be: *women whom Jane knew well enough to smile at.*

It is incorrect to try to hang a relative clause beginning with 'who' on to a noun in the possessive form. 'It is Jack's ball, who lives next door' will not do. Nevertheless an announcer tells us that 'prison staff and inmates are being questioned as part of the detailed investigation into Frederick West's death, who was a remand prisoner at Winson Green'. (*Radio 4*) The apostrophe must be removed from 'Frederick West's' if the relative clause is to be kept: *investigation into the death of Frederick West, who was a remand prisoner.*

whom. Misuse of 'whom' is less common that misuse of 'who', but 'we managed to acquire a Clark Gable lookalike, whom we thought would be right up her street' (*My Weekly*) should be either: *who, we thought, would be right up her street,* where the pronoun is the subject of the verb 'would be', or: *whom we thought to be right up her street,* where the pronoun is the object of the verb 'thought'.

whomever. 'Expanding that sector [owner-occupied housing] will pose some tricky problems for whomever ends up in Downing Street.' (*Radio 4*) It would be correct to say 'Give this to whomever you choose', where 'whomever' is the object of the verb 'choose', but 'whomever' cannot be the subject of the verb 'ends up': *will pose some tricky problems for whoever ends up in Downing Street.*

For the same reason when a political spokesman speaks of a 'notion that asylum-seekers from certain countries will be black-listed, whomever they are' (*Radio 4*), it should be: *whoever they are.*

who's/whose. 'Who's' is an abbreviation of 'who is' or 'who has' ('the chap who's in the lead' or 'the chap who's just won the race').

In '. . . a cat who's coat has become seriously matted is a pitiful sight' (*Wild About Animals*) there is no such abbreviation. It should be: *a cat whose coat has become matted.*

whose. *See* WHO'S.

will. We hear news of representatives 'arguing that the political and military will exercised by the international community in Bosnia needs to be repeated in Rwanda'. (*Radio 4*) 'Will' cannot be 'repeated': *needs to be applied again in Rwanda.*

will/would. There is a tendency to use the indicative tense where the conditional tense would be correct.

'If suppliers worked more closely with retailers at this level, they will find that they can achieve far more than they ever imagined.' (*Marketing Week*) This should be: *If suppliers worked more closely with retailers, they would find they could achieve far more.*

window. There was a time when politicians told us that a new avenue was being explored. Now they tell us that a new window is being opened.

Thus the Queen's speech-writer, if the BBC is to be trusted, arranged for Her Majesty, speaking in St Petersburg, to declare that 'now Russia's window on the west was open again, and was being joined by other windows throughout the land' (*Radio 4*). The image is of windows traversing the steppes to gather in the old capital. 'Being joined' will not do: *now Russia's window on the west was open again, and others were opening throughout the land.*

It appears that overuse of the expression 'window of opportunity' has now resulted in the assumption that 'window' is a synonym for 'opportunity'.

'Opportunities to carry out this dangerous operation were few and far between, but there was one short time window each week when it could be accomplished.' (*Yesterday*) The writer does not wish to repeat 'opportunity' so uses 'window' instead: *but there was one brief occasion each week when it could be accomplished.*

wish. Whereas 'I want to go' could be replaced by 'I wish to go', 'I want help' cannot be replaced by 'I wish help'.

But reporting on the Labour Party conference election for the executive committee a newsreader said, 'The addition of campaign group members at the expense of Blairite shadow cabinet members illustrates grassroots eagerness for a broader church than their leader may wish.'

(*Radio 4*). Neither the grassroots nor the leader can thus 'wish' a church: *broader church than their leader may want*.

wishful thinking. 'Possibly the new Dorman engine was wishful think-ing had the Castle-Four gone into production.' (*Automobile*) 'Wishful thinking' is a mental process, not the object of thought, such as an engine. *Possibly too the new Dorman engine would have remained a dream had the Castle-Four gone into production*.

with. Of the various current misuses of 'with' we treat the most easily corrigible.

THE INTRUSIVE 'WITH' The word 'with' is dragged in to perform a function beyond its grammatical scope, when what is needed is a simple participle construction.

'The company announced yesterday there had been a 33 per cent take up, with the balance left with the underwriters.' (*Independent*) 'With' is awkward, inelegant and unnecessary, and should go: *there had been a 33 per cent take up, the balance being left with the underwriters*.

In the same way 'With the history of the coaching inn inseparable from that of the development of the road network, it is perhaps no sur-prise that the heyday of the coaching era was also the high point of the popularity of these buildings' (*Heritage*) should become: *The history of the coaching inn being inseparable from that of the development of the road network, it is perhaps no surprise*.

This misuse is an epidemic in journalism. 'With no children, her hus-band was succeeded in the baronetcy by his brother' (*The Times*) should be: *Having no children, her husband was succeeded in the baronetcy by his brother*.

'The 3rd Duke, with some claim to the crown, was seen as a threat by Henry' (*Majesty*) should be: *The 3rd Duke, having some claim to the crown, was seen as a threat by Henry*.

'This hole is quite difficult to judge with the green exposed on a sort of table top' (*Lancashire Life*) should be: *difficult to judge, the green being exposed on a sort of table top*.

THE REDUNDANT 'WITH' Sometimes the appropriate change can be made merely by omitting 'with' and, if necessary, replacing it by a comma.

'The industry grew rapidly with the Napoleonic Wars creating an increased demand.' (*Traditional Homes*) Here is a case in point: *The industry grew rapidly, the Napoleonic Wars creating an increased demand*.

'The blocks are surprisingly durable with any damage almost always being caused by frost' (*Automobile*) should be: *surprisingly durable, any damage almost always being caused by frost.*

'More than 1,200 schools have entered The Calypso Cricket Cup competition with the national final being staged at a county ground' (*Lancashire Life*) should be: *entered the competition, the national final being staged at a county ground.*

'The Ombudsman said some of the complaints referred to his office were resolved as soon as his staff contacted the trust involved, with chief executives being embarrassed into action.' (*Nursing Standard*) Again omit 'with' here: *were resolved as soon as his staff contacted the trust involved, chief executives being embarrassed into action.*

THE SPURIOUSLY 'CAUSAL' WITH An increasingly popular abuse of 'with' combines the word with a participle and gives the whole a causal function.

'With the Queen opening the Sackler gallery at the Royal Academy, the Tate had to postpone its opening party for 24 hours.' (*The Times*) 'With the Queen opening' is a crude and clumsy evasion of the natural: *Since/Because the Queen was opening the Sackler gallery, the Tate had to postpone its opening party.*

'With the Prime Minister promising to reassert his leadership in a speech to Welsh Conservatives today, Tory MPs . . . gave Mr Major warm support.' (*Independent*) Again the construction is a crude evasion of the obvious: *Now that the Prime Minister is promising to reassert his leadership in a speech today.*

Similarly 'with' is quite out of place in 'Exports have clearly done very well this year but it is unlikely that the double digit growth figures we have been seeing can be sustained with Britain's major export markets set to grow by only around 6 per cent.' (*The Times*) This calls for the same treatment: *it is unlikely that the double digit growth figures can be sustained now that Britain's major export markets are set to grow by only 6 per cent.*

'The roadshow can only run in the summer months with the creatures needing to be kept warm' (*Lancashire Life*) should be: *since the creatures need to be kept warm.*

Sometimes 'with' is given a causal function even without attachment to a participle. 'With a very wide age gap, a lot of additional pressure is put on a relationship' (*New Woman*) should be: *Where there is a wide age gap.*

'With the new approach, they have become so popular' (*Viva*) should be: *As a result of their new approach.*

THE ANTICIPATORY 'WITH' A further misuse of 'with' occurs when the word is given an anticipatory function in relation to the substance that follows.

'With any cooking appliance, it's no use keeping it tucked away at the back of the kitchen cupboard.' (*Home Style*) Both 'with' and 'it' are unnecessary. *No cooking appliance should be kept tucked away at the back of the kitchen cupboard.*

'With a woman boss, there's a belief she'll be better, more caring and sharing.' (*Company*) Again both 'with' and 'she' should be removed. *A woman boss is expected to be better.*

'WITH' FOR 'WHEN' 'Headroom varies between a not unreasonable 5ft 2in and 5ft 7in even with the roof down. With it raised, that increases over a central area.' (*Caravan Magazine*) This should be: *When it is raised.*

THE ALL-PURPOSE 'WITH' A habit has developed of trying to turn 'with' into an all-purpose preposition that can be substituted for the appropriate one. 'With sugar beet terrain game was plentiful' (*Shooting Times*) should surely be: *On sugar beet terrain.*

THE WILDEST 'WITH' Perhaps worst of all is the 'with' that introduces an addition or consequence in the future. 'The next competition is a seasonal one: Treescapes, with the winner published in the July in View pages' (*The Artist*) should be: *Treescapes; and the name* [sic] *of the winner will be published in the July in View pages.*

with/by. The use of 'with' where 'by' is required suggests aural insensitivity. 'Robert Bridges, Emily Dickinson and Marlowe have been replaced with Emily Brontë and the Welsh poet Henry Vaughan.' (*The Times*) The subject is the National Curriculum: *have been replaced by Emily Brontë and the Welsh poet Henry Vaughan.*

with a view to. 'I want to learn the best way of investing a recently acquired annuity with a view to it earning a reasonable monthly income.' (*Moneywise*) This expression lures to error. Technically it would be correct to write 'with a view to its earning', but it is awkward. It would also be correct simply to omit 'it': *with a view to earning a reasonable monthly income.* But the expression is perhaps better avoided. *I want to learn the best way of investing a recently acquired annuity so that it may earn a reasonable monthly income.*

without. It is lax to use 'without' where 'unless' is really needed. 'West Germany . . . is heading for a recession without a rapid change of course.' (*Guardian*) If you said 'I am looking forward to a meal without potatoes', the function of 'without' would be clear. There are meals with potatoes and meals without potatoes. But there is no intention here to distinguish between two kinds of recession – recessions with a change of course and recessions without a change of course. The word 'unless' is needed: *West Germany is heading for a recession . . . unless there is a rapid change of course.*

There is a useful construction: 'He went abroad without my knowing'. It is a handy variant of 'He went away without my knowledge'. But since the 'knowledge' or the 'knowing' is what is lacking, we must be careful not to turn this into 'He went away without me knowing'. In fact this error is extremely common.

'I could wander round parks and art galleries . . . without him making any comment' (*Annabel*) should be: *without his making any comment.*

'Joanne ran to the settee without me having to repeat myself once' (*Annabel*) should be: *without my having to repeat myself once.*

'. . . your body is giving off that message without you even realising it' (*19*) should be: *without your even realising it.*

'And technology enabling bosses to access files on your computer without you even knowing has been around for some time' (*Bella*) should be: *without your knowledge.*

What applies to personal pronouns applies also to 'it'. 'Indeed, it is quite impossible for them to put on any kind of front without it being the cause of laughter' (*The Times*) should be: *without its being the cause of laughter. See also* GERCIPLES.

word of mouth. 'David continues to work through word of mouth.' (*Cumbria Life*) This is meant to convey that the artist does not advertise but relies simply on personal recommendation for getting known. It is not a matter of how he 'works' but of how he gets known. *David continues to get known through word of mouth.*

Word Order. SINGLE WORD MISPLACED Word order can be at fault even though there is no grammatical error.

'It, six centimetres wide, is about the same size as our smallest mammal.' (*Guardian*) The sensitive ear would surely want: *Six centimetres wide, it is about the same size as our smallest mammal.*

The placing of a single adjective can go badly astray. 'Nick, a second-hand London bookseller' (*Daily Telegraph*) should surely be: *Nick, a London second-hand bookseller.*

In the same way 'Railtrack has defended its safety standard in the face of a critical leaked report' (*Radio 4*) should be: *in the face of a leaked critical report.*

'Because the diseases tend to occur in concentrated areas rather than evenly throughout the moorland flocks, individual farmers can be even harder hit while others may escape any losses at all.' (*Dalesman*) It is not certain areas that are 'concentrated' but the incidence of disease among the sheep: *Because the diseases tend to be concentrated in certain areas.*

As an adjective should be placed close to the noun it qualifies, so too an adverb must be placed close to the verb it modifies.

'A study of 31 newly qualified doctors last year showed that fewer than half were capable of reviving someone who had collapsed effectively.' (*The Times*) It sounds as though it was the collapse that was effective: *fewer than half were capable of effectively reviving someone who had collapsed.*

PHRASE MISPLACED 'The impact of moving into towns upon the cat population should not be underestimated.' (*Country-side*) The space between 'impact upon' and 'cats' is uncomfortably wide. *The impact upon the cat population of moving into towns should not be underestimated.*

Sometimes, when a phrase is thus misplaced, it can attach itself to the wrong noun or verb. 'A film taken of him correcting an oesophageal abnormality for teaching purposes was once previewed by his staff.' (*The Times*) The surgeon surely was not correcting the abnormality 'for teaching purposes', as is suggested here: *A film, taken for teaching purposes, which showed him correcting an oesophageal abnormality.*

'The suggested menu this month is for a warm evening, probably eaten outside . . .' (*The Field*) Neither the menu nor the evening can be eaten outside. *The menu is for a meal to be eaten on a warm evening, perhaps outside.*

'Your card can also be used to withdraw cash from TSB and many other cash machines in the UK and abroad displaying the Visa sign for a small charge.' (*TSB circular*) The idea of having to pay in order to have the pleasure of seeing the Visa sign displayed is fetching. The bank means something different. *For a small charge your card can also be used to withdraw cash from TSB and many other cash machines in the UK and abroad displaying the Visa sign.*

CLAUSE MISPLACED It is awkward to distance a relative clause (beginning with 'which') from the noun it qualifies. '. . . Paraffin was unobtainable in Iceland, which these stoves used frugally.' (*Outdoors Illustrated*) This makes it sound as though the stoves used Iceland: *paraffin, which these stoves used frugally, was unobtainable in Iceland.*

working. 'Working with an Account Director, the job involves progressing design prints, promotion and liaison with clients.' (*The Times*) This error is widespread in advertisements for posts. The sentence implies that the job will work with an Account Director. If 'working' is kept, there must be a subject to agree with it. *Working with an Account Director, the appointee will be involved in progressing design prints.*

worn. 'A fur coat, worn by every well-off woman in Italy, hangs in the corner.' (*The Times*) Journalistic hedge-hopping surely goes a bit far here. The fur coat in question is presumably used by one owner only. *A fur coat, of the kind worn by every well-off woman in Italy, hangs in a corner.*

worthwhile. 'It may be worthwhile the taxpayer moving some savings.' (*Meridian*) This is colloquial short-hand for: *It may be worthwhile for the taxpayer to move.*

worthy. 'And finally the Sunday Times has been taking a closer look at some of the subjects deemed worthy for study by Britain's undergraduates.' (*Radio 4*) The prepositions are the wrong ones. Usage requires 'fit for' and 'worthy of': *some of the subjects deemed worthy of study.*

would. In sentences involving a conditional clause the conditional forms, 'should' and 'would', must be used in such a way that they are properly matched.

'If you become the First Prize winner, you would receive a message through official channels.' (*Reader's Digest*) This offer mismatches the indicative form 'become' with the conditional form 'would'. The writer should either stick to the indicative: *if you become the First Prize winner, you will receive a message*, or stick to conditionals: *if you were to become the First Prize winner, you would receive a message. See also* WILL.

wreak. *See* REEK.

Y

younger. 'The Eighties were an age of ambition – fostered by the boom, the change of pace in the workplace brought about by technology and promotion coming faster and younger.' (*Vogue*) 'Promotion' does not grow from infancy to old age. Neither technology nor promotion can be said to come 'younger'. The gerciple ('technology and promotion coming') is inadmissible: *the change of pace in the workplace brought about by technology and by earlier and rapider promotion.*

your. 'Your welcome to call in to our extensive showrooms.' (Yellow Pages) Here what is wanted is the abbreviated form of 'You are': *You're welcome to call in.*

yours. 'Whatsits paid for its space, but you got your's for free.' (*Precision Marketing*) 'Yours' is the equivalent of 'mine' or 'his' and, like 'hers', requires no apostrophe: *you got yours for free. See also* HERS.